Missing Persons

A missing person is an individual whose whereabouts are unknown and where there is some concern for his or her wellbeing. In the UK, around 250,000 people are reported missing every year, with the majority being children under the age of 18. Despite the fact that missing persons are a social phenomenon which encompasses vast areas of interest, relatively little is known about those who go missing, what happens to them while they are missing, and what can be done to prevent these incidents from occurring.

This groundbreaking book brings together for the first time ideas and expertise across this vast subject area into one interconnected publication. It explores the subjects of missing children, missing adults, the investigative process of missing person cases, and the families of missing persons.

Those with no prior knowledge or professionals with focused knowledge in some areas will be able to expand their understanding of a variety of topics relevant to this field through detailed chapters which advance our understanding of this complex phenomenon, discuss what is unknown, and suggest the best and most important steps forward to further advance our knowledge.

Karen Shalev Greene is the founder and Director of the Centre of the Study of Missing Persons at the University of Portsmouth. Her research focuses on missing persons and she collaborates with academics, law enforcement agencies and NGOs across the UK and internationally.

Llian Alys is a British Psychological Society Chartered Psychologist and Associate Fellow, a Full Associate of the International Academy for Investigative Psychology and a Fellow of the Higher Education Academy. She currently works as a Research Psychologist providing consultancy on defence and security issues. She has previous experience in academia (as a Lecturer in Forensic Psychology at the University of Bedfordshire) and in law enforcement (as Research and Policy Officer in the UK Missing Persons Bureau and Crime Analyst in the Serious Crime Analysis Section, both now part of the National Crime Agency).

Missing Persons

A handbook of research

Edited by Karen Shalev Greene and Llian Alys

Routledge
Taylor & Francis Group

LONDON AND NEW YORK

First published 2017
by Routledge
2 Park Square, Milton Park, Abingdon, Oxon OX14 4RN

and by Routledge
711 Third Avenue, New York, NY 10017

First issued in paperback 2017

Routledge is an imprint of the Taylor & Francis Group, an informa business

British Library Cataloguing in Publication Data
A catalogue record for this book is available from the British Library

Library of Congress Cataloging in Publication Data
Names: Shalev Greene, Karen, editor. | Alys, Llian, editor.
Title: Missing persons : a handbook of research / edited by Karen Shalev Greene & Llian Alys.
Description: Abingdon, Oxon ; New York, NY : Routledge, 2017. | Includes bibliographical references and index.
Identifiers: LCCN 2016016004| ISBN 9781409468028 (hardback) | ISBN 9781315595603 (ebook)
Subjects: LCSH: Missing persons.
Classification: LCC HV6762.A3 M574 2017 | DDC 362.8--dc23
LC record available at https://lccn.loc.gov/2016016004

ISBN 13: 978-1-138-49444-2 (pbk)
ISBN 13: 978-1-4094-6802-8 (hbk)

Typeset in Bembo and ITC Stone Sans by
Servis Filmsetting Ltd, Stockport, Cheshire

This book is dedicated to Laura, Danielle and Neve.

I fy ngŵr annwyl am ei holl gefnogaeth ac i'n merch fach arbennig.

The Great Eternal Silence

Missing in the darkness,
vanished without a trace,
with only the memories and photographs,
to fill an empty place.

Frequent prayer and fervent cries,
is there anyone there?
But the only sound
was the silent eternal fanfare.

For a long time
its deafening sound
subdued by a path
through lost and found.

Laughter and sorrow,
anguish and grief,
all the moments of a life
but with no relief.

Everything and nothing
one within and between all,
gentle, loving, pervading,
the eternal silence falls.

(Aquinas T. Duffy, 2000)

Contents

Contents

Figures

Tables

Contributors

Helen Alves developed the family support services at Missing People as Senior Services Manager. Having scoped families' wants and needs, and looked at academic understanding and best practice, Helen visited Australian service provision to consolidate understanding. This resulted in a new structure of support to families of missing people including a bespoke counselling service, online peer support and events for families to meet each other. Helen has delivered training around 'ambiguous loss' to therapeutic and search practitioners to enhance their insight into families' unique needs. Helen has eight years' experience working with families and those who are missing, and previous experience with asylum seekers and in youth work, mental health, and homelessness.

Llian Alys is a British Psychological Society Chartered Psychologist and Associate Fellow, a Full Associate of the International Academy for Investigative Psychology and a Fellow of the Higher Education Academy. She currently works as a Research Psychologist providing consultancy on defence and security issues. She has previous experience in academia (as a Lecturer in Forensic Psychology at the University of Bedfordshire) and in law enforcement (as Research and Policy Officer in the UK Missing Persons Bureau and Crime Analyst in the Serious Crime Analysis Section, both now part of the National Crime Agency).

Joe Apps leads, develops and manages the UK Missing Persons Bureau (National Crime Agency), supporting and advising on missing and found person enquiries nationally and internationally. He is a retired police officer with more than 40 years' experience in policing at a senior level, with extensive knowledge of missing person investigations and the missing phenomenon. He is undertaking a professional doctorate programme with the University of Dundee, researching 'missing'-related issues.

Jan Bikker is an experienced forensic anthropologist working with UK police forces on forensic anthropological casework and international Disaster Victim Identification operations. He contributed to the development of uniform international Disaster Victim Identification standards and the new INTERPOL Disaster Victim Identification forms and training programmes for police forces and forensic experts to identify missing persons/unidentified remains of disaster victims according to the internationally recognised standards.

Jane Birkett is an officer for the NCA, working as Policy and Research Officer for the UK Missing Persons Bureau from February 2012 to January 2015. During this time she worked on a memorandum of understanding between the police and coroners in an effort to provide an improved and more consistent service to identify bodies and body parts. Research involvement includes the seasonality of missing, associations between crime and missing, and the geography of missing. Prior to working in the Bureau Jane was a Crime Analyst in the Serious Crime Analysis Section, linking serious sex offences and murders nationally using offender behaviour. Alongside this Jane volunteered as a Special Constable for Thames Valley Police from 2009–2012, gaining experience of front-line policing. Jane has a BSc in Psychology from the University of Westminster and an MSc in Forensic Psychology from the University of Leicester and now works in the Economic Crime Command of the NCA.

Sue Black is Director of the Centre for Anatomy and Human Identification and Deputy Principal for public engagement at Dundee University. She is both an anatomist and a certified forensic anthropologist. Her research is multidisciplinary, covering a wide variety of subjects including the detailed gross, microscopic and biomolecular analysis of adult and juvenile remains to establish all aspects of biological and personal identity, including the sex, age at death, and disease and trauma status of the individual.

Philip Coales worked as a project associate for the Oxford Academic Health Science Network and as an intern and project support for Neighbourhood Return Scheme, which ended in 2014.

Naomi Eales works in the National Crime Agency's UK Missing Persons Bureau as an intelligence officer. She has gained an MSc in Forensic Psychology and is currently studying for her Professional Doctorate with the University of Portsmouth. Her thesis is examining the police risk assessment processes for missing person cases. As part of her work in the Bureau, she has completed an evidence-informed search tool (iFIND) to assist Police Search Advisers and trained search volunteers to locate missing persons.

Nicholas R. Fyfe is Director of the Scottish Institute for Policing Research and Professor in the School of Social Sciences at the University of Dundee. In addition to his work on missing persons he is also leading a four-year evaluation of police reform in Scotland and is co-editor of *Centralizing Forces? Comparative Perspective on Contemporary Police Reform in Northern and Western Europe.*

Graham J. Gibb is a retired police inspector. He is a former leader of the Grampian Police Mountain Rescue team and President of the Braemar Mountain Rescue Association. During his service with Grampian Police he pioneered the development and application of behavioural profiling for police-led missing person investigations. In 1996 he was awarded an MBE by Her Majesty the Queen in recognition of his services to mountain rescue.

Carol Hayden has researched a range of interconnecting themes around vulnerable children and families. Some of this research has focused specifically on children in the care system and the multiple disadvantages they face. She has researched the topic of children reported missing to the police and has a special interest in how the issue of children missing from residential care intersects with how this part of the care system operates.

Patricia Hynes is a principal lecturer and joint head of department in the Department of Applied Social Studies at the University of Bedfordshire. Prior to undertaking these roles she has worked for the National Society for the Prevention of Cruelty to Children, the Open Society Institute and in a range of roles within refugee camps across Southeast Asia. Her research interests include human rights and forced migration in all its forms, including trafficking, refugees and issues around asylum plus social exclusion, the sociology of human rights, the sociology of 'childhood', child abuse, child maltreatment and ethics during the research process.

Charlie Hedges is acknowledged as one of the UK's foremost experts on missing persons, particularly children and those who are abducted and trafficked. During a career spanning 36 years with the police and more lately with some of the UK's leading public bodies in this field, he has amassed a wealth of practical and theoretical experience, nationally and internationally. He currently runs his own consultancy, Charlie Hedges Advisory, working on missing, abducted and trafficked children and child alerts.

Lucy Holmes is Research Manager at UK charity Missing People, and Honorary Research Fellow at the Centre for the Study of Missing Persons, University of Portsmouth. Lucy's previous research interests include youth offending and desistance from crime, the regulation of street prostitution, and homelessness. Since focusing on missing persons Lucy has undertaken research into the impact on families of missing incidents, policing, mental health, dementia and the links between gang involvement and young people going missing.

Colin Hope is National Search Advisor with the Crime Operational Support section at the Organised Crime Command of the National Crime Agency (NCA). His remit is to provide advice, guidance and support in specialist search, strategies and tactics to senior investigating officers, police forces and other law enforcement agencies engaged in managing major crime investigations, suspicious and high-profile missing person cases.

Rupert McShane is a Consultant in Old Age Psychiatry based in Oxford. He has published data about people with dementia who get lost, explored the use of GPS tracking devices and founded the Neighbourhood Return Scheme, which ran for two years until 2014.

Geoff Newiss is the CEO of Action Against Abduction (previously known as PACT). His recent work on child abduction has focused on understanding the different types of child abduction and kidnapping in the UK. He has also published a critique of 'stranger danger' and has a strong interest in developing new evidence-based abduction avoidance strategies. Geoff has undertaken studies on the police response to missing persons, homicides which begin as missing persons, fatal disappearances, the characteristics of long-term missing persons, and men who go missing on a night out.

Francis Pakes is a professor in comparative criminology at the University of Portsmouth. He has a psychology degree from Groningen in the Netherlands and a PhD in social science from Leiden University in the Netherlands and has been working in the UK since 1998. Apart from comparative criminology he has written books on criminal psychology and has undertaken research into mental health services for offenders for the Home Office, the Ministry of Justice and several mental health foundation trusts and on mental health courts. He also has undertaken research to inform Lord Bradley's review of people with mental health problems or learning disabilities in the criminal justice system (2009).

Hester Parr is Professor of Human Geography at the University of Glasgow. She has worked on questions of mental health, geography and identity for over 20 years and was principal investigator for the Economic and Social Research Council (ESRC) funded 'Geographies of Missing People' research.

Dave Perkins and Pete Roberts have been active members of Northumberland National Park Mountain Rescue Team (NNPMRT) for over 40 years. In 1997 they formed a registered charity, the Centre for Search Research (TCSR), through which they teach their own search management and search skills courses throughout the UK and Ireland. They have made presentations at conferences in the UK, Ireland, Europe, the US and Canada. They co-authored the UK Missing Person Study along with a variety of associated search-related papers.

Chloe Setter is Head of Advocacy, Policy and Campaigns at the leading children's rights charity ECPAT UK, which campaigns against child exploitation and trafficking. She leads on policy for trafficking at the organisation, authors' research and briefings, and leads on several campaigns and European projects on human trafficking. She chairs the UK government's Child Trafficking Sub-Group, sits on various advisory groups, writes expert reports for child victims and is the organisational lead for the Anti-Trafficking Monitoring Group, a coalition of ten organisations monitoring the UK's response to trafficking and modern slavery.

Karen Shalev Greene is the Director of the Centre of the Study of Missing Persons at the University of Portsmouth. Her research focuses on missing persons and she collaborates with academics, law enforcement agencies and NGOs across the UK and internationally.

Nicola Sharp-Jeffs is a Research Fellow within the Child and Woman Abuse Studies Unit at London Metropolitan University. Her research interests include: birth registration; economic abuse as a form of coercive control within intimate partner violence; rebuilding lives after domestic violence; coordinated community responses to domestic violence; and 'going missing' in the context of woman and child abuse. Nicola is also a professional doctorate student at the University of Bedfordshire and has published book chapters and journal articles on her doctoral studies which explore the links between forced marriage, going missing and child sexual exploitation.

Olivia Stevenson is an honorary Research Fellow of the University of Glasgow and (acting) Head of Public Policy at University College London. She leads University of Central London's programme of public policy engagement to enhance the ways in which research can inform policy and practice spheres. Her research is centred on social and cultural geographies and she has published on missing people, geographies of suicide and family geographies.

Holly Towell is a policy and campaigning professional, with an academic background in history and psychology. She is presently in the voluntary sector, where she has worked on a number of policy areas, including missing persons, brain injury and cancer. This includes five years at UK charity Missing People, where Holly managed the successful campaign for the reform of presumption of death legislation in England and Wales, and was Vice Chair of the English Coalition for Runaway Children.

Louise Vesely-Shore is a senior officer for the UK Missing Persons Bureau. Following completion of a BSc in Psychology, she worked for the Serious Crime Analysis Section as a Crime Analyst linking serious sexual crimes through behaviour. She has worked for the Bureau since 2008, providing specialist support and advice to police investigating missing and unidentified cases. During this time Louise has completed an MSc in Forensic Psychology through the University of Surrey, undertaking a dissertation into predicting outcomes in missing person reports involving older individuals. She has also been responsible for managing a review of

outstanding unidentified bodies across the UK, and implementing procedures regarding colla-
tion of DNA and fingerprints for missing and unidentified persons.

Penny S. Woolnough is a Lecturer in Forensic Psychology at Abertay University where her
main area of research relates to the investigation and behaviour of missing persons. She is a
registered forensic psychologist and has provided operational advice and support to over 100
police-led missing person and equivocal death investigations. She is a Fellow of the International
Academy of Investigative Psychology.

Jo Youle led the development of family support services at Missing People as Director of
Services. As CEO Jo regularly works with families with a missing loved one and drives to
improve life for families left behind. The successful charity campaign 'Missing Rights' culmi-
nated in the Presumption of Death Act 2013 and the campaign for guardianship legislation seeks
to help families respond to important legal and practical issues. Jo is a regular media spokesper-
son and public speaker on the issue of missing with over ten years' experience working with
missing people and their families.

Foreword

When a loved one goes missing, time stops for those left behind. Past and present are sucked into a black hole of questions on what, why, where, how. Why did he or she go missing? Is there anything I should have done differently to prevent this? Is he or she still alive? Is there anywhere we haven't looked? Will I ever see him or her again?

People go missing for a wide variety of reasons. Some may leave their home intentionally, others may wander away due to mental health issues, or go missing as the result of an accident. Some may be groomed, others pushed away or thrown out. People may go missing if they are abducted, kidnapped, trafficked or murdered. And, in many cases, a complex mixture of situations, including push and pull factors, applies.

Missing persons can be adults and children of all genders, ages and races. While the majority of missing persons are found to be safe within a number of days after being reported missing, some are never found. For those left behind, 'not knowing' often makes it difficult, if not impossible, to go on. A page which can never be turned. For those missing, going missing is often the symptom of other, underlying problems, or a first step into a cycle of vulnerability, harm and abuse.

In all its complexity, the problem of missing persons is still too often underestimated, poorly understood, and at times trivialised by those in charge. Poor reporting and data collection practices make it difficult to paint a coherent picture of the scale of the problem. According to a study published by the European Commission in 2013, 250,000 children are reported missing in the EU each year.[1] A closer look at the data, however, reveals the problem may well be much wider, as countries with a similar number of inhabitants report dramatically different numbers on missing children.[2] Inconsistencies in the collection of data on missing adults are likely to be at least as important, if not worse.

The problem is also changing, with the increase in mobility in the EU and globalisation and migration at worldwide level having an undeniable impact. A data report published by Missing Children Europe in May 2015 on the caseload of hotlines for missing children highlights that an overall 25 per cent of the cases, reported to a total of 27 hotlines, are cross-border or international in nature.[3] While 79 per cent of the international or cross-border cases are considered to be intra-EU situations, it is clear that the problem of going missing is a global and increasingly cross-border phenomenon.

As is demonstrated by the variety of issues tackled in this book, any approach to the cross-cutting phenomenon of missing persons needs to face many different aspects of human society and life. Chapters in this volume touch upon challenges related to 'missing' in the context of children in care, child sexual exploitation, child trafficking, police practices and investigations, mental health issues, forced marriage, forensic identification, grief and more. This mirrors the need for any approach on missing persons to be multidisciplinary, taking into account the many layers and facets that are at stake when a person goes missing.

In bringing together research on the broader problem of missing persons from legal, psychological, criminological and sociological perspectives, this book sets the scene for more interdisciplinary research in the area. While operational support to missing persons, in particular to missing children, is slowly evolving in some European and other Western countries, research on the phenomenon is lagging behind. Too little is known about the root causes and risks of the different forms of disappearances, including the link between missing and exploitation, as well as of the effectiveness of legal and other instruments in dealing with the problem. Practitioners and policy makers including law enforcement authorities, child protection authorities, NGOs running specialised hotlines and helplines, and family mediators confronted with missing persons or those left behind require data and evidence to guide their work. Academics need to root their research in the challenges of those concerned.

I can, in the light of this, only applaud the work of the editors of this book, and the authors who contributed to it, for leading the way in developing evidenced, practice-oriented knowledge on 'going missing'. With increased knowledge and understanding we can do a better job at helping to prevent people from going missing, and bringing relief to those left behind.

Delphine Moralis
Secretary General, Missing Children Europe

Notes

1 See: European Commission – Directorate-General for Justice (2013). Missing children in the European Union: Mapping, data collection and statistics. http://ec.europa.eu/justice/fundamental-rights/files/missing_children_study_2013_en.pdf.

2 See: 'Missing children in the European Union: Mapping, data collection and statistics' p. 34: 'three countries with similar population sizes, France, Italy and the United Kingdom, provided very different figures: for 2012, France reports 50,326 cases, Italy only 5,513 and in the United Kingdom figures from just two-thirds of the local police forces already arrive at a total of 96,341 cases.

3 See: Missing Children Europe (2015). Missing children facts and figures 2014. Caseload data from missing children organisations and cross-border family mediators across Europe. http://missingchildreneurope.eu/Portals/0/Docs/Missing per cent20children per cent20facts per cent20and per cent20figures per cent202014.pdf.

Acknowledgements

The editors would like to thank all the authors for contributing to this book. We would also like to thank our families for their encouragement and support.

Abbreviations

ACPO	Association of Chief Police Officers
APPG	All-Party Parliamentary Group
CEOP	Child Exploitation and Online Protection Centre
DNA	Deoxyribonucleic Acid
EU	European Union
GPS	Global Positioning System
INTERPOL	International Criminal Police Organization
Ofsted	Office for Standards in Education, Children's Services and Skills
NCA	National Crime Agency
NGO	Non-Governmental Organisation
NPIA	National Policing Improvement Agency
SOCA	Serious Organised Crime Agency
UK	United Kingdom
US	United States of America

Introduction

Someone is recorded as missing in the UK every two minutes (NCA, 2014a). However, going missing is a global phenomenon and a human problem. While most people who go missing are found safe and well, a notable minority come to harm or may even lose their lives. The reasons why people go missing are diverse and the impact on the family and friends they leave behind is profound and often long-lasting. This book focuses on the subject of missing persons as it aims to highlight the complexity of this issue, draw attention to published research and identify gaps in knowledge, which will hopefully promote future examination by academics and professionals alike.

The definition of a missing person is a multifaceted one. As Edkins (2011) argued, 'missing-ness' is often experienced by the person reporting the incident, rather than the person being reported to the police. In the UK, a missing person is defined as 'anyone whose whereabouts cannot be established and where the circumstances are out of character or the context suggests the person may be the subject of crime or at risk of harm to themselves or another' (ACPO, 2013). Each year in the UK, over 300,000 reports are made to the police (NCA, 2014a, 2015; NPIA, 2012; SOCA, 2013). Shalev Greene and Pakes (2014) estimate that the annual cost of missing person investigations is well over £700 million and equates to 14 per cent of the total number of full-time police officers across the UK.

Thus, the scope of this problem is wide-ranging and concerns people from all ages and social and ethnic backgrounds. For example, a missing person case may include a young child who was abducted, a young woman who was trafficked for sexual exploitation, or an adult who has a mental health illness or is living with dementia.

While missing person reports are frequent and take up such a marked proportion of police time, there is relatively little research in this area. This book is a response to that and is a culmination of the coordinated work of academics and professionals who work in this area, either for law enforcement agencies or NGOs. This book centres its attention, for the most part, on cases where a person was reported missing, rather than a political, social or anthropological perspective of a multitude of people who are missing in war zones, are reported missing as a result of natural disaster, and so on.

This Collection

This book has 21 chapters and is divided into four parts: missing children (Chapters 1–5), missing adults (Chapters 6–11), investigation of missing person cases (Chapters 12–18), and families of missing persons (Chapters 19–22).

In the UK, around two-thirds of all missing person reports to the police are for children and young people who are under 18 years old (NCA, 2014b, 2015). Part I of this book focuses on them.

Children who go missing are a varied group, but children in care feature disproportionately in reports to the police. Chapter 1 focuses on this group of children and examines the common features of this group, and why children in care go missing. The chapter also discusses the past and present role of the police and children's services in managing these cases.

Child sexual exploitation is receiving increasing attention from the police and other professionals. This is due to a number of highly publicised cases over the past few years. Chapter 2 reviews current research literature to explore what is known about the association between these two public protection issues. In doing so it explores how understanding 'going missing' in the context of child sexual exploitation provides a potential method of identification, a route for intervention and additional legal mechanisms though which to prosecute offenders.

Chapter 3 examines the research literature on child abduction. It draws primarily on UK studies together with select research from overseas where the findings have relevance to the UK context. The chapter offers a review of the definitions of child abduction and the broader conceptual basis. The chapter also summarises the available data on the extent of abduction. Types of family and nonfamily abduction are highlighted in the third section, followed by a discussion of the implications for response and prevention.

Child trafficking is a global phenomenon and asylum-seeking children who go missing are particularly vulnerable to being exploited. Chapter 4 highlights the extent of the problem and discusses the importance of early identification of an unaccompanied or asylum-seeking child as a victim of trafficking. The chapter also discusses multi-agency practices across the UK and offers key recommendations to improve the safeguarding of these children.

'Where' children go when they go missing is a fundamental question that is at the core of any investigation into a child's disappearance. Chapter 5 explores what is known about the ways in which missing children in Western societies interact with and experience the environment. The chapter also examines how children travel, the distances they travel and where they go. Investigative strategies to maximise the gathering of '*where*' type information during cases of missing children are also provided.

According to national statistics, approximately 100,000 (NCA, 2014b, 2015) missing person reports relate to adults who go missing. Adults who go missing often present as vulnerable people, who may suffer from mental health issues, such as depression or dementia, or may be victims of crime, such as human trafficking. Part II of this book, therefore, focuses on missing adults.

The notion of intentionality, the degree to which people go missing deliberately, has long been used as a framework to understand missing person incidents. Chapter 6 explores in more depth what intentionality means and how it is not a fixed state. Someone may have different intentions during a missing incident. The chapter also outlines why intentionality is an important concept for missing persons and highlights the risks and benefits of understanding missing persons using this framework.

Chapter 7 discusses current mental health issues in relation to missing adults, including those who disappear to suicide, making reference to relevant research outside the policing domain (psychological autopsy research on suicide). The chapter also looks at two other vulnerable groups which the police encounter on a regular basis: absconders from hospitals and individuals who request the assistance of police forces and health services giving false details or claiming amnesia ('come to notice' persons).

People who live with dementia may go missing, especially if they are physically robust but have a poor topographical memory. If they do go missing, they are particularly vulnerable and may succumb to injury, existing health problems or the elements. Chapter 8 examines the association between dementia and going missing and discusses investigative and search strategies. Prevention strategies such as community first responders and tracking equipment are also discussed, along with the ethical considerations involved.

People who are forced to migrate across international borders include asylum seekers and those who are 'trafficked' for various forms of exploitation. Chapter 9 examines the association between going missing during the process of migration. The chapter will establish the extent of the problem and identify systems of support and surveillance of asylum seekers throughout the process of seeking asylum in the UK.

Over the past decade, a link between 'going missing' and associated public protection issues has been established. One public protection issue is forced marriage. Chapter 10 considers what going missing means in the context of forced marriage. The discussion then turns to implications for practice. Finally, appropriate forms of support for survivors are identified.

Whenever a person is reported missing to the police, there is an obvious need to locate an individual in space and time. Consequently, searching for a missing person can be a complicated process for any agency, involving interpreting the interplay of spatial, environmental and human elements at stake. In Chapter 11, the authors elaborate on these complexities and seek to use recent research evidence to shed new light on missing adult geographies and journeys.

The importance of dealing with missing persons properly is essential for the successful resolution of an investigation. All missing person reports must be assessed and understood to ensure that the response is appropriate in the circumstances (ACPO, 2013). Therefore, Part III focuses on the investigation of a missing person case.

Chapter 12 explains the procedures of a typical missing person investigation, drawing attention to policy considerations and good practice. The chapter discusses the process of initial assessment and response, the investigative process and the broader subject of management of a missing person investigation. The chapter also explores how to manage expectations (for example, those of the missing person's relatives) regarding what an investigation can and should include. There will also be discussion of challenging cases and the chapter will map the operational services available to support police investigations.

In the UK, the police service has the primary responsibility for coordinating the role of other agencies in search and rescue, including the specialist support provided by voluntary organisations. Chapter 13 reviews the role of search and rescue activities in missing person investigations. An outline of the processes involved during the initiation and management of a search and rescue operation is provided and the importance of the effective use of 'best assets' in search management is discussed.

From the police perspective, risk assessment of missing persons is an important topic as it provides the basis for how they prioritise cases and locate resources. Chapter 14 discusses the current process of risk assessment in missing person investigations and the challenges that police face. The chapter also highlights areas where future research activities will assist in developing better predictors of risk and improving early classification of risk.

While 99 per cent of missing person cases in the UK are solved within a year (NCA, 2014b), some cases remain open for prolonged periods of time. Those cases are often referred to as 'cold case' investigations, or a status more locally (pre-review) known as 'inactive', 'filed' or 'historic'. Chapter 15 provides an overview of the importance of conducting cold case reviews for missing person cases. It touches on the procedures in the UK, giving an idea of some of the good practice that is in place to ensure all relevant opportunities are progressed to resolve these cases, and then identifies some of the limitations and areas where further research could aid the search.

For the most part this book focuses on missing person cases where individuals are reported missing in the UK. However, each year hundreds of British citizens go missing overseas. Chapter 16 sets out circumstances in which people go missing, explaining the situation surrounding people who go missing abroad. The chapter describes the key agencies and bodies responsible for searching for missing people and investigating cases and the challenges and restrictions faced when conducting policing enquiries in other countries. British police procedures will also be explained. Also discussed is the support available to families, friends and found missing people from the voluntary sector both here in the UK and abroad. Meeting the expectations of families and friends is a crucial part of the investigative and supportive functions of the state and its third-sector partners, and comments on this issue are weaved into the sections of the chapter. Reconstructions of cases and case studies are used to illustrate work conducted to find and repatriate missing people.

Unfortunately, a very small proportion of missing person cases, up to 1 per cent of reports, will result in a fatality. The process of identifying of the deceased is a highly complex and sensitive procedure, yet essential for the resolution of the case as well as for the relatives of the missing person, who will then be able to come to terms with their loss of a loved one. Chapters 17 and 18 explore the process of forensic identification. Chapter 17 explores this issue in relation to individual cases where a body was found and is identified as a person who was reported as missing.

Chapter 18 explores the processes and procedures for recovering and identifying the deceased in a disaster. The chapter reviews the typical disaster response, the role of families in disaster cases and international coordination efforts in a disaster.

The emotional, financial and social impact on families when a loved one is missing is often significant. Therefore, Part IV focuses on the families of missing persons.

Chapter 19 explores the key themes in research about the emotional impact on families when someone goes, and stays, missing. Furthermore, the chapter introduces new testimony collected from 12 families of missing people, some of whom were interviewed in spring 2013. The chapter primarily focuses on people missing through accident, crime or individual choice.

Whilst there is a clear need to establish the whereabouts and safety of long-term missing people, it is important to additionally consider the wellbeing of the family that they leave behind. Further to the emotional repercussions, families of missing people can also encounter complex issues if there are not appropriate provisions in place to enable them to manage and protect the missing person's affairs whilst they are away, or to administer them if it is believed they have died. Chapter 20 explores the challenges families can encounter when attempting to manage or resolve a missing loved one's affairs (or their own if these are shared with the missing person). The chapter discusses the legal steps families may take, which include the presumption of death and guardianship of the missing person's affairs.

As we established earlier, the vast majority of missing person cases are resolved. Case resolution can take many forms, depending on the circumstances of the missing incident, the choices made by the missing person and the response of the people searching for them or the people to whom the missing individual reaches out. Chapter 21 explores the range of ways in which missing incidents can be resolved, the responses of authorities to the return of the person and the impact the return has on the person's family.

Throughout, the authors were encouraged to identify academic literature and highlight gaps in knowledge for the benefit of future research. Overall, the book illustrates how vast the subject area of 'missing persons' is and advocates that 'missing persons' should be regarded as a distinct research discipline within social sciences.

References

ACPO (2013). *Interim Guidance on the Management, Recording and Investigation of Missing Persons*. London: College of Policing.

Edkins, J.A. (2011). *Missing: Persons and Politics*. Ithaca: Cornell University Press.

NCA (2014a). *Missing Persons: Data and Analysis 2012/2013*.

NCA (2014b). *One Recorded Every Two Minutes: Missing Persons Figures*. Released 3 November 2014 (retrieved 9 September 2015). www.nationalcrimeagency.gov.uk/news/475–one-recorded-every-two-minutes-missing-persons-figures-released.

NCA (2015). *Missing Persons. High Level Data Reports 2014–2015*. UK Missing Persons Bureau. London: National Crime Agency. www.missingpersons.police.uk/download/53.

NPIA (2012). *Missing Persons: Data and Analysis 2010/2011*.

Shalev Greene, K. and Pakes, F. (2014). The cost of missing person investigations: Implications for current debates. *Policing: A Journal of Policy and Practice* 8(1): 27–34. doi: 10.1093/police/pat036.

SOCA (2013). *Missing Persons: Data and analysis 2011/2012*.

Part I
Missing Children

1

Children Missing from Care

Carol Hayden

Missing and Care

Children are more likely to be reported missing to the police than adults. In the UK, around two-thirds of all missing person reports to the police are for children and young people (NPIA, 2012). Research outside the UK confirms a similarly high number of children reported as missing. For example, American research shows that the great majority are children who have run away from home or care, rather than abductions and similar events (Patterson, 2008). Biehal and Wade (2000) point out that running away from child-care institutions is not new and that there is evidence across the centuries of children running away from charity schools, workhouses and foster placements.

Children who go missing are a varied group but research has clearly demonstrated that children in care feature disproportionately in reports to the police (Biehal and Wade, 2000; Hayden and Goodship, 2013). However, it is probable that children in care are more likely to be reported missing by carers, than parents reporting children missing from home, because of the professional role of care workers (Hayden and Goodship, 2013). Many of those not in care and reported missing are known to social services departments (Hayden and Goodship, 2013; The Children's Society, 2012a) and more than one-third are identified as being 'at risk of significant harm' (The Children's Society, 2012b). The risks of children going missing have been well established by a range of studies since the 1970s in the UK (see for example Sinclair, 1971) and by a series of reports and campaigns by The Children's Society (Safe on the Streets Research Team, 1999; Rees and Lee, 2005; Rees, 2011). A more recent focus in this field includes sexual exploitation (The Children's Society, 2012a, 2012b) and trafficking (Williams, 2012), issues that are dealt with in more depth in other chapters in this volume. Both of these latter issues interconnect with the circumstances and risks associated with being in care, particularly residential care.

'Care' encompasses a variety of environments including local authority, voluntary and independent sector residential care homes and foster care placements, as well as 'family and friends' placements, where a child is placed within the wider family or with significant others connected to the family. Existing evidence would suggest that although children are reported missing from all types of placement, children go missing more frequently from *residential* care (Biehal and Wade, 2000; Hayden and Goodship, 2013). There are just over 65,000 children in care in England at any one time, although around 90,000 a year pass through the care system, some for just a short period. Most of these children live in various types of foster care but around 7 per cent live in one of England's 1810 children's homes (Department for Education, 2012). Children's residential care is now predominantly (76 per cent of all homes) provided by the voluntary and independent sectors; only 24 per cent of homes are run by local authorities (Department for Education, 2012). There is great unevenness in the geographical distribution of children's homes: half of all homes in England are in three areas (North West, 25 per cent; West Midlands, 16 per cent; South East, 13 per cent) (Department for Education, 2012, p. 35). This latter situation means that 44 per cent of children are placed in homes outside the local authority that is responsible for them (Department for Education, 2012, p. 51). Around 42 per cent of children in care are aged under ten years of age; it follows that 58 per cent are over the age of ten (Department for Education, 2012).[1] Going missing tends to be concentrated in the teenage years (Biehal and Wade, 2000; Hayden and Goodship, 2013).

Prevalence and Frequency

Table 1.1 illustrates various recent estimates of the number of individual children reported missing from care in the UK as well as the number of incidents or reports. Local authorities have to report annually to central government on the children missing from care for more than 24 hours: this official data shows 930 individual children in 2011 (APPG, 2012). Police data shows higher numbers: 5,000 individual children and 17,000 incidents. The UK Missing Persons Bureau estimate is higher still as it includes children missing for short periods.

What Table 1.1 illustrates is how differently the scale of the issue can be configured, in relation to whether incidents or individual children are the focus of the analysis, and whether the child has been missing for over or under 24 hours. According to Rees and Lee (2005) young people living in residential care are approximately three times more likely to run away overnight compared with young people living with their birth families. Biehal and Wade (2000) estimated that overall around 30 per cent of those who go missing *and* are reported to the police are missing from care environments and most of these are missing from residential care.[2] They also found that the rate of going missing from residential care environments ranged from 20–25 per cent in two local authorities to 65 per cent in one large urban authority and 71 per cent in an inner London borough.

Research by the author (Hayden and Goodship, 2013) found a very similar proportion (to that of Biehal and Wade, 2000): 28.7 per cent of individual children were missing from care environments in a large police force that serves four local authorities. This police force had nearly 10,000 missing person reports in a one-year period, of which around three-quarters were reports on children. The perception was often that children in care accounted for a substantial

Table 1.1 Estimates of the scale of children missing from care and reported to the police in the UK

Source	Estimate
APPG (2012) police figures, > 24 hours	5,000 children
	17,000 incidents
APPG (2012) local authority figures, > 24 hours	930 children
UK Missing Persons Bureau (2012)	10,000 children
	42,000 incidents

proportion of their work, partly because of repeat incidents and partly because of the number of reports from a single address. Children in care accounted for 44.9 per cent of all *incidents* relating to children and 28.7 per cent of *individual children*. At least half the addresses that had the highest number of missing person reports each month (over a one-year period) were children's residential care homes. The number of reports from individual addresses ranged from 14 to 40 reports in a month from a single care home address. As most of these homes housed a maximum of six children and young people and not all went missing every month, the number of reports illustrates how multiple reports on a child are common, even in a short period like a month. Analysis of missing person reports across seven homes over a six-month period illustrated that although all homes had children reported missing in this period, the number of reports varied greatly (again endorsing the findings of Biehal and Wade, 2000). Shalev Greene and Hayden (2014) confirm these earlier studies and have also shown that 88 per cent of reports on children in care are repeat reports. The range in the prevalence across different local authorities suggests that the specific context of residential care (such as proportion of out-of-area and specialist placements) in these local authorities and in individual care homes (age of children, whether the home caters for short-term or long-term placements) are important issues to understand in order to reduce the number of children who go missing from care.

There is very little published research that focuses on children who go missing from foster care. Biehal and Wade (2000) found that there was no central recording in their four local authorities and overall recording by social workers was 'hit and miss' (2000, p. 214). They estimated that at least 5 per cent of children in foster placements went missing over a one-year period. The author found a much bigger proportion of carers (in a small-scale survey of 29 placements) had experienced a child going missing during 2010 (58 per cent) and that 78 per cent of foster carers had this experience at some point in their time as a carer. This local authority still had no central recording system for children missing from foster care; records were held by individual social workers.

More broadly, it is important to recognize that many children in care started to go missing *before* they entered the care system. The Social Exclusion Unit (2002, p. 14) found that 'while almost half of all young people in care are likely to have run away, many started running before they entered the care system'.

Why Do Children Go Missing from Care?

Children go missing from care for a variety of reasons, the most frequent of which relates to a desire to be somewhere else (often with friends and family) and for more freedom than they are allowed by their placement. Some aspects of the problem are created by the nature of residential care – for example, children in residential care cannot have a key to the home and there may not be enough staff to pick them up from a night out with friends (Hayden and Gough, 2010). Children and young people may be used to more freedom to come and go as they please than they find in both residential and foster care so react by not returning to their home when expected. Sometimes they are running away from bullying or arguments with other residents. Other reasons for going missing may relate to seeking adventure or excitement and trying to escape an accumulation of stress and anxiety. The importance of peer influence has been noted, particularly in relation to young girls. Children in care (particularly residential care) are also groomed by inappropriate adults who want to abuse them. Table 1.2 outlines the very different types of missing from care.

Adult involvement and sexual exploitation are possible in any of the situations depicted in Table 1.2, but the likelihood may well increase from situations 1 to 6. Trafficking is more likely to be an issue in disappearances from care. In July 2011, CEOP took the national lead for

Table 1.2 Different types of 'missing' and 'absent' from care

Type of incident	Example or explanation
1 Reported missing during the day	Do not go to school/leave the school site/do not come back from school but do not stay out overnight. Carers may or may not know where the child is.
2 Absent	Go to see family or friends, go to a party and do not return, often overnight or longer. Carers think they know where the young person is but either did not give their permission or expected them to have returned.
3 Missing from care overnight	Go out and do not return. Whereabouts *unknown* by carers.
4 Missing from care repeatedly	May relate to grooming and sexual exploitation or other dangerous activities (drugs, criminality).
5 Missing from care for longer periods	May relate to grooming and sexual exploitation or other dangerous activities (drugs, criminality).
6 Disappearance from care	May be related to trafficking.

missing children, acknowledging the link between going missing and child sexual exploitation. Going missing is increasingly recognized to be connected to the risk of sexual exploitation; and, in turn children who are sexually exploited are more likely to go missing (Sharp, 2012). For example, a study by Barnardo's (2011) estimated that around 50 per cent of the children and young people they worked with in relation to sexual exploitation went missing on a regular basis. CEOP (2011) in its national scoping study of grooming concluded that going missing frequently was in evidence in many cases and where it was not it is possible that parents had not reported their child missing. Similarly, the Children's Commissioner (2012) inquiry into child sexual exploitation in gangs and groups found evidence of children repeatedly reported missing in all 14 sites in the inquiry.

Morgan (2006, p. 19), as Children's Rights Director for England at the time, concluded from his consultations with children who had run away from home or care that:

> there are three very different sorts of running away – running away simply to enjoy yourself for a while before coming back; running to somewhere or someone you want to go to (like your family or a friend's); and, most worryingly, running away from where you have been placed because you can't cope with things or didn't feel protected there.

In 2013 it would be pertinent to add to these three groups – those who go missing because they are groomed for sexual exploitation or through trafficking or fall into these situations through going missing. Morgan's (2012) second report has more mentions of these latter possibilities, although the overall message is very similar.

Earlier research has generally concluded that going missing is a sign that something is wrong in young people's lives (Payne, 1995; Rees and Lee, 2005). This might include problems within a placement or at school, drug and alcohol use or offending behaviour.

Research conducted on reports to the Missing People charity in 2003 showed that 70 per cent of children who had been reported missing had run away by choice – this included those who stayed away from home without permission and without intending to leave for good. Biehal et al. (2003, p. 22), in a sample of 40 former young runaways, found that 'running away is more often a spontaneous reaction to hurt and frustration than a premeditated decision'. These researchers also found that one in eight runaways (12.5 per cent) reported having been physically hurt and one in nine (around 11 per cent) reported being sexually abused while running away (Biehal et al., 2003, p. 32).

Foster carers in the author's own research (referred to earlier, as part of the study reported in Hayden and Goodship, 2013) gave a wide range of reasons why children went missing from foster care:

> They run from school because they don't like school, they've run because they don't know the placement and they want to get home, they run to their pimp, they run to their best mates because that's where they've stayed for the last two weeks and they liked it there, they run to the previous foster carer, any number of reasons.

Other carers emphasized the excitement of going missing: 'They get high on running, you'd be surprised how addictive running away becomes.'

The location and well-documented lack of choice of care placements was another theme. Sometimes placements were too far away from family and friends (as is more often the case with residential cases); sometimes the placement was too nearby, as in the following case: 'I mean, placing a child with a foster carer who lives around the corner from mum, even if you are the only bed, is just a complete waste of time, you know they're going to run.' For some children, foster carers said that they liked the attention from the police, who could be very kind and understanding, sometimes even speaking up for the child when a carer was angry. Children were also said to enjoy a ride in a police car.

The Role of the Police and Children's Services in the UK

The great majority of children reported missing to the police in the UK are missing for very short-term periods (usually hours), but reports to the police are numerous and many happen later in the day or at night. This means that any judgement about risk and response has to be made in situations where there may be limited staff available to look for, locate and thereafter possibly transport children and young people home (Hayden and Goodship, 2013).

Central to the response to children in care in the UK is the way the police and children's services understand each other and react to children and young people who go missing. The police are often the default out-of-hours and emergency service when children go missing from care: the 'blue light social services'.

Hayden and Gough (2010) have noted that police call-outs to residential care are predominantly about children going missing, but that children who go missing are more likely to commit a crime. This latter situation can be explained in two main ways: first, 'survival crimes' (such as stealing) may be committed because the young person is away from their place of residence and has no money; second, being reported missing to the police by professional staff and the consequent contact and surveillance this brings is part of what has been described as the potentially 'criminogenic' environment in children's residential care (Hayden, 2010).

Following ACPO (2005) guidance, it was common practice for a few years for the police and children's services to make a distinction between 'unauthorized absence' and 'missing' in relation to children missing from care. In this situation adults would often know where they were or were likely to be (with friends or family) but they had not been given permission to be where they were and/or were unwilling to return to where they were supposed to be. In 2009 the NPIA (p. 8) guidance outlined a new position in which children and young people who were categorized as being 'absent without authority' but not missing would no longer be recorded as 'missing' by the police. However, in 2013 the concept of 'absent' made a return and was defined as: 'A person not at a place where they are expected to be' (ACPO/COP, 2013, p. 5). This position is qualified by stating that this category should be used where 'there is no apparent risk', and that such cases should not be ignored and must be monitored, escalating the case to 'missing' if there are any changes that increase the level of risk (p. 5).

This view illustrates the difficulty of the police position in relation to children in care. These children do account for a disproportionate number of reports to the police, many of which appear on the surface to be about lack of control in the care environment rather than children who are missing in the sense of whereabouts unknown. Nevertheless, children in care who are 'absent' from where they are supposed to be are unlikely to carry 'no apparent risk', partly because they have been taken into care because of highly problematic families and other circumstances, particularly as we know that the children are often returning to those same circumstances. This has led some children's charities to be critical of the 'absent' category. For example, Tucker (Head of Policy at the NSPCC, National Society for the Prevention of Cruelty to Children) is quoted as saying that:

> The length of time a child goes missing is irrelevant because they can fall into the clutches of abusers very quickly. We expect all professionals including the police to invest the right amount of time and take the necessary action to protect all children as soon as they go missing.
>
> (BBC, 2013, paras 12–13)

Recent Policy Developments and Responses to Children Going Missing from Care in the UK

There has been a flurry of activity around the issues of children missing from care in the UK in recent years. Children generally have had more attention in this policy area, particularly children going missing from residential care. What the various initiatives amount to overall is an attempt to develop more coherent policy and practice in this field, which should, in turn, enhance the safeguarding of children. Central to doing this is better inter-agency working and data sharing to inform the responses of police, children's social services and other agencies. Both the *Young Runaways Action Plan* (Department for Children Schools and Families, 2008) and the *Missing from Home and Care Guidance* (Department for Children Schools and Families, 2009) emphasized better support for young people who go missing, with the Department for Children, Schools and Families guidance promoting the use of return interviews and a named person who has responsibility for missing children at a local level.

In January 2008, it was announced that there would be an indicator relating to young runaways included in the National Indicator Set from April 2009. National Indicator 71 was introduced to create a focus on the provision of services to children who go missing from home and care settings. However, this national indicator was abolished by the incoming coalition government in May 2010.

Late in 2009, the National Policing Improvement Agency on behalf of the Association of Chief Police Officers (ACPO) launched a consultation on proposed revisions to the 2005 ACPO *Guidance on the Management, Investigation and Recording of Missing Persons* (NPIA, 2009). The key messages within this guidance were that going missing should be considered to be an indicator of other problems or criminality that impact on the person's life and contribute to their going missing, and the police investigation should be dealt with as a cycle, addressing safeguarding issues and reducing the potential for future missing incidents.

Section 6 of the more recent guidance (NPIA, 2012) focuses on working with other agencies in relation to missing persons and refers to the requirement to develop agreed local area protocols between the police, local authority children's services, other statutory agencies and relevant voluntary sector organizations. Protocols should be ratified by the Local Safeguarding Children Board (LSCB). Such protocols should cover both children who go missing from home and those who go missing from the care of the local authority.

The Children's Society (The Children's Society, 2012a) assessment of the state of play since the abolition of NI71 is as follows: 'Since the national assessment which measured local areas' performance in relation to runaway children was abolished, the responses to runaway and missing children and young people have been significantly downgraded' (p. 3). Ofsted (2013) inspections of ten local authorities concluded that: 'There is little or no reliable data on missing children … Most authorities were unable to evidence the impact of different interventions' (pp. 5–6). The Ofsted (2013) report illustrates that most of the key changes initiated in 2009 have not become established. Key information, such as 'safe and well' checks by the police are not always in evidence; in-depth return interviews are said to be 'rarely evident' (p. 6). Strategic planning is still said to be 'underdeveloped' and data systems are still 'unreliable' (p. 6). On the other hand, 'Inspectors saw evidence of some imaginative preventative work, mainly in schools, but the degree of attention paid to prevention was variable' (p. 6). Reducing the frequency of missing incidents is in everybody's interests. Where this was happening Ofsted (2013) found, not surprisingly, 'effective multi-agency cooperation, timely and persistent family support, continuity of workers, listening to and taking account of the views of children' (p. 5).

An additional and unresolved policy issue at the time of writing is cross-boundary placements (also known as 'out-of-area' placements), where children are placed outside their own local authority. In March 2013, 48 per cent of children in residential care (2,371 children) were placed outside their own local authority, an increase of 2 per cent on the previous year (Puffett, 2014). This increase has come about despite the desire to reduce the practice and the acknowledged risks of placing vulnerable children away from their home area. One of the problems of these placements is that they may put a big physical distance between the social worker responsible for a child and the child themselves. In many cases these placements result in reduced involvement of the placing social worker in a young person's life (APPG, 2012). A government consultation on improving the safeguarding of children in care (Department for Education, 2014b) has recently been completed. This consultation addresses the key issues of decision making in relation to cross-boundary placements – information exchange between placing and receiving local authorities. It is recommended that practice following any changes should be monitored, given the high number of children placed away from home.

At the time of writing it would seem that many of the long-documented and enduring problems about the evidence on and response to children missing from care are still present, particularly the lack of reliable data and the variability in response to this issue. However, the findings from the inquiry into victims of sexual exploitation (Children's Commissioner, 2012) has helped to bring a new urgency to the issue in England.[3]

Notes

1 For updated statistics see Department for Education (2014).
2 Children in care (foster and residential) make up less than 0.5 per cent of the population of children in the UK.
3 Also see HMIC (2016).

References

ACPO (2005). *Guidance on the Management, Investigation and Recording of Missing Persons*. London: ACPO.

ACPO/COP (2013). *Interim Guidance on the Management, Recording and Investigation of Missing Persons*. London: ACPO.

APPG (2012). *Report from the Joint Inquiry Into Children Who Go Missing From Care*. London: H. M. Government. www.gov.uk/government/uploads/system/uploads/attachment_data/file/175563/Report_-_children_who_go_missing_from_care.pdf (accessed 4 September 2013).

Barnardo's (2011). *Puppet on a String: The Urgent Need to Cut Children Free from Sexual Exploitation*. Ilford, Essex: Barnardos. www.barnardos.org.uk/ctf_puppetonastring_report_final.pdf (accessed 21 June 2013).

BBC (2013). Police shake-up over missing person cases. 20 March. www.bbc.co.uk/news/uk-21854549 (accessed 21 June 2013).

Biehal, N. and Wade, J. (2000). Going missing from residential and foster care: Linking biographies and contexts. *British Journal of Social Work*, 30, 211–225.

Biehal, N., Mitchell, F. and Wade, J. (2003). *Lost from View: Missing Persons in the UK*. Bristol: Policy Press.

CEOP (2011). *Scoping Report on Missing and Abducted Children*. London: CEOP. https://ceop.police.uk/Documents/ceopdocs/Missing_scopingreport_2011.pdf (accessed 4 September 2013).

Children's Commissioner (2012). *'I Thought I Was the Only One. The Only One in the World'. The Office of the Children's Commissioner's Inquiry into Child Sexual Exploitation in Gangs and Groups*. London: The Office of the Children's Commissioner. http://dera.ioe.ac.uk/16067/1/FINAL_REPORT_FOR_WEBSITE_Child_Sexual_Exploitation_in_Gangs_and_Groups_Inquiry_Interim_Report__21_11_12.pdf (accessed 4 September 2013).

Children's Society (2012a). *Ministers Give Evidence to Children Missing from Care Inquiry*. Press release, 9 May. www.childrenssociety.org.uk/news-views/press-release/ministers-give-evidence-children-missing-care-inquiry (accessed 21 June 2013).

Children's Society (2012b). *Make Runaways Safe: The Local Picture*. London: The Children's Society. www.childrenssociety.org.uk/what-we-do/policy-and-lobbying/children-risk/runaways (accessed 4 September 2013).

Department for Children, Schools and Families (2008). *Young Runaways Action Plan*. London: HMSO. http://webarchive.nationalarchives.gov.uk/20081107145633/The Department for Children, Schools and Families.gov.uk/publications/ (accessed 4 September 2013).

Department for Children, Schools and Families (2009). *Statutory Guidance on Children Who Run Away and Go Missing from Home or Care: Supporting Local Authorities to Meet the Requirements of National Indicator 71 – Missing from Home and Care*. London: The Department for Children, Schools and Families. www.education.gov.uk/consultations/downloadableDocs/Runaway%20and%20Missing%20from%20Home%20and%20Care%20Guidance.pdf (accessed 4 September 2013).

Department for Education (2012). *Children's Homes in England Data Pack*. London: H. M. Government.

Department for Education (2014a). *Children's Homes Data Pack*. www.gov.uk/government/uploads/system/uploads/attachment_data/file/388701/Childrens_Homes_data_pack_Dec_2014.pdf.

Department for Education (2014b). *Consultation on Improving Safeguarding for Looked After Children: Changes to the Care Planning, Placement and Case Review (England) Regulations 2010. Government Response*, January. London: Department for Education.

Hayden, C. (2010). Offending behaviour in care: Is children's residential care a 'criminogenic' environment? *Child and Family Social Work*, 13(4), 461–472.

Hayden, C. and Goodship, J. (2013). Children reported missing to the police: Is it possible to 'risk assess' every incident? *British Journal of Social Work*, 45(2), 440–456.

Hayden, C. and Gough, D. (2010). *Implementing a Restorative Justice Approach in Children's Residential Care*. Research Report. IC Portsmouth: IJS, University of Portsmouth.

HMIC (2016). *Missing Children: Who Cares? The Police Response to Missing and Absent Children*. http://www.justiceinspectorates.gov.uk/hmic/wp-content/uploads/missing-children-who-cares.pdf.

Morgan, R. (2006). *Running Away. A Children's View Report*. Newcastle-upon-Tyne: The Office of the Children's Rights Director.

Morgan, R. (2012). *Running Away. Young People's Views on Running Away from Care*. Manchester: Ofsted.

NPIA (2009). *Consultation Draft: Guidance on the Management, Investigation and Recording of Missing Persons*. London: ACPO/NPIA.

NPIA (2012). *Missing Persons: Data and Analysis 2010/2011*. London: NPIA/Missing Persons Bureau.

Ofsted (2013). *Missing Children* (February no. 120364). London: Ofsted. www.gov.uk/government/

uploads/system/uploads/attachment_data/file/419144/Missing_children.pdf (accessed 4 September 2013).

Patterson, G. T. (2008). Examining missing person police reports to identify the service needs of runaway youth and their families. *Journal of Human Behaviour and Social Environment*, 16(3), 73–88.

Payne, M. (1995). Understanding 'going missing': Issues for social work and social services, *British Journal of Social Work*, 25, 333–348.

Puffett, N. (2014). Out-of-area children's home placements on the rise. *Children and Young People Now*, 3 June.

Rees, G. (2011). *Still Running 3: Findings from the Third National Survey of Young Runaways*. London: The Children's Society.

Rees, G. and Lee, J. (2005). *Still Running 2: Findings from the Second National Survey of Young Runaways*. London: The Children's Society.

Safe on the Streets Research Team (1999). *Still Running: Children on the Streets in the UK*. London: The Children's Society.

Shalev Greene, K. and Hayden, C. (2014). *Repeat Reports to the Police of Missing People: Locations and Characteristics*. Research Report. Portsmouth: ICJS, University of Portsmouth. http://eprints.port.ac.uk/15145/1/Repeat_reports_to_the_police_of_missing_people.pdf.

Sharp, N. (2012). *Still Hidden? Going Missing as an Indication of Child Sexual Exploitation*. London: Missing People. www.nwgnetwork.org/resourcefilepublic.php?id=223&file=1 (accessed 4 September 2013).

Sinclair, I. (1971). *Hostels for Probationers*. Home Office Research Study Number 6. London: HMSO.

Social Exclusion Unit (2002). *Young Runaways*. 28 November. London: Office of the Deputy Prime Minister.

Williams, N. (2012). *MPs Investigate Why Trafficked Children Go Missing from Care*, 25 April. www.childrenssociety.org.uk/news-views/our-blog/mps-investigate-why-trafficked-children-go-missing-care (accessed 21 June 2013).

2

Hidden Links?

Going Missing as an Indicator of Child Sexual Exploitation

Nicola Sharp-Jeffs

Introduction

Child sexual exploitation (CSE) is receiving increased attention from the police and other professionals. This is due to a number of highly publicised cases such as Operation Span (Rochdale), Operation Retriever (Derbyshire), Operation Central (Rotherham), Operation Chalice (Telford), Operation Mansfield (Torbay) and Operation Bullfinch (Oxfordshire). It is also a consequence of significant government attention to the issue, including the development of the *Tackling Child Sexual Exploitation: Action Plan* (Department for Education, 2011).

At the same time, practitioners are frequently observing that many child sexual exploitation cases have a 'going missing' element to them. This chapter therefore presents a summary of what is known about the links between child sexual exploitation and going missing within the research literature. Since going missing is considered to include both intended and unintended incidents, literature related to running away, abduction and trafficking is explored. It is concluded that an awareness of the relationship between going missing and child sexual exploitation is useful not only in the identification of cases, but also in investigating, disrupting and prosecuting them.

What is Child Sexual Exploitation?

Ongoing research suggests changing and emerging forms of child sexual exploitation, leading Jago et al. (2011, p. 5) to conclude that there is no 'one model' of how young people are sexually exploited and no 'one method' of coercion. Since varying definitions of the boundaries of child sexual exploitation exist it is impossible to 'neatly segment' it into different forms (CEOP, 2011b, p. 86). The following definition therefore encompasses a number of different possible scenarios and is used in statutory safeguarding guidance on child sexual exploitation (DCSF, 2009, p. 9):

> Exploitative situations, contexts and relationships where young people (or a third person or persons) receive 'something' (for example, food, accommodation, drugs, alcohol, cigarettes, affection, gifts, money) as a result of performing sexual activities and/or another performing sexual activities on them ... In all cases those exploiting the child/young person have power

over them by virtue of their age, gender, intellect, physical strength and/or economic or other resources. Violence, coercion and intimidation are common, involvement in exploitative relationships being characterised in the main by the child or young person's limited availability of choice resulting from their social/economic and/or emotional vulnerability.

It is important to note that before the Sexual Offences Act (2003) child sexual exploitation was labelled 'child prostitution' (Adams et al., 1997). Yet this term ignored the inverse power relationships between adults and children, thereby dismissing the exploitive nature of this crime (Barrett, 1997). The Act extended the protection of the law so that no one under the age of 18 can consent to sexual activity where exploitation is involved. As a consequence, child sexual exploitation is now considered to be a form of child abuse (Jago and Pearce, 2008; Jago et al., 2011) and should never be considered to be a free 'adult' choice, leading to a lack of protective action (Harper and Scott, 2005).

Defining 'Going Missing' in the Context of Child Sexual Exploitation

'Going missing' is often used interchangeably with the term 'running away' when referring to children and young people. However, a number of commentators argue that there is a clear distinction between the two. For example, Rees and Lee (2005) note that the majority of children and young people who run away are not formally reported as missing. It is also observed that children and young people who are reported as missing do not fit the definition of running away (Smeaton, 2011), with scenarios ranging from children being abducted by family members or strangers, to teenagers who leave home to 'escape' something and to children who are 'misplaced' for periods of time – such as getting lost when shopping (Plass, 2007).

In recognition that the spectrum of 'missing children' events is indeed quite broad (Plass, 2007) this chapter adopts the missing continuum developed by Biehal et al. (2003). According to this model, missing incidents can range from an intentional break in contact which is deliberately chosen by the missing person (for example, running away from home) to an unintentional break in contact, which is not of their choosing (for example, trafficking or abduction).

It is further recognised that, in line with the Sexual Offences Act (2003), statutory guidance on children who run away and go missing from home or care protects children up to the age of 18 (Department for Education, 2014). This is in contrast to some definitions of 'running away' (see for example Rees, 1993; Smeaton, 2011) that apply the term only to young people who are aged 15 or younger. Such definitions are also problematic in the context of child sexual exploitation in that they apply only to those young people who 'have either run away or been forced to leave home and have stayed away overnight on at least one occasion' (Rees and Lee, 2005; Rees, 2011). Emerging evidence suggests that a missing child is believed to be at risk from child sexual exploitation, irrespective of the length of time they are away from home or a caring environment (Plass, 2007; CEOP, 2011b). Moreover, there is growing consensus that sexually exploited children and young people are likely to go missing from home or care on a regular basis and for short periods of time (CEOP, 2011a; Berelowitz et al., 2012).

Evidence of the Links between Going Missing and Child Sexual Exploitation

Risk factors indicating child sexual exploitation are well established in the research literature and are supported through analysis of child sexual exploitation cases (Beckett, 2011; CEOP, 2011a; Jago et al., 2011; Berelowitz et al., 2012). Barnardo's (2011b) identifies the 'top four' risk factors for child sexual exploitation as: going missing; substance misuse; disengagement from education, training or employment; and accommodation need.

Sexual exploitation cases may be characterised by one or a combination of any of these factors. Although care should be taken not to rely solely on going missing as an indicator since it will result in bias towards the identification of young women (who are more likely to go missing than boys: Office of the Children's Commissioner, 2012) the Child Exploitation and Online Protection Centre (CEOP 2011a, p. 47) nonetheless describes the overall coincidence of children and young people going missing and experiencing sexual exploitation as particularly 'striking'. Similarly, Scott and Skidmore (2006, p. 23) describe going missing in the context of child sexual exploitation as 'the most immediate indicator of vulnerability'.

Indeed, Jago et al.'s (2011) exploration of what actions are being undertaken by local partnerships to address child sexual exploitation concluded that a high proportion of sexually exploited young people 'go missing'. Snapshot data showed that well over half of sexually exploited young people using child sexual exploitation services on one day were known to have gone missing and, of those, over half had gone missing more than ten times.

The interim report of the Children's Commissioner's Inquiry into child sexual exploitation in gangs and groups also noted 'going missing' as a particular area of concern (Berelowitz et al., 2012). Here, 58 per cent of calls for evidence submissions stated that children had gone missing from home or care as a result of child sexual exploitation. In addition, all 14 site visits conducted as part of the inquiry revealed that children who were being sexually exploited were repeatedly going missing, in some cases three or more times within a two-week period.

The Nature of the Links Between Going Missing and Child Sexual Exploitation

It is unknown whether the nature of the link between going missing and child sexual exploitation is causal and/or linear. Some children and young people in the CEOP (2011b) scoping exercise, for example, began running away from home after having been groomed by an offender, while others were already engaged in a pattern of repeatedly running away prior to sexual exploitation.

Jago et al. (2011) and Beckett (2011) suggest that child sexual exploitation can operate in two directions. Children or young people may seek to get away from something (push factors) or to get to somewhere, someone or something (pull factors). This reflects the literature on running away and going missing which identifies 'push' and 'pull' factors as reasons for leaving. As such, sexual exploitation is considered to be both a cause and a consequence of going missing (CEOP, 2011a).

Push Factors: Towards Child Sexual Exploitation

Children and young people may be 'pushed' from home or care for a number of reasons. However, only a small proportion of children and young people who run away access help from statutory agencies (Rees, 2011) due to issues of trust and confidentiality and concerns about being immediately returned home if they are under the age of 16. Despite the existence of Section 51 of the Children Act (1989), which allows a young person to stay in a refuge for a maximum of 14 consecutive days and a maximum of 21 days in any three-month period, this form of support is inaccessible to the vast majority of young people since only two refuge places are available across the whole of England (Children's Society, 2011).

Whilst many young people will stay with families or friends (Rees, 2011) a number will find themselves in risky situations (Barnardo's, 2009) and will be vulnerable to the risk of sexual exploitation (Pearce et al. 2002; Jago and Pearce, 2008; Pearce, 2009; CEOP, 2011a). Plass (2007) suggests that running away from home, almost by definition, places any child in an unprotected and risky situation in which the likelihood of encountering a motivated offender is greatly increased (see also Payne, 1995; Liabo et al., 2000). A frequent form of child sexual exploitation in this context is the opportunistic abuse of a young person in need of help by an adult offering accommodation in return for sex (Stein et al., 1994; Payne, 1995; Barrett, 1997; Goulden and Sondhi, 2001; Harris and Robinson, 2007; Jago et al., 2011). However, it is also noted that, in some cases, perpetrators may specifically target locations that runaways are known to frequent (Kelly et al., 1995).

The 'Still Running' report by the Children's Society (Rees, 2011) found that one in nine young people said they had been hurt or harmed while away from home on the only or most recent occasion. One in six young people said that they had slept rough or stayed with someone they had just met for at least some of the time they were away. One in nine said they had done 'other things' in order to survive (in addition to stealing and begging). In addition there was significant overlap between these different experiences, such as being hurt or harmed, sleeping rough or with someone the young person had just met and risky survival strategies (Rees, 2011).

Pull Factors as Part of Child Sexual Exploitation

As well as being a situation that puts young people at risk, going missing can be a 'symptom' of sexual exploitation (Jago and Pearce, 2008; Jago et al., 2011). The involvement of young people in sexual exploitation does not begin overnight and overt force is rarely used by third parties (Scott and Skidmore, 2006). Instead, children and young people may be groomed by the offender to stay away from home for a short period of time, perhaps at the residence of the offender. In this scenario, the offender becomes a significant 'pull factor' by cultivating a sense of trust and affection before coercing the young person into sexual activity with friends and associates, leading to them being kept away from home for longer periods of time (CEOP, 2011a). Gifts received as part of the grooming process such as clothes, accommodation, money and mobile phones are also observed to enable young people to 'survive' away from home (Melrose, 2004).

CEOP (2011a) draws attention to the possibility that victim behaviour may be altered as a result of being groomed. Offenders may encourage children to go missing from home with the aim of deliberately causing conflict with parents/carers and creating an atmosphere which would encourage the victim to run away for longer periods of time. It is noted by the charity Pace (CROP, 2009) that even when victims of child sexual exploitation do not have a dysfunctional family life, the grooming process and subsequent changes in the behaviour of the victim can place families under significant stress.

Repeatedly going missing can therefore indicate a crucial transition period during which young people move back and forth 'between worlds'. Research by Beckett (2011) noted that some young people returning from missing episodes were observed to be tired, unkempt and undernourished and frequently agitated, upset or withdrawn. Furthermore, there was evidence that a number of young people were seriously self-harming on their return and this was suspected to be a reaction to some distressing experience while away.

Some young people will be reported missing from home or care dozens of times over a year or more. Although agencies may perceive that children or young people who repeatedly go missing from home or care are perhaps at less harm because they are 'streetwise', it is clear from the evidence that this assumption cannot be sustained (Barnardo's, 2009). Repeated missing episodes may in fact suggest that a child or young person is being groomed and therefore at very high risk of being sexually exploited (CEOP, 2011a). It is suggested that around 90 per cent of children and young people who have been subject to sexual grooming will go missing at some stage (DCSF, 2009). CEOP (2011a) state that it is vital for professionals to recognise this, since all too often the people who exploit children in this way will deliberately return victims home before their curfew in an attempt to avoid detection. Similarly, young people who go missing overnight will be returned to their residence in the morning (Evans et al., 2008).

Abduction

There is evidence to suggest that victims of child sexual exploitation may be abducted by their perpetrators (Pearce et al. 2002; Joseph Rowntree Foundation, 2003; Berelowitz et al., 2012). The Office of the Children's Commissioner for England (Berelowitz et al., 2012) notes that sexually exploited children may be abducted for periods of time and held with limited access to food, water and washing facilities. The Home Affairs Committee (2013) also heard evidence from a young woman that her exploiters had threatened to kidnap her for a few days to pay off money she owed them for drugs and alcohol.

Trafficking of Children Within the UK

It is recognised that child trafficking for the purposes of child sexual exploitation does not have to involve crossing international borders (Sillen and Beddoe, 2007). Research undertaken by Pearce et al. (2009) suggests that trafficking can be divided between children and young people who are trafficked from abroad and then internally trafficked within the UK (see also CEOP, 2007) and indigenous UK nationals who are trafficked within the UK. Under Section 58 of the Sexual Offences Act (2003), being moved for the purposes of child sexual exploitation within the UK is recognised as internal trafficking.

The purposeful movement of children for sexual exploitation within the UK is noted by Barnardo's (2009). The charity states that when a child or young person goes missing regularly or for several days at a time their case worker is always alert to the possibility that the young person may have been taken away to other towns. Some young people may report having been moved to a different location, others may be found in areas with which they have no known connection (Barnardo's, 2011a). CEOP (2011) observes how this can have a disorientating effect on the victim and is consistent with observations that movement into an unfamiliar area means that previous coping mechanisms based on local knowledge may become undermined.

Barnardo's (2011a) further describe how young people (who are often connected) are passed through networks, over geographic distances and between towns and cities where they may be forced into sexual activity with multiple men. In some cases internal trafficking for child exploitation may even involve the organised 'buying and selling' of young people by perpetrators who may not always be engaging in sexual activity themselves but are arranging for others to do so (CEOP, 2011).

Beckett (2011) identifies trafficking for the purposes of sexual exploitation in her exploration of the issue in Northern Ireland. In this study, a number of cases were reported of young people across the border of Northern Ireland after going missing, with concern expressed as to how young people were able to travel such distances without any obvious resources to do so. In some cases, abusers were reported to be explicitly facilitating this, through transporting young people themselves, arranging taxis and/or providing money for transport. Indeed, taxi firms have been implicated in a number of sexual exploitation cases (see Pearce et al., 2002; Barnardo's, 2011a; Berelowitz et al., 2012). Offenders are reported to be picking up victims from near their homes, on the street or from parks and driving them to other locations. In a number of cases, the taxi itself can be the location of the exploitation (CEOP, 2011).

CEOP notes how moving children and young people around the country may be part of a deliberate strategy by the perpetrator to prevent any single police force area obtaining a picture of the complete pattern of offending behaviour. Furthermore, the disorientating effect of being moved to multiple locations makes it harder for victims to report the identities and numbers of perpetrators involved (Berelowitz et al., 2012). This demonstrates the importance of effective information sharing.

Trafficking for Child Sexual Exploitation into the UK

A CEOP (2007) scoping report on child trafficking in the UK identifies migrant young people as a specific subset of children who go missing from care. This group is often called 'unaccompanied asylum seeking' or 'separated' children and is at particular risk of sexual exploitation, often having been trafficked into the UK for this purpose (Sillen and Beddoe, 2007; CEOP, 2010; Anti-Trafficking Monitoring Group, 2010). The missing episode is therefore often the first indicator that the child has been trafficked (APPG, 2012).

Research undertaken by Pearce et al. (2009) suggests that trafficked children and young people frequently go missing at the port of arrival into the country and then again after being placed in local authority care. After looking retrospectively at cases involving vulnerable children from abroad, Beddoe (2007) found that many were known or suspected to have been trafficked into the UK. Of 80 such cases, 60 per cent of children went missing from social services, usually within the first seven days of being in local authority care and in some cases within 24 to 72 hours.

A much larger scoping study by CEOP in the same year estimated that 56 per cent of 330 victims of trafficking had also gone missing without a trace. For those trafficked children who went missing and were later found, suspicion or evidence of abuse was recognised in the intervening period (CEOP, 2007). Similarly, 183 of 220 victims of trafficking identified by the government over an 18-month period went missing from social service care (Sillen and Beddoe, 2007), as did over half of 60 trafficking cases identified in West Sussex (Harris and Robinson, 2007).

Going missing can therefore be seen as a part of the trafficking process (Pearce, 2009). Beddoe (2007) suggests that young people may go missing as a consequence of following prearranged instructions given to them by the trafficker, who exerts control over the child and seeks to remove them as soon as possible. Once the child passes through immigration and is accommodated he or she is then collected, suggesting that there are persons expecting them in the UK (CEOP, 2007) who effectively use the care system as a 'holding pen' until they are ready to pick the child up (Home Affairs Committee, 2009). CEOP (2007) notes that those trafficking children for sexual exploitation tend to be linked to organised groups at varying levels, although there are also cases where children have been trafficked and sexually exploited by one person, highlighting individual opportunists who also engage in this trade.

Another scenario for trafficked children in local authority care is for them to choose to run away themselves. This may be out of fear of being found by the trafficker (Beddoe, 2007) or it may be because they are afraid of the possible repercussions of revealing information that will implicate the traffickers (Pearce, 2009). It is further noted that young people may run away because they are disturbed by the emotional impact of talking about traumatic experiences (Pearce et al., 2007).

Whatever their reason for running, these children remain at risk of further abuse and exploitation since they will not have any financial resources or identity papers (Beddoe, 2007). Local authorities may not have recorded any information about the child in the form of photos or other identifying details, making it difficult to look for them (Anti-Trafficking Monitoring Group, 2010). Indeed, in a strategic threat assessment, CEOP (2010) estimated that almost two-thirds of trafficked children are never found.

It has also been alleged that when trafficked children go missing, the police and children's services do not always respond in the same way that they would if a British child had gone missing (Home Affairs Committee, 2009). For example, local authorities may view child trafficking as an immigration issue (APPG, 2012).

In some cases children may even be sexually exploited whilst still under the care of the authorities. For example, children may be put in unsuitable accommodation and be seen to be disappearing at regular times of the day (CEOP, 2007; Berelowitz et al., 2012). Evidence to a recent APPG inquiry into children missing from care heard that trafficked children are being accommodated in provision such as bed and breakfast, hostels and supported lodgings, which do not have the level of supervision and specialist support needed to prevent trafficked children from going missing or being targeted for further exploitation (APPG, 2012).

Trafficking of Children Outside the UK

Links between going missing and trafficking for the purposes of sexual exploitation tend only to be recognised in cases where a young person has been trafficked into the UK and then subsequently disappears from local authority care (Arocha, 2010). However, another form of trafficking for the purposes of sexual exploitation is increasingly being recognised in the context of young British nationals being forced into marriage abroad (CEOP, 2010; Sharp, 2013). This is based on the argument that forced and underage marriage is in itself a form of child sexual exploitation since it too may be motivated by a third party receiving financial gain and is undertaken in the knowledge that movement of the child will almost certainly result in sexual violence (Mikhail, 2002; Asquith and Turner, 2008; Bokhari, 2009; HM Government, 2009).

The Child Exploitation Online and Protection Centre (CEOP) notes that it is possible that this trend is underreported as forcibly removing a young person from the UK for the purposes of marriage abroad may not always be considered to qualify as 'trafficking'. But a strategic threat assessment of child trafficking undertaken by the Centre identified a number of cases in which girls were believed to have been trafficked and forced into marriage (CEOP, 2010). There are therefore scenarios in which a young person may go missing from school (House of Commons, 2008; HM Government, 2009; HM Government 2010; NPIA, 2010).

Intervention

This analysis has provided an overview of how many different forms of 'going missing' are linked to child sexual exploitation. This suggests that, in exploitation cases where there is a 'going missing' element, specific tools may be used in investigating, disrupting and prosecuting it. For instance, it is recommended good practice that a return home interview is carried out with children and young people after a missing incident. Ideally undertaken by an independent person from outside the home/care environment, the interview can provide an opportunity for the young person to disclose experiences of exploitation. Not only does this assist in identifying the most effective follow-up support for the individual, but it is a useful tool for social services and the police to collect intelligence about perpetrators and locations where grooming, for example, may be taking place (Home Affairs Committee, 2013). This can then be used to improve the chance of conviction when perpetrators are identified.

Such intelligence can be gathered by social services and the police, recorded on IT systems and shared where appropriate. Increasingly, statutory and non-statutory agencies are recognising the importance of information sharing in this area and are identifying ways of working together. This may involve setting up joint protocols between agencies such as the police and children's care homes, co-locating agencies in multidisciplinary teams or setting up multi-agency forums such as Multi-Agency Safeguarding Hubs (MASH).

The use of Child Abduction Warning Notices is another way of disrupting those who seek to groom young people for sexual exploitation. Formerly known as Harbourers Warning Notices, these enable the police to disrupt undesirable activities of adults who are associating with young people against the wishes of the young persons' parent(s) or local authority carer. In essence, the Notices identify the child/young person and confirm that the suspect has no permission to associate with or to contact or communicate with the child and that if s/he continues to do so, s/he may be arrested and prosecuted for an offence under Section 2 of the Child Abduction Act (1984), Section 49 of the Children and Young Persons Act (1989) or for any other criminal offence committed in relation to that child.

The CPS observes that these Notices have provided useful evidence in many prosecutions, including in large-scale grooming cases. Whilst the Notices themselves have no statutory basis (they are part of an administrative process), they can, when issued properly, help to safeguard vulnerable youngsters and provide supportive evidence for criminal or other proceedings. Along with other mechanisms such as Harassment Warnings (Police Information Notices) and police cautions, their issuance can be used to help build a criminal case through establishing a pattern of behaviour and thereby undermining the credibility of defendants at prosecution.

Similarly, the use of trafficking legislation can help prosecute perpetrators of child sexual exploitation. As noted above, Section 58 of the Sexual Offences Act (2003) makes it an offence to move a child within the UK for sexual exploitation, regardless of the distance moved. This legislation was successfully used for the first time in Operation Span (Rochdale) illustrating that, where police have awareness of crimes that are associated with child sexual exploitation, they are able to approach the Crown Prosecution Service with more than a single charge, thus increasing the likelihood of a successful outcome. In this case the perpetrators were found guilty of a variety of crimes, including conspiracy to engage in sexual activity with a child, two rapes, aiding and abetting a rape, one sexual assault and trafficking within the UK for sexual exploitation.

Conclusion

As this chapter illustrates, there is a strong link between going missing and child sexual exploitation. When missing incidents are considered in relation to the missing spectrum, it is clear that professionals can also make use of abduction and trafficking legislation in their efforts to safeguard young people from exploitation. National police and statutory guidance exists to guide professionals through some of these complexities. Links should also be made with local sexual exploitation and missing person forums to establish protocols and help coordinate responses. Details about child sexual exploitation can be accessed via the NWG Network (www.nwgnetwork.org) and about missing persons via the charity Missing People (www.missingpeople.org.uk).

References

Adams, N., Carter, C., Carter, S., Lopez-Jones, N. and Mitchell, C. (1997). Demystifying child prostitution: A street view. In D. Barrett (ed.), *Child Prostitution in Britain*. London: The Children's Society.

Anti-Trafficking Monitoring Group (2010). *Wrong Kind of Victim? One Year On: An Analysis of UK Measures to Protect Trafficked Persons*. June. Northern Ireland: Anti-Slavery International.

APPG for Runaway and Missing Children and Adults and APPG for Looked After Children and Care Leavers (2012). *Report from the Joint Inquiry into Children Who Go Missing from Care*. London: APPG.

Arocha, L. (2010). Theoretical perspectives on understanding slavery: Past and present challenges. In *Human Trafficking in Europe* (pp. 30–40). Palgrave Macmillan UK.

Asquith, S. and Turner, E. (2008). *Recovery and Reintegration of Children from the Effects of Sexual Exploitation and Related Trafficking*. Geneva: Oak Foundation.

Barnardo's (2009). *Whose Child Now? Fifteen Years of Working to Prevent the Sexual Exploitation of Children in the UK*. London: Barnardo's.

Barnardo's (2011a). *Puppet on a String: The Urgent Need to Cut Children Free from Sexual Exploitation*. London: Barnardo's.

Barnardo's (2011b). *Reducing the Risk, Cutting the Cost: An Assessment of the Potential Savings from Barnardo's Interventions for Young People Who Have Been Sexually Exploited*. Research Briefing. London: Barnardo's.

Barrett, D. (ed.) (1997). *Child Prostitution in Britain: Dilemmas and Practical Responses*. London: The Children's Society.

Beckett, H. (2011). *Not a World Away: The Sexual Exploitation of Children and Young People in Northern Ireland*. October. Northern Ireland: Barnardo's.

Beddoe, C. (2007). *Missing Out: A Study of Child Trafficking in the North-West, North-East and West Midlands*. London: ECPAT UK.

Berelowitz, S., Firmin, C., Edwards, G. and Gulyurtlu, S. (2012). *'I Thought I Was the Only One. The Only One in the World.' The Office of the Children's Commissioner's Inquiry Into Child Sexual Exploitation in Gangs and Groups*. Interim report, November. London: Office of the Children's Commissioner.

Biehal, N., Mitchell, F. and Wade, J. (2003). *Lost from View: Missing Persons in the UK*. York: University of York.

Bokhari, F. (2009). *Stolen Futures: Trafficking for Forced Marriage in the UK*. London: ACPAT and Wise.

CEOP (2007). *A Scoping Project on Child Trafficking in the UK*. June. London: CEOP.

CEOP (2010). *Strategic Threat Assessment: Child Trafficking in the UK*. London: CEOP.

CEOP (2011a). *Out of Mind, Out of Sight: Breaking Down the Barriers to Understanding Child Sexual Exploitation*. CEOP Thematic Assessment. June. London: CEOP.

CEOP (2011b). *Scoping Report on Missing and Abducted Children*. London: CEOP.

Children's Society (2011). *Make Runaways Safe: Launch Report*. July. London: Children's Society.

CROP (2009). *The True Cost to Families of Child Sexual Exploitation*. Conference report. London: CROP.

Department for Education (2011). *Tackling Child Sexual Exploitation: Action Plan*. London: Department for Education.

Department for Education (2014). *Statutory Guidance on Children Who Run Away or Go Missing from Home or Care*. London: Department for Education.

Department for Children, Schools and Families (2009). *Safeguarding Children and Young People from Sexual Exploitation: Supplementary Guidance to Working Together to Safeguard Children*. London: HM Government.

Evans, K., Houghton-Brown, M. and Rees, G. (2008). *Stepping Up: The Future of Runaways Services*. London: The Children's Society.

Goulden, C. and Sondhi, A. (2001). *At the Margins: Drug Use by Vulnerable Young People*. In the 1998/99 Youth Lifestyles Survey. Home Office Research Study 228. Home Office Research, Development and Statistics Directorate. November. London: Home Office.

Harper, Z. and Scott, S. (2005). *Meeting the Needs of Sexually Exploited Young People in London*. Barkingside: Barnardo's.

Harris, J. and Robinson, B. (2007). *Tipping the Iceberg: A Pan Sussex Study of Young People at Risk of Sexual Exploitation and Trafficking*. London: Barnardo's.

HM Government (2009). *Multi-Agency Practice Guidelines: Handling Cases of Forced Marriage*. June. London: HM Government.

HM Government (2010). *The Right to Choose: Multi-Agency Statutory Guidance for Dealing with Forced Marriage*. January. London: HM Government.

Home Affairs Committee (2009). *The Trade in Human Beings: Human Trafficking in the UK*. London: House of Commons.

Home Affairs Committee (2013). *Child Sexual Exploitation and the Response to Localised Grooming*. Second Report of Session 2013–14. London: House of Commons.

House of Commons (2008). *Domestic Violence, Forced Marriage and 'Honour' Based Violence*. London: Home Affairs Select Committee.

Jago, S. and Pearce, J. (2008). *Gathering Evidence of the Sexual Exploitation of Children and Young People: A Scoping Exercise*. June. Bedford: University of Bedfordshire.

Jago, S., Arocha, L., Brodie, I., Melrose, M., Pearce, J. and Warrington, C. (2011). *What's Going On to Safeguard Children and Young People from Sexual Exploitation? How Local Partnerships Respond to Child Sexual Exploitation*. October. Luton: University of London.

Joseph Rowntree Foundation (2003). *The Choice and Opportunity Project: Young Women and Sexual Exploitation*. May. York: Joseph Rowntree Foundation.

Kelly, L., Wingfield, R., Burton, S. and Regan, L. (1995). *Splintered Lives: Sexual Exploitation in the Context of Children's Rights and Child Protection*. London: Barnardo's.

Liabo, K., Bolton, A., Copperman, J., Curtis, K. and Downie, A. (2000). *The Sexual Exploitation of Children and Young People in Lambeth, Southwark and Lewisham*. Barkingside: Barnardo's.

Melrose, M. (2004). Young people abused through prostitution: Some observations for practice. *Practice: Social Work in Action*, 16(1):17–29.

Mikhail, S. (2002). Child marriage and child prostitution: Two forms of sexual exploitation. *Gender and Development*, 10(1): 43–49.

NPIA (2010). *Guidance on the Management, Recording and Investigation of Missing Persons*, 2nd edition. London: National Policing Improvement Agency.

Office of the Children's Commissioner (2012). *Briefing for the Rt. Hon Michael Gove MP, Secretary of State for Education, on the Emerging Findings of the Office of the Children's Commissioner Inquiry into Child Sexual Exploitation in Gangs and Groups with a Special Focus on Children in Care*. July. London: Office of the Children's Commissioner.

Payne, M. (1995). Understanding 'going missing': Issues for social work and social services. *British Journal of Social Work*, 25, 333–348.

Pearce, J. (2009). *Young People and Sexual Exploitation: It Isn't Hidden, You Just Aren't Looking*. London: Routledge Falmer.

Pearce, J., Hynes, P. and Bovarnick, S. (2009). *Breaking the Wall of Silence: Practitioners' Responses to Trafficked Children and Young People*. London: NSPCC.

Pearce J., with Williams M., and Galvin C. (2002). *It's Someone Taking a Part of You: A Study of Young Women and Sexual Exploitation*. London: National Children's Bureau.

Plass, P. S. (2007). Secondary victimizations in missing children events. *American Journal of Criminal Justice*, 32, 30–44.

Rees, G. (1993). *Hidden Truths: Young People's Experiences of Running Away*. The Children's Society in Social Care, online. www.childrenssociety.org.uk/sites/default/files/tcs/research_docs/hidden_truths_summary.pdf.

Rees, G. (2011). *Still Running 3: Early Findings from our Third National Survey of Young Runaways*. London: The Children's Society.

Rees, G. and Lee, J. (2005). *Still Running 2: Findings from the Second National Survey of Young Runaways*. London: The Children's Society.

Scott, S. and Skidmore, P. (2006). *Reducing the Risk: Barnardo's Support for Sexually Exploited Young People. A Two-Year Evaluation*. London: Barnardo's.

Sharp, N. (2013). Missing from discourse: South Asian young women and sexual exploitation. In M. Melrose, and J. Pearce (eds), *Critical Perspectives on Child Sexual Exploitation and Related Trafficking*. London: Palgrave Macmillan.

Sillen, J. and Beddoe, C. (2007). *Rights Here, Rights Now: Recommendations for Protecting Trafficked Children*. London: UNICEF and ECPAT.

Smeaton, E. (2011). *A Review of Research Findings Addressing the Relationship between Running Away and Child Sexual Exploitation*. Unpublished.

Stein, M., Rees, G. and Frost, N. (1994). *Running the Risk: Young People on the Streets of Britain Today*. London: The Children's Society.

3

Child Abduction

Geoff Newiss

This chapter examines the research literature on child abduction. It draws primarily on UK studies together with select research from overseas where the findings have relevance to the UK context. The first section offers a review of the definitions of child abduction and the broader conceptual basis. The second section summarises the available data on the extent of abduction. Types of family and nonfamily abduction are highlighted in the third section, followed by a discussion of the implications for response and prevention.

Defining and Conceptualising Child Abduction

Child abduction is the unauthorised removal or retention of a minor from a parent or anyone with legal responsibility for the child. Child abduction covers a broad range of social phenomena. Not all fit within the relevant legal definitions or match broader public perceptions of child abduction.

Legal Definitions

The criminal offence of child abduction is defined in the provisions of the Child Abduction Act 1984. This applies, in different forms, in each of the four countries of the UK (see Parents and Abducted Children Together, n.d.). The Act makes it a criminal offence for anyone 'connected with' a child under the age of 16 to 'take or send' that child out of the UK without the appropriate consent. 'Connected with' includes parents, guardians or a person with a residence order or custody of the child. 'Appropriate consent' is the consent of the mother, the father (if he has parental responsibility), the guardian or anyone with a residence order, parental responsibility or the leave (permission) of the court.

Parental child abduction is usually treated as a civil matter. Legislation in each of the four countries of the UK gives effect to the Hague Convention[1] and other provisions relating to parental custody of, and contact with, children (see Official Solicitor and Public Trustee, 2011). The Child Abduction Act also makes it a criminal offence for 'other persons' to 'take or detain' a child under the age of 16 without lawful authority or reasonable excuse. 'Other persons' are people other than the child's parent, guardian or a person with parental responsibility for the child.

In addition to child abduction, Newiss and Traynor (2013) document other 'abduction related' offences. The offence of kidnapping exists in England and Wales and Northern Ireland, and is defined at common law as 'the taking or carrying away of one person by another, by force or fraud, without the consent of the person taken or carried away and without lawful excuse. It must involve an attack on or loss of that person's liberty' (Law Commission, 2011). Kidnapping overlaps with child abduction to a 'large extent' (see Law Commission, 2011, for a discussion of the legal overlap and Newiss and Traynor, 2013, for evidence of similarities in the types of cases recorded under each offence). An offence of kidnapping (which can be recorded for children and adults) may be recorded for older child victims (those aged 16 or 17 years old) for whom the offence of child abduction cannot be recorded.

In Scotland, the abduction of a child can also be recorded as a common law offence of abduction: 'the carrying off or confining of a person forcibly and without lawful authority' (Scottish Law Commission, 1987). Abduction can be recorded for child and adult victims. There appears to be little in the literature to examine the practice of crime recording between abduction and child abduction in Scotland. In addition, a common law offence of child stealing ('plagium') can be committed against children below the age of puberty (under 12 years for girls and under 14 years for boys) when the abductor has no parental responsibility for the child (Scottish Law Commission, 1987).

Serious Crime Involving Child Abduction

A recurring theme of the international literature is the need to distinguish offences meeting the public perception of child abduction (predominantly offences involving a predatory offender acting with a sexual motive, and in some cases resulting in the death of the victim) from other crimes that meet legal definitions, which may only require a child to be moved a short distance or for a brief duration (Finkelhor et al., 1992). Providing a clear account of the scale of different types of child abduction is necessary to inform public debate (Finkelhor et al., 1992) and for the development of effective prevention and safety measures (Boudreaux et al., 2000).

The US NISMART[2] series distinguishes the most serious offences of 'stereotypical kidnapping' from other nonfamily abductions (Sedlak et al., 2002). 'Stereotypical kidnapping' was defined in NISMART2 as occurring when 'a stranger or slight acquaintance perpetrates a nonfamily abduction in which the child is detained overnight, transported at least 50 miles, held for ransom, abducted with intent to keep the child permanently, or killed' (Sedlak et al., 2002). In the UK, processes to identify (and count) serious crimes (for example, rape and homicide) which begin with the abduction of a child victim are poorly developed (Newiss and Traynor, 2013). This limits our understanding of the risk of child abduction.

Perceived Victimhood

Not all individuals who experience child abduction may perceive themselves to have been victimised. For example, some children who are taken by a parent do not identify either themselves as a victim of abduction or the parent as an abductor (Freeman, 2006). Likewise, some young people may willingly go with, or to, a person they regard to be their boyfriend, and may resist attempts to disrupt what is perceived by authorities to be an exploitative relationship (see below). In other cases, individuals may be abducted but more readily identify themselves as victims of a sex offence, robbery, assault and so on.

Abduction and Missing

Abduction accounts for only a small fraction of all missing children cases. In the US, NISMART2 researchers reported that 9 per cent of children regarded as missing by their caretakers were abducted by a family member, and 3 per cent by a nonfamily member (Sedlak et al., 2002).

Likewise, not all children who are abducted will be recognised to be, or reported as, missing. Some incidents will not last long enough for a child to be considered missing. Some abductions do not necessarily result in the whereabouts of the child remaining unknown (for example if a child is retained by a parent). In the US, NISMART2 found that just over half of the children who were abducted by family or nonfamily members were regarded as missing by their care-taker, and just 21 per cent of nonfamily abductions and 28 per cent of family abductions were reported to the police or another agency for assistance in finding the child (Sedlak et al., 2002).

Extent of Child Abduction

Information on the extent of child abduction in the UK is available from different sources. These vary considerably in the type of incidents they cover and the limitations of the data.

Crime Statistics

The number of child abduction offences recorded in England and Wales rose dramatically between 2000/01 to 2004/05 to a high of 1,035 offences, before reducing back down to between 500 and 600 offences from 2007/08 to 2013/14 (Office for National Statistics, 2014a; see Figure 3.1). A similar trend was seen in Northern Ireland with a fall from 79 offences recorded in 2006/07 to 40 offences in 2013/14 (Police Service of Northern Ireland, 2014). It is not known whether these decreases are the result of a real fall in the number of crimes committed or are an artefact of crime recording practices (Newiss and Traynor, 2013; Newiss and Collie, 2015).

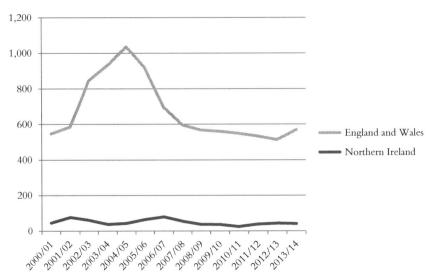

Figure 3.1   Police recorded offences of child abduction in England and Wales and Northern Ireland
Source: Office for National Statistics 2014a; Police Service of Northern Ireland, 2014

Over the last decade, the number of kidnappings recorded each year in England and Wales fell from over 3,000 (in 2002/03) to 1,727 in 2013/14 (Office for National Statistics, 2014a). Between 50 and 100 kidnappings were recorded each year in Northern Ireland over the same period (Police Service of Northern Ireland, 2014). It has been estimated that approximately one-fifth of all kidnappings recorded by police involve child victims (Newiss and Collie, 2015).

Likewise, in Scotland, it is not possible to distinguish child from adult victims of abduction in the data available from the Scottish government. For all abductions the trend again is a recent decline to 227 offences in 2012/13 compared to a peak of over 300 offences before 2006/07. Only three offences of child stealing/plagium (see above) were recorded in Scotland in 2012/13, compared to more than 40 offences recorded each year between 2001/02 to 2005/06 (Scottish Government Justice Analytical Services, personal communication, 25 September 2013).

Important limitations arise when using police recorded crime data as a measure of the extent of child abduction. Many abductions committed by family and nonfamily members are not reported to the police (see below). This inevitably means that police statistics offer only a partial account of all child abductions, and also suggests that police intelligence on offenders and offending patterns will have potential serious weaknesses.

Furthermore, police can generally only record a single crime for each incident (the Principal Crime Rule – see Home Office, 2014). Abductions which lead to a more serious offence being committed (for example, rape or homicide) will only be recorded as the more serious offence. Currently no means exist to identify and count serious crimes which involve child abduction. This limits a full understanding of the extent of abduction, particularly that with serious consequences.

Survey Data

Survey data highlights the gap between the number of child abduction offences recorded by police in the UK and the self-reported experiences of young people themselves. This may, in part, be explained by the use of broad, child-friendly definitions in surveys which do not match the legal criteria of child abduction. Whilst relatively few children are actually taken and suffer harm as a result, attempted abduction and incidents in which children fear for their own safety are far more common.

Radford et al. (2011) examined the prevalence of child abuse and neglect in the UK in 2009 using surveys of a random probability sample of 2,160 parents or guardians of children under 11 years of age; 2,275 young people between the ages of 11 and 17; and 1,761 young adults between the ages of 18 and 24. Respondents were asked if, at any time in their childhood, anyone had tried to kidnap them. Kidnapping was described to the participants as an incident when they were made to go somewhere, like into a car, by someone who they thought might hurt them. 0.2 per cent (1 in 500) of under 11s, 1.9 per cent (1 in 53) of 11 to 17 year olds, and 2.1 per cent (1 in 48) of 18 to 24 year olds reported an attempted kidnap. Nearly half of the attempted kidnappings (in each age group) were perpetrated by a stranger (Radford et al., 2011). In addition, Radford et al. (2011) asked young people about their experiences of a parent taking, keeping or hiding them from another parent; 1.1 per cent (1 in 91) of under 11s, 2.5 per cent (1 in 40) of 11 to 17 year olds, and 4.2 per cent (1 in 24) of 18 to 24 year olds reported such an experience.

Gallagher et al. (2008) carried out a survey of 2,420 school children in North West England in 1996/97. Forty-one children (1.7 per cent of the sample, or 1 in 59 children) reported that a stranger tried to get them to go with them when they did not want to at some point in their childhood. Four children (0.2 per cent of the sample, or 1 in 605 children) were made to go with a stranger against their wishes at some point in their childhood, three of whom were sexually assaulted. Gallagher et al. found that 60 per cent of victims of attempted abduction did not report the incident to the police.

Data on International Parental Child Abduction

Data on the number of international parental child abductions are available from numerous sources, including charities, government departments and legal and court agencies throughout the UK (Newiss and Traynor, 2013).

Reunite, the UK charity specialising in international parental child abduction, handles abductions to (and from) both Hague and non-Hague countries. In 2011 Reunite opened 512 new abduction cases, a rise of 47 per cent since 2001, involving 479 children abducted out of the UK, 189 children abducted into the UK and 16 children abducted between UK jurisdictions (Reunite, 2012). Similarly large increases in the number of abduction cases have been reported by the government units dealing with Hague cases (Lowe, 2011) and non-Hague cases (Foreign and Commonwealth Office, 2012).

Types of Child Abduction

Newiss and Traynor's (2013) study of 675 child abduction offences recorded by 49 UK police forces in 2011/12 illustrates how a simple categorisation of the relationship between the victim and offender (parent, other family, other known and stranger) masks a range of motivations and offence circumstances. Whilst most abductions perpetrated by a family member appear motivated by a desire for custody or contact with a child, some offences involve sexual abuse, a financial motive or domestic violence. Abductions perpetrated by a stranger can be motivated by financial gain and revenge as well as sexual abuse. Whilst the following section provides an overview of the broad types of child abduction, complexity between the victim–offender relationship and the motive/circumstances is ever present.

Much of the literature, particularly from the US, makes a distinction between family and nonfamily abduction and that same dichotomy is used below.

Abduction by a Parent or Family Member

Newiss and Traynor (2013) found that 19 per cent of child abductions recorded by police in 2011/12 were perpetrated by a parent of the victim. An additional 2 per cent of victims were abducted by another family member. There is little doubt that parental child abduction principally arises from a breakdown in the relationship between the parents of a child (Greif and Hegar, 1993; Plass, 1998; Hammer et al., 2002). NISMART2 findings indicate that only 4 per cent of family-abducted children were living with both parents at the time of abduction (Hammer et al., 2002). Divorce, separation, revenge, disputes over custody and broader cultural differences to bringing up children are all common factors in familial child abductions (Plass et al., 1997; Boudreaux et al., 2000; Lowenstein, 2002). Many abductions occur before a custody order has been made (Dalley, 2009; Redoglia, 2002). Some abduction occurs as a result of a parent (or occasionally both parents) seeking contact with a child who has been taken into care (Newiss and Traynor, 2013).

In other instances, abductions occur to remove a child from an abusing or violent parent (Weiner 2000; Lowenstein, 2002; Hoff, 2007; Mitchell-Miller et al., 2008). Girdner and

Johnston (1995) compared cases of parental abduction in California to high-conflict litigating divorce cases in which no child abduction occurred. The former exhibited higher rates of reported physical and sexual abuse, neglect, domestic violence and abductor criminal activity prior to the abduction than the latter.

In some cases familial abduction may arise from the perpetration of violence or abuse. Newiss and Traynor (2013) identified ten cases in which children, all aged under ten years old, were taken from, or held with, their mother, by their father or the mother's current or ex-partner, in situations involving violence or threatening behaviour. In addition, two fathers and three other relatives abducted children in order to sexually abuse them (Newiss and Traynor, 2013).

International Parental Child Abduction

Victims of international parental child abduction tend to be younger than children abducted in other circumstances. The 89 children abducted abroad by a parent in Newiss and Traynor's (2013) study had a mean age of five years (compared to 11 years across all types of abduction). Roughly equal numbers of boys and girls were abducted. Two-thirds of victims were from non-white ethnic backgrounds. Hegar and Greif (1994) report a dramatically higher rate of international parental child abduction for parents in interracial, ethnic and cross-cultural marriages than for other marriages in the US. The authors summarise a range of literature which indicates that relationships between partners from different national or ethnic backgrounds may be particularly vulnerable to stresses that might lead to the abduction of a child.

Lowe (2011) reports that the majority of (international) parental abductors (70 per cent globally) are mothers. The same author's analysis of Hague cases recorded by the Central Authority in England and Wales found that 40 per cent of abductors were the child's primary carer, 30 per cent the joint primary carer and 30 per cent the non-primary carer (Lowe, 2008). This presents an interesting contrast to the popular perception of an international parental child abductor typically being a non-resident father.

The Foreign and Commonwealth Office (2011b) reports that many abductions occur during school holidays when a child is not returned following a visit to the parent's home country ('wrongful retentions'). Compared to other types of abduction, children abducted abroad by a parent are likely to remain abducted for long periods. In Newiss and Traynor's (2013) sample over 70 per cent of children (where the duration was known) abducted abroad by a parent had not been returned to the UK at the time of data collection.

Assistance with resolving cases is provided by Reunite, the UK charity specialising in international parental child abduction; by the Foreign and Commonwealth Office (Child Abduction Section) for non-Hague cases; and by the Central Authorities in England and Wales (the International Child Abduction and Contact Unit at the Official Solicitor and Public Trustee, part of the Ministry of Justice), Scotland (at the Scottish government) and Northern Ireland (at the Northern Ireland Court and Tribunals Service) for Hague cases.

Nonfamily Abduction

Abductions by nonfamily perpetrators are equally diverse in nature.

Abduction by a Stranger

Newiss and Traynor (2013) collected data on 273 victims of stranger child abduction recorded by UK police in 2011/12 – 40 per cent of all child abductions recorded. A stranger was defined as someone who was not known to, or recognised by, the victim. Three-quarters of these cases involved an attempted abduction.

Victims in Newiss and Traynor's sample had a mean age of 11 years. Two-thirds involved female victims, echoing the findings from US studies (Finkelhor et al., 2002; Finkelhor and Ormrod, 2000; Mitchell-Miller et al., 2008). Nearly all abductions or attempted abductions by a stranger occur when the victim is outdoors, for example on the street or in a park (Newiss and Traynor, 2013; Gallagher et al., 2008).

Newiss and Traynor (2013) found that nearly two-thirds of attempted abductions by a stranger reported to police involved a perpetrator in a vehicle. Whilst most children suffered no injury, nearly half the victims were grabbed, dragged or held by the offender. Gallagher et al. (2008) found that nearly three-quarters of victims were with other children or adults at the time of an abduction or attempted abduction. Newiss and Traynor (2013) highlighted 22 cases in which young children were with their parent or carer when an attempt was made to take them, mostly from public places such as a shopping centre, play area or the street.

The motive for stranger-perpetrated offences, particularly attempted abductions, is often difficult to determine with certainty. However, a large proportion is believed to be sexually motivated (Newiss and Traynor, 2013; Finkelhor et al., 2002; Erikson and Friendship, 2002; Boudreaux et al., 1999). Newiss and Traynor (2013) collected data on 15 children who were actually abducted by a stranger in which the motive was clearly sexual. Five suffered a sexual assault or rape. Five victims first met the offender online, reflecting a growing concern about the use of mobile and internet technology, including social networking sites, in grooming people for sexual exploitation (Jago et al., 2011; Paskell, 2013).

Exploitation

More than one-quarter of child abductions recorded by police in the UK in 2011/12 occurred in the context of an exploitative relationship between the victim and perpetrator (Newiss and Traynor, 2013). In many cases the victim went willingly with the offender. Ninety per cent of victims were female, and three-quarters were 14 or 15 years old.

Abduction can occur in the context of inappropriate relationships (often involving a perpetrator who is significantly older than the victim); grooming and coercion from 'boyfriends' or peers; and organised networks of offenders in which victims can be transported – in some cases forcibly – for long distances to be abused (Pearce et al., 2002; Barnardo's, 2011; Jago et al., 2011; Paskell, 2013). Not all victims of exploitation will perceive themselves, or be perceived by others, to have been abducted. The use of Child Abduction Warning Notices (CAWNs)[3] is now an established police tactic for the disruption of grooming and child sexual exploitation (CEOP, 2011; Jago et al., 2011; Newiss and Traynor, 2013).

Involvement in, or with, gangs can also lead to abduction. Girls can be forcibly held or coerced into staying away from home in order to engage in sexual activity with gang members (Firmin, 2010; Berelowitz et al., 2012) or may be kidnapped and/or raped as a punishment or warning (Firmin, 2010, 2011). Male gang members also run the risk of abduction (often leading to serious violence) arising from disputes, retaliation and territorial matters (Department for Children, Schools and Families and Home Office, 2010).

The forced, coerced or manipulated movement of young people for sexual exploitation, domestic servitude, labour and criminal activity has also been reported in the literature on trafficking (see, for example, Beddoe, 2007; Dowling et al., 2007; CEOP, 2010).

Revenge or Dispute

Newiss and Traynor (2013) identified 42 children who were abducted for revenge or because of a dispute. These included abductions by someone known to the victim and by a stranger.

Victims had an average age of 15 years (older than victims of other types of abduction) and suffered a relatively high rate of injury, sometimes at the hands of multiple perpetrators.

Kidnap for Ransom

Whilst Newiss and Traynor (2013) found three victims who were kidnapped for ransom in their study, there appears to be little detailed research into this phenomenon in the UK. In the US, Finkelhor et al. (2002) found that 4 per cent of all (58,200) nonfamily abducted children and 5 per cent of all (115) victims of stereotypical kidnapping were held for ransom.

Child Abduction and Homicide

Only a small proportion of all child abductions result in homicide. Findings from NISMART2 suggest that there were 115 stereotypical kidnappings (see above) reported to police in 1997 in the US (this compares to over 58,000 victims of nonfamily abductions). Forty per cent of the victims of stereotypical kidnapping were killed (Finkelhor et al., 2002).

Sexual gratification appears to be the most common motive behind child abduction homicide offences in the US (Hanfland et al., 1997). Brown et al. (2006) found that three-quarters of victims of child abduction homicide were killed within three hours of being abducted. US research suggests that the majority of offenders have substantial criminal careers yet are versatile in their prior offending, including violence, property and drug offences, and offences committed against both child and adult victims (Beasley et al., 2009).

Unfortunately, there is little comparable research on child abduction homicide in the UK. Whilst the Office for National Statistics publishes data on child victims of homicide in England and Wales[4] (in 2012/13 there were 67 victims of homicide under the age of 16 years in England and Wales: Office for National Statistics, 2014b) no information is available on the proportion who were abducted prior to being killed.

Implications for Response and Prevention

The existing literature has highlighted numerous policy and practice implications arising from the different types of child abduction. The summary here focuses primarily on the UK context.

Dealing with the Effects of Abduction

Only children abducted by a parent for a short duration suffer apparently few detrimental effects (Sagatun and Barrett, 1990). Whilst effects may lessen with time (Greif, 1998), studies with clinicians and with adults who were abducted earlier in life indicate that children can experience severe trauma. Research from the US and UK documents physical impacts on children including symptoms of stress, such as sickness, headaches, alopecia and bed wetting; emotional impacts including anger, helplessness, guilt, loneliness, lack of trust and problems dealing with one or both parents; and social and behavioural difficulties (Greif, 2000, 2003, 2009; Freeman, 2006). As abducted children grow older they can experience relatively high levels of substance abuse, mental health and legal problems, issues with identity, and difficulties forging intimate relationships (Greif, 2000, 2003, 2009; Freeman, 2006). Left-behind parents and siblings can bear a similar toll of physical and emotional impacts both during an abduction episode and following any resolution, as well as considerable financial costs (Freeman, 2006; Bowers, 2007; Greif and Hegar, 1993; Spilman, 2006).

Greif and Bowers (2007) reported findings from a two-day focus group with five individuals whose siblings were abducted by nonfamily members (two were confirmed or believed to be dead and three were still missing at the time of the research). The participants reported considerable damage to family relationships, a loss of trust in the police, resentment and frustration with media portrayals of the abduction, dysfunctional coping strategies and a struggle to find meaning and purpose in life. These difficulties can extend to future generations of the same family.

Helping children, parents and families to recover from the effects of abduction is an emerging field of work. Freeman's (2006) interviews with ten children previously abducted by a parent found that whilst four had received services from a counsellor, psychologist or psychiatrist, only one reported this to be of any benefit. Greif and Bowers (2007) describe the implications for mental health workers in adapting their work to supporting siblings of children abducted by nonfamily members.

Greif (2012) proposes a framework of 'ambiguous reunification' as a way for professionals to conceptualise the process that families go through after lengthy separations. Whilst a child may be physically reunited with their family, either the child, parent(s) or siblings may be emotionally unprepared to accept the return and remain psychologically absent. Professionals working with families may encourage a grieving process to mark the time lost together, as well as encouraging family members to accept changes that have occurred which may result in new, often ambiguous, relationships, with divided loyalties.

Legal and Law Enforcement Agencies' Response

Freeman's (2006) research documented the frustration parents can experience with the legal processes for resolving international parental child abduction, and the need for specialist legal advice. The same author's work with abducted children highlights the need for children's views on return to be heard during the legal process and for their opinions to carry weight if the adverse effects of abduction are to be alleviated. Further research undertaken by Reunite indicates that specialist mediation, whilst not appropriate in all cases, can play an important role in helping some parents reach, and observe, an agreed solution, whilst minimising litigation and upheaval and the stress on children and parents (Reunite, 2006; Buck, 2012).

The police pursuit of criminal investigations in cases of international parental child abduction requires scrutiny (Newiss and Traynor, 2013). Research might examine whether police involvement helps to locate children or encourages parents to return an abducted child, or whether it delays resolution as abducting parents seek to evade contact with police.

The use of Child Rescue Alert[5] as a means of bringing information from the public into a police enquiry at the time a child remains missing has attracted growing attention (Newiss and Traynor, 2013; Laville, 2012; Casciani, 2014). In 2013 new guidance was released to clarify the basis for deploying Child Rescue Alert as the perception of 'imminent danger of serious harm or death' to a child (National Crime Agency CEOP Command and Police Scotland, 2013). This broadens the potential use of Child Rescue Alert to all types of child abduction, including parental abduction. Whilst Child Rescue Alert is still in its infancy in the UK, there has been debate overseas about the effectiveness of alert systems in locating and safeguarding children (Griffin and Miller, 2008; Pashley et al., 2010; Shalev Greene and Hedges, 2016).

The use of Child Abduction Warning Notices to disrupt child sexual exploitation has also attracted scrutiny. The Office of the Children's Commissioner (2012) asked the government to consider extending the use of Child Abduction Warning Notices in cases involving children up to the age of 18 (rather than up to the age of 16 as is presently allowed) and to permit them to be served without parental consent where necessary. A parliamentary inquiry into the effectiveness of legislation for tackling child sexual exploitation and trafficking within the UK recommended that the government place Child Abduction Warning Notices on a statutory footing and create an offence of breaching the conditions of a Child Abduction Warning Notices (Barnardo's, 2014). Newiss and Traynor (2013) recommend an evaluation of the impact of Child Abduction Warning Notices.

Global attention has been paid to rare cases of children being recovered alive years after being abducted (for example, the release of Amanda Berry, Gina DeJesus and Michelle Knight in Cleveland, Ohio, US, in May 2013 – see Walker, 2013; Jaycee Lee Dugard in California, US, in 2009 – see Batty, 2011; and Natascha Kampusch in Vienna, Austria, in 2006 – see Fickling, 2006). These cases raise important questions about the long-term response of the police and other agencies looking for missing and abducted children, as well as how agencies can support recovered children.

Prevention

Agencies continue to report large increases in cases of international parental child abduction (see above), highlighting the importance of prevention. Raising awareness of the effects of child abduction on both children and the parents involved is one component (see, for example, Foreign and Commonwealth Office, 2013). Some abducting parents are unaware that their actions may be unlawful and may be detrimental to their long-term prospects of securing custody (Freeman, 2006; Buck, 2012). In 2014, the European Commission produced two short films to explain the need for international couples with children who are separating to decide on child custody and visiting rights so as not to commit parental child abduction (European Commission, 2014).

Parents suspecting that their child may soon be abducted need immediate help, and there is evidence that early intervention can indeed prevent an abduction from occurring (Foreign and Commonwealth Office, 2013). Police forces and UK border staff need to be fully aware of the role they can play in preventing an abductor leaving the country (Newiss and Traynor, 2013). Parents need expert legal advice quickly. Poor legal advice, from solicitors without expertise in the field of parental abduction, can hinder steps to prevent an abduction taking place (Freeman, 2006).

Initiatives to prevent nonfamily abduction of children have tended to focus on the risk posed by strangers (Moran et al., 1997). The UK government released several public information films in the 1970s and 1980s to warn children of the dangers of going with, and talking to, strangers (see Parents and Abducted Children Together, 2013). National and local charities made, and continue to make, teaching resources available (see, for example, Elliott, 2000).

Child safety teaching programmes have focused on raising children's awareness of risky situations (for example, a stranger presenting a lure), instilling avoidance behaviours (saying 'no', walking away), and encouraging children to report incidents to parents, teachers and so on (see, for example, Holcombe et al., 1995; Miltenberger and Olsen, 1996). Effective teaching methods (for example, verbal reasoning, modelling, role play), teaching environments (individual or group training, parent/teacher or expert instructor), and factors that indicate maintenance of the behaviours have been examined.

However, other research (e.g. Collie and Shalev Greene, 2016) highlights the difficulties of a 'stranger'-based approach. Mayes et al. (1990) found that (particularly young) children demonstrate only a tenuous grasp of the concept of a stranger and nonstranger and differentiate poorly between them. Moran et al. (1997) studied the verbal responses of 168 children (aged 6, 8 and 10 years old) to video sequences of various child and known/not known adult interactions. They found worryingly high levels of compliance with adult approaches, even amongst older children. A recent review of the issues in teaching children to stay safe from stranger child abduction was published by Newiss (2014).

Understanding the circumstances of child abduction, who commits it, why and how, is vital to the development of effective, tested prevention strategies and materials (Boudreaux et al., 2000). A growing public policy concern is the role the internet plays in facilitating abuse and harm (CEOP, 2013; Lilley and Ball, 2013). A UK survey (part of the EU Kids Online programme) of 1,031 nine- to 16-year-olds who use the internet, found that 4 per cent had met in person with an individual they first encountered online (Livingstone et al., 2010). A significant challenge facing those concerned with abduction prevention is the development of teaching resources and strategies that cover the breadth of circumstances in which abduction occurs and inspire the appropriate avoidance behaviour.

Fear and Parenting

Cases of child abduction, particularly nonfamily abduction, can command enormous media attention (Soothill et al., 2004). This can impact on the public perception of where the actual risk to children lies (Slovic, 2000; Gill, 2007), and can create disproportionate levels of fear (Valentine, 1997; Furedi, 2001). Constraints on children's movement and outdoor activities, and the serious consequences on children's social, psychological and physical development, have been reported (Hillman et al., 1990; Gill, 2007).

For some commentators, these are symptoms of a 'moral panic' which is creating increasingly 'paranoid parents' (Furedi, 2001). In contrast, others have argued that a large part of children's fears is grounded in their actual experience of victimisation within their immediate social geography (Pain, 2006). These debates will continue to frame the development of abduction prevention initiatives and the broader public policy response to child abduction.

Conclusion

Child abduction covers a broad spectrum of social and criminological phenomena. Motives, circumstances and the relationships between victims and perpetrators are diverse and interwoven. Data on the extent of abduction are available from numerous though disparate sources, each with significant limitations. The situation impairs any accurate assessment of prevalence or trends. The UK literature specifically on child abduction is relatively sparse.

However, some broad patterns are apparent. Abduction by a stranger, resulting in murder or sexual assault, is a rare occurrence. However, survey findings and police data indicate that several hundred attempted abductions are perpetrated by strangers each year. Prevention measures must be grounded in the specific contexts in which stranger abduction occurs. In cases of attempted abduction, when there exists no prior relationship between the victim and the offender, the motive is often assumed (perhaps with little certainty) to be sexual. However, sexually motivated child abduction does occur in different circumstances, for example as a result of grooming, inappropriate relationships or involvement with gangs. Each presents its own challenges for policy development and prevention.

Many hundreds of child abductions are perpetrated by parents each year. There is evidence that international parental child abduction is a growing problem, which has substantial adverse effects on the children abducted and family members left behind. Key issues for agencies involved are prevention and awareness raising, methods to expedite resolution, and strategies for assisting children and families to recover and reunify where possible.

Notes

1 The 1980 Hague Convention on the Civil Aspects of International Child Abduction is an agreement between countries which aims to ensure the return of an abducted child to the country where he or she normally lives, so that issues of residence (custody) and contact (access) can be decided by the courts of that country (Foreign and Commonwealth Office, 2011a).

2 The National Incidence Studies of Missing, Abducted, Runaway and Thrownaway Children (NISMART) provide national estimates of missing children based on surveys of households, juvenile facilities and law enforcement agencies. The series provides statistical profiles of different types of missing children including their demographic characteristics and the circumstances of their disappearance (Sedlak et al., 2002). NISMART1 provided estimates for 1988. NISMART2 provided estimates for 1999.

3 A Child Abduction Warning Notice (CAWN) can be used by police to disrupt the activities of an individual who repeatedly associates with a young person (under the age of 16 if living at home, or under the age of 18 if living in the care of a local authority). A CAWN alerts the individual that they have no permission to associate, contact or communicate with a named young person, and that if they continue to do so then they may be arrested and prosecuted (CEOP, 2011).

4 The number of recorded homicides is published annually by the Scottish Government and by the Police Service of Northern Ireland. However, no further information is made available on the age of victims, the relationship between victims and offenders or how many victims were abducted.

5 Child Rescue Alert is a scheme to alert members of the public to an abduction or other high-risk disappearance, and to provide a mechanism for the police to handle a high volume of calls. CRA has been running as a nationally coordinated system in the UK since 2010 and is managed by the National Crime Agency CEOP Command on behalf of police forces (see National Crime Agency CEOP Command and Police Scotland, 2013).

References

Barnardo's (2011). *Puppet on a String: The Urgent Need to Cut Children Free from Sexual Exploitation.* Barkingside: Barnardo's.

Barnardo's (2014). *Report of the Parliamentary Inquiry into the Effectiveness of Legislation for Tackling Child Sexual Exploitation and Trafficking within the UK. Chaired by Sarah Champion MP.* Barkingside: Barnardo's.

Batty, D. (2011). Jaycee Dugard kidnapper handed long jail term. *The Guardian*, 2 June: www.theguardian. com/world/2011/jun/02/jaycee-dugard-us-phillip-garrido (accessed 28 July 2014).

Beasley, J. O., Hayne, A. S., Beyer, K., Cramer, G. L., Berson, S. B., Muirhead, Y. and Warren, J. I. (2009). Patterns of prior offending by child abductors: A comparison of fatal and nonfatal outcomes. *International Journal of Law and Psychiatry*, 32(5): 273–280.

Beddoe, C. (2007). *Missing Out. A Study of Child Trafficking in the North West, North East and West Midlands.* London: ECPAT UK.

Berelowitz, S., Firmin, C., Edwards, G. and Gulyurtlu, S. (2012). '*I Thought I Was the Only One. The Only One in the World.' The Office of the Children's Commissioner's Inquiry into Child Sexual Exploitation in Gangs and Groups, Interim report.* London: Office of the Children's Commissioner.

Boudreaux, M., Lord, W. and Dutra, R. (1999). Child abduction: Age based analyses of offender, victim, and offence characteristics in 550 cases of alleged child disappearance. *Journal of Forensic Sciences*, 44: 539–553.

Boudreaux, M., Lord, W. and Etter, S. (2000). Child abduction: An overview of current and historical perspectives. *Child Maltreatment*, 5: 63–71.

Bowers, D. T. (2007). *A Child is Missing: Providing Support for Families of Missing Children.* Alexandria, VA: National Center for Missing and Exploited Children.

Brown, K., Keppel, R., Weis, J. and Skeen, M. (2006). *Investigative Case Management for Missing Children Homicides: Report 2.* Washington, DC: US Department of Justice, Office of Juvenile Justice and Delinquency Prevention.

Buck, T. (2012). *An Evaluation of the Long Term Effectiveness of Mediation in Cases of International Parental Child Abduction.* Leicester: Reunite.

Casciani, D. (2014). Child rescue alerts: How they work [online]. *BBC News*, 17 January: www.bbc. co.uk/news/uk-25781623 (accessed 24 March 2014).

CEOP (2010). *Strategic Threat Assessment Child Trafficking in the UK*. London: CEOP.

CEOP (2011). *Out of Mind, Out of Sight: Breaking Down the Barriers to Understanding Child Sexual Exploitation*. CEOP thematic assessment. London: Child Exploitation and Online Protection Centre.

CEOP (2013). *Threat Assessment of Child Sexual Exploitation and Abuse*. London: Child Exploitation and Online Protection Centre.

Collie, C. J., and Shalev Greene, K. (2016). The effectiveness of victim resistance strategies against stranger child abduction: An analysis of attempted and completed cases. *Journal of Investigative Psychology and Offender Profiling*.

Dalley, M. (2009). *Missing Children Reference Report* [online]. National Missing Children Services, Royal Canadian Mounted Police: www.rcmp-grc.gc.ca/pubs/omc-ned/an-ra/annrep-rappann-09-eng.htm (accessed 16 June 2012).

Department for Children, Schools and Families and Home Office (2010). *Safeguarding Children and Young People Who May Be Affected by Gang Activity*. London: HM Government.

Dowling, S., Moreton, K. and Wright, L. (2007). *Trafficking for the Purposes of Labour Exploitation: A Literature Review*. Home Office Online Report 10/07. London: Home Office.

Elliott, M. (2000). *Feeling Happy Feeling Safe: A Safety Guide for Young Children*. London: Home Office.

Erikson, M. and Friendship, C. (2002). A typology of child abduction events. *Legal and Criminological Psychology*, 7: 115–120.

European Commission (2014). *Parental Child Abduction* [online]. EU Justice Portal: https://e-justice.europa.eu/content_parental_child_abduction-309-en.do (accessed 18 September 2014).

Fickling, D. (2006). Kidnapped girl found alive after eight years. The Guardian, 24 August: www.theguardian.com/world/2006/aug/24/davidfickling (accessed 28 July 2014).

Finkelhor, D. and Ormrod, R. (2000). Kidnapping of Juveniles: Patterns from NIBRS. Juvenile Justice Bulletin. Washington, DC: US Department of Justice, Office of Juvenile Justice and Delinquency Prevention.

Finkelhor, D., Hotaling, G. and Sedlak, A. (1992). The abduction of children by strangers and non-family members: Estimating the incidence using multiple methods. *Journal of Interpersonal Violence*, 7: 226–243.

Finkelhor, D., Hammer, H. and Sedlak, A. (2002). *Nonfamily Abducted Children: National Estimates and Characteristics*. Washington, DC: US Department of Justice.

Firmin, C. (2010). *Female Voice in Violence Project: A Study into the Impact of Serious Youth and Gang Violence on Women and Girls*. London: Race on the Agenda.

Firmin, C. (2011). *This Is It. This Is My Life … Female Voice in Violence Final Report: On the Impact of Serious Youth Violence and Criminal Gangs on Women and Girls Across the Country*. London: Race on the Agenda.

Foreign and Commonwealth Office (2011a). *International Parental Child Abduction*. London: Foreign and Commonwealth Office.

Foreign and Commonwealth Office (2011b). Campaign launched to help tackle international parental child abduction [online]. Gov.UK, 29 June 2011: www.gov.uk/government/news/campaign-launched-to-help-tackle-international-parental-child-abduction (accessed 18 September 2014).

Foreign and Commonwealth Office (2012). Parental child abduction is a worldwide problem [online]. Gov.UK, 12 December 2012: www.gov.uk/government/news/parental-child-abduction-is-a-worldwide-problem (accessed 18 September 2014).

Foreign and Commonwealth Office (2013). New FCO figures show parental child abduction cases on the rise [online]. Gov.UK, 12 December 2013: www.gov.uk/government/news/new-fco-figures-show-parental-child-abduction-cases-on-the-rise (accessed 18 September 2014).

Freeman, M. (2006). *International Child Abduction: The Effects*. Leicester: Reunite.

Furedi, F. (2001). *Paranoid Parenting: How Anxiety Prevents Us from Being Good Parents*. London: Allen Lane.

Gallagher, B., Bradford, M. and Pease, K. (2008). Attempted and completed incidents of stranger-perpetrated child sexual abuse and abduction. *Child Abuse and Neglect*, 32: 517–528.

Gill, T. (2007). *No Fear: Growing Up in a Risk Averse Society*. London: Calouste Gulbenkian Foundation.

Girdner, L. and Johnston, J. R. (1995). *Risk Factors for Family Abduction and Child Recovery*. Washington, DC: American Bar Association, Centre for Children and the Law and Centre for the Family in Transition.

Greif, G. L. (1998). The long-term impact of parental abduction on children: Implications for treatment. *The Journal of Psychiatry and Law*, 26: 45–55.

Greif, G. L. (2000). A parental report on the long-term consequences for children of abduction by the other parent. *Child Psychiatry and Human Development*, 31: 59–78.

Greif, G. L. (2003). Treatment implications for adults who were parentally abducted when young. *Family Therapy*, 30: 151–165.

Greif, G. L. (2009). The long-term aftermath of child abduction: Two case studies and implications for family therapy. *The American Journal of Family Therapy*, 37(4): 273–286.

Greif, G. L. (2012). Ambiguous reunification: A way for social workers to conceptualize the return of children after abduction and other separations. *Families in Society: The Journal of Contemporary Social Services*, 93(4): 305–311.

Greif, G. L. and Bowers, D. T. (2007). Unresolved loss: Issues in working with adults whose siblings were kidnapped years ago. *The American Journal of Family Therapy*, 35(3): 203–219.

Greif, G. L. and Hegar, R. L. (1993). *When Parents Kidnap: The Families Behind the Headlines*. New York: Free Press.

Griffin, T. and Miller, M. K. (2008). Child abduction, AMBER alert, and crime control theater. *Criminal Justice Review*, 33(2): 159–176.

Hammer, H., Finkelhor, D. and Sedlak, A. J. (2002). *Children Abducted by Family Members: National Estimates and Characteristics*. Washington, DC: US Department of Justice, Office of Justice Programs, Office of Juvenile Justice and Delinquency Prevention.

Hanfland, K. A., Keppel, R. D. and Weis, J. G. (1997). *Cases Management for Missing Children Homicide Investigations*. Olympia, WA: Attorney General of Washington.

Hegar, R. L. and Greif, G. L. (1994). Parental abduction of children from interracial and cross cultural marriages. *Journal of Comparative Family Studies*, 25(1): 135–142.

Hillman, M., Adams, J. and Whitelegg, J. (1990). *One False Move: A Study of Children's Independent Mobility*. London: Policy Studies Institute.

Hoff, P. (2007). 'UU' UCAPA: Understanding and using UCAPA to prevent child abduction. *Family Law Quarterly*, 41: 2–17.

Holcombe, A., Wolery, M. and Katzenmeyer, J. (1995). Teaching preschoolers to avoid abduction by strangers: Evaluation of maintenance strategies. *Journal of Child and Family Studies*, 4: 177–191.

Home Office (2014). *Home Office Counting Rules for Recorded Crime: General Rules* [online]. Gov.UK: www.gov.uk/government/uploads/system/uploads/attachment_data/file/340315/count-general-july-2014.pdf (accessed 18 September 2014).

Jago, S., Arocha, L., Brodie, I., Melrose, M., Pearce, J. and Warrington, C. (2011). *What's Going On to Safeguard Children and Young People from Sexual Exploitation*? Luton: University of Bedfordshire.

Laville, S. (2012). April Jones: Abduction triggers child rescue alert [online]. *The Guardian*, 3 October: www.theguardian.com/uk/2012/oct/02/april-jones-child-rescue-alert (accessed 24 March 2014).

Law Commission (2011). *Simplification of Criminal Law: Kidnapping*. Consultation Paper No. 200. London: The Law Commission.

Lilley, C. and Ball, R. (2013). *Young Children and Social Networking Sites: A Blind Spot*. London: NSPCC.

Livingstone, S., Haddon, L., Görzig, A. and Ólafsson, K. (2010). *Risks and Safety for Children on the Internet: The UK Report Full Findings from the EU Kids Online Survey of UK 9–16 Year Olds and Their Parents*. LSE, London: EU Kids Online.

Lowe, N. (2008). *A Statistical Analysis of Applications Made in 2003 Under the Hague Convention of 25 October 1980 on the Civil Aspects of International Child Abduction Part 2 – National Reports* [online]. International Child Abduction Database (INCADAT): www.hcch.net/upload/wop/abd_pd03ef2007.pdf (accessed 24 September 2012).

Lowe, N. (2011). *A Statistical Analysis of Applications Made in 2008 Under the Hague Convention of 25 October 1980 on the Civil Aspects of International Child Abduction Part 3 – National Reports* [online]. International Child Abduction Database (INCADAT): www.hcch.net/upload/wop/abduct2011pd08c.pdf (accessed 25 September 2012).

Lowenstein, L. F. (2002). Parental child abduction: A literature review. *Police Journal*, 75(3): 234–244.

Mayes, G. M., Gillies, J. B. and Warden, D. A. (1990). *An Evaluative Study of a Child Safety Training Programme*. Final report to ESRC, award number R000232018.

Miltenberger, R. G. and Olsen, L. A. (1996). Abduction prevention training: A review of findings and issues for future research. *Education and Treatment of Children*, 19: 69–82.

Mitchell-Miller, J., Kurlycheck, M., Hansen, J. and Wilson, K. (2008). Examining child abduction by offender type patterns. *Justice Quarterly*, 25: 521–543.

Moran, E., Warden, D., Macleod, L., Mayes, G. and Gillies, J. (1997). Stranger danger: What do children know? *Child Abuse Review*, 6, 11–23.

National Crime Agency, CEOP Command and Police Scotland (2013). *Child Rescue Alert. Practitioners' Manual of Guidance*. London: Association of Chief Police Officers.

Newiss, G. (2014). *Beyond Stranger Danger: Teaching Children about Staying Safe from Stranger Child Abduction*. London: Parents and Abducted Children Together and Child Exploitation and Online Protection Centre.

Newiss, G. and Collie, C. (2015). *Police Recorded Child Abduction and Kidnapping 2012/13 to 2013/14 England, Wales and Northern Ireland*. London: Parents and Abducted Children Together.

Newiss, G. and Traynor, M. (2013). *Taken: A Study of Child Abduction in the UK*. London: Parents and Abducted Children Together and Child Exploitation and Online Protection Centre.

Office for National Statistics (2014a). *Crime in England and Wales, Year Ending March 2014* [online]. Office for National Statistics: www.ons.gov.uk/ons/rel/crime-stats/crime-statistics/period-ending-march-2014/stb-crime-stats.html (accessed 18 September 2014).

Office for National Statistics (2014b). *Chapter 2 – Homicide* [online]. Office for National Statistics: www.ons.gov.uk/ons/rel/crime-stats/crime-statistics/focus-on-violent-crime-and-sexual-offences--2012-13/rpt---chapter-2---homicide.html (accessed 18 September 2014).

Office of the Children's Commissioner (2012). *Briefing for the Rt Hon Michael Gove MP, Secretary of State for Education, on the Emerging Findings of the Office of the Children's Commissioner's Inquiry into Child Sexual Exploitation in Gangs and Groups, with a Special Focus on Children in Care*. July 2012. London: Office of the Children's Commissioner.

Official Solicitor and Public Trustee (2011). *Child Abduction Law* [online]. Ministry of Justice: www.justice.gov.uk/protecting-the-vulnerable/official-solicitor/international-child-abduction-and-contact-unit/child-abduction-law (accessed 24 March 2013).

Pain, R. (2006). Paranoid parenting? Rematerializing risk and fear for children. *Social and Cultural Geography*, 7(2): 221–243.

Parents and Abducted Children Together (n.d.). *Child Abduction: The Legislative Jigsaw* [online]: http://childabduction.org.uk/index.php/briefing-papers (accessed 24 December 2015).

Parents and Abducted Children Together (2013). *Stranger Danger Archive* [online]: www.actionagainstabduction.org/cause/safe-not-scared-time-move-stranger-danger/ (accessed 24 December 2015).

Pashley, V., Enhus, E. and Leys, M. (2010). *Child Alert: Public Information Dissemination of Child Disappearances*. Research report. Brussels: Child Focus.

Paskell, C. (2013). *The Tangled Web: How Child Sexual Exploitation Is Becoming More Complex*. Barkingside: Barnardo's.

Pearce J., Williams, M. and Galvin, C. (2002). *It's Someone Taking a Part of You: A Study of Young Women and Sexual Exploitation*. London: National Children's Bureau.

Plass, P. S. (1998). A typology of family abduction events. *Child Maltreatment*, 3(3): 244–250.

Plass, P. S., Finkelhor, D. and Hotaling, G. T. (1997). Risk factors for family abduction: Demographic and family interaction characteristics. *Journal of Family Violence*, 12(3): 333–348.

Police Service of Northern Ireland (2014). *Trends in Police Recorded Crime in Northern Ireland 1998/99 to 2013/14*. Belfast: Police Service of Northern Ireland.

Radford, L., Corral, S., Bradley, C., Fisher, H., Bassett, C., Howat, N. and Collishaw, S. (2011). *Child Abuse and Neglect in the UK Today*. London: NSPCC.

Redoglia, E. (2002). Children abduction in case of separation and divorce. *Psicologia e Giustizia*, 3: 1–14.

Reunite (2006). *Mediation in International Parental Child Abduction: The Reunite Mediation Pilot Scheme*. Leicester: Reunite.

Reunite (2012). Reunite sees a sharp increase in the number of children parentally abducted [online]. Press release, 19 January 2012: www.reunite.org/news/reunite_sees_a_sharp_increase_in_the_number_of_children_parentally_abducted.asp (accessed 18 September 2014).

Sagatun, I. J. and Barrett, L. (1990). Parental child abduction: The law, family dynamics, and legal system responses. *Journal of Criminal Justice*, 18: 433–442.

Scottish Law Commission (1987). *Child Abduction*. Cm64. Edinburgh: Scottish Law Commission.

Sedlak, A., Finkelhor, D., Hammer, H. and Schultz, D. (2002). *National Estimates of Missing Children: An Overview*. Washington, DC: US Department of Justice.

Shalev Greene, K. and Hedges, C. (2016). The more eyes the better? A preliminary examination of the usefulness of child alert systems in the Netherlands, United Kingdom (UK), Czech Republic and Poland. *Analysis Report*. University of Portsmouth.

Slovic, P. (2000). *The Perception of Risk*. London: Earthscan.

Soothill, K., Peelo, M. T., Pearson, J. and Francis, B. (2004). The reporting trajectories of top homicide cases in the media: A case study of The Times. *The Howard Journal of Criminal Justice*, 43(1): 1–14.

Spilman, S. K. (2006). Child abduction, parents' distress, and social support. *Violence and Victims*, 21: 149–162.

Valentine, G. (1997). Oh yes you can, oh no you can't: Children and parents' understanding of kids' competence to negotiate public space safely. *Urban Geography*, 17: 205–220.

Walker, T. (2013). Ariel Castro sentenced to life plus 1,000 years in prison for abduction of Amanda Berry, Gina DeJesus and Michelle Knight. *The Independent*, 1 August: www.independent.co.uk/news/world/americas/ariel-castro-sentenced-to-life-plus-1000-years-in-prison-for-abduction-of-amanda-berry-gina-dejesus-and-michelle-knight-8741054.html (accessed 28 July 2014).

Weiner, M. H. (2000). International child abduction and the escape from domestic violence. *Fordham Law Review*, 69(2): 593–706.

4

Unaccompanied Asylum-Seeking Children and Trafficked Children

Chloe Setter

Introduction

The internationally agreed definition of human trafficking originates from the Protocol to prevent, suppress and punish trafficking in persons, especially women and children, that supplements the United Nations Convention against Transnational Organized Crime, which the UK and the majority of countries around the world have adopted. A child is defined by the Palermo Protocol and the United Nations Convention on the Rights of the Child as any person under the age of 18.

The trafficking of children is a process comprised of two distinct stages: the Act and the Purpose. This is the 'recruitment, transportation, transfer, harbouring or reception of persons, including the exchange or transfer of control over those persons … for the purpose of exploitation'. The definition of child trafficking differs slightly from that of adults, which requires an extra stage for trafficking to be present, that of the Means, 'of the threat or use of force or other forms of coercion, of abduction, of fraud, of deception, of the abuse of power or of a position of vulnerability or of the giving or receiving of payments or benefits to achieve the consent of a person having control over another person'. The Means stage is not required for the definition of child trafficking. This is not to say that this stage does not occur for child victims, but the definition recognises that a child cannot give informed consent to his or her own exploitation, even if he or she agrees to travel or understands what has happened.

Trafficking can occur across international borders but also within borders. The latter is commonly known as internal trafficking. This means that children who are moved around the UK for the purposes of exploitation, whether they are children from abroad or citizen children, can be considered victims of trafficking. Many children may have been trafficked to other countries prior to arriving in the UK.

Trafficking is a global phenomenon and it is estimated that 1.2 million children are trafficked worldwide each year (International Labour Organization, 2002). Children account for about one-quarter of all trafficking victims discovered in the UK (National Crime Agency, 2014) and the global child trafficking market is valued at over $12 billion a year (International Labour Organization, forced labour statistics quoted in National Crime Agency, 2014).[1] In the UK, it is difficult to estimate the true number of children trafficked. The National Crime Agency identified nearly 700 potential child victims of trafficking, for example, in 2014, but itself acknowledged that around two-thirds of victims do not go through the official identification process (SOCA and UK Human Trafficking Centre, 2013). Government estimates put the total number of adult and child victims of modern slavery in the UK at about 13,000.[2] Charities and support providers claim the official statistics are the 'tip of the iceberg' figure because of issues around identification, which will be explored later in this chapter.

The majority of child victims of trafficking in the UK are not British nationals and are trafficked into the UK across the border. In the year 2014, the top countries of origin for children trafficked in the UK were Albania, Vietnam, UK, Slovakia, Nigeria, Bangladesh, Eritrea, Romania, Afghanistan, China and the Democratic Republic of Congo. However, since 2009, there have been children identified from more than 50 countries across the world.

Some trafficked children may arrive in the UK from abroad unaccompanied, while others are accompanied by adults, including those who are trafficked by their own family and may be travelling with their parents, close relatives or strangers claiming to be a relative (Department for Education, 2014). An unaccompanied asylum-seeking child is defined as a child who has been separated from both parents and other relatives and is not being cared for by an adult who, by law or custom, is responsible for doing so (UNICEF, 2008). A separated child has been separated from both parents, or from their legal or customary primary caregiver, but not necessarily from other relatives (UNICEF, 2008). Most children trafficked to the UK are 'separated children', which encompasses the term 'unaccompanied asylum-seeking children'. Trafficked children may or may not seek asylum on arrival in the UK. They may not need to, for example if they are from a European Union country and have a right to reside in the UK (ECPAT UK, 2009). Some travel on false documents or someone else's documents provided by the trafficker, while others are smuggled in without any identification documents. Others may have travelled using an approved visa, such as a student visa or visitor visa. They can arrive via air, boat, rail or land. It is therefore unhelpful to classify all potential victims of trafficking as asylum-seeking children and to view them from an immigration perspective. This may lead to a risk that those children who do not have immigration issues at the border, or who are accompanied, are overlooked.

Trafficking can affect children of all ages, although research indicates that most children are aged over 12 when identified. Statistics for 2012 (SOCA and UK Human Trafficking Centre, 2013) show that nearly half of the children identified are aged 16–17, with one-third aged 15 and under (10 per cent of these were under 10). Generally, girls are more likely to be trafficked to the UK than boys (CEOP, 2010) but the number of males is thought to be on the increase. Children are trafficked for a variety of types of exploitation, including: sexual; forced labour; domestic servitude; enforced criminality and begging; organ removal; forced marriage; and illegal adoption.

Child trafficking is child abuse and trafficked children, who are particularly vulnerable, will need the care and protection of the state. Under Section 17 of the Children Act 1989, local authorities have a duty to safeguard and promote the welfare of all children in their area who are in need. Also under the Children Act 1989, local authorities have a duty to investigate when they are informed of a child who is suffering or likely to suffer significant harm under Section 47. Harm in this context can be defined as exploitation, detention in an immigration removal centre, enforced removal to face persecution or breaches of rights under the European Convention on Human Rights (Crawley, 2012).

Unaccompanied and trafficked children are usually accommodated under Section 20 of the Children Act 1989, which requires local authorities to look after under 16s who cannot be appropriately looked after by someone else – children who have no parents or children whose parents (or adults with parental responsibility) are unable to care for them. Those over

16 who have been assessed as vulnerable will also be accommodated under Section 20. When looking after a child under Section 20, the local authority is acting as the child's 'corporate parent'. If a young person who has been looked after by a local authority for 13 weeks or more turns 18, the local authority continues to have a duty to provide them with assistance until they are 21 (or up to 25 if they are in full-time education). Under Section 47 of the Children Act (1989) a local authority should initiate a joint inquiry with the police where a child is believed to be at risk of serious harm.

Missing as an Indicator of Trafficking

Children who are in care are three times more likely to run away than other children (APPG for Runaway and Missing Children and Adults and the APPG for Looked After Children and Care Leavers, 2012) with the APPGs' Joint Inquiry in 2012 finding: 'Trafficked children from abroad are particularly being let down and their needs ignored because the authorities view child trafficking as an immigration control issue. Hundreds of them disappear from care every year and the majority are never found again.'

These issues are still of huge concern, despite research over many years highlighting the problem. Research by the children's charity ECPAT UK in 2001 highlighted early concerns about trafficked children going missing from local authority care and called for improved measures of safe accommodation. The stark reality of the situation was highlighted in a later report, which found that nearly two-thirds (60 per cent) of child victims of trafficking from a sample population in the North West, North East and West Midlands went missing from local authority care (ECPAT UK, 2007, p. 5). In 2009, a Home Affairs Select Committee report on human trafficking highlighted that traffickers may be using the 'care home system for vulnerable children as holding pens for their victims until they are ready to pick them up' (Home Affairs Committee, 2009, p. 58). In the same year, the then Prime Minister Gordon Brown described this situation as 'completely unacceptable' (House of Commons debate, 6 May 2009, c163).

The NSPCC's Child Trafficking Advice Centre received 715 child referrals from 13 September 2007 to 19 April 2012 (NSPCC, 2012). One hundred and sixty-one of those referred had been reported missing at some time. Of those missing trafficked children, 73 are still missing, 26 have been found, 11 returned and 18 classed as 'unknown'. Of the children who went missing, 58 per cent were being exploited for criminal activity (street-based crimes) and cannabis cultivation. These statistics highlight a growing trend in trafficking for forced criminality, which uses children to commit crimes, such as pickpocketing, theft, shoplifting, ATM theft and cannabis cultivation. These children are often first identified via police raids or arrests and are often treated as criminals and not victims of trafficking. If bailed or once out of custody, the children often go missing and are retrafficked. The Crown Prosecution Service has issued guidance on the nonprosecution of victims of trafficking in line with European legislation on the issue in 2011, 2012 and 2013 (Crown Prosecution Service, 2011, 2013). Despite this, convictions still take place (RACE in Europe Project, 2014). Tackling the criminalisation of victims should be an immediate priority for the UK government and relevant agencies, particularly in light of a recent Court of Appeal judgment that quashed the convictions of three Vietnamese children who had been trafficked to work in cannabis factories in the UK (*R v L and others*, 2013).

Concern over the number of children who are potential victims of trafficking going missing from care has been highlighted in the media, for example the case of 77 Chinese children who disappeared from one London local authority between 2006 and 2009, with several of the girls later found being exploited in brothels (Booth, 2009). The large proportion of children of Vietnamese ethnicity featured on the Missing Kids website has also been highlighted

(Judah, 2013). At the time, ECPAT UK identified that, of 118 children listed as missing on this site, 24 were Vietnamese (20 males, 4 females) and 14 were Chinese (4 males and 10 females). Yet, media attention when these young people go missing is often low, especially in comparison to their British counterparts. Vietnam was the top country of origin for trafficked children in the UK in 2013 with 76 victims identified, rising to 109 in 2014 (second only to Albania), and the fear is that, in the context of a huge rise in the number of cannabis farms found by police in the UK (ACPO, 2012), many of these children are being trafficked and retrafficked to work as 'gardeners' in these illegal and dangerous farms. In the county of Kent, 28 Vietnamese children went missing from care in 2010, according to research by the Office of the Children's Commissioner for England, with 60 per cent of the young people going missing within three days of entering care. The Children's Commissioner recommended that, due to the fact that virtually all unaccompanied Vietnamese children in Kent went missing (and the only ones recovered to date had been found in cannabis factories), 'all unaccompanied Vietnamese children should be regarded, prima facia, as having being trafficked' (APPG Inquiry, 2012, pp. 2–3).[3]

Control of the Traffickers

Most victims go missing within one week of being in care, many within 48 hours and often before being registered with social services (APPG Inquiry, 2012). The main reason cited for their disappearance is the fact they are 'groomed so effectively by their traffickers that the children are so terrified of what might happen to them or their families if they break their bond or tell the authorities' that they run back into the hands of their traffickers (p. 13).

In order to understand and attempt to tackle the issue of child victims of trafficking missing from care, it is vital to look at the reasons why children go missing in the context of their trafficking experience and lives in their countries of origin, in particular looking at how the traffickers operate and their control methods. Some traffickers abduct or kidnap their victims, but frequently children and their families are deceived into believing the child will gain education or respectable work, such as in a restaurant or as a domestic servant. Often the traffickers will seek to control the child by removing their documents and threatening that the child will be deported if he or she tries to escape. In addition, the creation of a false identity can give the trafficker direct control over every aspect of the child's life, particularly if they claim to be a parent or family member. Traffickers control their victims in a number of other ways, such as direct violence, or threats of, to both the child and his or her family. They often keep the child isolated, which may be made easier by the child's inability to speak English. Often children are told that they owe large amounts of money and they must work to pay this off – sometimes these sums are impossibly large. In many cases, particularly from Africa, voodoo, witchcraft or juju (a traditional West African belief) is used to frighten the children, who are told they or their families may die if they speak about what is happening to them (ECPAT UK, 2011). The long-term impact of such terror can be devastating for children.

The main reason why children are trafficked is for financial gain. This can include payment from or to the child's parents and can place the child in debt bondage to the traffickers. Commonly, the trafficker receives payment from those wanting to exploit the child once he or she is in the UK. Traffickers frequently operate as part of an organised crime network in which many 'agents' or 'facilitators' play a role in enabling trafficking. Some organised crime groups are very complex and strategic, trafficking a number of victims in many countries.

It is important to note that child victims of trafficking are actually witnesses to a serious crime, one that is currently punishable by up to life in prison under the new Modern Slavery Act

(England and Wales), the Northern Ireland Human Trafficking and Exploitation Act and the Human Trafficking and Exploitation (Scotland) Act. When children are identified as suspected victims, those tasked with protecting and supporting them must consider this as part of their protection plan, particularly as the traffickers, in most instances, have not been prosecuted and are still at large. This means children are faced with the fear of what might happen if someone finds out they have been identified. Some professionals may view being 'rescued' as the end of the young person's journey, but for most children it is just another stage that they must pass through in order to fulfil what they have been told they must do in order to 'win back' their safety or freedom.

Identification of Child Victims of Trafficking

Early identification of children is critical but it is not an easy task. Child victims are unlikely to give direct disclosures and their accounts may be confused and sometimes contradictory – often because they are traumatised or scared of telling the truth. Child victims of trafficking in the UK may come to the notice of the authorities through a wide range of sources, including the health, legal, education, welfare, police and immigration sectors, together with NGOs and the wider public.

In 2009, as a result of the UK ratifying the Council of Europe Convention on Action against Human Trafficking, a system for formal identification of child and adult victims was introduced called the National Referral Mechanism. It is a framework for identifying victims of trafficking and ensuring they receive the appropriate protection and support. The National Referral Mechanism is also the mechanism through which the UK Human Trafficking Centre collects data about victims. In the same way as any child protection referral, the referral will be made with or without the child's consent, but it is best practice to discuss the referral with the child and try to explain the process and seek their consent.

ECPAT UK has criticised the way the National Referral Mechanism operates for children. Awareness of the National Referral Mechanism among front-line workers is very low, which often means children are not referred and so there are no reliable statistics to give an accurate picture of the scale of the problem. There are also serious concerns about the way decisions on victim status are made for children, particularly as decisions involving non-EU children, or where immigration is an issue, are made by what was the UK Border Agency (UK Border Authority), now mainly Home Office Immigration and Visas. This department within the Home Office is primarily tasked with protecting the UK's borders and has been criticised widely for operating with a 'culture of disbelief' when processing National Referral Mechanism cases (Children's Society, 2012). ECPAT UK has also raised the issue of a lack of child-specific knowledge within the Home Office and the UK Human Trafficking Centre. There is also no formal appeals process in the National Referral Mechanism. In 2014, the Home Office completed a review of the National Referral Mechanism, publishing recommendations for a revised system that is currently being trialled in South West England and West Yorkshire.

Early and robust identification of child victims of trafficking is essential for trust to be developed to enable the child to disclose their experiences, which then enables practitioners to safeguard the child effectively and for evidence to be gathered for a criminal investigation. The reaction of practitioners to a suspected trafficked child will have an important bearing on the child's perception of UK authorities. Many children are not believed when they do disclose their experiences, often because their accounts seem too horrific. Discrepancies in accounts can lead to accusations that the child has made up the story in order to improve a potential claim for asylum in the UK. It is paramount to document and act on all information given by the child, particularly any disclosure of abuse/exploitation.

Many children trafficked to the UK arrive on false documents and this makes determining age very difficult. In addition, some children have been in the UK for long periods of time and do not know how old they are, while others are told to say they are adults in order to cross borders more easily and to attract less attention. If a child is wrongly age assessed the child could be placed in adult or unsupervised accommodation. They may receive no direct support from a social worker and be at risk of further harm and retrafficking (Anti-Trafficking Monitoring Group, 2013). Under European trafficking legislation, to which the UK is bound, 'where the age of a person subject to trafficking is uncertain, and there are reasons to believe it is less than 18 years, that person should be presumed to be a child and receive immediate assistance, support and protection'. This principle is also enshrined in UK domestic legislation.

Being identified as a potential child victim of trafficking early is crucial to determining the type of accommodation needed for the child. ECPAT UK has identified that there are no commonly agreed safety and protection standards across the UK for the placement of children who are suspected or known to be trafficked (ECPAT, 2011). Barely any research has been conducted into the provision of safe accommodation for sexually exploited or trafficked young people (Brodie et al., 2011). In light of this, the type of accommodation required for each child must be decided on a needs-based assessment (p. 2). There are many factors that must be taken into account in order to keep the child safe and these must be discussed with the young person. Children may be placed in residential care, foster care, specialist foster care, or hostels/bed and breakfast accommodation. The latter is often used for those children who are over 16 but has been frequently criticised as not being appropriate or safe for victims of trafficking. The Deputy Children's Commissioner, Sue Berelowitz, claimed inappropriate accommodation left trafficked children 'desperately vulnerable' to further exploitation (APPG, 2012).

In 2011 Barnardo's received Department for Education grant funding for a two-year pilot project to deliver specialist foster care for sexually exploited/trafficked young people. An independent evaluation found there was 'clear potential for specialist placements to be cost effective' and, where developed as part of a model of specialist support, can effectively protect trafficked young people and help them recover from abuse (Shuker, 2013). Although the pilot itself was small, it was recommended that the model should continue in order to ensure more young people could benefit from the provision and to generate further learning. Specialised foster care may be the most effective option for trafficked children, but a shortage of trained and available foster carers continues to be an issue. Research has found that foster placements with young people are more likely to succeed where social workers provide useful support to foster carers, and where carers have good social support networks (Brodie et al., 2011). A separate piece of research suggests that the most effective foster placements for sexually exploited children are out of authority, where they are forced to break their links with pimps/clients (Farmer and Pollock, 2003). This is supported by practitioners (Anti-Trafficking Monitoring Group, 2010), who support the idea that the location is kept a secret and a distance from the area in which the child is discovered. To reduce the number of children going missing, research has suggested that children are less likely to go missing from foster care if the carer is present full time (Pearce et al., 2009).

The risk of missing is exacerbated by a general lack of awareness, training and joined-up practice on human trafficking and its indicators among front-line practitioners, such as social workers, police, immigration officials, teachers, health professionals and foster carers (see Case Study: Dalal).

Case Study: Dalal

Dalal (not her real name) is a young person from China. Dalal told her support worker in Wales that she was given away as a child to foster parents because she was female. The foster parents later sold her to a female trafficker in China who kept her locked up with many other girls. Dalal was then passed on to a man who took her on a ship to another destination, where she was passed on to another man. This man kept Dalal locked up for some time; he did not harm her but she was made to watch videos of children being beaten. This man then brought her to the UK by plane and warned her to tell anyone who asked her age that she was 21, and that if she did not she would be returned to China. When they arrived at Heathrow, Dalal hid in the lavatories until she was found by security. Dalal had a passport with her that stated that she was 21 years old; however, she claimed to be 16. Dalal was treated as an adult by the UK Border Authority which sent her to a city in Wales where she was placed in initial Home Office accommodation.

Soon afterwards, Dalal was required to move to another city in Wales by the UK Border Authority and was placed in accommodation with several adult females. The voluntary sector organisations that came into contact with Dalal, including ECPAT UK, expressed concern at how young she appeared to be and estimated that her true age was between 15 and 16 years. Dalal was age assessed by social services, which concluded that she was over 18; a subsequent medical assessment was inconclusive. Voluntary sector agencies were concerned at her history and current vulnerabilities. At least three referrals were made to the local authority social work team and to the police. A child protection strategy meeting was held and it was agreed that a police officer would visit Dalal and talk to her about her experiences. Given the concerns about the case, a number of agencies and professionals became involved, including the Office of the Children's Commissioner for Wales. For over two months, the Office repeatedly asked for information and for the relevant police force to visit, but no visit took place. Then, it was reported that Dalal had a man staying with her in the accommodation. The housing manager went to investigate and found a Chinese man hiding in her wardrobe. Dalal claimed that he was her brother but it is thought by at least one of the voluntary agencies that he was the trafficker. Shortly afterwards, Dalal disappeared and is now officially recorded as a missing person. Three years on, Dalal is still missing and, in May 2012, the Labour AM Mick Antoniw told the National Assembly in Wales that Dalal, who had been housed in adult accommodation in Newport, was '**missing, presumed dead** because local authorities and police did not take responsibility for a suspected victim of trafficking because she was age disputed'.

The importance of multiagency working has been highlighted as key to successfully supporting victims of trafficking. The 2011 guidance, *Safeguarding Children who may have been Trafficked* (Department for Education and Home Office, 2011), states: 'All practitioners who come into contact with children and young people in their everyday work need to be able to recognise children who have been trafficked and be competent to act to support and protect these children from harm.' In January 2014, the Department for Education issued statutory guidance on children who run away or go missing from home or care, which includes a chapter on looked after children trafficked from abroad. This states that this cohort of children are at 'high risk of going missing' and says any assessment of the risk of going missing should inform a child's care plan and information of this should be shared with relevant agencies (p. 24). The use of Multi-Agency Safeguarding Hubs is recommended as an effective way of safeguarding children and processing the risks faced by children (Anti-Trafficking Monitoring Group, 2013). It is noted that a multiagency approach from the time the child is identified can reduce the number of times a trafficked child has to disclose their ordeal, which can be very traumatic and lead to only partial disclosure in line with the focus of the assessment, as well as inconsistencies.

Practical steps have been taken in some areas to implement effective multiagency practice and procedures with regard to child victims of trafficking. The London Borough of Harrow updated its Good Practice for Trafficked Children in Care in 2011 (Harrow Council, 2011), which reinforces the need for placements away from the trafficker's location and gives practical steps to try to mitigate the risks of retrafficking and missing. This includes, but is not limited to, steps such as: obtaining key identity information/photographs immediately in case the child goes missing; restricted access to phones/mobile phones, with an explanation of why, to break the contact between the child and the trafficker; keeping the location of the placement confidential and on a need-to-know basis; giving the child information about the risks of returning to the traffickers and details of how to get back in contact with the local authority/police if they do go missing; CCTV monitoring outside the placement; and regularly reviewing a child's placement in an environment where they can speak freely and feel safe. Carers must also be sensitive to the possibility that the young person is suffering from post-traumatic stress disorder, and that random things may trigger fear or panic (Fursland, 2009).

A Trafficked Children's Toolkit was developed and piloted by the London Safeguarding Children Board in 12 local authority areas across the UK to act as an assessment framework with guidance to support practitioners and policymakers working with suspected victims of child trafficking in line with existing child protection procedures (London Local Safeguarding Children's Board, 2011). It states: 'At the heart of this framework is multiagency working, which recognises that trafficking is a complex form of child abuse and requires a proactive response supported by specialist training and input from professionals, voluntary groups and community agencies alike' (p. 7). It found that, despite pockets of good practice in some areas, identification of trafficked children was 'a major challenge for pilot local authorities in a context of low public awareness, professional reluctance to accept child trafficking as a live issue in the UK, inconsistent levels of multiagency engagement, and the rapid speed with which trafficked children can go missing' (p. 7). The Toolkit and Guidance, updated in 2011, recommends that all accommodation placements be given a copy of its guidance to mitigate the risk of children going missing.

A lack of knowledge among front-line staff combined with a lack of agreed safety standards can place a child at huge risk and increase the likelihood of them going missing and being retrafficked, either within the UK or out of the UK to other countries. Budget constraints in local authorities and a culture that prioritises immigration control and criminal prosecution over child protection combined with a lack of specialist accommodation are known to also contribute to the inadequate support that trafficked children receive (APPG, 2012).

Data Collection

The available statistics on child trafficking are not regarded as indicative of the true scale of the problem in the UK. Awareness of the National Referral Mechanism is low among front-line practitioners and ECPAT UK understands that hundreds of children each year are not referred and not formally identified (Joint Committee on Human Rights, 2013). Information and statistics of missing trafficked children are 'incomplete and patchy' (APPG, p. 13), which makes it difficult to assess the real scale of the problem. Data collection on all missing children is complex. The APPG inquiry revealed a 'startling discrepancy' in what is recorded and how data is recorded (p. 28). It reported that the Department for Education data for 2011 reported 930 children in care having gone missing from care, yet the UK Missing Persons Bureau, based on police data, suggested 10,000 individual children were responsible for around 42,000 missing incidents in a year (pp. 28–29). This huge gap in data is accounted for by a number of factors. For example, local authorities must submit annually details of every child in their care but this form only records missing incidents of more than 24 hours. The APPG Inquiry noted this was an 'arbitrary' figure. But the UK Missing Persons Bureau data, even when children who went missing for less than 24 hours are removed from police figures, suggests 5,000 children went missing in 17,000 incidents, which is still significantly higher than the Department for Education data. The number of missing incidents for each child is not published by the Department for Education so it is impossible to tell whether a child has gone missing once or hundreds of times. As an additional complexity, only just over half of England's police forces use a searchable database (COMPACT) and can record individual children who are reported missing. Those not using this database can only record the number of incidents.

Data collection in each local authority is compounded by the use of out-of-borough placements of children. For example, if a child placed in one local authority is reported missing at a police station in another local authority area, this may not be recorded in the home authority, therefore police data does not always correlate with that of the local authority. Of 64 local authorities that responded to the APPG Inquiry only two collected centralised data on whether children had been trafficked, with only five collecting the nationality of children in care who go missing (p. 30). This is hugely disappointing, particularly given the known missing risk associated with certain nationalities. The Inquiry recommended a comprehensive and independent national system of data collection on trafficked children who go missing to address these issues.

Recommendations

The widely reported concerns about missing trafficked children led ECPAT UK to formulate ten child-centred principles concerning the safe accommodation of suspected child victims of trafficking (2011):

1   The best interests of the child should be at the centre of all decisions regarding the provision of accommodation and related support.
2   Children should be asked about what makes them feel safe.
3   Children should be given sufficient information to help them make informed decisions about their accommodation and care.
4   Safety measures should be implemented to reduce a child's risk of going missing, especially within 24–72 hours after first contact with the child.
5   Safe accommodation should be understood as multifaceted, involving physical and psychological elements, with particular recognition of the impact of trauma on a child's perception and behaviour.
6   A child's accommodation and safety needs will change over time and should be regularly assessed.
7   A child should not feel punished or overly restricted by measures taken to help keep them safe in accommodation.
8   A child should be given access to a range of psychological, educational, health, social, legal, financial and language support that 'brings safety to the child' and helps them recover.
9   Everyone working with child victims of trafficking should be trained to recognise and respond appropriately to their needs.
10 Efforts to keep children safe should involve the wider community in ways that create an environment that is difficult for traffickers to operate in.

ECPAT UK recommends that, using these principles, the government should introduce a national standard of safe accommodation for children who may have been trafficked. In 2014, the Department for Education issued statutory guidance on children who run away or go missing from home or care. This contains a brief chapter on trafficked children from abroad, which stresses the need for an informed care plan that analyses the vulnerability of the child to going missing and calls for close working with other statutory bodies. However, it is not known how this guidance is being used in practice and the guidance does not contain much detail about the risks and how to mitigate them.

It is also recommended that all separated children should be given a legal guardian immediately on arrival or when coming to the notice of authorities (ECPAT UK, 2014). Separated children, who are often victims of trafficking, find themselves alone in the UK, without parents, and the level of support provided to them varies widely and is often woefully inadequate. A legal guardian would be able to improve identification of victims of trafficking, assist in ensuring age disputes were carried out lawfully and with the full participation of the young person, ensure the child's rights are upheld and advocate in their best interests while holding key agencies and authorities to account (ECPAT UK, 2014). A legal guardian would be someone they could trust and who would be a constant amongst the daunting multitude of individuals and agencies the child must encounter.

The UK is taking steps to move towards implementing statutory guardianship systems but each administration in the UK is taking a different approach that caters for different groups of children and none of these systems are up and running yet.

In January 2015, Northern Ireland passed new human trafficking legislation that provides for an independent legal guardian for trafficked and separated children who arrive in Northern Ireland without a parent or primary caregiver (and where that separation may put the child at risk of harm).[4] Scotland has operated a nonstatutory system of 'guardianship' for children who arrive in Scotland unaccompanied (some of whom are trafficked). However, this service does not provide a service for those separated children from within the European Union. Legislation on human trafficking, which contains provision for a statutory guardianship service in Scotland, is currently before the Scottish Parliament. It is expected that the legislation will be similar to that in Northern Ireland; however, it may not provide for Scottish national children who are trafficked to be allocated a guardian. The Modern Slavery Act 2015 (in England and Wales) contains an enabling mechanism for Independent Child Trafficking Advocates. A trial is currently under way in 23 local authority areas that is being independently evaluated by the University of Bedfordshire. However, only those children who are trafficked qualify for an advocate, so unaccompanied and separated children would not be allocated a guardian under this provision. British national children who are trafficked internally would qualify for an advocate.

The UK must also improve data collection, both in terms of human trafficking and also missing children, implementing a national system of data on missing trafficked children, ensuring local authorities and police record key identity information and nationality when a child goes missing, prioritising investigating missing trafficked children and improving referrals into the National Referral Mechanism. ECPAT UK and other key charities support the call for an Anti-Trafficking/Slavery Commissioner for the UK (Anti-Trafficking Monitoring Group, 2013). This should be an independent mechanism that ensures the systematic collection, monitoring and analysis of comprehensive and disaggregated data, with full accountability to Parliament. This would also improve the sharing of intelligence among police and local authorities of key profile groups of victims, known traffickers in an area and detailed information on risk that would help to inform practitioners developing safety plans for trafficked children.

Awareness of trafficking and its indicators remains low across front-line agencies. Mandatory, regular and quality training must be delivered to all social workers, police, lawyers, foster carers, immigration officers, teachers and health professionals, as well as raising awareness among the general public about the existence and indicators of trafficking in their communities. Social workers and police in particular must be fully trained about the risks posed to child victims of trafficking with regard to going missing and be informed of how to reduce this risk while working alongside other key agencies and voluntary organisations. Multi-Agency Safeguarding Hubs, or equivalent multiagency teams, should be better able to assess risk and trained on how to provide a multidisciplinary response to concerns of trafficking. Additionally, there should be further investigation into the effectiveness of specialist foster care for trafficked children, as demonstrated in Barnardo's recent pilot (Shuker, 2013). The Joint Committee on Human Rights recommended that this pilot should be rolled out across the UK for all trafficked children.

Conclusion

It is clear that safe accommodation must encompass more than the mere provision of adequate placements for trafficked children. It should include consideration of the child's physical, psychological, legal, language and security needs. Most importantly, perhaps, it must take into account the child's own perception of safety. The ongoing scandal of trafficked and unaccompanied children going missing from care has been given some attention in the wake of the 2012 APPG Inquiry. There is no single answer to solve the problem of children missing from care. However, urgent and prioritised action is needed to implement the above recommendations as part of a holistic response to the needs of child victims of trafficking who are some of the most vulnerable children in the UK. It is the duty of front-line agencies to identify, protect and support them. If we are not able to help trafficked children break the control of the adults who seek to manipulate and exploit them we will be condemning them to lives of abuse, danger and trauma. Trafficked children must first be treated as victims of abuse and crime – not asylum seekers, immigrants or criminals. Only then will they be able to recover and rebuild their lives in a safe environment.

Notes

1 This figure was given by the Director of Europol to the EU STOP/International Labour Organization conference on trafficking in 2002. Note that it relates only to the profits from hiring out services and structures. The ILO estimated in 2005 that the average annual profits generated by trafficked forced labourers was just under $32 billion (A global alliance against Forced Labour, Global Report under the Follow up to the ILO Declaration on Fundamental Principles and Rights at Work, Geneva, 2005).
2 www.gov.uk/government/news/true-scale-of-modern-slavery-in-uk-revealed-as-strategy-to-tackle-it-published.
3 For more information about this topic in a broader European context see Shalev Greene and Toscano (2016) and O'Donnell and Mikaela (2013).
4 www.legislation.gov.uk/nia/2015/2/section/21/enacted.

References

ACPO (2012). *National Problem Profile: Commercial Cultivation of Cannabis 2012*. www.acpo.police.uk/documents/crime/2012/20120430CBACCofCPP.pdf.

Anti-Trafficking Monitoring Group (2010). *Wrong Kind of Victim? One Year On: An Analysis of UK Measures to Protect Trafficked Persons*. www.antislavery.org/includes/documents/cm_docs/2010/f/full_report.pdf.

Anti-Trafficking Monitoring Group (2013). *In the Dock: Examining the UK's Criminal Justice Response to Trafficking.* www.antislavery.org/includes/documents/cm_docs/2013/i/inthedock_final_small_file .pdf.

APPG for Runaway and Missing Children and Adults and the APPG for Looked After Children and Care Leavers (2012). *Report from the Joint Inquiry into Children Who Go Missing from Care.* www.childrenssociety.org.uk/sites/default/files/tcs/u32/joint_appg_inquiry_-_report…pdf.

Booth, R. (2009). Revealed: 77 trafficked Chinese children lost by home. *The Guardian*, 5 May. www.theguardian.com/world/2009/may/05/trafficked-chinese-children-crime.

Brodie, I., Melrose, M., Pearce, J. and Warrington, C. (2011). *Providing Safe and Supported Accommodation for Young People Who Are in the Care System and Who Are at Risk of, or Experiencing, Sexual Exploitation or Trafficking for Sexual Exploitation.* www.beds.ac.uk/__data/assets/pdf_file/0008/120788/SafeAccommodationreport_finalOct2011IB_1.pdf.

CEOP (2010). *Strategic Threat Assessment Child Trafficking in the UK.* Available: www.ceop.police.uk/Documents/ceopdocs/Child_Trafficking_Strategic_Threat_Assessment_2010_NPM_Final.pdf.

Children's Society (2012). *Into the Unknown: Children's Journeys through the Asylum Process.* www.childrenssociety.org.uk/sites/default/files/tcs/into-the-unknown--childrens-journeys-through-the-asylum-process--the-childrens-society.pdf.

Crawley, H. (2012). Working with children and young people subject to immigration control: Guidelines for best practice. *Immigration Law Practitioners' Association.* www.ilpa.org.uk/pages/publications.html.

Crown Prosecution Service (2011). *CPS Policy for Prosecuting Cases of Human Trafficking.* www.cps.gov.uk/publications/docs/policy_for_prosecuting_cases_of_human_trafficking.pdf.

Crown Prosecution Service (2013). *Legal Guidance. Human Trafficking, Smuggling and Slavery.* www.cps.gov.uk/legal/h_to_k/human_trafficking_and_smuggling/.

Department for Education and Home Office (2011). *Safeguarding Children who May Have Been Trafficked.* www.gov.uk/government/uploads/system/uploads/attachment_data/file/177033/DFE-00084-2011.pdf.

Department for Education (2014). *Care of Unaccompanied and Trafficked Children: Statutory Guidance for Local Authorities on the Care of Unaccompanied Asylum Seeking and Trafficked Children.* July. www.gov.uk/government/uploads/system/uploads/attachment_data/file/330787/Care_of_unaccompanied_and_trafficked_children.pdf.

ECPAT UK (2007). *Missing Out: A Study of Child Trafficking in the North West, North East and West Midlands.* www.ecpat.org.uk/sites/default/files/missing_out_2007.pdf.

ECPAT UK (2009). *Frequently Asked Questions on Child Trafficking.* www.ecpat.org.uk/content/faqs-child-trafficking.

ECPAT UK (2011). *On the Safe Side: Principles of Safe Accommodation for Child Victims of Trafficking.* www.ecpat.org.uk/sites/default/files/on_the_safe_side.pdf.

ECPAT UK (2014). *Fundamental Rights Agency. Guardianship for Children Deprived of Parental Care: A Handbook to Reinforce Guardianship Systems to Cater for the Specific Needs of Child Victims of Trafficking.* http://ec.europa.eu/dgs/home-affairs/e-library/docs/guardianship_for_children/guardianship_for_children_deprived_of_parental_care_en.pdf.

Farmer, E. and Pollock, S. (2003). Managing sexually abused and/or abusing children in substitute care. *Child and Family Social Work*, 8: 101–112.

Fursland, E. (2009). *Caring for a Young Person Who Has Been Trafficked: A Guide for Foster Carers.* London: British Association for Adoption and Fostering.

Harrow Council (2011). *Good Practice Guidance for Trafficked Children in Care.* www.harrowlscb.co.uk/guidance_and_procedures.aspx.

Home Affairs Committee – Sixth Report (2009). *The Trade in Human Beings: Human Trafficking in the UK.* www.publications.parliament.uk/pa/cm200809/cmselect/cmhaff/23/2302.htm.

ILO (2012). *Trafficking in Children.* www.ilo.org/ipec/areas/Traffickingofchildren/lang--en/index.htm.

Joint Committee on Human Rights (2013). *Human Rights of an Unaccompanied Migrant Children and Young People in the UK.* First report of the session 2013–14, London. www.publications.parliament.uk/pa/jt201314/jtselect/jtrights/9/9.pdf.

Judah, S. (2013). Why are so many of the UK's missing teenagers Vietnamese? BBC News Magazine, 17 June. www.bbc.co.uk/news/magazine-22903511.

London Local Safeguarding Children's Board (2011). *London Safeguarding Trafficked Children Toolkit.* www.londonscb.gov.uk/trafficking/.

National Crime Agency (2014). *National Referral Mechanism Statistics – End of Year Summary 2014.*

London: National Crime Agency. www.nationalcrimeagency.gov.uk/publications/national-referral-mechanism-statistics/502-national-referral-mechanism-statistics-end-of-year-summary-2014/file.

NSPCC (2012). *Response to All Party Parliamentary Group on Runaway and Missing Children and Adults.* www.nspcc.org.uk/globalassets/documents/consultation-responses/nspcc-response-missing-children-inquiry.pdf.

O'Donnell, R. and Mikaela, H. (2013). Identification, Reception and Protection of Unaccompanied Children. CONNECT Project Report. www.connectproject.eu/PDF/CONNECT-Project_Report.pdf.

Pearce, J., Hynes, P. and Bovarnick, S. (2009). *Breaking the Wall of Silence: Practitioners' Responses to Trafficked Children and Young People.* London: NSPCC.

R v L and others [2013] EWCA Crim 991.

RACE in Europe Project (2014). *Trafficking for Forced Criminal Activities and Begging in Europe: Exploratory Study and Good Practice Examples.* www.ecpat.org.uk/sites/default/files/race_report_english.pdf.

Shalev Greene, K. and Toscano, F. (2016). *SUMMIT Report: Best Practices and Key Challenges on Interagency Cooperation to Safeguard Unaccompanied Children from Going Missing.* http://missingchildreneurope.eu/catalog/categoryid/9/documentid/348.

Shuker L. (2013). *Evaluation of Barnardo's Safe Accommodation Project for Sexually Exploited and Trafficked Young People.* Bedford: University of Bedfordshire.

SOCA and UK Human Trafficking Centre (2013). *United Kingdom National Referral Mechanism Provisional Statistics 2012.* www.soca.gov.uk/about-soca/library/doc_download/474-nrm-provisional-statistics-2012.

UNICEF (2008). *Toolkit Child Protection in Emergencies: A Guide for Field Workers. Section 4 Separated And Unaccompanied Children.* www.crin.org/docs/Toolkit%20on%20Child%20Protection%20in%20Emergencies%20%20A%20guide%20for%20fiel.pdf.

5

Geography of Missing Children

Penny S. Woolnough and Graham J. Gibb

Introduction

Having a child go missing is every parent or guardian's worst nightmare. Immediate questions concerning why the child has disappeared, where they may have gone and who they may be with are the source of immense anguish for those responsible for the child's safeguarding, but are critical to forming an immediate and focused search for the missing child.

We know that the actions of adults mediate the ways in which children interact with their environment and that children and young people experience places, spaces and things in different ways to adults (James 1990; Skelton and Valentine 1998; Holloway and Valentine, 2000). Furthermore, when adults are not present the behaviour of children may significantly alter. Even when children share the same settings as adults, such as the home or public space, parks and shopping centres, what they expect and what they are expected to do there are likely to differ, and thus we see variations in ways in which children and adults experience the same environment (James, 1990, p. 279). Nevertheless, very little research has specifically focused on the geographical aspects of missing children, despite the importance of 'where'-type questions to family and police search strategies.

In this chapter we draw upon a diverse literature to argue that knowledge of the specific places and spaces of children's lives is central to our understanding and response to cases of missing children. In particular, knowing how missing children's journeys are socially and spatially structured is critical to ensuring appropriate mechanisms are in place to prevent, protect and provide for children at risk of or reported missing (Gibb and Woolnough, 2007). Consequently, we explore what is known about the ways in which children in Western societies, from which the data and literature in this chapter are drawn, interact with and experience the environment including how they travel, the distances they travel and where they go. In order to do this, we provide an overview of relevant issues in relation to typologies of missing children, child development and child mental health, followed by a description of the use of geospatial profiling by the police in cases of missing children. Investigative strategies, to maximise the gathering of 'where'-type information during cases of missing children, are also provided.

Typologies of Missing Children

Children may be reported missing for very varied reasons, all of which have a direct impact on their behaviour and geographies. For example, a child or young person who is intentionally missing (has run away from home) will interact with space and time very differently from one who is unintentionally missing (lost or abducted) (Biehal et al., 2003). In this section we present a brief overview of the different typologies of missing children and how these may impact on their behaviour and missing geographies.

Unintentionally Missing Children

It is not uncommon for children, especially young children, to wander off, become disoriented and lost. Becoming lost in supermarkets and shopping centres is something most young children have done, but they may also wander from their own home or school, perhaps caught by the lure of something more exciting or in the bustle of a group (Gibb, 2010). Some children may be given parental authority to play unsupervised within a predetermined range of the home (Anderson and Tindal, 1972), but may not adhere to this and travel beyond its outer limits into less familiar territory and subsequently become lost (Hart, 1979). Once lost, the child may try to get home or make contact with whoever is their guardian but be unable to do so or may be too young to know how to return home or make contact (Sedlak et al., 2002).

In addition to becoming lost, children are often missing for benign reasons resulting from misunderstanding or miscommunication. For example, very young children may hide from their guardian thinking they are playing a game. Small children can secrete themselves into very small spaces and sometimes fall asleep resulting in them being hard to find (they may not wake even with loud noise or calling) (Koester, 2008; Gibb, 2010). Alternatively, a miscommunication may arise over the expected time of return of an older child from school or whether they are spending time with friends (under the perceived supervision of a friend's guardian) (Biehal and Wade, 2002).

Of critical importance in the disappearance of any child is the possibility that a third party may be responsible for the disappearance (Newiss and Traynor, 2013). While this could be as a result of a family abduction (due to the violation of custodial rights) it could also be the result of a nonfamily abduction where a child is taken by a stranger or slight acquaintance (for example, kidnapping/ransom demands, sexual assault or murder). In such cases, the relationship between geography and time is of paramount importance as research indicates a window of between three and six hours exists from time of abduction to murder (Brown et al., 2006; National Center for Missing and Exploited Children, 1994, 1998).

Intentionally Missing Children

Those children categorised as intentionally missing tend to be older children who have consciously removed themselves from a situation, often arising from an unauthorised absence from home or substitute care (Wade et al., 1998). While this is generally described in terms of running away from something (for example, running from care or school) it can also relate to failing to turn up at an expected time (such as at the end of a curfew) or 'running to' a situation (such as wishing to be with friends or a boyfriend/girlfriend) (Biehal and Wade, 2002). Of particular concern, the link between running and child sexual exploitation is increasingly becoming clear (see Sharp, 2012; CEOP, 2012). Alternatively, the child or young person may have been 'thrown away' or forced to leave by their parents or carers (Safe on the Streets and Stein, 1999).

In either circumstance, although relatively uncommon, it is not unheard of for young people to leave to suicide (Greydanus and Calles, 2007; Juhnke et al., 2010).

While the intentionality behind a missing child's episode can illuminate their associated behaviour and geographies, the intentionality may not be immediately apparent. Interrelated with intentionality, understanding a child or young person's stage of physical and psychological development can provide additional critical insight into motivations for missing and subsequent behaviour and geographies, which we discuss below.

The Importance of Age: Physical and Psychological Development

A child's age and associated stage of psychological and physical development will affect their understanding, and utilisation of and interaction with the environment and those around them (see Doherty and Hughes, 2009; Lindon, 2012). For example, there are significant differences between the behaviour of young children and older adolescents, where the latter's psychological needs and risk taking (for example, sexual, criminal, substance abuse) are more developed (see American Psychological Association, 2002). Consequently, in order to understand how children and young people behave in missing circumstances, it is essential to consider their stage of physical and psychological development.

Preschool-Age Children

While it has been suggested that children younger than about seven are 'preoperational', and so cannot handle the basic 'operations' that are supposedly required for spatial cognition and behaviour (Downs and Liben, 1987, 1988; Liben and Downs, 1989, 1991), there is an increasing body of literature which suggests that young children can learn map skills and macro spatial concepts (Blaut and Stea, 1971; Blaut, 1997; Blades et al., 1998). Nevertheless, there is a higher probability of a preschool child becoming lost compared to an older child. In relation to this, developmental psychologists have conducted experimental research to explore children's wayfinding abilities. Young children are more likely to be able to navigate their way back to a specific location if route features where the child should continue or change direction have been previously specified to them (Cornell et al., 1989). As age increases, children become more adept at route finding and navigation. For example, in terms of route reversal navigation, younger children perform poorer than older children when specified route landmarks are removed prior to retracing (Heth et al., 1997). At intersections, younger children are also less likely to know the direction to return. Older children also wander off route less than younger children when distant orientation cues have been pointed out to them (Cornell et al., 1989) and older children more often report using additional landmarks than those specified compared to younger children (Heth et al. 1997). In older preschool children the mind is a mixture of reason, fantasy and logic, and definite interests, which may draw their attention, begin to develop (Koester, 2008). The younger the child, the closer to the 'place missing from' they are likely to be found (Gibb and Woolnough, 2007) and while they do not usually travel far, even very young children have been known to utilise transport and travel reasonably large distances (Roberts, 2004).

School-Age Children

Once children begin to attend school the potential for being reported missing from school itself arises. School children learn about new areas and may begin to travel further as part of their natural everyday lives. In addition, they make new friends and guardians are unlikely to always know with whom they are associating. Consequently, when children are reported missing it may be necessary to interview children's school friends by checking with the school for class lists (Gibb, 2010). Children in this age group are less likely to become lost and the wayfinding performance of 12-year-old children has been shown to not markedly differ from adults (Cornell et al., 1992). From around age five onwards children tend to learn to ride bicycles, which may facilitate them travelling longer distances reasonably quickly compared to a child travelling on foot (Gibb, 2010). Children may also use buses to travel to school (Pabayo and Gauvin, 2008) and may become confident enough to use wider public transport. The independent mobility of children is affected by individual families' attitudes towards risk (Valentine, 2004) as well as the ease and safety with which they can access local destinations. Well-connected low-traffic streets, access to recreational facilities and retail destinations have all been shown to increase 10–12-year-olds' independent mobility (O'Brien et al., 2000; Timperio et al., 2004; Villanueva et al., 2012). Consequently, as age increases the distance between place missing from and location found also increases (Gibb and Woolnough, 2007).

Adolescents

At this age, young people explore their own identities and a variety of spaces may be important to this process (Skelton and Valentine, 1998). Of particular relevance, adolescents in care may be placed in care homes at a distance from previous or familial addresses, increasing the tendency for the child to run away to their previous location, to be with their real family or friends (Wade, 2003; Rees, 2011). This often increases distances travelled, especially for urban cases, when children are likely to be more confident using public transport (Gibb, 2010). The ease with which young people can travel is enhanced by the increasing use of mobile phones. Mobile internet access has revolutionised the way in which children and young people communicate and socialise, with more than three-quarters of adolescents in the US and UK estimated to have personal mobile phones, with almost half being smartphones (Madden et al., 2013; Ofcom, 2012). Indeed, mobile phone ownership is thought to create an 'anytime, anywhere' link between young people and their caregivers, which has been perceived to increase the distances travelled by young people (Pooley et al., 2005). This communication revolution, coupled with the fact that adolescents and college-age individuals take more risks than children or adults (Steinberg 2004; Reyna and Farley, 2006), as well as the potential for young runaways to become involved with drugs and alcohol (Rees and Lee, 2005) and crime (Shalev, 2011), may strongly influence the behaviour and geographies of missing adolescents. Furthermore, as set out below, mental health issues, which become more prominent during adolescence, may also impact upon a young person's risk of missing and subsequent behaviour and geographies while missing.

The Effects of Mental Health

Research suggests that approximately one in ten British children and adolescents have at least one mental health problem involving a level of distress or social impairment that warrants treatment (Ford et al., 2003; Meltzer et al., 2000). While a wide range of mental health problems may be encountered, more common problems include Attention Deficit Hyperactivity Disorder (ADHD), generalised anxiety disorder, autism spectrum disorders, depression, self-harm and eating disorders, and are often a direct response to what is happening in the child's life (Mental Health Foundation, 2013). Furthermore, it is not unusual for a child to have more than one disorder (Meltzer et al., 2003a). In this section we present a brief overview of three of the most common child mental health issues and how these may impact on children's geographies of missing.

Autistic Spectrum Disorder

Autistic Spectrum Disorder (ASD), as suggested by its name, covers a wide spectrum of conditions, from those requiring 24-hour care at one end of the scale to very mild sufferers at the other (Cummine et al., 2010). The disorder is typified by communication deficits, including responding inappropriately in conversations, misreading nonverbal interactions, and having difficulty building friendships. Children with ASD may be overly dependent on routines and familiar routes, highly sensitive to changes in their environment, or intensely focused on inappropriate items (American Psychological Association, 2013; Gerland, 2000). By the very nature of their condition, these children are all vulnerable and will behave differently from other children. They may be dressed inappropriately (for example, no shoes, coat, or in nightwear), have no fear and no concept of time. Their communication difficulties result in them preferring to be alone and they will often leave a group. In particular, they become easily upset in noisy environments, often resulting in attempts to escape (Koester, 2008). Children suffering from ASD are at risk of bullying, particularly as they get older, and may suffer from depression (Zablotsky et al., 2013). They may become anxious and have a tendency to not let parents or school teachers know what is going on and may go off without telling anyone. In such cases they will tend to use familiar routes to head for a 'safe place' known to them which they enjoy or find familiar such as a playing field or somewhere they can watch traffic or animals (Gibb, 2010). However, while they can be very happy to stay settled in one place for a long time, they are extremely vulnerable to being tempted to go with a stranger. In particular, those in adolescence can suffer from sexual frustration, which may result in them responding inappropriately to sexual invitations (Ruble and Dalrymple, 1993; Hellemans et al., 2007).

Attention Deficit Hyperactive Disorder

Children who are consistently overactive, behave impulsively and have difficulty paying attention may have Attention Deficit Hyperactivity Disorder (ADHD). While more boys than girls are affected, the causes of ADHD are not fully understood (Mental Health Foundation, 2013). Although signs of ADHD are often present in preschool children, diagnosing the disorder in very young children is difficult. Consequently, diagnoses are not usually made until children are at primary school. Children with ADHD who go missing can be at greater risk because their awareness of danger is reduced, which can lead them to engage in physically dangerous activities, such as playing near fast-flowing rivers or railway lines. They can be impulsive, often acting before they think, and are easily distracted and often forgetful (see National Institute for Health and Clinical Excellence, 2009). Children with ADHD have a tendency to travel further than missing children of a similar age without ADHD (Gibb and Woolnough, 2007). Their poor social skills may make it difficult for them to ask for help or to engage with others. Because the effects of ADHD medication last for around four to five hours, it is imperative to establish early on in any missing person enquiry when the child last took his or her medication (Gibb, 2010). Due to the impulsive nature of their condition and their tendency to be distracted by irrelevant things, it is difficult to predict the places that they will be found. Therefore, it is extremely important for those searching to establish what their interests are, as these may provide vital clues as to the places they are likely to go to or the activities they might indulge in (Gibb and

Woolnough, 2007). Importantly, children with ADHD are all different, they act in different ways and the problems associated with ADHD appear in different ways at different ages (Taylor and Sonuga-Barke, 2008).

Depression, Self-Harm and Suicide

Depression in youth is a valid clinical phenomenon which is more common in adolescents than younger children and can affect anybody, although it is more common in girls compared to boys. Looked after children and young people also have a higher prevalence of depression (Meltzer et al., 2003b). Depression can occur for multiple reasons, including: family problems; abuse; bullying; neglect; long-term health problems; problems at school; a major life change such as moving house; friendship or boyfriend/girlfriend relationship problems; and alcohol or drug use (BUPA, 2013). Self-harm, when someone injures or harms themselves on purpose, often co-occurs with depression and affects at least one in 15 young people in the UK (NSPCC, 2009). A proportion of young people who self-harm do so because they wish to end their lives. They may have broader mental health or personality difficulties and, while the suicide attempt often follows a stressful event in the young person's life, the young person may not have shown any previous signs of difficulty. The risk of suicide is higher if the young person is depressed or has a serious mental illness; is using drugs or alcohol when they are upset; has previously tried to kill themselves, or has planned for a while how to die without being saved; or has a relative or friend who tried to kill themselves (Royal College of Psychiatrists, 2013). While the behavioural manifestations of depression, self-harm, and suicide can be very varied, they are often characterised by withdrawal from normal social interactions and activities. Consequently, while the number of young people who suicide is relatively small, when a young person is reported missing it should always be considered a possibility that they may have gone off to suicide.

Geospatial Profiling of Missing Children

Risk assessment and response to reports of missing children are a significant challenge to the police. While a very young child will always be assigned a high-risk status and an immediate response deployed, an older child with a history of running away may be assigned a lower risk or be classified as absent (ACPO, 2013) but nevertheless poses unique challenges and their running behaviour may be indicative of issues of wider risk such as sexual exploitation (Sharp, 2012; CEOP, 2012). Time may be important in either circumstance as the window of opportunity between child abduction and murder is estimated to be just three to six hours (Brown et al., 2006; National Center for Missing and Exploited Children, 1994, 1998). Taking account of these issues and in order to bring a more evidence-based approach to the police's response to missing persons, research conducted by Grampian Police (now part of Police Scotland) presented the first attempt to provide normative temporospatial profiles to specifically aid police missing person investigations by providing explicit timescales, distances and likely locations for finding missing people (ACPO, 2006; Gibb and Woolnough, 2007; see also Shalev et al., 2009). Using methodology developed in wilderness search and rescue research (Syrotuck, 1975, 1976; Hill, 1991, 1999) and based on a UK-wide analysis of closed police recorded missing person cases, Gibb and Woolnough (2007) present behavioural probabilities using predictive variables (age, sex and mental condition) to predict outcome characteristics (distance travelled, where they are likely to be located, how they will be traced/found and likelihood of suicide). In terms of children, they present behavioural probabilities for five distinct age groupings (1–4 year olds; 5–8 year olds; 9–11 year olds; 12–14 year olds; 15–16 year olds) and for children diagnosed

Children aged 1 to 4 years

TABLE 1:
Time taken to locate missing children

Cumulative percentage of cases	Time lapse between report and location
20%	8 minutes
40%	11 minutes
50%	20 minutes
70%	26 minutes
80%	40 minutes
95%	65 minutes
99%	196 minutes

TABLE 2:
Distance between places missing & found

Cumulative percentage of cases	Time lapse between report and location
30%	160 m
50%	400 m
70%	750 m
80%	900 m
98%	1.2 Km

TABLE 3:
Likely places children are found

Cumulative percentage of cases	Time lapse between report and location
58%	Playing in the street
18%	At a friend's/relative's/neighbour's address
15%	Within home address
9%	Traced playing in places where they were not immediately visible (playing fields, small wooded areas etc.)

THINGS TO CONSIDER:

- The younger the child, the closer to the 'place missing from' they are likely to be found.
- Children traced beyond 900 metres were either the subject of a 'parental abduction' or with some other appropriate adult, and reported missing as a result of a genuine misunderstanding.
- In this sample, the gender split was 37% female and and 63% male.
- 87% went missing on foot, 10% on their bicycles. 73% went missing from home, 10% went missing whilst at shopping centres.
- 37% were found by police, 30% by relatives and 27 % by members of the public.

Figure 5.1 Temporospatial tables for missing 1 to 4 year olds
Source: Gibb and Woolnough, 2007

with ADHD, setting out the timescales within which children in each group should be located, the distance they are likely to have travelled from the place missing from (generally the home address), and the places they are most likely be found (see Figure 5.1).

Table 1 within Figure 5.1 shows the timescales within which a child aged one to four years either returns home or is located by the police or other party. For example, from the time a child in this category is reported missing 50 per cent were traced within 20 minutes and 81 per cent within 40 minutes. Based on the data presented, it is extremely important to monitor the passage of time from when a child is reported missing; if a child in this age group has not been traced within one hour of being reported missing the incident becomes a critical one, and the likelihood of a third party being involved increases dramatically. Table 2 shows that 70 per cent of children in this age group are found within 750 metres of the place from which they went missing; 88 per cent are found within 900 metres and 98 per cent are found within 1,200 metres. By aligning the centre of these search parameters with the place the child went missing from, a realistic search area can be established. A visual understanding can be achieved by superimposing the suggested search parameters onto an appropriate map (see Figure 5.2). Finally, Table 3 within Figure 5.1 lists, in order of priority, the most likely places within the established search area that a child of this age is likely to be found.

In terms of how this data works in action, looking at Figure 5.2 and concentrating the search for a missing 1–4-year-old within the area bordered by the 70 per cent circle, placing priority on the known places likely to be found combined with a given time frame (such as 40 minutes),

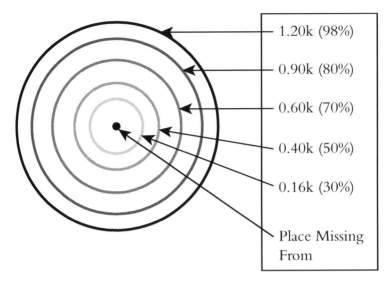

1.20k (98%)

0.90k (80%)

0.60k (70%)

0.40k (50%)

0.16k (30%)

Place Missing
From

Figure 5.2   Search area for missing 1 to 4 year olds
Source: Gibb and Woolnough, 2007

provides very clear parameters within which the police can manage the initial response to the case. If a search within the 70 per cent circle is not successful, the officer in charge has the option of extending the search out to and beyond the 80 per cent probability zone. However, at this stage strong consideration should be given to upgrading the incident and allocating additional resources. This information provides clearer justification for decision making and may enable officers leading enquiries to establish very quickly whether they are dealing with a critical out-of-the-ordinary incident and make associated evidence-based decisions regarding the nature and scale of the subsequent enquiry, for example by issuing a Child Rescue Alert (NPIA, 2010).

When used in conjunction with broader personal characteristics and circumstantial information, as illustrated in the earlier paragraphs of this chapter, these three sets of quantitative information provide extremely useful information for search/enquiry planning and case management, bringing an evidence-based approach to the deployment of resources.

Conclusion

Children represent one of the most vulnerable groups at risk of missing and present unique challenges to those responsible for their safeguarding (ACPO, 2010, 2013; CEOP, 2011, 2012). The scale of the problem is also significant, with over 200,000 incidents of missing children recorded by police in the UK alone during 2011–12 (SOCA, 2013). In this chapter we have provided a brief overview of some of the key issues relevant to the geographies of missing children. While it has not been possible to cover issues in any depth, it is hoped that this chapter highlights the importance of specifically considering how children's use of space differs from that of adults and how this may manifest itself in different behaviour and geographies when children are missing. We have attempted to highlight the impact that a child's stage of physical and psychological development has upon their personal geographies and how this changes with age. In addition, the influence of mental health problems, especially in older children, is provided to illustrate the wide range of issues relevant to children's missing episodes and subsequent geographies.

When considered together, all of these factors offer pertinent and valuable insight into the possible and likely behaviours and geographies of a missing child, which may prove critical to a successful search and their location. Faced with the challenge of responding to complex cases and with multiple competing demands, the police and other search related agencies are increasingly becoming more innovative in the way in which they respond to missing persons. The emerging use of spatial profiling has been presented to illustrate one way in which the police have improved their response to this very vulnerable population. However, this initial spatial research needs to be substantially built upon using broader methodological approaches. Further research in relation to qualitative aspects of missing children's geographies, for example, would be particularly beneficial (see also Chapter 11 in this volume). Critically, by learning more about the geographies of missing children, those responsible for their safeguarding will be better placed to prevent, protect and provide for this very vulnerable population.

Acknowledgements

We would like to thank Olivia Stevenson and Jason Holland for a critical reading of the final draft of this chapter.

References

ACPO (2006). *Practice Advice on Search Management and Procedures*. Wyboston: National Centre for Policing Excellence.

ACPO (2010). *Guidance on the Management, Recording and Investigation of Missing Persons*. Wyboston: National Policing Improvement Agency.

ACPO (2013). *Interim Guidance on the Management, Recording and Investigation of Missing Persons*. Wyboston: College of Policing.

American Psychological Association (2002). *Developing Adolescents: A Reference for Professionals*. Washington, DC: APA.

American Psychological Association (2013). *Diagnostic and Statistical Manual of Mental Disorders* (5th edition). Washington, DC: APA.

Anderson, J. and Tindal, M. (1972). The concept of home range: New data for the study of territorial behaviour. In W. Mitchell (ed.), *Environmental Design: Research and Practice*. Los Angeles: University of California Press.

Biehal, N. and Wade, J. (2002). *Children Who Go Missing: Research, Policy and Practice*. London: Department of Health.

Biehal, N., Mitchell, F. and Wade, J. (2003). *Lost from View: A Study of Missing Persons in the UK*. York: University of York Social Work Research and Development Unit.

Blades, M., Blaut, J. M., Darvizeh, Z., Elguea, S., Sowden, S., Soni, D., Spencer, C., Stea, D., Surajpaul, R. and Uttal, D. (1998). A cross cultural study of young children's mapping abilities. *Transactions of the Institute of British Geographers*, 23(2): 269–277.

Blaut, J. M. (1997). The mapping abilities of young children. *Annals of the Association of American Geographers*, 87(1): 152–158.

Blaut, J. M. and Stea, D. (1971). Studies of geographic learning. *Annals of the Association of American Geographers*, 61: 387–393.

Brown, K. M., Keppel, R. D., Weis, J. G. and Skeen, M. E. (2006). *Case Management for Missing Children Homicide Investigation*. Washington, DC: US Department of Justice, Office of Juvenile Justice and Delinquency Prevention, Office of Justice Programs.

BUPA (2013). Depression in children and young people. http://www.bupa.co.uk/health-information/directory/d/depression-in-children-and-young-people (accessed 25 July 2013).

CEOP (2011). *Scoping Report on Missing and Abducted Children*. London: Child Exploitation and Online Protection Centre.

CEOP (2012). *2012/13 Threat Assessment of Child Sexual Exploitation and Abuse*. London: Child Exploitation and Online Protection Centre.

Cornell, E. H., Heth, C. D. and Broda, L. S. (1989). Children's wayfinding: Response to instructions to use environmental landmarks. *Developmental Psychology*, 25(5): 755–764.

Cornell, E. H., Heth, C. D. and Rowat, W. L. (1992). Wayfinding by children and adults: Response to instructions to use look back and retrace strategies. *Developmental Psychology*, 28(2): 328–336.

Cummine, V., Leach, J. and Stevenson, G. (2010). *Autism in the Early Years. A Practical Guide*. New York: Routledge.

Doherty J. and Hughes M. (2009). *Child Development: Theory and Practice*. Harlow: Pearson Education.

Downs, R. and Liben, L. (1987). Children's understanding of maps. In P. Ellen and C. Thinus-Blanc (eds), *Cognitive Processes and Spatial Orientation in Animal and Man*, vol. 2, *Neurophysiology and Developmental Aspects*. Dordrecht: Martinus Nijhoff.

Downs, R. and Liben, L. (1988). Through a map darkly: Understanding maps as representations. *Genetic Epistemologist*, 16: 11–18.

Ford, T., Goodman, R. and Meltzer H. (2003). The British and adolescent mental health survey 1999: The prevalence of DSMIV disorders. *Journal of the American Academy of Child and Adolescent Psychiatry*, 42(10): 1203–1211.

Gerland, G. (2000). *Finding Out About Asperger Syndrome, High Functioning Autism and PDD*. London: Jessica Kingsley Publishers.

Gibb, G. J. (2010). *Profiling the Behaviour of Missing Children*. Paper presented to the Police National Search Centre, London. July 2010.

Gibb, G. and Woolnough, P. (2007). *Missing Persons: Understanding, Planning, Responding*. Aberdeen: Grampian Police.

Greydanus, D. E. and Calles, J. (2007). Suicide in children and adolescents. *Primary Care: Clinics in Office Practice*, 34(2): 259–273.

Hart, R. (1979). *Children's Experience of Place*. New York: Irvington.

Hellemans, H., Colson, K., Verbraekan, C., Vermeiren, R. and Deboutte, D. (2007). Sexual behaviour in high functioning male adolescents and young adults with autism spectrum disorder. *Journal of Autism and Developmental Disorders*, 37(2): 260–269.

Heth, C. D., Cornell, E. H. and Alberts, D. M. (1997). Differential use of landmarks by 8- and 12-year-old children during route reversal navigation. *Journal of Environmental Psychology*, 17(3): 199–213.

Hill, K. (1991). *Predicting the Behaviour of Lost Persons*. Paper presented at the 20th Annual Conference of the National Association for Search and Rescue, Fairfax, Virginia.

Hill, K. (1999). *Lost Person Behaviour*. Ottawa: National Search and Rescue Secretariat.

Holloway, S. L. and Valentine, G. (eds) (2000). *Children's Geographies: Playing, Living, Learning*. London: Routledge.

James, S. (1990). Is there a 'place' for children in geography? *Area*, 22(3): 278–283.

Juhnke, G. A., Granello, D. H. and Granello, P. F. (2010). *Suicide, Self-Injury, and Violence in the Schools: Assessment, Prevention, and Intervention Strategies*. Hoboken: Wiley.

Koester, R. (2008). *Lost Person Behavior: A Search and Rescue Guide on Where to Look for Land, Air and Water*. Charlottesville, VA: dbS Productions LLC.

Liben, L. and Downs, R. (1989). Understanding maps as symbols: The development of map concepts in children. *Advances in Child Development and Behavior*, 22: 145–201.

Liben, L. and Downs, R. (1991). The role of graphic representations in understanding the world. In R. M. Downs, L. S. Liben, and D. S. Palermo (eds), *Visions of aesthetics, the environment and development: The legacy of Joachim F Wohlwill*. Hillsdale, NJ: Erlbaum.

Lindon, J. (2012). *Understanding Children's Behaviour: 0-11 Years*. London: Hodder Education.

Madden, M., Lenhart, A., Duggan, M., Cortesi, S. and Gasser, U. (2013). *Teens and Technology 2013*. Washington, DC: Pew Research Center.

Meltzer, H., Gatward, R., Corbin, T., Goodman, R. and Ford, T. (2003a). *Persistence, Onset, Risk Factors and Outcomes of Childhood Mental Disorders*. London: Office for National Statistics.

Meltzer, H., Gatward, R., Corbin, T., Goodman, R. and Ford, T. (2003b). *The Mental Health of Young People Looked After by Local Authorities in England*. London: The Stationery Office.

Meltzer, H., Gatward, R., Goodman, R. and Ford T. (2000). *The Mental Health of Children and Adolescents in Great Britain*. London: The Stationery Office.

Mental Health Foundation (2013). Children and young people. www.mentalhealth.org.uk/help-information/mental-health-a-z/C/children-young-people/ (accessed 4 July 2013).

National Centre for Missing and Exploited Children (1994). *Deceased Child Project*. Arlington, VA: National Center for Missing and Exploited Children.

National Centre for Missing and Exploited Children (1998). *Deceased Child Project, Part 2*. Arlington, VA: National Center for Missing and Exploited Children.

National Institute for Health and Clinical Excellence (2009). *Attention Deficit Hyperactivity Disorder: Diagnosis and Management of ADHD in Children, Young People and Adults*. London: National Institute for Health and Clinical Excellence.

Newiss, G. and Traynor, M. (2013). *Taken: A Study of Child Abduction in the UK*. London: Parents and Abducted Children Together (PACT).

NPIA (2010). *Child Rescue Alert Activation Protocol*. London: National Policing Improvement Agency.

NSPCC (2009). *Young People Who Self Harm: Implications for Public Health Practitioners*. London: National Society for the Prevention of Cruelty to Children.

O'Brien, M., Jones, D., Sloan, D. and Rustin, M. (2000). Children's independent spatial mobility in the urban public realm. *Childhood*, 7(3): 257–277.

Ofcom (2012). *The Communications Market 2012*. London: Ofcom.

Pabayo, R. and Gauvin, L. (2008). Proportions of students who use various modes of transport to and from school in a representative population based sample of children and adolescents, 1999. *Preventative Medicine*, 46(1): 63–66.

Pooley, C. G., Turbull, J. and Adams, M. (2005). *A Mobile Century? Changes in Everyday Mobility in Britain in the Twentieth Century*. Aldershot: Ashgate.

Rees, G. (2011). *Still Running 3: Children on the Streets in the UK*. London: The Children's Society.

Rees, G. and Lee, J. (2005). *Still Running 2: Findings from the Second National Survey of Young Runaways*. London: The Children's Society.

Reyna, V. and Farley, F. (2006). Risk and rationality in adolescent decision making: Implications for theory, practice, and public policy. *Psychological Science in the Public Interest*, 7: 1–44.

Roberts, G. (2004). Great train toddlers. *Aberdeen Evening Express*, 30 March, pp. 1–2.

Royal College of Psychiatrists (2013). Self-harm in young people: information for parents, carers and anyone who works with young people. Mental health and growing up factsheet 20. www.rcpsych. ac.uk/expertadvice/parentsandyouthinfo/parentscarers/self-harm.aspx (accessed 25 July 2013).

Ruble, L. and Dalrymple, N. (1993). Social/sexual awareness of persons with autism: A parental perspective. *Archives of Sexual Behavior*, 22(3): 229–240.

Safe on the Streets Research Team and Stein, M. (1999). *Still Running: Children on the Streets of the UK*. London: The Children's Society.

Sedlak, A. J., Finkelhor, D., Hammer, H. and Schultz, D. (2002). *National Estimates of Missing Children: An Overview*. Washington, DC: US Department of Justice.

Shalev, K. (2011). Children who go missing repeatedly and their involvement in crime. *International Journal of Police Science and Management*, 12(4): 29–36.

Shalev, K., Schaefer, M. and Morgan, A. (2009). Investigating missing person cases: How can we learn where they go or how far they travel? *International Journal of Police Science and Management*, 11(2): 123–129.

Sharp, N. (2012). *Still Hidden? Going Missing as an Indicator of Child Sexual Exploitation*. London: Missing People.

Skelton, T. and Valentine G. (1998). *Cool Places: Geographies of Youth Culture*. London: Routledge.

SOCA (2013). *Missing Persons: Data and Analysis*. London: Serious Organised Crime Agency.

Steinberg, L. (2004). Risk taking in adolescence: What changes, and why? *Annals of the New York Academy of Sciences*, 1021: 51–58.

Syrotuck, W. G. (1975). *An Introduction to Land Search: Probabilities and Calculations*. Mechanicsburg, PA: Barkleigh Productions, Inc.

Syrotuck, W. G. (1976). *Analysis of Lost Person Behavior: An Aid to Search Planning*. Mechanicsburg, PA: Barkleigh Productions, Inc.

Taylor, E. and Sonuga-Barke, E. (2008). Disorders of attention and activity. In M. Rutter, E. Taylor and J. S. Stevenson (eds), *Rutter's Child and Adolescent Psychiatry* (5th edition). London: Blackwell.

Timperio A., Crawford, D. and Telford A. (2004). Perceptions about the local neighbourhood and walking and cycling among children. *Preventative Medicine*, 38(1): 39–47.

Valentine, G. (2004). *Public Space and the Culture of Childhood*. Aldershot: Ashgate.

Villanueva, K., Giles-Corti, B., Bulsara, M., Timperio, A., McCormack, G., Beesley, B., Trapp, G. and Middleton, N. (2012). Where do children travel to and what local opportunities are available? The relationship between neighborhood destinations and children's independent mobility. *Environment and Behavior*, 45: 679–705.

Wade, J. (2003). Children on the edge. Patterns of running away in the UK. *Child and Family Law Quarterly*, 15(4): 343–352.

Wade, J., Biehal, N., Clayton, J. and Stein, M. (1998). *Going Missing: Young People Absent from Care*. Chichester: Wiley.

Zablotsky, B., Bradshaw, C., Anderson, C. and Law, P. (2013). The association between bullying and the psychological functioning of children with autism spectrum disorders. *Journal of Developmental and Behavioral Pediatrics*, 34(1): 1–8.

Part II
Missing Adults

6

Intentionality and Missing Adults

Lucy Holmes

intentional /ɪnˈtɛnʃ(ə)n(ə)l / adjective [ORIGIN French or medieval Latin]

1. Of or pertaining to intention; existing (only) in intention.
2. In scholastic logic and (later) phenomenology: of or pertaining to the operations of the mind; existing in or for the mind.
3. Done on purpose; deliberate.

(Shorter Oxford English Dictionary, 2007)

The notion of intentionality, the degree to which people go missing deliberately, has long been used as a framework to understand missing person incidents. Research about missing persons, across a range of disciplines, has developed a typology of 'missing' based around the concept of intentionality. Different approaches have been adopted, all of which have tried to encapsulate the ways that different 'types' of missing incident seem to suggest different levels of intentionality on the part of the missing person.

This chapter will explore in more depth what intentionality means and how it is not a fixed state; someone may have different intentions during a missing incident. It will also outline why intentionality is an important concept for missing and to highlight the risks and benefits of understanding missing using this framework.

The degree to which people choose to go missing, and the conceptualisation of this intentionality by others, is a theme running through much of the literature about missing persons (Payne, 1995; Henderson et al., 2000; Biehal et al., 2003; James et al., 2008; Holmes, 2008). Payne, for example, conceived of five categories of missing person: 'Runaway (missing people); Throwaways (rejected missing people); Pushaways (people forced to go missing); Fallaways (people who have lost contact); Takeaways (people forced out of contact)' (Payne, 1995, p. 337). Tarling and Burrows similarly suggested a range of reasons why people disappear, including both 'push' and 'pull' factors, such as relationship breakdown, abuse at home, peer group pressure and other external influences (Tarling and Burrows, 2004, p. 17). Guidance for police officers similarly highlights the importance of considering the range of push and pull factors, emphasising that a missing incident is likely to have been 'precipitated by a problem in the person's life' (ACPO, 2010, p. 18).

Figure 6.1   The missing continuum
Source: Adapted from Biehal et al., 2003, p. 3

Perhaps the most nuanced approach has been that taken by Biehal et al. (2003) who devised a continuum to describe the various degrees of intent, whilst also acknowledging that 'some situations are particularly complex' and may not easily be fitted into the continuum.

The concept of intentionality also depends on the way in which the person has been defined as missing, whether they see themself as a missing person and whether anyone has reported them missing. 'Missingness' is 'indelibly relational', an entirely attributed state which may be imposed on an absent adult without their knowledge (Parr and Fyfe, 2013, p. 3). There is a substantive difference between cases in which family members have realised that they are unable to contact another family member following a history of sporadic or infrequent contact, and cases where someone who is usually in regular contact (or whose patterns of whereabouts are normally known) disappears very suddenly. Arguably, if the missing person is unaware that they are missed, it may not be at all helpful to consider their intent; if they were to become aware, and then to choose to resume contact or to stay away, then intent becomes relevant. This is addressed in the missing continuum by the 'drifted' category (Biehal et al., 2003, p. 3).

The continuum has been applied to empirical work, leading to estimates of the proportion of adults who go missing intentionally and unintentionally. Biehal et al. found that, in a sample of nearly 200 formerly missing adults, 64 per cent had 'decided' to go missing, 19 per cent had 'drifted' out of contact, 16 per cent had gone missing 'unintentionally' and the remaining 1 per cent had been forced away (Biehal et al., 2003, p. 14).

Difficulties with Assessing Intentionality

While intentionality has become entrenched in research about missing, it is a difficult notion to apply to individual circumstances and disappearances. During a disappearance it is, by definition, impossible to consult the missing person about what caused them to go missing and evidence may be sought to try to establish intent (or lack thereof). There are four main reasons why assessing intent is troublesome:

1   The tension between individual agency and structural factors may render assessment of intent moot.
2   The concept of intentionality is reliant on the missing person's mental capacity, which is difficult to assess in absentia.
3   Unless there is evidence left behind, there is no proof of intent until the missing person is found.
4   Intent may change over time so a correct assessment may become incorrect.

The following section explores these reasons in more depth.

Discussion of intentionality has generally relied on the construct of missing adults as rational actors. In the field of criminology, the rational choice theory of offending and desistance (which positions offending as a rational choice made by offenders, who weigh up potential costs and benefits) has been shown to be significantly lacking. Rational Choice Theory of offending and desistance (Clarke and Cornish, 1985; Cusson and Pinsonneault, 1986, cited in Maruna, 1999) has largely been overtaken by social bonds and narrative approaches to understanding why offenders reduce and cease their offending. However, some work has been undertaken to explore the links between going missing and social exclusion. A recent Canadian paper found that groups at risk of social exclusion are also at risk of going missing. Social exclusion refers to 'structural processes that prevent particular people and groups from participating in the economic, social, cultural, and political activities that other people in that society access thereby resulting in a poor quality of life' (Percy–Smith, 2000, cited in Kiepal et al., 2012, p. 141). The Canadian findings suggest that structural factors, over which individuals have little or no control, may influence the likelihood of going missing, therefore throwing doubt on the framing of the 'intentionally' missing person as a rational actor: 'Even if it appears that people choose to go missing, their decision is often motivated by adverse events over which they have little control' (Kiepal et al., 2012, p. 140).

Reliance on the concept of intentionality requires assumptions that a person who appears to have gone missing deliberately not only has the capacity to make a choice, but may also ignore the externally imposed factors that contribute to the likelihood of disappearance. This is reflected in the recent Geographies of Missing People research project: 'whilst some people might make a conscious decision to leave, the situations that people go absent from are not entirely of their own making' (Stevenson et al., 2013, p. 39). This may not be a significant point during an individual missing episode, but bears consideration by anyone examining the phenomenon as a whole.

This links to the question of whether the object of intent is relevant to any categorisation. An adult who decides to leave a violent home, or to flee a perceived threat of violence, may indeed intend to remain 'hidden' from the people who pose the risk. However, they may hope not to be reported missing, and they may choose to stay in contact with some family or friends. Further, there is a question around whether the intention to leave also reflects a desire to leave their home. It may be the case, instead, that they feel that they have been forced to leave by the threat of violence, when they would have preferred the perpetrator to leave instead. The decision to leave may indeed be rational and deliberate, but it does not follow that the departure from home is chosen.

One could also imagine an instance whereby an adult loses contact with family as a result of multiple deprivations such as family breakdown, homelessness or substance use. While that person may not have chosen to be missing, and their lack of contact might have been caused by both individual and social factors, that individual may not be identified as missing or reported for some time, if at all. It is also possible that, at some point, that person might consciously choose not to reinstate contact, at which point they arguably become an intentionally missing person, even if those left behind have not identified them as such.

It is difficult to assess intentionality without full knowledge of the missing person's mental wellbeing and capacity at the time of disappearance. The law presumes that adults have the right to make decisions unless they lack the capacity to do so. The Mental Capacity Act 2005 (in England and Wales) 'provides a framework to empower and protect people who may lack capacity to make some decisions for themselves' (Ministry of Justice, 2012). The decision to leave or break off contact would be an example of a decision that requires mental capacity. Capacity, however, is fluid and may change over time and in different circumstances. This means that someone who seemed not to have capacity before leaving might, in fact, have been capable of deciding to leave. The opposite is also true; someone who, when last seen by family, was capable of making decisions might have subsequently experienced a change in their capacity.

> It really wasn't possible to tell, but it didn't appear that it was a bag packed and walked out, it really appeared that for some reason he'd popped out. Either because he'd got frightened by something if he was feeling delusional, or because he just felt a need to go out for something and for some reason just never went back. So I always got the sense that he hadn't left the house, that it was while he was out something prevented him from going back, something in his mind probably.
>
> (Sister of a missing man, interview data associated with Holmes, 2008)

Mental illness and other matters covered in standard police risk assessments, such as substance use, do not, per se, mean that an adult lacks capacity to make decisions. It may also be the case that someone who lacks capacity to make some decisions is nonetheless able to follow through a planned course of action in a way that appears intentional. Departure during a significant mental health crisis may take place at a time when the individual does not have capacity to choose to become missing, or to keep themselves safe, but may be capable of collecting belongings and travelling some distance. The act of leaving, in this case, could be identified as either deliberate and intentional, or unintentional, depending on the perspective and knowledge of those making the judgement.

Certain types of evidence or information may suggest a high level of intent to leave on the part of the missing adult. This may be explicit, such as a letter or other communications made to family members stating that the missing adult intended to leave. Alternatively, evidence may be implicit; evidence left behind when an adult goes missing that suggests they made preparations to leave. Cash withdrawals in the days before a disappearance, or taking crucial items (such as medication, bank cards, a passport, suitable clothing) may suggest planning, while leaving important items behind may suggest a low degree of intentionality. Similarly, in some cases it is clear that departure would have required significant effort (such as absconding from a secure hospital ward), which may also indicate a deliberate disappearance. It is not known what proportion of missing person cases involves evidence of explicit or implicit intent. It is also important to acknowledge that evidence might also be sought to establish an absence of intent; in some cases there may be evidence that a perpetrator has forced an adult to leave.

Where evidence of intent is unavailable, assessment of intent is likely to rely on family and friends' knowledge of the missing person's character and behaviour patterns. Friends and family members may also be well positioned to make judgements about a person's mental wellbeing immediately prior to a disappearance. Previous research has found that family members of missing people showed a tendency to draw conclusions about the degree of intent involved in a disappearance based on the missing person's character and behaviour (Holmes, 2008).

There is, however, a risk in relying on informants' judgements; while they know the missing person well, and may be able to make good observations about their state of mind or character, friends or family members may (deliberately or inadvertently) act to protect the memory of their relationship with that person, and may be unable to countenance the idea that they left on purpose (through loyalty or self-preservation). Families may disagree on their judgements, and informants' and family members' thoughts on intent may vary over time.

The ways in which people become missing vary, and research has found that for many people it is an impulsive act, an instantaneous decision to leave home, to get away, to walk or travel aimlessly, rather than a decision to become a missing person (Stevenson et al., 2013). However, missing adults may face further decision points during a missing episode. An example of a decision point would be the realisation or discovery that the police have opened an investigation. Similarly, as people move between places and make choices about which road to walk along or which train to board, they may be deciding and redeciding to stay away from home. Importantly for police and support providers, these decision points may provide an opportunity to reach out to the missing adult with information and compassion.

As capacity may change over time, so might intent to be missing or away from home. It is entirely possible, for example, that an adult who intended to leave could subsequently fall victim to crime, accident or illness which renders them unable to return had they so wished. Similarly, it is also possible that adults who do not intend to leave for a long period later decide to evade the people searching for them, and to continue to be out of contact. It is also worth considering, if a disappearance is deemed intentional, what the object of that intent might have been. If an adult intends to leave a difficult situation but does not anticipate that they will be reported missing to the police, should that be described as an intentional disappearance?

The Impact of the Concept of Intentionality

Despite the many difficulties with using the concept of intentionality to categorise disappearances, it endures for several reasons: because it is central to the missing person's experience; because of the potential impact perceptions of intentionality might have on the work of search and support agencies; and because perceptions of intentionality can be significant to families left behind.

The level of intent involved in leaving or staying missing may affect the extent to which the missing adult is willing to engage with the people and agencies searching for them. For a missing adult, the way in which they became missing is likely to strongly influence their experience whilst away and may have some bearing on the way in which they return or are found. The missing person's decisions whilst away, including how they respond to search efforts, may depend on whether, and how strongly, they wish to remain out of contact. It is important to note, however, that research suggests that some missing adults may remain out of contact not because they have made a positive choice to go or stay missing, but because they fear the consequences of police involvement (Stevenson et al., 2013). This may be because of previous negative experiences with police, fear of getting arrested or being in trouble, or fear of unknown consequences.

Categorisations that are rooted in assumptions about intent have also informed search strategies on the part of police and other search agencies. A number of valuable resources that support profiling and search strategies work with categories of lost missing people which are underpinned with the notion of intentionality, such as Gibb and Woolnough, 2007, which used police missing person and suicide reports; Centre for Search Research, 2011, based on data collected from UK mountain rescue teams; and Koester, 2008, which used data collected from the International Search and Rescue Incident Database (ISRID). In this sense, the available evidence (explicit or implicit) about the missing person's intent is used to support scenario-based risk assessment and search planning. The potential problems in this approach have already been rehearsed earlier in this chapter, but in the absence of proof, perception of intent is treated as relevant and operationally useful.

There are risks inherent in too strong reliance on categorising missing incidents as intentional or unintentional. One such risk is that the perception of intent could influence the decision whether to report someone missing to police or others, through families not wishing to distress a missing person, not believing that the incident warrants police involvement, or fearing that the police will not be willing to search for an intentionally missing adult. It is also possible that members of the police or other search and support agencies might be unduly influenced by perceptions of intent. Certainly this is a concern for informants:

> We think the police have just put him down as 'he's only an alcoholic, he'll turn up'. And they never took us at all seriously.
>
> (Daughter-in-law of a missing man)

> I was really was surprised, pleasantly surprised by how much interest the police were prepared to show in it, because it wasn't a vulnerable person in the traditional sense […] at the end of the day an adult who was capable of making his own decisions had walked away from his own house and had walked away from his debts.
>
> (Sister of a missing man, interview data associated with Holmes, 2008)

Importantly, while most adults have the legal right to break contact with their family, and for their whereabouts to remain confidential, it may still be relevant for the police to investigate a disappearance. Risk assessment procedures will define the operational police response to any missing person report. Implicit or explicit evidence of intent may inform the police investigation, but concerns about the missing person's welfare must take priority in terms of the police response.

A further risk with categorising missing people by degrees of intent is that, in absentia, the extent of intentionality may be incorrectly assessed. The police are advised 'if in doubt, think murder' in order to remind them that, in the absence of evidence to the contrary, it is always possible that a missing person has gone missing as a result of force or accident and sound investigation requires positive action (ACPO, 2010, p. 15).

Not only has the notion of intentionality informed police behaviour, it is also relevant for providers of support services. Missing People (2012) acknowledges the importance that the concept can have for families left behind.

> Missing People supports those who are missing and their families across the whole continuum. We recognise the importance of perceived 'intent' to leave. Even though this intent is generally assumed rather than known by a family, it has a huge effect on their feelings and their ability to cope.
>
> (Missing People, 2012, p. 5)

Perception of intent may also matter to family and friends left behind because it may affect their behaviour (reporting, telling others, searching, publicising), their emotional response (triggering anger, guilt, worry, hope), their expectation of the person returning, and their help-seeking behaviour. Research has also found that contrasting perceptions of intent within a family can have a divisive effect (Holmes, 2008, p. 21). The charity Missing People has explored the effects of families' perceptions of intent and found that families' perceptions of intentionality may be linked to their beliefs about whether the missing person is still alive, or whether they have died whilst missing (Holmes, 2008, p. 24). Figure 6.2 represents the different effects of families' perceptions of intent and outcome and how these can affect behaviour, emotional response and expectation of finding the missing person.

It is also possible that family members' perceptions of intent might inform their approach to dealing with legal and practical affairs. Across the UK Presumption of Death legislation provides a legislative framework to allow families to administer a missing person's affairs. Whether and when families decide to use such processes may be influenced by their perceptions of intent as well as outcome.

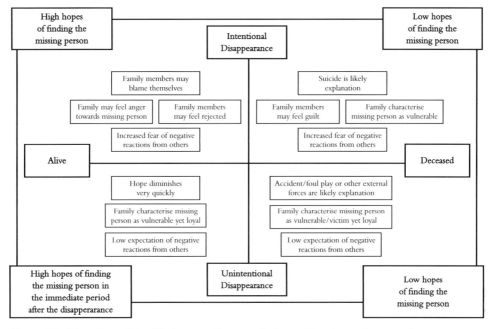

Figure 6.2 The effect of families' perceptions on their emotional reaction to a disappearance
Source: Holmes, 2008, p. 30

Conclusion

While there are risks associated with making judgements about intent there are a number of reasons why understanding intent may be helpful. First, consideration of intent is based on the understanding that adults who are not subject to a legal constraint have the right to choose to leave. Commitment to protecting this right should underpin the work of all search and support agencies. Missing adults may be reassured to know that they are within their rights to leave, and will not normally face any legal proceedings as a result of being missing.

By exploring the notion of intent, and bearing in mind the nature of 'decision points', those involved in searching for and supporting missing adults may also gain insight into the best ways to reach out to missing people. The charity Missing People, for example, makes clear in all communication with missing adults that it recognises their right to be missing, and that choosing to remain missing does not prevent missing adults from accessing support services.

For service providers, such as the police and charities working in the field, consideration of intent will raise a number of questions. How can perceptions of intent provide benefit to an investigation or search without introducing unacceptable risks? How might the decision points faced by missing adults be used as intervention or safeguarding opportunities? How might understanding of the nuance of intent inform the support provided to people left behind when someone is missing? Further investigation of risk assessment, crime detection (including development of hypotheses, as discussed in ACPO, 2005) and missing adult behaviour in relation to missing person enquiries may go some way to addressing such questions.

References

ACPO (2005). *Practice Advice on Core Investigative Doctrine*. Cambourne: National Centre for Policing Excellence.

ACPO (2010). *Guidance on the Management, Recording and Investigation of Missing Persons* (2nd edition). London: National Policing Improvement Agency.

Biehal, N., Mitchell, F. and Wade, J. (2003). *Lost from View*. Bristol: The Policy Press.

Centre for Search Research (2011). *The UK Missing Person Behaviour Study*. Northumbria: Centre for Search Research.

Clarke, R. V. and Cornish, D. B. (1985). Modeling offender's decisions: A framework for research and policy. In M. Tonry and N. Morris (eds), *Crime and Justice: An Annual Review of Research*. Chicago: University of Chicago Press.

Cusson, M. and Pinsonneault, P. (1986). The decision to give up crime. In D. B. Cornish and R. V. Clarke (eds), *The Reasoning Criminal*. New York: Springer-Verlag.

Gibb, G. and Woolnough, P. (2007). *Missing Persons: Understanding, Planning, Responding*. Aberdeen: Grampian Police.

Henderson, M., Henderson, P. and Kiernan, C. (2000). Missing persons: Incidence, issues and impacts. *Trends and Issues in Crime and Criminal Justice*, 144. Canberra: Australian Institute of Criminology.

Holmes, L. (2008). *Living in Limbo: The Experiences of, and Impacts on, the Families of Missing People*. London: Missing People.

James, M., Anderson, J. and Putt, J. (2008). *Missing Persons in Australia*. Research and public policy series no. 86. Canberra: Australian Institute of Criminology.

Kiepal, L., Carrington, P. J. and Dawson, M. (2012). Missing persons and social exclusion. *Canadian Journal of Sociology/Cahiers canadiens de sociologie*, 37(2): 137–168.

Koester, R. J. (2008). *Lost Person Behavior: A Search and Rescue Guide on Where to Look – For Land, Air, and Water*. Charlottesville, VA: dbS Productions LLC.

Maruna, S. (1999). Desistance and development: The psychosocial process of 'going straight'. In *British Criminology Conferences: Selected Proceedings*, Vol. 2, papers from the British Criminology Conference, Queens University, Belfast, July 1997. www.britsoccrim.org/volume2/003.pdf (accessed 27 August 2015).

Ministry of Justice (2012). Mental Capacity Act (England and Wales) 2005, www.justice.gov.uk/protecting-the-vulnerable/mental-capacity-act (accessed 12 June 2014; last updated 16 April 2014).

Missing People (2012). *An Uncertain Hope*. London: Missing People.

Parr, H. and Fyfe, N. (2013). Missing geographies. *Progress in Human Geography*, October 2013, 37(5): 615–638.

Payne, M. (1995). Understanding 'going missing': Issues for social work and social services. *British Journal of Social Work*, 25: 333–348.

Percy-Smith, J. (2000). *Policy responses to social exclusion: Towards inclusion?*. McGraw-Hill Education.

Oxford Dictionaries (2007). *Shorter Oxford English Dictionary*. Oxford: Clarendon Press.

Stevenson, O., Parr, H., Woolnough, P. and Fyfe, N. (2013). *Geographies of Missing People: Processes, Experiences, Responses*. Glasgow: University of Glasgow.

Tarling, R. and Burrows, J. (2004). The nature and outcome of going missing: The challenge of developing effective risk assessment procedures. *International Journal of Police Science and Management*, 6(1): 16–26.

7

Mental Health Issues and Missing Adults

Penny S. Woolnough, Llian Alys and Francis Pakes

Introduction

> A lot of it is to do with mental illness. That's my personal experience and a lot of people aren't comfortable admitting it, but I have to because it's the only way I'm going to manage not to be reported missing again.
>
> > (Andrew's story: being missing for 4 weeks[1])

> I disenfranchised myself and it came and went in phases and a lot of it is to do with mental illness. Every time I felt trapped and confined. It felt that way to me but that's not actually the way it was. Inside my own head I felt like everything was closing down on me and the only escape was to run.
>
> > (Rhona's story: a life of missing experience[2])

People go missing or become reported missing for many different reasons. As James et al. (2008, p. 2) illustrate:

> While it is not a crime to go missing, there may be factors relating to the criminal justice system, either underpinning the motives of the missing person, or relating to the outcome of the missing person investigation. On the other hand, the explanation may be totally removed from any criminal dimension and could include social problems associated with mental health issues, alcohol use, child psychological abuse, child neglect or parental rejection of a child. It could be a combination of both criminal activities and social problems … It could involve an older person with Alzheimer's disease or dementia. It may be a homicide or a suicide or be the result of an accident … The list is seemingly endless.

Endeavouring to make sense of this wide range of circumstances, Biehal et al. (2003) set out a conceptualisation of missing along a continuum from intentional (decided) to unintentional (forced), with drifted (lost contact over a period of time) along the continuum. They indicate that at any point along the continuum a person can be vulnerable, stating that mental health problems were one of the main reasons for adults going missing. Indeed, they found that more than half of individuals who had 'unintentionally' gone missing experienced dementia or other mental health problems. Echoing this, it has been suggested that the three groups most at risk of going missing are those living with a mental illness, young people and older people with dementia or memory loss (James et al., 2008). Furthermore, approximately 12,000 individuals are reported missing from NHS care in the UK every year and a high proportion of these will have a mental health problem (Home Office, 2011). Consequently, there are clear indications that adults reported as missing to the police may suffer mental health problems which may contribute to their vulnerability as a missing person, affect their behaviour and have significant resource implications for police, social services and health care providers.

In this chapter we discuss current mental health issues in relation to missing adults, including those who disappear to suicide, making reference to relevant research outside the policing domain (such as psychological autopsy research on suicide). We also look at two other vulnerable groups which the police encounter on a regular basis, absconders from hospitals and individuals who request the assistance of police forces and health services giving false details or claiming amnesia ('come to notice' persons).

The Prevalence and Nature of Mental Health in the Adult Missing Person Population

Government data consistently indicate that one in four adults in the UK will experience a mental health problem in any given year (Meltzer et al., 1995; Self et al., 2012). Unfortunately, high-level figures such as these are not yet available from government or third sector agencies in relation to missing persons and mental health. However, a small number of studies have touched on the issue and, although findings vary, they provide some indication of the extent of the issue.

Compared to the general population, research suggests that unemployment, disability and mental health issues are more prevalent amongst adults who go missing (Biehal et al., 2003; Tarling and Burrows, 2004). The first study which touched on missing and mental health was an analysis of a year's worth of police missing person reports from a large city in the US, which found that 18.8 per cent of adults had a mental health problem (Hirschel and Lab, 1988). These figures are reasonably consistent with a study of cases recorded by the UK Missing People charity (then the National Missing Persons Helpline), which suggested that around 11 per cent of adults had mental health problems (Biehal et al., 2003). However, these cases related only to those referred to the charity and may not have been officially reported to the police. More recent research using police data suggests that the prevalence of mental health issues amongst missing adults is much higher than this. Gibb and Woolnough (2007) conducted an in-depth content analysis of police reports from across the UK and found that approximately 80 per cent of adults who go missing are thought to have some form of mental illness based on clinical diagnoses and general diagnoses by family members and friends. In terms of clinical diagnoses alone, 63 per cent of adult cases involved a mental health issue (Woolnough and Gibb, 2013). In line with this, using electronically retrieved data from two English police forces Holmes et al. (2013) also found that just under 60 per cent of adults had a clinically diagnosed recorded mental health problem.

In addition to research using police recorded data, follow-up research with families of missing persons and located missing persons suggests that the prevalence of mental health difficulties in the adult missing population is high. Henderson and Henderson (1998) found that in 62 per cent of adult missing person cases families and friends identified the missing person as having one or more special needs. Recently completed research involving in-depth qualitative interviews with located missing people suggests figures in line with the Gibb and Woolnough (2007) work, with 76 per cent of the interviewees reporting themselves to have mental health problems (Stevenson et al., 2013).

Despite the variation across these studies, it is clear that the prevalence of mental health problems in the adult missing person population appears to be higher than the general population and could be as high as 80 per cent. It is also clear that missing people experience a wide range of mental health conditions. Gibb and Woolnough (2007) categorised adult missing persons based on diagnoses of depression, bipolar disorder, psychosis/schizophrenia, dementia and Attention Deficit Hyperactivity Disorder. In their study of charity held cases, Biehal et al. (2003) found that of those who responded to a self-report post-incident questionnaire, just over one-fifth (22 per cent) reported depression and around one in 12 (9 per cent) reported having other mental health problems. Biehal et al. (2003) also found that adults aged 60 and over were even more likely to be vulnerable, as over half were suffering from dementia or mental health problems. Similarly, from a sample of police reports and a survey of families and friends of missing persons, Henderson and Henderson (1998) identified depression and age-related disorders such as Alzheimer's disease. Furthermore, during interviews with located missing persons 67 per cent reported mood disorders (including bipolar and depression) and 23 per cent reported schizophrenia and other psychotic disorders (Stevenson et al., 2003).

The Importance of Mental Health Throughout the Missing Journey

This accumulating evidence for a relationship between mental health and missing raises important questions and challenges for researchers, policy makers and practitioners. What impact does mental health have in terms of risk of going missing? What impact might mental health have on a person's decision making and behaviour while they are missing? What associated risks might this present and what safeguarding measures are required? What implications are there for the police and other agencies? What impact does the experience of missing have on a missing person's mental health and wellbeing and what support measures are required before, during and after missing episodes? Although there have been very few studies which have explored the broader issues of mental health and missing (Gibb and Woolnough, 2007; Holmes et al., 2013), in this section we explore what is currently known about the importance and impact of mental health throughout the missing journey.

Reasons for Going Missing

Biehal et al. (2003) found that the primary reason for adults going missing was due to relationship breakdown within their family, followed by drifting away, mental health issues and escaping a negative situation. Others lost touch through drifting into a transient lifestyle, often connected to mental health, drug or alcohol problems. Mental health problems and substance abuse are also common issues that link homelessness and missing (Crisis, 2002; Rees, 2009). During in-depth interviews, located missing adults elucidate on this, talking about the importance of historic and current traumatic experiences as well as strong emotions of being unable to cope, feeling trapped and unable to talk about or share their feelings (Stevenson et al., 2013). Some missing persons report that deciding to leave creates a moment of calm and clarity, as well as short-term mental and physical relief (Stevenson et al., 2013). However, decisions to go missing are not always present. Biehal et al. (2003) found that while most adults with depression had left intentionally, a few of those with mental health problems left unintentionally and had not really been aware of what they were doing at the time, particularly those suffering from dementia. Henderson and Henderson (1998) also identified that dementia sufferers were at risk of going missing on more than one occasion.

Police Risk Assessment and Response

From a policing point of view, mental health is a critical factor which should be taken into account as part of the risk assessment and response to any missing person. Specific advice should be sought from qualified medical staff when adults who are accommodated in residential care situations or are day patients at hospital, including accident and emergency departments, go missing, including likely outcomes if they do not receive treatment/medication and their ability to look after themselves or to survive (ACPO, 2010). While these factors are identified as central to the police response, risk assessment and understanding of the implications of mental health in adult missing person cases are limited by a paucity of research in this area. In an attempt to address this, Gibb and Woolnough (2007) (see also ACPO, 2006) presented the first operational guidance for police officers containing spatial profiles and investigative strategies for missing persons with: depression, bipolar disorder, psychosis/schizophrenia, dementia, Attention Deficit Hyperactivity Disorder and cases of suicide. Based on a UK-wide analysis of 2,198 closed police recorded missing person cases, Gibb and Woolnough (2007) used 'predictive' variables (such as age, sex, suicide attempts, previous missing episodes and mental condition) to 'predict' outcome characteristics (such as distance travelled, where they will be located, and timescales in which they will be traced/found). This work is currently used by police and search and rescue agencies throughout the UK (ACPO, 2006; Gibb and Woolnough, 2007).

Duration Missing

Due to the sparseness of research on mental health and missing, little is known about whether the presence or absence of mental health diagnoses has an impact upon the duration of missing episodes. While duration missing will vary across cases, some research suggests that mental health may be an important factor influencing the length of a person's missing episode. In their study of cases reported to the National Missing Persons Helpline (now Missing People), Biehal et al. (2003) found that vulnerable adults were usually found more quickly than other missing people, and the majority were found within six months. In their operational guidance, Gibb and Woolnough (2007) set out time parameters in which officers should expect to locate missing adults (from the time reported to the police) if they had not suffered an accident or fatal outcome.

As can be seen from Table 7.1, these figures suggest that adult missing persons diagnosed with bipolar disorder have longer missing episodes than those with psychosis/schizophrenia

Table 7.1 Timescales to locate missing adults with mental illness

Mental illness	Timescales to locate
Dementia	70% within 3 hours and 50 minutes
	99% within 14 hours
Psychosis/schizophrenia	70% within 4 hours and 10 minutes
	99% within 12 hours and 50 minutes
Bipolar disorder	70% within 16 hours and 10 minutes
	99% within 71 hours

Source: Gibb and Woolnough, 2007

or dementia (who have the shortest durations missing). Use of transport increases all of the timescales and associated parameters are given in the guidance (see also ACPO, 2006). Further research on this issue is urgently needed as knowledge of the timescales associated with missing episodes has important implications for police risk assessment and response, highlighting when cases may be 'out of the ordinary' and facilitating the allocation of additional resources (Gibb and Woolnough, 2007).

Hiding, Encounters and Seeking Help While Missing

Very little is known about the impact of mental health upon missing behaviour while adults are missing. However, a recent study utilising in-depth interviews with located missing adults has provided valuable qualitative insights (see Stevenson et al., 2013; Parr and Stevenson, 2014). The interviews reveal that adults may or may not be aware they have been reported missing to the police and even when unaware their missing journeys involved a degree of hiding behaviours with adults hiding from a range of actors, including the police, family members, mental health workers, friends and colleagues (Stevenson et al., 2013). Encounters reported on missing journeys were both accidental and deliberate with acquaintances or friends, and adults who were absconding from mental health facilities would at times abscond with others (Stevenson et al., 2013). Over half of the interviewees attempted to seek help in relation to the risks they felt were associated with their own mental health and did so by seeking out 'sympathetic' people who would understand the issues associated with their mental health. However, fear of being 'sectioned' prevented adults with mental health issues from approaching family or friends. In relation to this, adults reported missing on more than one occasion were often aware of police procedures and those absconding from mental health wards knew that the police had the potential to section and return them if located (Stevenson et al., 2013).

Issues of Return

While the safe location of a missing person is the principal aim of any police-led missing person enquiry, the discovery of a person's whereabouts should not be the sole consideration. Stevenson et al. (2013) highlight that the police handling of the return is critical to feelings of guilt and shame in the missing person, and may be important for continuing mental health or repeat missing events and future police contact. Repeatedly missing adults with mental health issues experienced high levels of police intervention and were more aware of police procedure. Those interviewees with mental health problems who challenged the police in relation to return by questioning police procedure were provided with limited response. For those adults who were not being returned to a ward, interviewees reported feelings of shock that prohibited them from asking about police involvement. This highlights the importance of not rushing initial conversations, being nonjudgemental and talking with sensitivity about the individual's missing journey (Stevenson et al., 2013). Biehal et al. (2003) also reported how missing adults were anxious about returning and ashamed of the distress they had caused. Mitigating this to some extent, they found that the mediation of the National Missing Persons Helpline (now Missing People) sometimes helped to give people the confidence to return. Echoing this, a recent study by the Missing People charity highlights the importance of a sensitive, tailored and holistic approach to reconnecting missing people with families and that this may need to happen in a number of ways and over a period of time (Holmes, 2014). Importantly, while ACPO (2010) guidance talks about the importance of conducting a return interview with children, especially those with mental health issues, as soon as possible and in any case within 72 hours of the child being located or returning, there is no mention of the importance of such an interview with located adults. Clearly, as Stevenson et al. (2013) indicate, an appropriate return interview for adults is also of vital importance to ongoing safeguarding and prevention efforts. This is particularly illustrated by the finding that when services were accessed on return it was often to assess medication and talk about mental health issues rather than about missing experiences. Consequently, the chance to talk about missing experiences did not always present itself and interviewees spoke about how they felt they would have benefited from this (Stevenson et al., 2013).

Suicide and Missing

The risk of suicide is a key consideration for investigators when adults go missing (see Hedges, 2002; ACPO, 2005), particularly if there is a history of mental health issues. However, not all individuals who attempt suicide when missing will have experienced mental health problems or will have been diagnosed as such (Missing People, 2013) and neither will all individuals with mental health issues who go missing attempt suicide (Gibb and Woolnough, 2007). Individuals with mental health issues may, however, be more likely to be reported missing due to greater supervision by carers and loved ones (for example, Sveticic et al., 2012).

Newiss' (2011) examined cases reported to both the charity Missing People and the police, and, consistent with national suicide rates (for example, Office of National Statistics, 2014), most missing suicide victims were male with an average age of 42 years. One-quarter of the suicide victims were known to be under stress due to family or relationship issues and some had experienced a critical life event such as a death or the departure of a loved one (Newiss, 2011). Gibb and Woolnough (2007) refer to such events as possible triggers and advise investigators to consider problems in all areas of the missing person's life (personal, psychological, physical, familial, social, education and employment-related). A critical event might have occurred recently or in the past; an anniversary, for example, might make the date of disappearance significant (Gibb and Woolnough, 2007).

Indicators of Risk

Previous behaviour is often described as the best predictor of future behaviour; as such, having a previous history of suicide attempts and no previous history of missing episodes are considered 'red flags' for a suicide attempt (Gibb and Woolnough, 2007). Leaving behind everyday items which an individual would normally carry (for example, wallet and keys) might indicate a suicide attempt (Gibb and Woolnough, 2007; Newiss, 2011). Gibb and Woolnough (2007) consider leaving a suicide note and communication of suicidal intent as strong indicators but caution that these are not necessary precursors. Other more subtle behaviours, of which family members may not realise the relevance, include being more affectionate prior to going missing, uncharacteristically leaving wedding rings in obvious places and putting personal affairs like finances in order.

An Australian study by Foy (2006, cited in Sveticic et al., 2012) compared missing persons who had completed or attempted suicide with those who had run away and those who had been subject to foul play. Missing persons who had attempted suicide were more likely to be male, aged between 41 and 65 years, single, without children, suffering from depression and with a previous history of suicide attempts or threats and a number of acute and chronic stressors in their lives. In most cases, the disappearance was considered out of character and in almost 80 per cent of cases the person reporting to the police suggested suicide as a possible motive, suggesting that family members and friends might be aware of a suicidal missing persons' intentions. Foy (2006, cited in Sveticic et al., 2012) tried to identify reasons for going missing from a number of identified indicators but was only able to accurately predict 59 per cent of suicide cases (greater predictive success was had with 'foul play' and 'runaway' cases).

Gibb and Woolnough (2007) provide an aide memoire to guide investigators in assessing risk of suicide through consideration of indicators of intent, personal and familial history of suicide attempts, mental health issues, drugs and medication, and details of the case (for example, location, access to transport, access to suicide methods). Gibb and Woolnough (2007) caution that while the presence of some indicators of suicidal intent may contribute to the risk assessment, their absence should not preclude consideration that the missing person may attempt suicide. As alluded to by other authors (for example, Newiss, 2011), reliance on indicators is likely to lead to a number of 'false positives' (as the overall base rate of fatal missing episodes is so low compared to nonfatal occurrences) and there might be a risk of 'false negatives' for cases where no obvious indicators are apparent. Newiss (2011) advocates adopting a 'scenario-based risk assessment' which encourages the investigator to create narrative accounts of the disappearance based on the missing person and the circumstances of the missing episode.

Searching for Missing Persons at Risk of Suicide

When it is unclear whether the missing person wants time to think or is intending to attempt suicide, Gibb and Woolnough (2007) advocate a 'twin track' search strategy focusing on both possibilities. This is prudent given that Stevenson et al. (2013) found that an individual's behaviour following a suicide attempt or change of mind resembled that of other 'nonsuicidal' missing persons. If a suicide note is present, there may be clues to the individual's whereabouts (though the individual may have included misleading information to avoid interruption) (Gibb and Woolnough, 2007).

Gibb and Woolnough (2007) propose that individuals will choose a suicide location based on practical (convenience or need for a body of water to drown) or personal reasons (the location has a personal significance). Stevenson et al. (2013) interviewed individuals who had been missing and found that some who intended to commit suicide had decided on a specific (usually familiar) location which on occasion had been chosen some time previously (for example, when planning earlier suicide attempts). Others went to a familiar location but had not necessarily planned to go there specifically.

If an individual has decided to attempt suicide, they may try to evade searchers. For example, previously missing individuals who were intent on suicide (interviewed by Stevenson et al., 2013) said that they wore dark clothing to avoid drawing attention at night. This should be considered when searching for the missing person. Police will attempt to make contact with the missing person but recognise that, sometimes, the person may not want to engage with the authorities (or may be scared of doing so). West Mercia Police explored a partnership with the Samaritans to try to address this issue. With the consent of the missing person's next of kin, the police could share the missing person's mobile phone number with the charity, which could offer support to the individual by text message (Home Office, 2011). This unfortunately may not work on all occasions as individuals may purposely turn off or abandon their phones and, if contemplating suicide, it might not be appropriate to ask them to confirm that they are 'OK' (Stevenson et al., 2013).

Patients Missing from Hospital

Individuals missing from hospital (particularly mental health establishments) or 'hospers' are one of the most common missing person issues encountered by the police (Henderson and Henderson, 1998; Newiss, 1999). While adults can 'choose' to go missing, this is not the case if they are sectioned under the Mental Health Act 1983 (Missing People, 2013).

There have been a number of Independent Police Complaint Commission inquiries regarding individuals missing from hospital (Independent Police Complaint Commissioner, 2007, 2008, 2011) demonstrating the risks involved and the sometimes critical nature of these incidents. It is perhaps not surprising, therefore, that 'absconding', as it is referred to in the literature (or less frequently 'elopement', Brumbles and Meister, 2013), has been the focus of much research, particularly in the area of health (for reviews of this literature, see Bowers et al., 1998; Muir-Cochrane and Mosel, 2008; Stewart and Bowers, 2010).

Rates of absconding as high as 34.5 and 38.7 per 100 patients have been reported (Neilson et al., 1996; Bowers et al., 1998, respectively, as cited in Bowers et al., 2003). However, different studies use different means to calculate absconding rates (Muir-Cochrane et al., 2011) and some methods of calculation (like Molnar and Pinchoff's, 1993) do not distinguish between single or repeat incidents and length of stay is not taken into account, which could lead to biased results.

Bowers et al.'s (1998) review of the literature found that absconders are 'generally young, single and male, and tend to come from disadvantaged groups within the wider society' (p. 349). Disadvantaged populations may include ethnic minorities (see Bowers et al., 2000; Falkowski et al., 1990) and individuals with previous contact with forensic services (see Bowers et al., 1999c).

Previous absconders are at greater risk of absconding (Bowers et al., 2000; Meehan et al., 1999), as are 'new' patients; one of the periods at which a person may be most at risk of absconding is the first three weeks following admission (Bowers et al., 1999b). Certain mental health conditions have been linked to absconding (specifically schizophrenia, Bowers et al., 2000; Falkowski et al., 1990), as have suicide attempts and self-harm (Bowers et al., 1999c; Milner, 1966). Bowers et al. (2000) also suggest behavioural 'red flags' that an individual might be at risk of absconding, for example refusal of medication and involvement in officially reported ward incidents in the week prior to the absconding incident. Bowers et al. (1999b) also found that 58 per cent of the absconders in their study had communicated an intention to leave within 24 hours of the incident.

As in the general literature on missing persons, both 'push' and 'pull' factors (Tarling and Burrows, 2004) for absconding have been proposed (for example, running from the hospital and running to a family member). Some absconders appear to be expressive and impulsive (for example, in anger following delay of leave or discharge) while others appear instrumental (for example, the patient leaves specifically to carry out some activity outside the hospital; Bowers et al., 1999a, 1999b, 1999c, 2000; Clark et al., 1999). Absconders from Stevenson et al.'s (2013) interview study demonstrated different degrees of planning. For a review of influences and motivations for absconding including internal (patient characteristics), personal, social and external (relating to care, treatment or the institution), see Bowers et al. (1998). Manchester et al. (1997) propose an interaction between environmental triggers, organic factors and psychological characteristics, while Meehan et al. (1999) propose that environmental and situational factors are likely to be more influential than any characteristics of the patient.

Bowers et al. (1999b) interviewed absconders and found that many went home and engaged in 'normal' activities such as housework, sleeping, eating, watching television and socialising. Very few appeared to have absconded without an idea of where to go. Absconding might be positive from the patient's perspective, providing 'freedom', a decrease in negative thinking and emotion associated with the hospital or ward (paranoia, unease), reassurance or relief from concerns about loved ones and property, and the positive experience of seeing loved ones (Bowers et al., 1998).

Fortunately, most absconders do not come to direct physical harm (Bowers et al., 1999c). However, in some cases there may be a risk of harm to the absconder (Crammer, 1984; Aspinall, 1993) or harm to others (Milner, 1966; Powell et al., 1994). Violence towards others during absconding has received much media attention and inquiries have been held to examine cases involving murder and serious harm (Sheppard, 1996); however, such cases are comparatively rare. In terms of harm to self, the individual may die from exposure or serious self-neglect (Aspinall, 1993) and also suicide.

Absconding appears to increase the risk of attempted and completed suicide for patients (King et al., 2001; Stewart et al., 2011). Bowers et al. (2008a) argue however that the association between absconding and suicide is not necessarily causal as the absconding may not be separable from the individual's intention to suicide; for example, King et al. (2001) found that 75 per cent of absconding suicides occurred immediately after absconding from psychiatric hospitals. Nonetheless, there remains a proportion of individuals who do not complete suicide immediately and Bowers et al. (2008a) propose that these may be 'ambivalent or impulsive acts that are stimulated by features of the out of hospital environment, or enabled to be enacted because of the absence of staff support and supervision at a critical moment' (p. 22).

In most cases, absconders return by themselves or through assistance from ward staff, relatives, friends or the police within a day or two of absconding (Bowers et al., 1999b, 1999c). In Bowers et al.'s study (1999c), some of those who returned by themselves did so due to pressure from others and expectations that the police would become involved. Others had nowhere to go or were cold, hungry or unwell or were in need of medication or treatment for medication side effects.

Prevention and Intervention of Absconding

Incidents of absconding can highlight issues with security and oversight in the hospital – patients walking away from open wards or recreational activities (Kernodle, 1966) or absconding when shifts change (Bowers et al., 1999b). High perimeter fences can be an obstacle to absconders but Enser and MacInnes (1999) concluded that, overall, the design of a building is not a main factor in absconding. While locked wards might seem the answer, Stewart and Bowers (2011) caution that, conversely, they can lead to more volatile environments (Folkard, 1960) and can be associated with depression (Haglund and Von Essen, 2005), self-harm (Bowers et al., 2008b) and feelings of stigmatisation and reduced perception of staff support (Bowers et al., 2007; Bowers et al., 2008b).

Patient observation is not effective in preventing absconding in all cases (Bowers et al., 1999b; Hunt et al., 2010) and findings concerning the role of staffing levels are mixed (Siegal et al., 1982; Walsh et al., 1998). It may not be the number of staff that is important but the type of staff (how experienced they are) (Siegal et al., 1982; Meehan et al., 1999).

Physical security measures alone appear not to be sufficient to prevent absconding. Bowers et al. (1999b, p. 210) suggest that 'professional patient relationships' and psychosocial support may be just as important (see also the National Mental Health Development Unit's Strategies to Reduce Missing Patients; Bartholomew et al., 2009; Joanna Briggs Institute, 2007). Hunt et al. (2010) suggest that support is particularly important at the time of admission. Other suggestions for reducing absconding include medication management and visit facilitation (Farragher et al., 1996), behavioural management plans (Blass et al., 2001) and token economies (LePage, 1999), for which there are varying degrees of evidential support (Muir-Cochrane and Mosel, 2008).

Bowers et al. (1998) compared evaluations of interventions to decrease absconding and proposed that the generalisability of findings was limited; however, Bowers et al. (2003) evaluated the impact of 'The Anti-Absconding Package' intervention and reported that the rate of absconding fell by 25 per cent. It is important to remember that one size will not fit all with regards to absconding. For example, Bowers et al. (2008a) propose that individuals who abscond in order to suicide may not be amenable to general absconding interventions (Bowers et al., 2005; Bowers et al., 2003).

A number of police forces in the UK have or are developing joint mental health protocols with health services in their area (ACPO, 2010) which encourage joint working and set out the roles and responsibilities of the agencies involved in relation to absconding and any police-related incidents involving individuals with mental health issues. In 2004, the Home Office (2004) published guidance on developing such protocols along with a model police health local protocol template. ACPO (2010) report that such protocols have resulted in fewer reports of absconding from health care and improved working practices.

Come to Notice Individuals

As this chapter indicates, issues of mental health and missing and the link between the two can be multifaceted. In light of that it makes sense to consider individuals who, in a way, represent a rather paradoxical group. There is a seemingly small group of individuals who, rather than go missing, instead 'come to notice'. Come to notice is a term used in the UK by police to describe individuals that come to their attention for a variety of reasons, ranging from intending to suicide, being found in a dishevelled state to checking into hospitals with real or imagined complaints. The UK National Missing Persons Bureau maintains the UK 'Come to Notice' database which holds information on these individuals for operational purposes. The Come to Notice database forms an appendix to the main National Missing Persons database. Consequently, when a police report is received that resembles the circumstances or behaviour of an individual contained in the latter database a connection can be made and the establishment of the identity of a missing person or someone classed as 'unidentified alive' can be achieved. The database contains case notes and photographs but, as it relies on police input, does not usually contain specific medical information beyond that initially recorded by the police officer.

In 2013 the Come to Notice database consisted of some 140 individuals. These are persons who repeatedly come to notice and frequently report real or imagined illnesses or emergencies (Pakes et al., 2014); however, they typically go missing before any diagnosis can be made or intervention put in place. Through a thematic analysis of 15 individuals from the UK database who are prolific in such behaviour Pakes et al. (2014) found that the lives of these individuals is governed by mobility and anonymity. Many travel from place to place but often without pleasure or purpose. Most suffer from physical and mental health difficulties. Many have experienced loss and trauma and only when experiencing further crisis do they give up their autonomy and anonymity to seek help. However, when the crisis subsides, the need to 'be away' seems to drive these people away from the very services that can help them. Pakes et al. (2014) argue that interventions involving this group may be modelled on successful interventions with homeless persons as issues of autonomy and distrust of official agencies may be shared by both groups. Furthermore, timing may be of the essence as well as an understanding that officialdom represents a threat to such people. At the same time, however, there is no doubt that there is a great deal of unmet need within this group and that it may require both persistence and creativity to engage with them effectively.

Conclusion

In this chapter we have attempted to give an overview of the key issues of relevance to understanding and responding to issues of mental health and adult missing persons. Although only a small number of studies have looked at or touched upon this issue, there are clear indications that adults reported as missing to the police may suffer mental health problems which may contribute to their vulnerability as a missing person, affect their behaviour and have significant resource implications for police, social services and health care providers. Furthermore, the prevalence of mental health problems in the adult missing person population appears to be higher than the general population, with indications that it could be high as 80 per cent (Gibb and Woolnough, 2007), and covers a range mental health issues including depression, bipolar disorder, psychosis/schizophrenia, anxiety and dementia (Gibb and Woolnough, 2007; Holmes et al., 2013; Stevenson et al., 2013).

Where there is a history of mental health issues the risk that an adult missing person may cause harm to themselves or others must be a key consideration for investigators (Hedges, 2002; ACPO, 2005). The relative importance of mental health to adults' decisions (or otherwise) to go missing, behaviour while missing and potential needs upon return have been highlighted by in-depth interviews with located missing adults (Stevenson et al., 2013; Parr and Stevenson, 2014). In particular, the need for sympathetic opportunities to discuss their mental health issues while missing and to talk about missing experiences after return were raised by many of the interviewees. Consequently, Stevenson et al. (2013) suggest that campaigns to raise awareness of going missing should be targeted at staff working within the health service as there is a need for mental health services to anticipate and respond to missing experience through early identification of warning signs. Indeed, while some protocols already exist (ACPO, 2010), protocols between police, hospitals and mental health units and charities should be introduced as standard practice across the UK, facilitating health care workers to also share their knowledge and expertise of mental health and suicide indicators to assist police in risk assessing such missing cases (Stevenson et al., 2013). One innovative illustration of an information-sharing arrangement is the Westminster Protocol, which allows the charity UK Missing People and partner organisations within Westminster, London, to share information to try to locate missing adults and to identify unidentified service users where there are concerns for their mental wellbeing by sharing information in two ways: requests to trace and requests to identify (see Holmes and Diamond, 2011).

As indicated by studies of patients missing from care (Bowers et al., 1999b; Bowers et al., 2003), adults may exhibit patterns of behaviour or signs that they are at risk of or intending to go absent through verbal and/or behavioural cues. Learning to recognise these signs and developing sensitively orientated and evidence-informed 'talk don't walk' campaigns or other targeted interventions would promote prevention (Stevenson et al., 2013). Prevention efforts would also be greatly facilitated by sensitive and targeted follow-up/engagement with located missing adults or patients who have 'come to notice'. While the mediation services provided by Missing People have been shown to be very helpful (Biehal et al., 2003), there is a need for the police or associated charitable organisations to endeavour to conduct return interviews as standard practice with located adults as they currently are with children (see ACPO, 2010).

As well as mental health being a key issue for missing people themselves, for every missing person reported at least 12 others are affected, whether emotionally, psychologically, physically or financially (Henderson and Henderson, 1988; Holmes, 2008). Raising general awareness of missing issues through developing cultures of talk and providing resources that help with this is important not just for families but everyone who might be involved in missing journeys, from families, to mental health services, to the police, to the Missing People charity, to the media (Stevenson et al., 2013).

Finally, while the amount of research on missing persons has slowly increased over the past decade, as this chapter highlights we still know very little about the important relationship between mental health and adult missing persons. Consequently, policy and practice in this area remain underdeveloped. The need for researchers, policy makers and practitioners to continue to advance knowledge and practice in this area is without doubt for the continued 'prevention', 'protection' and 'provision' of adult missing persons (Home Office, 2011).

Notes

1 'Andrew's story: being missing for 4 weeks' is taken from the Missing Voices report by Parr and Stevenson (2014), published as part of the Geographies of Missing Project (see www.geographiesofmissingpeople. org.uk).

2 'Rhona's story: a life of missing experience' is taken from the Missing Voices report by Parr and Stevenson (2014), published as part of the Geographies of Missing Project (see www.geographiesofmissingpeople. org.uk).

References

ACPO (2005). *Guidance on the Management, Recording and Investigation of Missing Persons*. Bramshill: National Centre for Policing Excellence. http://library.college.police.uk/docs/acpo/Missing-Persons-2005-ACPO-Guidance.pdf.

ACPO (2006). *Practice Advice on Search Management and Procedures*. Bramshill: National Centre for Policing Excellence. http://library.college.police.uk/docs/npia/search-management-practice-advice-2006.pdf.

ACPO (2010). *Guidance on the Management, Recording and Investigation of Missing Persons* (2nd edition). Wyboston: National Policing Improvement Agency. www.acpo.police.uk/documents/crime/2011/201103CRIIMP02.pdf.

Aspinall, P. (1993). When a vulnerable patient absconds. *Journal of Clinical Nursing*, 3: 115–118.

Bartholomew, D., Duffy, D. and Figgins, N. (2009). *Strategies to Reduce Missing Patients: A Practical Workbook*. London: National Mental Health Development Unit.

Biehal, N., Mitchell F. and Wade J. (2003). *Lost from View*. Bristol: The Policy Press.

Blass, D. M., Steinberg, M., Leroi, I. and Lyketsos, C. G. (2001). Successful multimodality treatment of behavioral disturbance in a patient with advanced Huntington's disease. *American Journal of Psychiatry*, 158: 1966–1972.

Bowers, L., Jarrett, M. and Clark, N. (1998). Absconding: A Literature Review. *Journal of Psychiatric and Mental Health Nursing*, 5: 343–353.

Bowers, L., Jarrett, M., Clark, N., Kiyimba, F., and McFarlane, L. (1999a). 1. Absconding: Why patients leave. *Journal of Psychiatric and Mental Health Nursing*, 6: 199–206.

Bowers, L., Jarrett, M., Clark, N., Kiyimba, F. and McFarlane, L. (1999b). 2. Absconding: How and when patients leave the ward. *Journal of Psychiatric and Mental Health Nursing*, 6: 207–212.

Bowers, L., Jarrett, M., Clark, N., Kiyimba, F. and McFarlane, L. (1999c). 3. Absconding: Outcome and risk. *Journal of Psychiatric and Mental Health Nursing*, 6: 213–218.

Bowers L., Jarrett, M., Clark, N., Kiyimba, F. and McFarlane, L. (2000). Determinants of absconding by patients on acute psychiatric wards. *Journal of Advanced Nursing*, 32: 644–649.

Bowers, L., Alexander, J. and Gaskell, C. (2003). A trial of an anti-absconding intervention in acute psychiatric wards. *Journal of Psychiatric and Mental Health Nursing*, 10(4): 410–416.

Bowers, L., Simpson, A. and Alexander, J. (2005). Real world application of an intervention to reduce absconding. *Journal of Psychiatric and Mental Health Nursing*, 12: 598–602.

Bowers, L., Whittington, R., Nolan, P., Parkin, D., Curtis, S., Bhui, K., Hackney, D., Allan, T., Simpson, A. and Flood, C. (2007). *The City 128 Study of Observation and Outcomes on Acute Psychiatric Wards. Report to the NHS SDO Programme*. London: NHS SDO Programme.

Bowers, L., Nijman, H. and Banda, T. (2008a). *Suicide Inside: A Literature Review on Inpatient Suicide: Report from the Conflict and Containment Reduction Research Programme*. London: City University. www.iop.kcl. ac.uk/iopweb/blob/downloads/locator/l_436_LitRevSuicide.pdf.

Bowers, L., Whittington, R., Nolan, P., Parkin, D., Curtis, S., Bhui, K., Hackney, D., Allan, T. and Simpson, A. (2008b). The relationship between service ecology, special observation and self-harm during acute inpatient care: The city 128 study. *British Journal of Psychiatry*, 193: 395– 401.

Brumbles, D. and Meister, A. (2013). Psychiatric elopement: Using evidence to examine causative factors and preventive measures. *Archives of Psychiatric Nursing*, 27(1): 3–9.

Clark, N., Kiyimba, F., Bowers, L., Jarrett, M. and McFarlane, L. (1999). Absconding: Nurses' views and reactions. *Journal of Psychiatric Mental Health Nursing*, 6(3): 219–224.

Crisis (2002). *Home and Dry? Homelessness and Substance Use*. London: Crisis.

Crammer, J. L. (1984). The special characteristics of suicide in hospital inpatients. *British Journal of Psychiatry*, 145: 460–463.

Enser, J. and MacInnes, D. (1999). The relationship between building design and escapes from secure units. *Journal of the Royal Society for the Promotion of Health*, 119(3): 170–174.

Falkowski, J., Watts, V., Falkowski, W. and Dean, T. (1990). Patients leaving hospital without the knowledge or permission of staff: Absconding. *British Journal of Psychiatry*, 156: 488–490.

Farragher, B., Gannon, M. and Ahmad, I. (1996). Absent without leave: Can we predict those who go AWOL? *Irish Journal of Psychological Medicine*, 13: 28–30.

Folkard, S. (1960). Aggressive behaviour in relation to open wards in a mental hospital. *Mental Hygiene*, 44: 155–161.

Foy S. (2006). *A Profile of Missing Persons in New South Wales.* Sydney (Unpublished doctoral thesis). Charles Sturt University, Australia.

Gibb, G. J. and Woolnough, P. (2007). *Missing Persons: Understanding, Planning, Responding.* Aberdeen: Grampian Police.

Haglund, K. and Von Essen, L. (2005). Locked entrance doors at psychiatric wards – advantages and disadvantages according to voluntarily admitted patients. *Nordic Journal of Psychiatry*, 59: 511–515.

Hedges, C. (2002). *Missing You Already: A Guide to the Investigation of Missing Persons.* London: Home Office.

Henderson, M. and Henderson, P. (1998). *Missing People: Issues for the Australian Community.* Canberra: Commonwealth of Australia.

Hirschel, J. D. and Lab, S. P. (1988). Who is missing? The realities of the missing persons problem. *Journal of Criminal Justice*, 16(1): 35–45.

Holmes, L. (2008). *Living in Limbo: The Experiences of, and Impacts on, the Families of Missing People.* London: Missing People.

Holmes, L. (2014). *When the Search is Over: Reconnecting Missing Children and Adults.* London: Missing People.

Holmes, L. and Diamond, F. (2011). *Missing People Information Sharing Protocol.* Westminster pilot evaluation report. London: Missing People.

Holmes, L., Woolnough, P., Gibb, G., Lee, R. and Crawford, M. (2013). *Missing Persons and Mental Health.* Paper presented to the 1st International Conference on Missing Adults and Children, June 2013, Portsmouth, UK.

Home Office (2004). *General Principles to Inform Local Protocols between the Police and Health Services on Handling Potentially Violent Individuals* (Home Office Circular 017 / 2004). www.gov.uk/government/publications/general-principles-to-inform-local-protocols-between-the-police-and-health-services-on-handling-potentially-violent-individuals.

Home Office (2011). *Missing Children and Adults: A Cross Government Strategy.* London: Home Office.

Hunt, I. M., Windfuhr, K., Swinson, N., Shaw, J., Appleby, L., Kapur, N. and the National Confidential Inquiry into Suicide and Homicide by People with Mental Illness (2010). Suicide amongst psychiatric inpatients who abscond from the ward: A national clinical survey. *BMC Psychiatry*, 10(14): 1–6.

Independent Police Complaints Commission (2007). Learning the lessons: Death of Mr S. (Case 2.9 Bulletin 2). www.learningthelessons.org.uk.

Independent Police Complaints Commission (2008). Learning the lessons: Killing by woman missing from a psychiatric hospital (Case 2.3 Bulletin 5). www.learningthelessons.org.uk.

Independent Police Complaints Commission (2011). Learning the lessons: Dealing with abscondees from secure hospitals (Case 8 Bulletin 12). www.learningthelessons.org.uk.

James M., Anderson, J., and Putt, J. (2008). *Missing Persons in Australia.* Canberra: Australian Institute of Criminology Research and Public Policy Series, No. 86.

Joanna Briggs Institute (2007). *Absconded Patient: Recommended Practice.* Adelaide, Australia: The Joanna Briggs Institute.

Kernodle, R. W. (1966). Nonmedical leaves from a mental hospital. *Psychiatry*, 29: 25–41.

King, E. A., Baldwin, D. S., Sinclair, J. M. A. and Campbell, M. J. (2001). The Wessex recent inpatient suicide study, 2: Case control study of 59 inpatient suicides. *British Journal of Psychiatry*, 178: 537–542.

LePage, J. P. (1999). The impact of a token economy on injuries and negative events on an acute psychiatric unit. *Psychiatric Services*, 50: 941–944.

Manchester, D., Hodgkinson, A., Pfaff, A. and Nguyen, G. (1997). A nonaversive approach to reducing hospital absconding in a head injured adolescent boy. *Brain Injury*, 11: 271–277.

Meehan, T., Morrison, P., and McDougall, S. (1999). Absconding behaviour: An exploratory investigation in an acute inpatient unit. *Australian and New Zealand Journal of Psychiatry*, 33: 533–537.

Meltzer, H., Gill, B., Petticrew, M. and Hinds, K. (1995). *OPCS Surveys of Psychiatric Morbidity in Great Britain, Report 1: The Prevalence of Psychiatric Morbidity among Adults Living in Private Households*. London: HMSO.

Milner G. (1966). The absconder. *Comprehensive Psychiatry*, 7: 147–151.

Missing People (2013). *Missing and Mental Health* (Missing People Information Sheet). www.missingpeople. org.uk/about-us/about-the-issue/information-statistics/77-relatedissues2.html.

Molnar, G. and Pinchoff, D. M. (1993). Factors in patient elopements from an urban state hospital and strategies for prevention. *Hospital and Community Psychiatry*, 44: 791–792.

Muir-Cochrane, E. C. and Mosel, K. A. (2008). Absconding: A review of the literature 1996–2008. *International Journal of Mental Health Nursing*, 17(5): 370–378.

Muir-Cochrane, E. C., Mosel, K. A., Gerace, A., Esterman, A. J. and Bowers, L. (2011). The profile of absconding psychiatric inpatients in Australia. *Journal of Clinical Nursing*, 20(5–6): 706–713.

Neilson, T., Peet, M., Ledsham, R. and Poole, J. (1996). Does the nursing care plan help in the management of psychiatric risk? *Journal of Advanced Nursing*, 24: 1201–1206.

Newiss, G. (1999). *Missing Presumed...? The Police Response to Missing Persons*. Police Research Series, paper 114. London: Home Office.

Newiss, G. (2011). *Learning from Fatal Disappearances: A Report by Missing People*. London: Missing People. www.missingpeople.org.uk/files/Research%20publications%20and%20presentations/Learning_from_Fatal_Disapearances_2011.pdf.

Office of National Statistics (2014). *Suicides in the United Kingdom, 2012 Registrations* (Statistical Bulletin). www.ons.gov.uk/ons/dcp171778_351100.pdf.

Pakes, F., Shalev Greene, K. and Marsh, C. (2014). Crisis, trauma and loss: An exploratory study of those of 'come to notice' to police and health service professionals and subsequently abscond. *International Journal of Police Science and Management*, 16: 297–307.

Parr, H. and Stevenson, O. (2014). Sophie's story: Writing missing journeys. *Cultural Geographies*, 21: 565–582.

Powell, G., Caan, W. and Crowe, M. (1994). What events precede violent incidents in psychiatric hospitals? *British Journal of Psychiatry*, 165: 107–112.

Rees, S. (2009). *Mental Ill Health in the Adult Single Homeless Population: A Review of the Literature*. London: Crisis.

Self, A., Thomas, J. and Randall, C. (2012). *Measuring National Well Being: Life in the UK*. London: Office for National Statistics.

Sheppard, D. (1996). *Learning the Lessons* (2nd edition). London: The Zito Trust.

Siegal, R. L., Chester, T. K. and Price, D. B. (1982). Irregular discharges from psychiatric wards in a VA medical center. *Hospital and Community Psychiatry*, 33: 54–56.

Stevenson, O., Parr, H., Woolnough, P. and Fyfe, N. (2013). *Geographies of Missing People: Processes Experiences and Responses* (Unpublished project report). www.geographiesofmissingpeople.org.uk/downloads/Stevenson-et-al.pdf.

Stewart, D. and Bowers, L. (2010). *Absconding from Psychiatric Hospitals: A Literature Review: Report from the Conflict and Containment Reduction Research Programme*. London: Institute of Psychiatry at the Maudsley. www.kcl.ac.uk/iop/depts/hspr/research/ciemh/mhn/projects/litreview/LitRevAbsc.pdf.

Stewart, D. and Bowers, L. (2011). Absconding and locking ward doors: Evidence from the literature. *Journal of Psychiatric and Mental Health Nursing*, 18: 89–93.

Stewart, D., Ross, J., Watson, C., James, K. and Bowers, L. (2011). Patient characteristics and behaviours associated with self-harm and attempted suicide in acute psychiatric wards. *Journal of Clinical Nursing*, 21: 1004–1013.

Sveticic, J., Too, L. S. and De Leo, D. (2012). Suicides by persons reported as missing prior to death: A retrospective cohort study. *British Medical Journal Open*, 2(2): 1–7.

Tarling, R. and Burrows, J. (2004). The nature and outcome of going missing: The challenge of developing effective risk assessment procedures. *International Journal of Police Science and Management*, 6(1): 16–26.

Walsh, E., Rooney, S., Sloan, D., McAuley, P., Mulvaney, F., O'Callaghan, E. and Larkin, C. (1998). Irish psychiatric absconders: Characteristics and outcome. *Psychiatric Bulletin*, 22: 351–353.

Woolnough, P. and Gibb, G. (2013). *Missing an Opportunity: Exploring the Importance of Mental Health in Cases of Missing Persons*. Paper presented to the Scottish Mental Health Nursing Research Conference, May 2013, Aberdeen, UK.

8

Missing People with Dementia

Combining New and Traditional Responses

Philip Coales and Rupert McShane

According to the Office of National Statistics (2015), more than 10 million people in the UK were aged 65 or over in 2013, which will increase to 19 million people by 2050. One in six people over the age of 80 in the UK lives with a form of dementia. However, there are more than 40,000 people under the age of 65 with dementia (Alzheimer's Society, 2013a). Individuals with dementia–related diseases are at risk of going missing, especially if they are physically robust but have a poor topographical memory (Alzheimer's Society, 2013b). Given their vulnerability, it is imperative that these individuals are found quickly before they succumb to injury, existing health problems or the elements. This chapter will examine the association between dementia and going missing and will discuss investigative and search strategies. Prevention strategies such as community first responders and tracking equipment will also be discussed, along with the ethical considerations involved.

Actor Simon Russell Beale prepared for the 2014 National Theatre production of *King Lear* by sitting down with a nephew who was training in geriatric medicine at St Bartholomew's Hospital. He realised that the 'sudden outbursts of rage' associated with dementia 'seemed to tie very well' with Shakespeare's most famous old man (Furness, 2014). Lear gets discarded after passing on his throne to his daughters and wanders the heath with a Fool, a blind Earl, and Tom O'Bedlam. Mad, lost and impotent, the Lear of the seventeenth century, read today, seems easy enough to diagnose. We see our own fears in his character: fear of losing control, of incomprehensibility, of becoming obsolete. In the same way that we appreciate Lear frenetically railing against the world around him, we must appreciate that there are a host of reasons for elderly people to exhibit unusual and challenging behaviour, even if the objectives are not easily discernible. To understand how we can best respond to incidences of missing people who live with dementia, we must first appreciate that behaviour we perceive to be aimless, and refer to as 'wandering', is very often neither (Algase et al., 2004, 2007).

The Alzheimer's Society (2013b) advises against using the term 'wandering', preferring instead 'walking about'. Activities ranging from attempting to leave unfamiliar surroundings (such as a care home) to heading off in search of a memory from earlier in life (such as a previous house) are often triggered by confusion, and may be problematic, especially given the tendency of people with dementia to experience difficulties in navigation. A severe case might be one in which a person living with dementia sets off in the middle of the night, inappropriately dressed, and in inclement weather conditions, to find a place of past significance, in a location far from where they now reside. They may forget to take their medication and could trip or fall. In a scenario where so many risk factors are present, the most appropriate course of action for a relative, carer or neighbour noticing them missing would be to immediately alert the emergency services.

Half of all people with dementia who are missing for more than 24 hours die or are seriously injured (Koestler, 1998). A review by Rowe and Bennett (2003) of the deaths of 93 people with dementia who had been reported missing found that in 75 per cent of cases the person had been missing for over a day when their body was discovered, with the vast majority (87 per cent) being located in secluded areas such as woodland, where these individuals attempted to find a secluded spot, where they remained until they succumbed to the elements.

People not being where they are expected to be, due to a desire to expend excess energy, boredom or a slight deviation in an everyday routine, could in each case produce anxiety in friends and relatives, especially as the length of absence extends. But long, unpredictable, and treacherous journeys, the behaviours we think of when we use the term 'wandering', only account for the minority of missing person incidents amongst the elderly. A 999 call is not necessarily the most effective method of finding the person who is missing. In some cases a more appropriate response can come from community first responders, relatives, friends, or volunteers, who may not be trained lifesavers but are able to offer important situation-specific information.

Strategies of prevention and risk management particular to elderly missing people have increased and improved radically in the past 30 years, but there remains an urgent need for an additional societal response. The responsibility for looking after the 850,000 people living with dementia in the UK (Alzheimer's Society, 2015a) at the moment lies not just with the traditional emergency services, nor with developers, care providers, or community members. It is shared by all these groups. A strategy of breadth and of collaboration, and the promotion of innovation, are vital as is understanding the nature and the nuances of the differing conditions that fall under the umbrella term 'dementia'.

Research conducted by the Alzheimer's Society (2013a) suggests that Alzheimer's disease, as clinically diagnosed, accounts for 62 per cent of incident dementia, whilst vascular dementia contributes a further 17 per cent, and dementia with Lewy bodies, 4 per cent. Ten per cent of people with dementia have a combination of different types, including rarer forms such as fronto-temporal dementia. Regular symptoms across all of these include memory loss, difficulty communicating, and mood fluctuation, although, as the rate of mixed dementias and the variety of forms suggest, there may be a significant difference in behaviour between any two people with dementia. A systematic review conducted by Robinson et al. (2007) found that 15 per cent of people with dementia will go missing from their usual place of residence at least once, with 5 per cent doing so regularly, according to McShane et al. (1998).

Additionally, the Alzheimer's Society (2013c) suggests that between 5 and 20 per cent of older people have some form of mild cognitive impairment at any one time. Often referred to as mild cognitive impairment, this is a term that indicates a person has some problems in one or more areas of cognitive function, such as speech, memory and attention, but where the effects on everyday living are only slight. It can indicate an early form of Alzheimer's disease, as is estimated by the Society to be the case for 10–15 per cent of people with mild cognitive impairment each year, but could also result from stress or as a side effect of medication. People with mild cognitive impairment encounter difficulties in activities such as planning and remembering, albeit less frequently than someone with a dementia diagnosis, though, again, drawing a line under the numbers is complicated, this time because the number of people living with dementia is thought to be significantly higher than diagnoses confirm. A November 2013 report produced by the

Department of Health suggests that only 48 per cent of people with dementia in England have actually been diagnosed. This figure is as low as 39 per cent in Wales, and as high as 63 per cent in Northern Ireland.[1] Therefore, when we talk about elderly people going missing, we are likely to be consistently underestimating the size of the association with dementia.

Traditional emergency services alone struggle to shoulder the cost of responding to calls relating to missing elderly people. The range of conditions, and of possible motivations for going missing, coupled with the difficulty in monitoring the progression of unusual behaviours in an ageing population, complicates the process of deciding upon the best response. On Dartmoor, the local search and rescue team, set up to assist missing walkers, now spends over half its time searching for people with dementia and other mental health conditions (BBC News, 2013). The 36 trained searchers have provided support for Devon and Cornwall Police, who themselves dealt with 616 incidents of missing people with dementia between July 2010 and 2013. The Dartmoor Search and Rescue Team now predominantly search in lowland and urban areas, as do other members of the national Association of Lowland Search and Rescue teams (ALSAR UK). Trained search and rescue personnel, along with Police Search Advisors (PolSAs), are usually best equipped to respond to reports of missing people, and their expertise needs to be incorporated into both local and national strategies for supporting elderly people at risk, and their carers and communities.

Confusion and frailty on Dartmoor are the ingredients for an easily identifiable emergency situation. In other areas it is far less easy to determine the risk factor of a situation, and given the high incidence of elderly missing people this requires police forces to use a degree of discretion in responding to reports. For instance, the missing persons policy of Thames Valley Police was developed with an intention to 'protect individuals who are at risk' and to 'ensure that police resources are used appropriately and effectively to investigate missing person reports'.[2] Their aim is to risk assess all reports of missing people within four hours of a report. What happens in this window is crucial in determining the severity of a missing person's situation, as it is when they are most likely to be found. But whilst all reports of missing people with dementia are treated as high risk and as requiring an immediate response, this is an unsustainable approach. There is a need for a strategy which results in an early reaction because this is the best means of ensuring a positive response, and yet the chances are relatively high that limited mobility, or predictably habitual behaviour, mean the person could be retrieved without emergency assistance within this window.

In a US context, a study of 53 carers of people with dementia over a 12-month period resulted in 25 per cent reporting that the person they were caring for made at least one unattended exit during the period, and 57 per cent of those were found off property; all were found in their own neighbourhood (Rowe et al., 2008). Rowe et al. (2011) investigated the use of an American community response project, known as Safe Return, which sought to meet the need for an immediate search for a missing elderly person by encouraging members of their neighbourhood to become involved as early as possible. In it, 87 per cent of people found were within five miles of home, and only 7 per cent were more than ten miles away. And whereas 33 per cent were retrieved by the police, 36 per cent were found by a 'Good Samaritan'.

A similar first response project was launched in Oxfordshire in November 2012. Neighbourhood Return worked by getting volunteers to sign up as potential 'searchers' should a person with memory problems be reported missing in their area. It was set up as a first response service for carers to contact as soon as someone they cared for went missing, the concept being to relieve some of the pressure on Thames Valley Police, who were involved in some capacity in the majority of their 18 callouts. The cooperation was not initially seamless, with police searchers sometimes unaware either that Neighbourhood Return searchers were involved, or of how to get in touch with the person search coordinator. Additionally, operational problems and difficulties in controlling costs and sustainability meant that the service was withdrawn at the end of its pilot stage in April 2014.

The service had expanded to five areas (Berkshire, Buckinghamshire, Northamptonshire, Waltham Forest in London, and Oxfordshire), and had proved to be a very attractive volunteering opportunity for the public, recruiting 6,888 volunteers in 18 months. Half of these had never volunteered for anything before. This suggests that its purpose, focusing as it did on the elderly, struck a chord with the general public. Although the project overreached, its closure offers a valuable opportunity to reflect on how the various different groups involved in searching for elderly people might best coordinate their efforts in future. With Neighbourhood Return's impressive early growth, and health secretary Jeremy Hunt setting a target of one million 'Dementia Friends',[3] able to spot symptoms of, and assist people with, dementia, there is scope for community members to assist, particularly in nonemergency cases.

Registration for Neighbourhood Return was encouraged in advance of a missing person incident, and information about carers and people with memory problems was recorded. The contact details of volunteers were taken too. Carers were encouraged to report a missing person as soon as possible, which they did by calling up the service's telecare providers. The telecare service operator would then establish some vital information about the missing person, expedited if they had already been registered, and undertake a brief risk assessment. A high-risk result would mean passing on the relevant information to the local police search advisor. A lower risk result led to a search beginning, managed on the Neighbourhood Alert community messaging system, used elsewhere in the UK by the Neighbourhood and Home Watch Network, as well as by various local police forces. Volunteers within a one- to three-mile radius of the last known location would be sent a message by text, telephone message, or email, depending on their contact preference, which would invite them to participate in the search. If they were able to participate, they would be added to the map by the telecare operator, who would be able to send out relevant information pertaining to the missing person, and track the progress of the searchers, by asking them to search in various locations and moving their icon correspondingly. The service was called into action 18 times by a pool of 357 people with memory problems. Unlike ALSAR, it was unable to provide each volunteer with any more training than a brief online guide and over-the-phone advice.

The service reported considerable impact on the peace of mind of carers. In a September 2013 survey of 48 carers registered with the service, 52 per cent said their worries about the person they cared for going missing had been reduced by either 'a great deal' or 'a fair amount', and 44 per cent replied that their worries had been reduced 'a little'; 90 per cent claimed that they would call the service before contacting the police. This is similar to the 80 per cent of 145,000 carers registered with US scheme Safe Return between 1993 and 2007 who reported that they signed up in order to feel safer (Bass et al., 2008).

Neighbourhood Return registrations were generated through outreach to local memory clinics and other community health-care teams, as well as via Thames Valley Police advising previously missing adults with memory problems to sign up for the service, and by advertising through events and publications put on by local care support organisations, such as the Oxford Dementia Awareness campaign's county tour. By using telecare, online mapping, and a community messaging platform to provide a first response service with the ability to involve local volunteers in a very short period of time (which cost nothing to its end users and did not rely on any formal registration requirements for any participants), Neighbourhood Return provided a blueprint for the integration of various service types. Its recruitment of 6,888 volunteers was one success of the service. This was in part attributable to the strategy of working with a neighbourhood charity which already used a community messaging system: 45 per cent of volunteers were recruited through this link. The low time commitment for volunteers, who were able to reply 'No' if they were unavailable to search, was also a factor in recruiting so many volunteers, specified as such by 69 per cent of volunteers surveyed (of a pool of 98 volunteers, interviewed over summer 2013). A new twist on the recipe of community engagement and technology-supported first response systems could provide the emergency services with sufficient support to allow them to focus only on the emergency cases, and could be extended to provide support for other categories of missing persons.

One of the innovations of Neighbourhood Return was the combination of telecare with real-time location tracking. It did not use Global Positioning System (GPS) satellite data, instead relying on telecare operatives moving pins on a map, based on the feedback of volunteer searchers. Tracking via GPS can provide additional peace of mind for carers and has the further benefit of reducing a potentially resource-intensive search party to a single relative equipped with a mobile phone. Depending on surroundings (tall buildings can reduce accuracy), a signal can be transmitted by someone wearing a GPS device within nanoseconds, at any time of day, anywhere in the world (Dana and Penrod, 1990). Harry Cayton (1994), writing from the 'Director's Desk' in the Alzheimer's Society's July 1994 newsletter, argued that 'it may be that electronic surveillance will become available but, have no doubt, it will be because it suits the professionals not people with dementia'.

Writing in the *British Medical Journal* nine years later, O'Neill rehearses his argument, claiming that the convenience of GPS tracking benefits the carer and is not patient centred (O'Neill, 2013). Conversely, Coltharp et al. (1996) and Cohen-Mansfield and Werner (1998) have made the case that promoting and assisting safer walking can offer more freedom than attempting to prevent any possible unattended exits. Allowing people with dementia relatively unrestricted movement, and using technology as a safeguard, may be appropriate in some circumstances. A study conducted by White et al. (2010) found that carers prefer to use tracking as a back-up strategy to close supervision and locked doors, unless they felt the risk of injury resulting from getting lost to be low, in which case the carers interviewed reported an enhanced sense of independence, both for themselves and the person they were caring for. Yet the same study found issues with the reliability of GPS devices.

With wearable technology devices becoming more advanced, to the extent that health tracking applications, including heart rate monitors and GPS activity trackers, are featured heavily in the promotional campaigns of both Samsung and Apple's flagship mobile phones for 2014, there is the potential for unobtrusive devices, such as GPS watches, bracelets, or necklaces, designed specifically to update family members in the case of a fall or an exit from a specific geographic area, to become a normalised and widely used care device, void of the stigma associated with 'tagging' (McShane, 2013). That, however, depends on the uptake of wearable health trackers. Confidence in technological solutions for the observation of vulnerable people is not currently sufficient for assistive technology to be the primary way of countering the risk of injury present when someone with dementia is allowed free movement within and outside of their home. Although there are a wide range of wearable devices already provided, many of which are catalogued at the AT Dementia library of assistive technology (www.atdementia.org.uk), the importance of confidence and of widespread adoption derives from the importance of first response. Hospitalisation, and institutionalisation, can easily stem from just one missing incident, which can of course happen before diagnosis. When someone starts getting lost outside their home, there is both an increased chance of their movements being restricted to the home and an increased probability of institutionalisation, as has been demonstrated in the longitudinal study produced by McShane et al. (1998) and the case studies reported by Rowe et al. (2004), as well as being determined by Scherer et al. (2008) as the behaviour most likely to precipitate admission.

Rowe recommends that an intensive search begins as quickly as possible when a cognitively impaired adult is reported as missing, to minimise exposure to the elements and the opportunity for the missing person to find a secluded hiding place. The case studies discussed involved searches for three missing people in which members of the local community were contacted by telephone and invited to help out in the search, and in each case the search was inadvertently hampered by the suggestions of family members about where to search. The Safe Return study found that various other factors are difficult to predict. Whilst almost half the people found by search teams went missing in the afternoon, 18 per cent went out at night. The time between the preregistration of the person and them being reported missing ranged from 0 to 56 months, with the mean being 15 months. There was also an increased chance of a missing incident when a cognitively impaired person was in an unfamiliar environment, their carer was distracted, or if they lived with a child as opposed to a partner, though unattended exits were still reported in situations of advanced monitoring, such as professional care environments (16.8 per cent). The stress placed upon any carer by the difficulty of anticipating when an elderly person may go missing cannot be removed by technology, but when the risk is recognised, precautions such as GPS tracking and community messaging can provide the rapid responses necessary to reduce it.

Twenty years on from Cayton's editorial, the Alzheimer's Society now recommends that tracking and alarm technologies are viewed not just as preventative or responsive but also as assistive technology (2013d, 2015b). These technologies (for example, GPS tracking devices, telecare, in-home movement sensors, and tags that send out alerts when they are taken outside of a particular 'geofenced' area) have been developed to support the existing emergency services. Satellite navigation capability is now common in mobile phones and can help carers retain peace of mind once the risk of getting lost is recognised. Sold on a one-off fee or subscription basis, either by private companies or in partnership with carers' organisations, they can offer a more appropriate and efficient method of responding in lower-risk situations.

These methods can indeed assist in encouraging physical activity, combatting the isolation of being locked indoors, and promoting independence. Further assistance is required from the wider community, whether that is in the form of preregistered volunteers or Dementia Friends, or in the form of collaborations between developers of apps, care services, and experts trained to search for missing people. No one service can provide all the support needed to anticipate the risk of getting lost and then provide a quick and effective response, both of which are key in reducing hospitalisation, institutionalisation, and the associated social and economic costs. McShane (2013, p. 246) stresses the 'big if' of even realising the risk in the first place. For although the Alzheimer's Society (2015b) has a wealth of information available online and via their community support groups, and police forces provide an information sheet for carers of people living with dementia, advising them on how to report a missing person, how to monitor potential behavioural risk indictors, and what to do when a missing person with dementia returns home (UK Missing Persons Bureau, 2013), preventative information is only useful if it is in place at the earliest possible stage. Each of the partners described above would do well to realise the potential of open platforms, such as the Alzheimer's Association (US)'s Comfort Zone,[4] which enables carers to view location data collated from a variety of devices made by different manufacturers on one website. This provides support for family members of healthy elderly people, who may enjoy kayaking or driving, right through to those with advanced dementia.

Meanwhile, in the UK, GPS tracking device manufacturer Buddi pulled out of a contract that would have seen them provide the hardware for a £1 billion Ministry of Justice scheme, which would have enabled 24-hour tagging of offenders. Buddi cited prohibitive terms: they did not want to hand over their intellectual property without the assurance that the government wouldn't allow access to other organisations participating in the scheme (Quinn, 2014). More needs to be done to encourage joint ventures and to foster a culture of collaboration in the vein of Comfort Zone and Neighbourhood Return. Where assistive technology developers and community-based care services converge, we are most likely to see effective responses reaching potentially affected older adults at an earlier stage. The stimulus for innovation and integration already exists, with £2.4 million being spent on the Dementia Friends campaign, an initiative aimed at tackling the £23 billion bill for dementia care the UK faces each year (Alzheimer's Society, 2014). Realising that we are all stakeholders with an interest in supporting the elderly in the most effective and efficient way possible, ought to encourage further collaboration between developers and care-focused organisations, with a view to integrating each of their offers and providing a more coherent response strategy.

Notes

1 'State of the Nation' (November 2013). Diagnosis rates are from the government's QOF (Qualities and Outcomes Framework) data for 2012/13, which is the number of people registered with GPs as living with dementia. Dementia prevalence rates are from the 2007 Dementia UK report.
2 Thames Valley Police Missing Persons policy (2008, 2013). The 2008 version contains only these two intentions, to which a third was added in 2013 – 'record, monitor and share information relating to absent persons' (available at www.thamesvalley.police.uk/misper_policy_250613.pdf). The updated policy was released seven months into the Oxfordshire trial of Neighbourhood Return, with which a Service Level Agreement had been made, outlining the information-sharing protocol for the two organisations.
3 The new target for Dementia Friends is four million (2015). www.dementiafriends.org.uk/
4 US Alzheimer's Association Comfort Zone: www.alz.org/comfortzone/.

References

Algase, D. L., Son, G. R., Beattie, E., Song, J. A., Leitsch, S. and Yao, L. (2004). The interrelatedness of wandering and wayfinding in a community sample of persons with dementia. *Dementia and Geriatric Cognitive Disorders*, 17(3): 231–239.
Algase, D. L., Moore, D. H., Vandeweerd, C. and Gavin- Dreschnack, D. J. (2007). Mapping the maze of terms and definitions in dementia related wandering. *Aging Mental Health*, 11(6): 686–698.
Alzheimer's Society (2013a). Factsheet: Young People with Dementia www.alzheimers.org.uk/site/scripts/download_info.php?fileID=1766.
Alzheimer's Society (2013b). Factsheet: Walking About. www.alzheimers.org.uk/site/scripts/download_info.php?fileID=1790.
Alzheimer's Society (2013c). Mild Cognitive Impairment. www.alzheimers.org.uk/site/scripts/download_info.php?fileID=1773.
Alzheimer's Society (2013d). Safer Walking Technology. www.alzheimers.org.uk/site/scripts/documents_info.php?documentID=579.
Alzheimer's Society (2014). Dementia UK. www.alzheimers.org.uk/dementiauk.
Alzheimer's Society (2015a). Statistics. www.alzheimers.org.uk/statistics.
Alzheimer's Society (2015b). Factsheet: Assistive technology, Devices to Help with Everyday Living. www.alzheimers.org.uk/site/scripts/download_info.php?fileID=1779.
Bass, E., Rowe, M. A., Moreno, M. and McKenzie, B. (2008). Expanding participation in Alzheimer's Association Safe Return by improving enrolment. *American Journal of Alzheimers' Disease and Other Dementia*, 23(5): 447–450.
BBC News (2013). Dartmoor rescuers see rise in dementia searches. 22 August 2013. www.bbc.co.uk/news/uk-england-devon-23789179.
Cayton, H. (1994). Alzheimer's Disease Society Newsletter.

Cohen-Mansfield, J. and Werner, P. (1998). Predictors of aggressive behaviors: A longitudinal study in senior day care centers. *Journal of Gerontology: Psychological Science*, 53B(5): 300–310.

Coltharp, W., Richie, M. F. and Kaas, M. J. (1996). Wandering. *Journal of Gerontological Nursing*, 22(11): 5–10.

Dana, P. H. and Penrod, B. M. (1990). The role of GPS in precise time and frequency dissemination, *GPS World*, 1–6. www.pdana.com/phdwww_files/gpsrole.pdf.

Furness, H. (2014). Could King Lear have suffered Lewy body dementia? *The Telegraph,* 7 February 2014. www.telegraph.co.uk/culture/theatre/william-shakespeare/10622547/Could-King-Lear-have-suffered-Lewy-body-dementia.html.

Koester, R. J. (1998). The lost Alzheimer's and related disorders subject: New research and perspectives. Response 98, *NASAR Proceedings*, National Association of Search and Rescue, Chantilly, Virginia, 165–181. www.dbs-sar.com/SAR_Research/ALZ.pdf.

McShane, R. (2013). Should patients with dementia who wander be electronically tagged? Yes. *British Medical Journal*, 346. www.bmj.com/content/bmj/346/bmj.f3603.full.pdf.

McShane, R., Gedling, K., Keene, J., Fairburn, C., Jacoby, R. and Hope, T. (1998). Getting lost in dementia: A longitudinal study of a behavioural symptom. *International Psychogeriatrics*, 10(3): 253–260.

Office of National Statistics (2015). Mid 2014 Population Estimates. www.ons.gov.uk/people populationandcommunity/populationandmigration/populationprojections/compendium/national populationprojections/2015-10-29/summaryresults.

O'Neill, D. (2013). Should patients with dementia who wander be electronically tagged? No. *British Medical Journal*, 346.

Quinn, J. (2014). Buddi withdraws from Ministry of Justice tagging contract. *The Daily Telegraph*, 5 March 2014. www.telegraph.co.uk/finance/newsbysector/supportservices/10678028/Buddi-withdraws-from-MoJ-tagging-contract.html.

Robinson, L., Hutchings, D., Dickinson, H. O., Corner, L., Beyer, F., Finch, T., Hughes, J., Vanoli, A., Ballard, C. and Bond, J. (2007). Effectiveness and acceptability of non-pharmacological interventions to reduce wandering in dementia: A systematic review. *International Journal of Geriatric Psychiatry*, 22(1): 9–22.

Rowe, M. A. and Bennett, V. (2003). A look at deaths occurring in persons with dementia lost in the community. *American Journal of Alzheimer's Disease and Other Dementias*, 18(6): 343–348.

Rowe, M. A., Feinglass, N. G. and Wiss, M. E. (2004). Persons with dementia who become lost in the community: A case study, current research and recommendations. *Mayo Clinic Proceedings*, 79(11): 1417–1422.

Rowe, M. A., Ahn, H., Benito, A. P., Stone, H., Wilson, A. and Kairalla, J. (2008). Injuries and unattended home exits in persons with dementia: A 12-month prospective study. *American Journal of Alzheimer's Disease and Other Dementias*, 25(1): 27–31.

Rowe, M. A., Vandeveer, S. S., Greenblum, C. A., List, C. N., Fernandez, R. M., Mixson, N. E. and Ahn, H. C. (2011). Persons with dementia missing in the community: Is it wandering or something unique? *BMC Geriatrics*, 11(1): 28.

Scherer, R. K., Scarmeas, N., Brandt, J., Blacker, D., Albert, M. S. and Stern, Y. (2008). The relation of patient dependence to home health aide use in Alzheimer's disease. *The Journals of Gerontology Series A: Biological Sciences and Medical Sciences*, 63(9): 1005–1009.

UK Missing Persons Bureau (2013). *Has Someone You Know Gone Missing? Information for Carers of People Living with Dementia.* Factsheet no.13. www.missingpersons.police.uk/download/47.

White, E. B., Montgomery, P. and McShane, R. (2010). Electronic tracking for people with dementia who get lost outside the home: A study of the experience of familial carers. *The British Journal of Occupational Therapy*, 73(4): 152–159.

9

Missing Adults
Asylum Seekers and Human Trafficking

Patricia Hynes

Introduction

People who are forced to migrate across international borders include asylum seekers and those who are 'trafficked' for various forms of exploitation. This chapter will examine the association between going missing during the process of migration for adults seeking refuge from persecution – referred to in policy terms as 'asylum seekers' when awaiting the outcome of refugee status determination procedures – and adults who are 'trafficked' for exploitative purposes. To do this, systems of support and surveillance of asylum seekers throughout the process of seeking asylum are highlighted and contrasted to the clandestine character of trafficking into, within and out of the UK.

Adults fleeing persecution are legally defined within Article 1 of the 1951 United Nations Convention relating to the Status of Refugees (hereafter the 1951 Refugee Convention) as applying to any person who:

> owing to a well-founded fear of being persecuted for reasons of race, religion, nationality, membership of a particular social group or political opinion, is outside the country of his nationality and is unable or, owing to such fear, is unwilling to avail himself of the protection of that country; or who, having a nationality and being outside the country of his former habitual residence … is unable or, owing to such fear, is unwilling to return to it.

This UN Refugee Convention was finalised by European states in July 1951 and entered into force in April 1954, restricted at the time to people who became refugees prior to the events of 1951 within Europe. This European focus was made universal in October 1967 when a Protocol relating to the Status of Refugees came into force extending the temporal and geographical limitations of the 1951 Refugee Convention (Goodwin-Gill, 1996, 2014). The United Kingdom is party to both and domestic legislation in 1993 – the Asylum and Immigration Appeals Act – incorporated the 1951 Refugee Convention into domestic law.

Adults who are trafficked are defined under different legal arrangements adopted in 2000 – the Convention against Transnational Organized Crime, supplemented by the Protocol to Prevent, Suppress and Punish Trafficking in Persons, Especially Women and Children, the latter

Protocol commonly referred to as the Palermo Protocol. This legal definition provided the first internationally agreed definition of human trafficking and in Article 3 defines those who are trafficked:

> Trafficking in persons shall mean the recruitment, transportation, transfer, harbouring or receipt of persons, by means of the threat or use of force or other forms of coercion, of abduction, of fraud, of deception, of the abuse of power or of a position of vulnerability or of the giving or receiving of payments or benefits to achieve the consent of a person having control over another person, for the purpose of exploitation.

This definition contains three interrelated yet distinct elements, the act (recruitment, transportation and transfer), means (use of violence, threats or other use of force or coercion) and purposes (a range of forms of exploitation which include sexual exploitation, forced labour and other practices similar to slavery or servitude) of trafficking. As such trafficking is seen as a process, not a one-off national bounded event (Hynes, 2011). The Palermo Protocol was signed by the United Kingdom in December 2000, coming into force in February 2006. The United Kingdom also ratified the Council of Europe Convention on Action against Trafficking, becoming operational in April 2009.

These legal definitions and competing legal frameworks frame those who are seeking asylum from persecution and those who are trafficked for exploitative purposes separately. However, there is overlap, an example of which would be persons who claim asylum on the basis of the inherent persecution involved with being trafficked. A further confusion lies in the differences between 'smuggling' and 'trafficking' which in recent months has played out in the Mediterranean where there has been a conflation between being 'trafficked' rather than 'smuggled'. To be a refugee there is a need to be outside the country of the person's former habitual residence, whereas trafficked persons include those who are trafficked across borders and people trafficked within national boundaries.

Much of the literature also relates to either those seeking asylum or those trafficked (Anderson, 2012, 2014; Bloch and Schuster, 2005; Hynes, 2011; Lewis, 2009; Lewis et al., 2013; Zetter et al., 2003). Statistics are also recorded separately for people seeking asylum and those who have experienced trafficking. In 2014, there were 31,300[1] applications for asylum in the UK and 4,015[2] final non-EU applicants were granted refugee or another form of humanitarian status. In the same year, 2,340[3] potential cases of trafficking were referred to a National Referral Mechanism, which was introduced in 2009 in the UK, designed in part to help identify 'victims' of 'trafficking'. Of these, 1,669 were adults and 671 'minors',[4] with forms of exploitation for adults divided into 'sexual exploitation', 'domestic servitude', 'labour exploitation', 'organ harvesting' and 'unknown exploitation'.

Anti-trafficking efforts run parallel to a broader immigration and asylum agenda that has seen an increasing tightening of policy and legislation since the mid-1990s (Bloch and Schuster, 2005; Bloch and Solomos, 2010; Hynes, 2009; Lewis, 2007). Since this time, the portrayal of asylum seekers as 'bogus' or 'genuine' claimants has entered public consciousness, leading to narratives of 'undeserving' and 'deserving' refugees (Sales, 2002). Consequently, an appreciation of the more structural 'harms' of state asylum and immigration policy whereby further exploitation can occur and vulnerabilities be exacerbated, is also essential to an understanding of anti-trafficking efforts (Anderson, 2012; O'Connell Davidson, 2013).

Definitional differences, distinct legal frameworks, separate recording of statistics, different literatures and policy agendas surrounding asylum and trafficking make looking at going missing complex. However, in practice, these populations overlap and distinctions become blurred in reporting and the lived realities of people. To unpick this, sections on people seeking asylum and people who have experienced trafficking will outline potential reasons and literature on going missing. A final section comparing the reasons for going missing will highlight the absence of literature[5] on the interrelation between asylum, trafficking and going missing.

People Seeking Asylum

Permission to enter and remain in the UK can be sought for various reasons including joining a spouse, to study or to work. However, if fleeing persecution on any of the tenets of the 1951 Refugee Convention, asylum is a method of protection given by states, such as the UK. There are no legal routes available to seek asylum other than lodging a claim for asylum upon arrival in the UK. An asylum seeker may arrive 'at port' (airport, port or rail terminal) or 'in country' (in IND offices in Croydon or Liverpool). At present, all who wish to submit an application for asylum must travel to Croydon, to the Asylum Screening Unit,6 no matter where their initial point of entry into the UK was. Since April 2013, the government has introduced a new Asylum Operating Model wherein applications go through a triage process at the initial screening interview and are given 'decision pathways' based on the perceived simplicity or complexity of the case.

For asylum seekers, the trajectory of legislation and policy since the mid-1990s has been designed within an overarching framework of deterrence. Increasingly used, deterrence measures have included detention, compulsory dispersal to urban centres outside London and the south-east of England, enforced destitution and deportation (Blinder, 2014; Bloch and Schuster, 2005; Garrett, 2006; Hynes, 2011; Lewis, 2007, 2009; Lewis et al., 2013; Silverman and Hajela, 2015; Zetter et al., 2003).

In 2013, approximately 30,400 people entered detention under Immigration Act powers[7] (Silverman and Hajela, 2015); 8,660 people who were removed or forced to depart were asylum cases (Blinder, 2014); 20,687 were in dispersal accommodation and 2,772 received subsistence-only support (Refugee Council, 2014); and an unknown number enter into destitution for an unquantifiable period of time.

The UK immigration detention estate is one of the largest in Europe and holds between 2,000 and 3,500 migrants in detention at any given time (Silverman and Hajela, 2015). The rationale for detention includes reducing the risk of absconding. Asylum seekers can be detained following an initial interview if it is considered by the Home Office that the decision to grant or refuse asylum can be provided quickly. Campaigning groups and the United Nations High Commission for Refugees (UNHCR) have argued that this process is highly inadequate given that victims of torture are unlikely to disclose details of their abuse during an initial screening interview. People can also be detained on arrival, upon presentation at an immigration office within the UK and during routine reporting.

Globally, there is growing evidence that the detention of asylum seekers is associated with negative mental health outcomes, particularly in relation to depression, anxiety and post-traumatic stress disorder (PTSD) (Filges et al., 2014; Physicians for Human Rights, 2003). Methodological difficulties and ethical considerations preclude studies based around randomised control trials (Filges et al., 2014) but decades of research into pre- and post-migration trauma include the negative impact of detention and potential of detention experiences to reactivate and exacerbate previous traumas (Medical Foundation for the Care of Victims of Torture, 1994).

The detention of children has been a particularly controversial aspect of UK asylum policy (Campbell et al., 2013; Crawley and Lester, 2005; Fazel and Stein, 2004). Since the Borders, Citizenship and Immigration Act 2009 the UK Borders Agency has a duty to safeguard and promote the welfare of children. Research carried out after this Section 55 duty continues to document children being separated from parents during indefinite periods of detention (Campbell et al., 2013).

Sigona and Hughes (2012) estimate that some 120,000 irregular migrant children live in the UK. These are children who are born in the UK or who have migrated to the UK at an early age and who do not have a legal immigration status. Their study was exploratory and mainly qualitative, focusing on interviewees from Afghanistan, Brazil, China, Jamaica and Nigeria and Kurds from Turkey, Iran and Iraq. Living without documentation – or being 'undocumented' – places children in positions of extreme vulnerability (Sigona and Hughes, 2012). They found that fear of detection and potential deportation by immigration authorities 'played a central role in the everyday lives of migrants' (Sigona and Hughes, 2012, p. 41) and suggest that 'a major concern for parents is shielding their children from the negative consequences of a lack of status', which include difficulties enrolling in school and access to health care (pp. 41–42). The motivation to avoid detention by remaining invisible to authorities is an under-researched area, as is the impact this has on children.

Before the Asylum and Immigration Act 1999, asylum applicants were supported through the mainstream benefits system and the issue of asylum seekers going missing was therefore not a probability. However, following this Act, a new agency – the National Asylum Support Service (NASS) – was set up, providing a parallel welfare and support structure specifically for asylum seekers. Under Section 95 of the Act, asylum seekers are paid between 65 per cent and 70 per cent of the rate of income support provided to UK nationals (Boswell, 2001). Asylum seekers needing accommodation were dispersed across England by NASS. Surveillance mechanisms built into this policy response included checks by local authority, social and private landlords on the occupancy of accommodation, legal requirements on landlords to report to the Home Office if the occupant was away for more than three days from accommodation provided through NASS, as well as the requirement that asylum seekers regularly report to Reporting Centres (Hynes, 2009, 2011). Incidents of asylum seekers going missing are therefore associated with opting out of an asylum process that offers little hope or perceived justice to those moving through it as well as a threat of detention if found to be failing to comply with the conditions attached to receipt of accommodation. Since its introduction in April 2000 the compulsory dispersal of asylum seekers has entailed less accommodation provision provided by local authorities and social landlords, with large contracts now awarded exclusively to large companies such as SERCO, G4S and Clearel under the Home Office's Commercial and Operational Managers Procuring Asylum Support Services (COMPASS) contracts.

As outlined by Lewis (2007, 2009), destitution of asylum seekers is a persistent concern across the UK. As Lewis (2007) highlights, destitute asylum seekers rely on friends, charity and their own 'communities' for basic needs and are often forced to find undocumented and potentially exploitative work to survive. People at all stages of the asylum system have reportedly experienced destitution, including those awaiting a decision if unable to access support, those whose appeal rights have been exhausted but are unable to return to their country of origin and those who have been granted refugee or another form of leave to remain who have to leave their accommodation and enter mainstream welfare provision to access a National Insurance number (House of Commons Home Affairs Committee, 2013). As Lewis (2007) found, periods of rough sleeping are common for some whose asylum cases have been refused and people remain in vulnerable positions for protracted periods. Blitz and Otero-Iglesias (2011) have argued that 'when denied state protection, refused asylum seekers endure an existence not unlike stateless people'. His study, conducted in Oxford and London, highlighted how refused asylum seekers and 'overstayers'[8] lose their entitlement to protection and become de facto stateless. There is a distinct lack of research on what it means to be undocumented and how going missing relates to this.

Increasingly, private sector contractors control and maintain the oversight of asylum seekers, in many cases through to deportation. As of January 2015 there were 11 Immigration Removal Centres, four of which were managed by the Prison Service and seven managed by private firms – Mitie, GEO, G4S and Serco – on contract to the Home Office (Silverman and Hajela, 2015). Deportation, 'administrative removal' and voluntary departures are categories within UK immigration rules, classified primarily by the method by which removal or departure takes place (Blinder, 2014). Beyond the known 8,660 asylum seekers who were removed or forced to depart the UK during 2013, it is unclear how many others remained invisible to authorities as a strategy of survival and avoidance of persecution on return.

On arrival into the UK, asylum seekers do not have the right to work and relationships with the informal economy are therefore largely unexplored. Literature is however emerging that demonstrates how refused asylum seekers remain in the UK with no right to work or recourse to public funds, which again makes people susceptible to unscrupulous employers (Lewis, 2009; Lewis et al., 2013). Going missing in this instance relates to the need to survive and, potentially, work in insecure, difficult and dangerous contexts. Instances of forced labour amongst asylum seekers and refugees have, until recently, not been recognised (Lewis et al., 2013). This interfaces with the experiences of those who have been trafficked for the purposes of forced labour.

People Who Have Experienced Trafficking

Trafficking is, by its very character, a clandestine phenomenon and the policy imperative is to identify people as trafficked to enable support and protection of 'victims' or 'survivors'. Remaining invisible, becoming undocumented and going missing from the view of services and authorities is consequently highly likely. In the UK, as outlined above, a relationship with asylum and immigration control is evident.

Research conducted in three south-eastern European countries (Brunovskis and Surtees, 2007) suggests that 'victims' of trafficking may decline or avoid support and assistance due to their personal circumstances (such as seeing assistance standing in the way of further migration), difficulties in protection systems (such as the 'one size fits all' nature of assistance provided) and differing social contexts and personal experiences (such as the stigma of receiving assistance; problems around identification and lack of trust in those providing assistance). Each of these reasons may result in a 'victim' of trafficking going missing in the eyes of authorities and those providing assistance.

In the UK, statistics available for those who are referred to a National Referral Mechanism show a range of exploitative explanations including being trafficked for sexual exploitation, labour exploitation, domestic servitude and a range of other exploitative practices (NCA, 2015). A new Modern Slavery Act which received Royal Assent in early 2015 in the UK has defined 'trafficking' and 'exploitation', provided for an Independent Anti-Slavery Commissioner, and outlined the protection of 'victims'. It is of note that, for children and young people, independent child trafficking advocates are one of the new provisions outlined in the Act.

For children, going missing from local authority care is a key indicator of potential trafficking and is explicitly incorporated into risk assessments such as the London Safeguarding Trafficked Children Toolkit. The issue of children going missing and the link to trafficking has been outlined in 'grey' literature (Pearce et al., 2009), some academic literature (Bokhari, 2008; ECPAT UK, 2007, 2009; Kelly and Bokhari, 2012; Pearce et al., 2013) and government reports where children were found to 'go missing' or 'abscond' within the first 48 hours of arrival into the UK when placed in temporary accommodation and remain missing thereafter (CEOP, 2007, 2009). In 2008 the Care Leavers' Association surveyed 172 local authorities in England and Wales and found that 41 of these had children and young people who were missing from their care. The highest number of these were unaccompanied asylum seekers.[9] Given such evidence, plus the increasing disclosures of child sexual exploitation and trafficking in cities across the UK such as Rotherham, Manchester and Oxford in recent months, it is of concern that some argue child trafficking to be a 'moral panic' that draws attention away from 'more difficult issues confronting social work' (Cree et al., 2014).

For adults who have experienced trafficking, there is no equivalent matrix and a lack of literature relating specifically to going missing. Seen initially as a problem surrounding sexual exploitation, trafficking debates in the UK now include other forms such as labour exploitation, forced labour, cannabis farming, domestic servitude, organ sale, forced begging and pickpocketing (Craig, 2014). Craig's (2014) review of the contribution to research in understanding 'modern slavery' in the UK outlines three major reports in the 'grey' literature from a consortium of NGOs – the Anti-Trafficking Monitoring Group (ATMG). Each of these reports, *Wrong Kind of Victim?*, *All Change* and *Hidden in Plain Sight*, progressively document areas for improvement in prevention, identification and protection of those who have been trafficked. Individuals going missing due to flaws within the process of identification are implicit in these reports.

Debates around trafficking of adults in the UK have historically focused on sexual exploitation and are highly polarised (Anderson, 2014). On one side, feminists argue that 'sex work' should be legalised and a rights approach adopted (Andrijasevic, 2010; Doezma, 2010). On the other, feminists argue that prostitution is a symptom of patriarchy and voluntary consent is not possible. Agustin (2007) argues that the label of 'trafficking' invokes a victimising discourse and does not accurately describe those who do sex work. She also argues that 'helpers' and moral agendas surrounding 'rescuing' those involved deny agency and make those involved passive 'victims'.

Work on different forms of trafficking are now emerging. Human trafficking and forced labour are both said to be modern forms of slavery which sometimes overlap but are not identical (Craig, 2014; Skrivankova, 2014). Research funded by the Joseph Rowntree Foundation (JRF) has resulted in a collection of independent studies on the nature, scale and scope of forced labour, including the work of Dwyer et al. (2011), Geddes et al. (2013) and Skrivankova (2010).

Dwyer et al. (2011) demonstrate the ways particular immigration statuses make people vulnerable to forced labour. A further study by this team into the precarious lives of asylum seekers and refugees illustrated for the first time how this group of migrants are 'susceptible to exploitation in various forms of severely exploitative and, in some cases, forced labour in England' (Lewis et al., 2013). They found that the experience of forced labour is an assumed necessity for refugees and asylum seekers in order to meet the basic needs of themselves and their families with payment below the National Minimum Wage a 'normalised reality' for those with 'compromised sociolegal status' which 'repeatedly pulled them back into precarious work'. Geddes et al. (2013) provide a summarising report bringing evidence on policy, practice and law together. Whilst the body of JRF's research challenged the notion that forced labour is a hidden phenomenon, facets of this, when applied to those with insecure immigration status, could easily result in people remaining invisible, staying hidden or 'going missing'.

Skrivankova's (2010) contribution outlines a continuum of exploitation between decent work (the optimum position) and forced labour (the most severe forms of labour exploitation). This continuum provides a framework for understanding the interaction between an individual's vulnerability and the setting within which the individual works, is exploited, discovered and/or prosecuted. Staying hidden in such exploitative work relates closely to the defining characteristics of forced labour as per the ILO's 1930 Forced Labour Convention No.29. Facets of this include actual or threats of physical harm, restrictions of movement or confinement to the workplace, debt bondage, withholding of wages, retention of identifying documents and/or threats of denunciations to the authorities. The issue of 'debt bondage' is often central to trafficking and fees paid to agents, brokers and others require repayment. Without the ability to work legally under the current immigration and asylum regime, recourse to the informal economy is one explanation as to why individuals may actively remain hidden from view. Such purposeful isolation at work was found to be a strong indicator of forced labour as was the fear of deportation. The provision of accommodation, money and authorisation to work by employers are also ways in which the power imbalance can be maintained and become exploitative.

Asylum, Trafficking and 'Going Missing'

The interface between asylum and trafficking is a relatively unexplored area (Morrison and Crosland, 2001; Lewis et al., 2013). It is clear that this interface warrants much further investigation. The link between going missing and asylum seekers being pushed into the informal economy remains largely unexplored, with the notable exception of Lewis et al. (2013). Adding the frame of 'going missing' into the territory of trafficking outlines a research area where there is, with the exception of some literature on children, no previous literature.

The creation of what has become termed a 'hostile environment' for asylum seekers will do little to assist in the identification of those who are trafficked, nor will it enable work on asylum seekers who go missing, become undocumented and are subsequently vulnerable to exploitation. Mistrust of asylum seekers undermines UK government policies that require engagement with different communities to address issues around trafficking, forced marriage and 'honour' crimes, as well as broader debates around social cohesion and social exclusion (Hynes, 2009). Trust is a key need for effecting such policies.

Both asylum seekers and people who are trafficked will continue to go missing in order to avoid detection by authorities and prevent themselves being detained or deported. For those who become destitute, having no recourse to public funds, again, avoidance of detention will involve taking steps to avoid being too visible. Taking up informal sector work, which may be highly exploitative, may become the only means of survival. As Lewis et al. (2013) suggest, because of their compromised sociolegal status asylum seekers and refugees are susceptible to exploitation in various forms, including forced labour, various forms of precarious work and, potentially, sexual exploitation. These forms of exploitation are also experienced by those trafficked into, within and out of the UK.

It is not known how many people go missing as a consequence of the different policies for asylum and trafficking. Becoming undocumented, 'going underground', and/or becoming exploited are consequently unknowns in the literature. Asylum seekers may also wish to move away from the stigmatising label of being an 'asylum seeker' (Hynes, 2011) and move towards an ordinary or normal life. Not knowing who to trust may affect all.

There are several unexplored reasons why people who have experienced trafficking may go missing. This may be due to debt incurred during the journey to the UK and the need to pay back agents. They may also go missing to escape exploitation, the threat of exploitation and exploiters. Escaping from abusive histories, avoiding the shame and stigma associated with the label of 'trafficking' to live a normal life could be another reason. Avoiding detection from the authorities who frame such actions as 'absconding' and avoiding detection, detention and deportation could be another.

There is no comparative literature specifically in relation to missing adults moving through these processes and there is also a gap in knowledge about why asylum seekers and trafficked persons go missing. Overall, lack of cumulative or reliable data on asylum seekers or the more clandestine number of people who are trafficked means that there is also no accurate picture on which to base estimates of the numbers of people going missing in the process.

Conclusion

There are separate legal frameworks, definitions, bureaucratic labels, policy agendas and recording of those who have experienced persecution and are claiming asylum to those who have experienced trafficking. In practice, the distinction between the two populations is less distinct. As outlined above, the care and control of asylum seekers is a difficult process which can lead to exploitative circumstances. The clandestine character of trafficking into, within and out of the UK can overlap with the asylum and immigration regime. Visibility or invisibility to those who offer support, and to the authorities, is complex.

There are similarities and differences in the reasons for going missing that relate closely to such visibility or invisibility. With asylum, visibility is built into the system largely based on control and surveillance inherent in policies enacted to deter those seeking protection from persecution safety and rights under the 1951 Refugee Convention written into domestic law. With trafficking, by its very nature, people remain invisible on arrival and only become visible to services and authorities if 'rescued' or presenting themselves for protection purposes.

The rationale in much of asylum policy is about reducing the risk of asylum seekers 'absconding', ensuring compliance, maintaining surveillance and control and keeping asylum seekers visible to the various agencies and authorities involved. It is unsurprising that 'strategies of invisibility' (Malkki, 1995, p. 155) are regarded by asylum seekers as positive coping strategies, essential for survival to ensure protection from persecution if removed to their countries of origin. This entails what Arendt (2004) refers to as 'rightlessness' – the loss of the right to have rights and entitlements afforded to others within a nation state – and leads to state harms and vulnerabilities that create spaces where exploitation can, and does, occur.

Being invisible or going missing may often be a rational decision to avoid detection or detention. This is an under-researched area, as is the impact this has on children. It is clear that there is further research to be done on the interface between asylum, trafficking and going missing.

Notes

1 UNHCR (2015), UNHCR Asylum Trends 2014: Levels and Trends in Industrialized Countries, Geneva: UNHCR.
2 Source: Eurostat (online data code: migr_asydcfina).
3 National Crime Agency (2015) National Referral Mechanism Statistics – End of Year Summary 2014, NCA and UK Human Trafficking Centre (UKHTC).
4 Seventeen or under at the time of first claimed exploitation.
5 Searches conducted on SocINDEX, Applied Social Sciences Index and Abstracts (ASSIA), International Bibliography of the Social Sciences (IBSS) revealed no literature combining the three topics.
6 Those who are considered particularly vulnerable can on occasion be screened in regional offices but instances of this are rare.
7 The most common category of immigration detainees is people who have sought asylum in the UK.
8 The term 'overstayers' refers to people who have stayed longer than their visas allow.
9 Further details: www.careleavers.com/general/74-missing.

Bibliography

Agustin, L. M. (2007). *Sex at the Margins: Migration, Labour Markets and the Rescue Industry*. London and New York: Zed Books.

Anderson, B. (2012). Where's the harm in that? Immigration enforcement, trafficking and the protection of migrants' rights. *American Behavioral Scientist*, 56(9): 1241–1257.

Anderson, B. (2014). Trafficking. In E. Fiddian-Qasmiyeh, G. Loescher, K. Long and N. Sigona (eds), *The Oxford Handbook of Refugee and Forced Migration Studies*. Oxford: Oxford University Press.

Andrijasevic, R. (2010). *Migration, Agency and Citizenship in Sex Trafficking*. London: Palgrave Macmillan.

Anti-Trafficking Monitoring Group (2010). *Wrong Kind of Victim? One Year On: An Analysis of UK Measures to Protect Trafficked Persons*. London: Anti-Trafficking Monitoring Group.

Anti-Trafficking Monitoring Group (2012). *All Change: Preventing Trafficking in the UK*. London: Anti-Trafficking Monitoring Group.

Anti-Trafficking Monitoring Group (2013). *Hidden in Plain Sight: Three Years On: Updated Analysis of UK Measures to Protect Trafficked Persons*. London: Anti-Trafficking Monitoring Group.

Arendt, H. (2004). *The Origins of Totalitarianism*. New York: Schocken Books.

Blinder, S. (2014). *Deportations, Removals and Voluntary Departures from the UK*. Migration Observatory briefing. Oxford: COMPAS, University of Oxford.

Blitz, B. and Otero-Iglesias, M. (2011). Stateless by any other name: Refuges asylum seekers in the United Kingdom. *Journal of Ethnic and Migration Studies*, 37(4): 657–673.

Bloch, A. and Schuster, L. (2005). At the extremes of exclusion: Deportation, detention and dispersal. *Ethnic and Racial Studies*, 28(3): 491–512.

Bloch, A. and Solomos, J. (2010). *Race and Ethnicity in the 21st Century*. Basingstoke and New York: Palgrave Macmillan.

Bokhari, F. (2008). Falling through the gaps: Safeguarding children trafficked into the UK. *Children and Society*, 22: 201–211.

Boswell, C. (2001). *Spreading the Costs of Asylum Seekers: A Critical Assessment of Dispersal Policies in Germany and the UK*. London: Anglo-German Foundation for the Study of Industrial Society.

Brunovskis, A. and Surtees, R. (2007). *Leaving the Past Behind? When Victims of Trafficking Decline Assistance*. Fafo AIS (Oslo) and NEXUS Institute (Vienna).

Campbell, S., Boulougari, A. and Youngeun, K. (2013). *Fractured Childhoods: The Separation of Families by Immigration Detention*. London: Bail for Immigration Detainees.

CEOP (2007). *A Scoping Project on Child Trafficking in the UK*. London: CEOP.

CEOP (2009). *Strategic Threat Assessment Child Trafficking in the UK*. London: CEOP.

Craig, G. (2014). Modern slavery in the UK: The contribution of research. *Journal of Poverty and Social Justice*, 22(2): 159–164.

Craig, G., Gaus, A., Wilkinson, M., Skrivankova, K. and McQuade, A. (2007). *Contemporary Slavery in the UK: Overview and Key Issues*. York: Joseph Rowntree Foundation.

Crawley, H. and Lester, T. (2005). *No Place for a Child. Children in UK Immigration Detention: Impacts, Alternatives and Safeguards*. London: Save the Children UK.

Cree, V. E., Clapton, G. and Smith, M. (2014). The presentation of child trafficking in the UK: An old and new moral panic? *British Journal of Social Work*, 44: 418–433.

Daniel, E. V. and Knudsen, J. C. (eds) (1995). *Mistrusting Refugees*. Berkeley, Los Angeles and London: University of California Press.

Doezma, J. (2010). *Sex Slaves and Discourse Masters: The Construction of Trafficking*. London: Zed Books.

Dwyer, P., Lewis, H., Scullion, L. and Waite, L. (2011). *Forced Labour and UK Immigration Policy: Status Matters?* York: Joseph Rowntree Foundation.

ECPAT UK (2007). *Missing Out: A Study of Child Trafficking in the North West, North East and West Midlands*. London: ECPAT UK.

ECPAT UK (2009). *Bordering on Concern: Child Trafficking in Wales*. London: ECPAT UK.

ECPAT UK (2012). *Child Trafficking and Private Fostering*. London: ECPAT UK.

Fazel, M. and Stein, A. (2004). UK immigration law disregards the best interests of children. *The Lancet*, 363: 1749–1750.

Filges, T., Lindstrom, M., Montgomery, E., Kastrup, M. and Jorgenson, A. K. (2014). *The Impact of Detention on the Health of Asylum Seekers: A Protocol for a Systematic Review*. Ottawa, Canada; Bryn Mawr, USA; Oslo, Norway: The Campbell Collaboration.

Garrett, P. M. (2006). Protecting children in a globalized world: 'Race' and 'place' in the Laming Report on the death of Victoria Climbie. *Journal of Social Work*, 6(3): 315–336.

Geddes, A., Craig, G., Scott, S., Ackers, L., Robinson, O. and Scullion, D. (2013). *Forced Labour in the UK*. York: Joseph Rowntree Foundation.

Goodwin-Gill, G. (1996). *The Refugee in International Law*. Oxford: Clarendon Press.

Goodwin-Gill, G. (2014). The international law of refugee protection. In E. Fiddian-Qasmiyeh, G. Loescher, K. Long and N. Sigona (eds), *The Oxford Handbook of Refugee and Forced Migration Studies.* Oxford: Oxford University Press.

House of Commons Home Affairs Committee (2013). *Asylum: Seventh Report of Session 2013–14.* London: The Stationery Office.

Hynes, T. (2003). *The Issue of 'Trust' or 'Mistrust' in Research with Refugees: Choices, Caveats and Considerations for Researchers.* United Nations High Commissioner for Refugees (UNHCR), Evaluation and Policy Analysis Unit, Working Paper No. 98.

Hynes, P. (2009). Contemporary compulsory dispersal and the absence of space for the restoration of trust. *Journal of Refugee Studies*, 22(1): 95–121.

Hynes, P. (2010). Global points of 'vulnerability': Understanding processes of the trafficking of children and young people into, within and out of the UK. *The International Journal of Human Rights*, 14(6): 952–970.

Hynes, P. (2011). *The Dispersal and Social Exclusion of Asylum Seekers: Between Liminality and Belonging.* Bristol: Policy Press.

Kelly, E. and Bokhari, F. (2012). *Safeguarding Children from Abroad: Refugee, Asylum Seeking and Trafficked Children in the UK.* London and Philadelphia: Jessica Kingsley Publishers.

Lewis, H. (2007). *Destitution in Leeds: The Experiences of People Seeking Asylum and Supporting Agencies.* York: Joseph Rowntree Charitable Trust.

Lewis, H. (2009). *Still Destitute: A Worsening Problem for Refused Asylum Seekers.* York: Joseph Rowntree Charitable Trust.

Lewis, H., Dwyer, P., Hodkinson, S. and Waite, L. (2013). *Precarious Lives: Experiences of Forced Labour among Refugees and Asylum Seekers in England.* University of Leeds and University of Salford: ESRC.

Malkki, L. (1995). *Purity and Exile.* Chicago: University of Chicago Press.

Medical Foundation for the Care of Victims of Torture (1994). *A Betrayal of Hope and Trust: Detention in the UK of Survivors of Torture.* London: Medical Foundation for the Care of Victims of Torture.

Meetoo, V. and Mirza, H. S. (2007). There is nothing 'honourable' about honour killings: Gender, violence and the limits of multiculturalism. *Women's Studies International Forum*, 30: 187–200.

Morrison, J. and Crosland, B. (2001). *The Trafficking and Smuggling of Refugees: The End Game in European Asylum Policy?* Working Paper No. 39, New Issues in Refugee Research, UNHCR, Geneva.

NCA (2015). *National Referral Mechanism Statistics – End of Year Summary 2014.* London: National Crime Agency.

O'Connell Davidson, J. (2013). Troubling freedom: Migration, debt, and modern slavery. *Migration Studies*, 1(2): 176–195.

Pearce, J., Hynes, P. and Bovarnick, S. (2009). *Breaking the Wall of Silence: Practitioners' Responses to Trafficked Children and Young People.* London and Luton: NSPCC and University of Bedfordshire.

Pearce, J. J., Hynes, P. and Bovarnick, S. (2013). *Trafficked Young People.* London and New York: Routledge.

Physicians for Human Rights and the Bellevue/NYU Program for Survivors of Torture (2003). *From Persecution to Prison: The Health Consequences of Detention for Asylum Seekers.* New York: Bellevue/NYU.

Refugee Council (February 2014). *Asylum Statistics.* London: Refugee Council.

Sales, R. (2002). The deserving and the undeserving? Refugees, asylum seekers and welfare in Britain. *Critical Social Policy*, 22(3): 456–478.

Sigona, N. and Hughes, V. (2012). *No Way Out, No Way In: Irregular Migrant Children and Families in the UK.* Oxford: Centre on Migration, Policy and Society, University of Oxford.

Silverman, S. J. and Hajela, R. (2015). *Immigration Detention in the UK.* Migration Observatory briefing. Oxford: COMPAS, University of Oxford.

Skrivankova, K. (2010). *Between Decent Work and Forced Labour: Examining the Continuum of Exploitation.* York: Joseph Rowntree Charitable Trust.

Skrivankova, K. (2014). *Forced Labour in the United Kingdom.* York: Joseph Rowntree Charitable Trust.

Zetter, R., Griffiths, D., Ferretti, S. and Pearl, M. (2003). *An Assessment of the Impact of Asylum Policies in Europe.* Home Office Research Study No. 259. London: Home Office.

10

To Honour and Obey?

Forced Marriage, Honour-Based Violence and Going Missing

Nicola Sharp-Jeffs

Introduction

Since the introduction of multidisciplinary public protection units, a more intelligence-led approach to missing person investigations has been adopted which recognises the importance of linking 'going missing' with associated public protection issues, including forced marriage (Hedges, 2002, ACPO/NPIA, 2008; H. M. Inspectorate of Constabulary, 2008; Jago et al., 2011).

This chapter begins by defining the term 'forced marriage' before considering what going missing means in this context. Next, the links between forced marriage and going missing are presented using the concepts of 'intentional' and 'unintentional' missing incidents (as defined by Biehal et al., 2003). The discussion then turns to implications for practice. Here it is argued that the police and other professionals working in statutory agencies (education, health, housing and benefits) need to recognise that forced marriage can be both a cause and a consequence of going missing and that the dynamics and risks surrounding this and other forms of 'honour'-based violence should be considered in training and investigation. Finally, appropriate forms of support for survivors are identified.

It should be noted that the literature cited in this chapter primarily refers to South Asian females since this group is highly visible within reported cases of forced marriage (Kazimirski et al., 2009). This is likely to reflect the fact that there is a large and established South Asian community in the UK and a relatively high proportion of young people in the British Bangladeshi and Pakistani communities who are at marriageable age (Samad and Eade, 2002). However it is important to acknowledge that forced marriage and other forms of so-called 'honour'-based violence also affect people from African, Middle Eastern and certain Eastern European communities (Kazimirski et al., 2009; Ministry of Justice, 2010; Sharp, 2010). Thus many of the issues discussed here are equally important to consider when responding to survivors from any group.

Defining Forced Marriage

The predominant policy approach to the threat or reality of a forced marriage in the UK has been to encourage individuals to exit the abusive situation (Phillips and Dustin, 2004). Multiagency practice guidelines recognise that both male and female victims of forced marriage may feel that running away is their 'only option' (H. M. Government, 2014). This was first acknowledged in policy discussions by the Working Group on Forced Marriage when politicians heard evidence of the 'plight of many young women who had run away to escape forced marriage' (Home Office Communications Directorate, 2000, p. 15). At around the same time, concern was expressed by police forces that young females from some ethnic minority groups were 'running away from arranged marriages, domestic violence within such marriages or the prospect of an arranged marriage' (Newiss, 1999, p. 33).

Use of the term 'arranged marriage' here highlights the complexities around defining forced marriage. The UK government definition of forced marriage refers to a situation in which one or both spouses do not (or, in the case of children and some adults with disabilities, cannot) consent to the marriage and duress is involved. Duress can include physical, psychological, sexual, financial and emotional pressure (H. M. Government, 2014). In contrast, the practice of arranged marriage involves the families of both spouses taking a leading role in arranging the marriage but the choice of whether or not to accept the arrangement remains with the prospective spouses. Therefore, if someone is described as running away from the prospect of an arranged marriage this would suggest that they are being forced into a marriage that they do not want (even if they initially agreed to the marriage).

Forced marriage is recognised as a form of so-called 'honour'-based violence. This term encompasses a range of violent or abusive acts committed in the name of 'honour' including assault, imprisonment and in extreme cases murder (an 'honour killing'). 'Honour' in this context is essentially about defending 'family honour', although this is often extended to reflect the 'honour' of the community. Such violence is perpetrated mainly (although not exclusively) against women who transgress traditional forms of acceptable female behaviour. When a woman's behaviour is deemed to be 'immoral' then she will be seen to have brought shame on her family and in doing so damaged its 'honour'. 'Honour' is therefore used as a motivation, justification or mitigation for violence against women – a mechanism used to control female sexuality and autonomy (Siddiqui, 2005).

Siddiqui (2005) observes that whilst boys and men also come under pressure to conform to prescribed forms of male behaviour, they do not generally face the same consequences for transgressing these norms as women do. Moreover, in cases where a male is killed for refusing to carry through a promise of marriage the motivation often lies in the fact that he or his family has ruined the woman's reputation. It is also important to note that the repercussions of being forced into marriage are very different for males and females, since many women will go on to suffer violence, rape, forced pregnancy and forced childbearing (H. M. Government, 2014).

Notions of 'honour' exist in all communities, including the UK, although its prevalence has diminished in many Western countries. Whilst white men continue to use cultural defences in the context of perpetrating violence against women, they do not refer to 'honour' as a motivating factor. However, the underlying justification of this behaviour is also rooted in the use of violence to maintain patriarchal power and control over women's behaviour, with defences resting on the notion of women's socially unacceptable behaviour, for example perceived adultery. This means that even if there are differences in the explanations given to justify acts of violence, these acts should not be understood in isolation but as rooted in a 'continuum of violence' (Kelly, 1988) through which power and control is exerted by males over females of all ethnicities.

Defining 'Missing' in the Context of Forced Marriage

The 'missing continuum' developed by Biehal et al. (2003, p. 6) is used as a guiding framework. This is because the definition which underpins the continuum recognises the varying levels of individual agency within different types of missing incident as well as the role played by others: 'A break in contact which; either the missing person or someone else defines as going missing and which may be either intentional or unintentional.' Forced marriage cases can involve both decided intentional and/or forced unintentional forms of going missing, as illustrated by the case of 17-year-old Shafilea Ahmed. This account demonstrates how forced marriage often comes to light when an individual is reported missing.

Case Study: Shafilea

Shafilea ran away from her family home in order to escape the threat of forced marriage on at least three separate occasions. As part of her parents' attempts to get her to 'agree' to marriage, Shafilea also went missing from school as a result of false imprisonment, was abducted by her father outside of school, and was drugged and taken to Pakistan against her will. Shafilea continued to resist being forced into marriage and was later reported missing by a former teacher after disappearing from the family home. It was later proven that Shafilea's parents had murdered her in the name of honour and instructed their children to tell police that Shafilea had run away again, this time with a boy.

Intentional Missing: Running Away

Going missing to escape abuse is recognised and accepted as a protective response to forced marriage by adults. Police statistics on going missing suggest that broadly equal numbers of men and women go missing (SOCA, 2012). However, a study by Biehal et al. (2003), which included analysis of nonreported as well as police reported cases, found a significant relationship between gender and ethnic origin among those who go missing between the ages of 18 and 24. This suggested that women of Asian origin are more likely to go missing than women from other ethnic age groups following conflict with their parents regarding entering into or remaining in a marriage. The researchers found that some women had gone missing to avoid being coerced into marriage and a few were escaping the threat of violence from relatives attempting to enforce family decisions regarding marriage.

In contrast to adults, the behaviour of young people who run away as a consequence of abuse is often framed within a deficit-focused, problem model. This is because young people under the age of 18 are believed to be inherently vulnerable and therefore in need of additional protection from the risks posed to them by different forms of harm (Barter et al., 2009). Although all young people are understood to experience challenges associated with the development of independence and autonomy in respect of family relationships (Coleman and Hagell, 2007; O'Brien and Scott, 2007), it is reported that South Asian teenagers may be subject to particularly restrictive parenting. Parental rejection of boyfriends and girlfriends emerges as a distinct issue for this group alongside threats of forced marriage in a minority of cases (Safe on the Streets Research Team, 1999; Akhtar, 2002; Social Exclusion Unit, 2002; Biehal et al., 2003; Jha, 2004; Barter et al., 2009).

For young people there is overlap in the profiles of forced marriage victims and those who go missing; most commonly young women aged between 12 and 17 years of age (Kazimirski et al., 2009; SOCA, 2012). The picture in relation to ethnicity is, however, more mixed. Reported forced marriage cases in England overwhelmingly involve females (96 per cent) of Asian ethnicity (97 per cent). Yet data on missing incidents indicate that the majority of those who go missing under the age of 18 are white (Stein et al., 1994; Goulden and Sondhi, 2001; Tarling and Burrows, 2003; Biehal et al., 2003).

Jha (2004) suggests that the 'problem' of runaway boys and girls affects only a very small part of the Asian population. This is reinforced by self-reported surveys which consistently appear to indicate significantly lower rates of running away amongst young people of Indian, Pakistani and Bangladeshi origin (Abrahams and Mungall, 1992; Rees, 1993; Rees and Lee, 2005; Rees, 2011).

Brandon and Hafez (2008) suggest that many girls and women are discouraged from leaving in the first place because they know that if they are subsequently found by their families they will be at even greater risk of violence. This is because they may be viewed as having defied the Asian code of behaviour, bringing shame both on themselves and their families (Jha, 2004). As a consequence, young Asian people are more likely to become disowned by family and community than is the case for other ethnic groups (Kelly et al., 1995; Kelly and Regan, 2000). It is therefore believed that this group may be more likely to continue coping with a difficult home situation and only leave as a last resort (Safe on the Streets Research Team, 1999; Akhtar, 2002; Izzidien, 2008).

Franks (2004) further suggests that lower lifetime running away rates amongst the South Asian community may be connected to a high degree of surveillance experienced by some young women, making it more difficult for them to leave (see also Akhtar, 2002; Gangoli et al., 2009). Kazimirski et al. (2009) observe that victims of forced marriage, in particular, are often severely restricted in their movements. In this scenario, it is believed that girls and young women have to make a premeditated escape (Safe on the Streets Research Team, 1999; Akhtar, 2002; Sharp, 2010) and may require more intensive support in living away from home compared to their white counterparts (Franks, 2004; Jha, 2004).

However, as Akhtar (2002) notes, Asian young people may be less likely to be reported as missing by their families due to concerns related to preserving family 'honour'. Indeed, when considering both police reported *and* nonpolice reported missing cases, Biehal et al. (2003) found significant differences in runaway rates of ethnic groups when age was considered. Research findings suggested that minority ethnic groups were more likely to go missing as teenagers. In this study, 26 per cent of Asian young people who had gone missing did so between 13 and 17 years of age, compared to just 14 per cent of white teenagers in the same age group.

It is certainly the case that research undertaken by the Safe on the Streets Research Team (1999) suggests a more mixed picture in relation to missing Asian young people. Professionals working with runaways identified broadly similar rates of running away across ethnic groups but felt that this behaviour might be less visible amongst Asian groups compared to white young people. For instance, Akhtar (2002) notes how young runaways from Asian communities may not hang around on the streets for fear of the risk of being seen by somebody who knows their family.

Unintentional Missing: Abduction

It is widely accepted that policy initiatives facilitating escape from abusive situations are crucial. Yet the 'exit' approach has been criticised for a number of reasons, not least because it imposes the burden of resolving the conflict on the individual without addressing the power relations that generate individual cases (Shachar, 2001). This is believed to result in an ongoing risk of harm to the individual and an overwhelming focus on protection (Philips and Dustin, 2004). Indeed it is noted that many women continue to live in fear of their families finding them after escaping a forced marriage (Home Office Communications Directorate, 2000).

Evidence suggests that some families will go to considerable lengths to find and bring back females who have fled a forced marriage (Home Office Communications Directorate, 2000; Izzidien, 2008; H. M. Government, 2009; Ministry of Justice, 2010). In many cases this will involve using subterfuge to locate them. Family members may report them as 'missing' or accuse them of a crime such as theft, believing that the police will disclose the whereabouts of the victim or return them home (NPIA, 2009; Bokhari, 2009). In other cases, private investigators or bounty hunters may be employed to track the missing person down.

There is evidence to suggest that some families will use organised networks of people to locate the missing person. These include family and community members, taxi drivers and shopkeepers, together with people who have access to official records such as staff from benefits and tax offices, GP and dentist surgeries, schools and colleges and local housing authorities. There may also be occasions when the missing person's family members ask a third party such as a family friend, councillor, MP or someone with influence within the community to request information about the missing young person. The third party may be given a very plausible reason by the family for needing to know the whereabouts of the person and the third party may unwittingly think they are helping the family by disclosing details of where the missing person is (Home Office Communications Directorate, 2000; Akhtar, 2002; H. M. Government, 2009; H. M. Government, 2010; NPIA, 2010).

Women and girls who go missing as a consequence of exiting a forced marriage situation may, therefore, be at risk of abduction by family members seeking to find them. Domestic violence refuges and local authorities have reported cases in which females have been abducted from accommodation services (Bokhari, 2009; Ministry of Justice, 2010). Similarly the police report incidents of women being forcibly removed from interview rooms by their families (H. M. Government, 2009).

After being located and/or abducted the young person may be falsely imprisoned until they 'agree' to the marriage (Philips, 2007). In order to restore the family 'honour', the primary objective of some parents may also be to bring forward the intended marriage (Akhtar, 2002; Jha, 2004; Brandon and Hafez, 2008). In cases where it is rumoured that the missing female was enjoying sexual relationships when missing she may be sent abroad, where her reputation is less likely to be damaged (Brandon and Hafez, 2008; Khanum, 2008; Bokhari, 2009). In this way, forced marriage is used as a mechanism to control deviant behaviour (Brandon and Hafez, 2008) and protect against the social rejection associated with being labelled a prostitute (Kazimirski et al., 2009; Richardson et al., 2009). Berelowitz et al. (2012) note cases in which sexually exploited young people from minority ethnic backgrounds have reported being controlled by abusers who play on their fear of bringing shame on their families and the threat of forced marriage if they disclose the abuse.

In extreme cases, women who escape a threatened or actual forced marriage may be killed (Akhtar, 2002; Philips, 2007; Brandon and Hafez, 2008). This is in line with research which identifies a strong link between homicides in a domestic violence context and 'attempts to leave' (Coordinated Action Against Domestic Abuse, 2009). But whilst the 'typical' pattern of domestic homicide within the UK is of a man killing his ex-partner or wife, some minority ethnic women are also at risk of violence from family and community members who may kill them in the name of 'honour' (Phillips, 2007).

Forced marriage cases reported in the press illustrate how the discovery of plans to run away have resulted in some young South Asian women being murdered by family members and, in many cases, reported as 'missing' in an attempt to cover up the crime (ACPO/NPIA, 2008, 2010). During its inquiry into domestic violence, forced marriage and 'honour'-based violence, the Home Affairs Select Committee (2008) heard that the Metropolitan Police Service was undertaking a review of 109 cases of murder, suicide and missing persons over a ten-year period in an attempt to identify previously unrecognised 'honour' killings.

Unintentional Missing: Trafficking

Other forms of 'going missing' also feature in forced marriage cases. For example, the parents of a young person may take them out of the UK against their will or trick them into going abroad (for example, being told that an elderly relative is dying) and then force them to marry (Kazimirski et al., 2009). It is observed that some British Asian young women may simply disappear from school in these circumstances, particularly during the summer holidays (Akhtar, 2002; Home Affairs Select Committee, 2008; H. M. Government, 2009; The Department for Children, Schools and Families, 2008; Kazimirski et al., 2009; H. M. Government, 2010). Victims of forced marriage have also recounted being kidnapped by relatives while visiting family abroad (Brandon and Hafez, 2008).

Although parental abduction, kidnapping and associated crimes such as theft of a passport are recognised by professionals within the range of criminal offences relevant to cases of forced marriage[1] (Home Affairs Select Committee, 2008; Gangoli et al., 2009; Ministry of Justice, 2009; H. M. Government, 2010), there is less recognition that taking a young person abroad for the purposes of forced marriage can be defined as a form of trafficking for child sexual exploitation under the Sexual Offences Act, which was introduced in 2003 (CEOP, 2010). This is because the Sexual Offences Act (2003) defines trafficking for sexual exploitation as involving circumstances in which the travel of a young person into, within or out of the UK is arranged in the belief that it is likely that rape or a child sexual offence will be committed against them.

It is common for trafficking into the UK for the purposes of underage and forced marriage to be noted within the research literature (Kapoor, 2007; CEOP, 2010; Brandon and Hafez, 2008). A number of cases have been reported in which under-18s are trafficked into the UK for the purposes of forced marriage and then subsequently disappear from local authority care (Arocha, 2010). A small-scale study undertaken by Beddoe (2007), for example, identified 80 known or suspected children who had been trafficked into the UK and found that 48 of these children had later gone missing from the care of the local authority, among them seven Somali girls who had been trafficked into the UK to be forced into marriage.

Yet there is little reference within the literature to young people who are taken out of the UK or moved within the UK for the same purpose. One notable exception is a strategic threat assessment of child trafficking undertaken by CEOP which identified eight cases where girls were believed to have been trafficked and forced into marriage. Three of these cases were related to British Asian girls living in the East Midlands, two of whom were to be married in Bangladesh and one who was to be taken to Leicester to get married (CEOP, 2010; see also Sharp, 2013, for a discussion on the links between going missing, forced marriage and child sexual exploitation).

Focus on Protection: Implications for Practice

In light of the risks outlined above, it is clear that all professionals require training in order to understand the dynamics of forced marriage and other forms of 'honour'-based violence and how these need to be considered when responding to missing incidents.

Guidance exists for the police on investigating missing persons (ACPO/NPIA, 2010) and forced marriage/honour-based violence (ACPO/NPIA, 2008). In addition, all professionals are bound by statutory guidance on children who run away and go missing (Department for

Education, 2014) as well as multiagency statutory guidance for dealing with forced marriage (H. M. Government, 2014). Such guidance highlights the importance of considering the connections between the linked public protection issues of missing and forced marriage to ensure professionals' responses do not inadvertently put victims at risk.

When a missing incident is reported by a friend, family member, partner or agency and is linked to forced marriage concerns, it is important that professionals make discreet enquiries before approaching the family. Simply visiting the family home without knowing the circumstances may put the person at risk of harm. It may result in violence towards the person reported missing or the marriage being brought forward. It may also mean that the missing person is removed to a new location, including overseas. As such, professionals should seek to collect intelligence first – exploring whether there has been a history of domestic violence or previous missing person incidents within the family, including the missing person's siblings.

In addition, any enquiries should only be shared with practitioners aware of the need to handle such information in a confidential manner. The police and other professionals should identify and constantly be aware of any possible breaches of confidentiality in missing person cases within a forced marriage context. This includes protecting against leaks of information to the missing person's family from within the police and other relevant statutory agencies (H. M. Government, 2014), including those attending Multi-Agency Risk Assessment Conferences (Ministry of Justice, 2010). Professionals from the same ethnic background of the missing person can be put under enormous pressure to divulge information and face conflict in circumstances where professional duties are compromised by strong family and community ties (Ministry of Justice, 2009).

Brandon and Hafez (2008) report that women's groups in some parts of the UK are reluctant to go to the police to report a missing person as safe and well because they cannot trust Asian police officers not to disclose the whereabouts of the victim to family members searching for them. Similar concerns have been highlighted within social services, with young runaway women failing to disclose forced marriage due to fears that social workers may be prone to sympathising with their family and breach confidentiality by revealing to their family where they are. For these reasons, cultural awareness and the possible repercussions of disclosing a victim's whereabouts are vital in encouraging victims to seek the support of statutory agencies (Franks, 2004; Jha, 2004; Akhtar, 2002).

Police guidance further advises officers to exercise caution in contacting their counterparts if a missing person is being held overseas. This is because there may also be collusion between overseas organisations, including respected bodies such as the police, and the person's family. In handling these cases, it is recommended that agencies liaise closely with the Forced Marriage Unit based within the Foreign and Commonwealth Office.

Forced Marriage Protection Orders may be a useful tool to use as a disruption technique in forced marriage cases. The Forced Marriage Civil Protection Act (2007) makes provision for the family courts to make a Forced Marriage Protection Orders to prevent a forced marriage taking place or to offer protective measures when a forced marriage has already taken place. The Forced Marriage Protection Orders are not an alternative to the work of the police and Crown Prosecution Service in investigating and prosecuting crimes but can be used to obtain court orders compelling families of forced marriage victims to hand over all passports (where there is dual nationality) and birth certificates, stop someone from being taken abroad and reveal the whereabouts of a person (Ministry of Justice, 2009).

When a missing person returns or is located, the management of this process is critical. Whilst, historically, police officers and professionals have treated allegations of forced marriage as a 'domestic dispute' and sought to encourage victims to return home, it is important to note that current guidance recognises that victims of forced marriage should never be encouraged to do so against their wishes (ACPO/NPIA, 2008; H. M. Government, 2014; ACPO/NPIA, 2010). Similarly, the practice of attempting to resolve cases through family counselling, mediation, arbitration and reconciliation is dangerous in forced marriage cases (H. M. Government, 2009) due to imbalances of power. The first concern should always be for the welfare of the missing person and the significant harm they may face if they are returned to their family. The police and others should therefore not disclose the missing person's location if it is against their wishes.

Safe and well checks undertaken by the police following a missing incident aim to establish whether a person has suffered harm whilst they have been away and make sure they are not in danger. For missing persons fleeing forced marriage, safe and well checks should be conducted in a neutral place and not adjacent to areas that have public access where there might be a risk of abduction. In addition, professionals should be aware that there may be situations in which they may be approached by prominent members of the community and asked to provide information to families who are trying to trace females who have been found 'safe and well' but who have chosen not to go home.

Caution should also be exercised in the use of interpreters if the missing person does not speak English. Police and professionals need to be aware that relatives, friends, community leaders, neighbours and those with influence in the community should never be used as interpreters or advocates. The missing person may feel embarrassed to discuss personal issues in front of them and sensitive information may be passed on to others and place the person in danger. Furthermore, such an interpreter may deliberately mislead practitioners and/or encourage the person to drop the complaint and submit to their family's wishes (H. M. Government, 2009).

Against this backdrop, forced marriage case records should always be restricted. Crime reports should be 'sanitised' and a note made highlighting the need not to disclose the victim's whereabouts. Police guidelines state that the location of domestic violence refuges should never be revealed to family members in missing person cases (ACPO/NPIA, 2008). Professionals should refuse to pass gifts and letters to a victim of forced marriage from their family.

Support for Victims

For many victims of forced marriage, accessing appropriate accommodation is vital since they may perceive statutory intervention as representing a stark choice between the 'security' of staying with their family or homelessness (Ministry of Justice, 2010). Professionals should seek to support victims with this, although in practice finding safe and secure accommodation may be challenging. This is due to a nationwide shortage of spaces in refuge accommodation as well as difficulties in locating culturally specific service provision (Coy et al., 2007; Coy et al., 2009; Quilgars and Pleace, 2010).

Identifying appropriate accommodation is further complicated in circumstances where a forced marriage victim leaves home with a partner of their choice (Akhtar, 2002) as only one specialist service exists for male and female couples fleeing family violence, including in cases of 'honour'-based violence (Quilgars and Pleace, 2010). Similarly, there are very few accommodation-based services for male victims of forced marriage so the use of hostels may be the only alternative (H. M. Government, 2009).

Young people, especially those aged 16 and 17, are another group that may present specific difficulties to agencies as there may be occasions when it is appropriate to use both child and adult protection frameworks to respond to forced marriage cases. Statutory guidance recognises that forced marriage is a form of domestic violence and, where it affects children and young people, child abuse (H. M. Government, 2010). However, although a child protection response may be appropriate in cases of domestic violence where one parent is abusing another, this will not be the case when teenagers are experiencing domestic violence within their own intimate relationships. Moreover, young people can, with parental consent, be married at 16 in England and Wales (Home Office, 2011). In recognition of this the government recently took the decision to lower the age within the domestic violence definition from 18 to 16 (Home Office, 2012).

Despite the fact that Section 31 of the Children Act (1989) provides for care and protection orders to be made by the courts to place a child under the age of 17 into the care of a local authority, many children's social care departments find it hard to locate appropriate housing or foster placements for this age group (H. M. Government, 2009; Ministry of Justice, 2010). Some 16- and 17-year-olds may not wish to enter the care system but prefer to access refuge accommodation (H. M. Government, 2009). Yet this is not always straightforward since few refuges will accept young women aged 17 and under (Izzidien, 2008; Gangoli et al., 2009; Home Office, 2011).

Evidence further shows that access to mainstream services for young runaways from minority groups is hindered because such services are not publicised in an appropriate way (Izzidien, 2008). Due to their 'white nature' there is perceived to be a lack of cultural awareness and sensitivity amongst agency workers towards these groups (Safe on the Streets Research Team, 1999; Franks, 2004). It may even be the case that children's services are unwilling to get involved in forced marriage cases involving 16–17-year-olds who are able-bodied and mentally stable (Kazimirski et al., 2009). Cases of threatened forced marriage without associated physical abuse also tended to be seen as lower priority. Meetoo and Mirza (2007) cite Radford and Tsutsumi (2004) who assert that, while feminists have seen the 'risk discourse' as an opportunity for opening up a dialogue with key agencies, uncovering violence and getting it taken seriously by the police and the courts, it has also meant rationing strategies to women who are deemed 'most at risk', thus denying protection to the majority (Coy and Kelly, 2011).

Scenarios like these may lead to a lack of clarity regarding who should take responsibility for responding to this age group (ACPO/NPIA, 2008). This highlights the importance of multiagency working in forced marriage cases. Information-sharing and referral protocols should be developed and implemented and links with domestic violence service providers of refuge, outreach and independent advocacy should be established via local domestic violence forums.

Finally, professionals should always be aware that, once placed in refuge or other form of safe accommodation, some victims of forced marriage may choose to go home as a consequence of missing their family and friends. If this is the case then they should be reminded of the services available to them if they change their mind. Safety measures can also be put in place through the police putting markers on their address and professionals checking in on them regularly.

Conclusion

This chapter highlights a variety of ways in which going missing and forced marriage may overlap and some of the complexities that arise when they do. National police and statutory guidance exists to guide professionals through some of these complexities. Links should also be made with local domestic violence and missing person forums to establish protocols and help coordinate responses. Details about national and local resources can be accessed via the freephone 24-hour National Domestic Violence Helpline – 0808 2000 247 (run in partnership between Women's Aid and Refuge) and 116 000 – the 24-hour and confidential helpline run by the charity Missing People.

Note

1 The act of forcing someone into marriage has also recently been criminalised within Section 10 of the Anti-Social Behaviour, Crime and Policing Act 2014.

References

Abrahams, C. and Mungall, R. (1992). *Runaways: Exploding the Myths*. London: NCH-Action for Children.

ACPO/NPIA (2008). *Guidance on Investigating Domestic Abuse*. www.acpo.police.uk/documents/crime/2008/2008-cba-inv-dom-abuse.pdf.

ACPO/NPIA (2010). *Guidance on the Management, Recording and Investigation of Missing Persons* (2nd edition). www.acpo.police.uk/documents/crime/2011/201103CRIIMP02.pdf.

Akhtar, S. (2002). *No One Asked Us Before!* Manchester: The Children's Society.

Arocha, L. (2010). *Wrong Kind of Victim? One Year On: An Analysis of UK Measures to Protect Trafficked Persons*. London: Anti-Trafficking Monitoring Group. www.antislavery.org/includes/documents/cm_docs/2010/a/1_atmg_report_for_web.pdf.

Barter, C., McCarry, M., Berridge, D. and Evans, K. (2009). *Partner Exploitation and Violence in Teenage Intimate Relationships*. Bristol: University of Bristol School for Policy Studies/NSPCC. www.nspcc.org.uk/Inform/research/findings/partner_exploitation_and_violence_report_wdf70129.pdf.

Beddoe, C. (2007). *Missing Out: A Study of Child Trafficking in the North West, North East and West Midlands*. London: ECPAT. www.ecpat.org.uk/sites/default/files/missing_out_2007.pdf.

Berelowitz, S., Firmin, C., Edwards, G. and Gulyurtlu, S. (2012). *I Thought I Was the Only One. The Only One in the World. The Office of the Children Commissioner's Inquiry into Child Sexual Exploitation in Gangs and Groups*. Interim report. London: Office of the Children's Commissioner. www.childrenscommissioner.gov.uk.

Biehal, N., Mitchell, F. and Wade, J. (2003). *Lost from View: Missing Persons in the UK*. London: Policy Press.

Bokhari, F. (2009). *Stolen Futures: Trafficking for Forced Marriage in the UK*. London: ECPAT. www.ecpat.org.uk/sites/default/files/stolenfutures_ecpatuk_2009.pdf.

Brandon, J. and Hafez, S. (2008). *Crimes of the Community: Honour Based Violence in the UK*. London: Centre for Social Cohesion. www.londonscb.gov.uk/files/resources/.../crimes_of_the_community.pdf.

CEOP (2010). *Strategic Threat Risk Assessment: Child Trafficking in the UK*. www.ceop.police.uk/Documents/ceopdocs/Child_Trafficking_Strategic_Threat_Assessment_2010_NPM_Final.pdf.

Coleman, J. and Hagell, A. (eds) (2007). *Adolescence, Risk and Resilience: Against the Odds*. London: Wiley.

Coordinated Action Against Domestic Abuse (2009). *Domestic Abuse, Stalking and Harassment and Honour Based Violence Risk Identification and Assessment and Management Tool*. www.caada.org.uk/marac/RIC_with_guidance.pdf.

Coy, M. and Kelly, L. (2011). *Islands in the Stream: An Evaluation of Four London Independent Domestic Violence Advocacy Schemes*. London: Child and Woman Abuse Studies Unit. www.cwasu.org/filedown.asp?file=IDVA+Main+Report(1).pdf.

Coy, M., Kelly, L. and Foord, J. (2007). *Map of Gaps: The Postcode Lottery of Violence Against Women Support Services*. London: Equality and Human Rights Commission. www.equalityhumanrights.com/uploaded_files/research/map_of_gaps1.pdf.

Coy, M., Kelly, L. and Foord, J. (2009). *Map of Gaps 2: The Postcode Lottery of Violence Against Women Support Services*. London: Equality and Human Rights Commission. www.equalityhumanrights.com/uploaded_files/research/map_of_gaps2.pdf.

Department for Children, Schools and Families (2008). *Young Runaways Action Plan*. http://webarchive.nationalarchives.gov.uk/20130401151715/https://www.education.gov.uk/publications/standard/publicationDetail/Page1/RUNAWAYS08.

Department for Education (2014). *Statutory Guidance on Children Who Run Away or Go Missing from Home or Care*. www.gov.uk/government/uploads/system/uploads/attachment_data/file/307867/Statutory_Guidance_-_Missing_from_care__3_.pdf.

Franks, M. (2004). *The Work of Safe on Our Streets with Minority Ethnic Runaways: An Analysis of Work Carried Out with Four Young Women from South Asian, Muslim Backgrounds*. London: The Children's Society. www.childrenssociety.org.uk/sites/default/files/tcs/work_with_four_south_asian_young_women.pdf.

Gangoli, G., McCarry, M. and Razak, A. (2009). Child marriage or forced marriage? South Asian communities in North East England. *Children and Society*, 23: 418–429.

Goulden, C. and Sondhi, A. (2001). *At the Margins: Drug Use by Vulnerable Young People in the 1998/99 Youth Lifestyles Survey*. London: Home Office Research Study 228.

Hedges, C. (2002). *Missing You Already: A Guide to the Investigation of Missing Persons*. London: Home Office.

H. M. Government (2009). *Multi-Agency Practice Guidelines: Handling Cases of Forced Marriage*. June. London: H. M. Government.

H. M. Government (2010). *The Right to Choose: Multi-Agency Statutory Guidance for Dealing with Forced Marriage*. January. London: H. M. Government.

H. M. Government (2014). *The Right to Choose: Multiagency Statutory Guidance for Dealing with Forced Marriage*. www.gov.uk/government/uploads/system/uploads/attachment_data/file/322310/HMG_Statutory_Guidance_publication_180614_Final.pdf.

H. M. Inspectorate of Constabulary (2008). *Protecting Vulnerable People*. www.hmic.gov.uk/media/protecting-vulnerable-people-20080131.pdf.

Home Affairs Select Committee (2008). *Domestic Violence, Forced Marriage and 'Honour' Based Violence*. Sixth Report of Session 2007–08. London: House of Commons. www.publications.parliament.uk/pa/cm200708/cmselect/cmhaff/263/263i.pdf.

Home Office (2011). *Cross Government Definition of Domestic Violence: A Consultation*. www.gov.uk/government/uploads/system/uploads/attachment_data/file/157800/domestic-violence-definition.pdf.

Home Office (2012). *Cross Government Definition of Domestic Violence: A Consultation – Summary of Responses*. www.gov.uk/government/uploads/system/uploads/attachment_data/file/157800/domestic-violence-definition.pdf.

Home Office Communications Directorate (2000). *A Choice by Right: The Report of the Working Group on Forced Marriage*. London: Home Office.

Izzidien, S. (2008). *'I Can't Tell People What Is Happening At Home'. Domestic Abuse within South Asian Communities: The Specific Needs of Women, Children and Young People*. London: NSPCC. www.nspcc.org.uk/Inform/research/findings/icanttellfullreport_wdf57889.pdf.

Jago, S., Arocha, L., Brodie, I., Melrose, M., Pearce, J. and Warrington, C. (2011). *What's Going On to Safeguard Children and Young People from Sexual Exploitation? How Local Partnerships Respond to Child Sexual Exploitation*. Luton: University of Bedfordshire. www.beds.ac.uk/__data/assets/pdf_file/0004/121873/wgoreport2011-121011.pdf.

Jha, K. (2004). Runaway Asian girls in Glasgow: The role and response of the community. *Scottish Affairs*, 48: 66–80.

Kapoor, A. (2007). *A Scoping Project on Child Trafficking in the UK*. London: CEOP/Home Office. http://ceop.police.uk/Documents/child_trafficking_report0409.pdf.

Kazimirski, A., Keogh, P., Kumari, V., Smith, R., Gowland, S., Purdon, S. and Khanum, N. (2009). *Forced Marriage: Prevalence and Service Response*. London: National Centre for Social Research, Department for Children, Schools and Families. www.gov.uk/government/uploads/system/uploads/attachment_data/file/222192/THE DEPARTMENT FOR CHILDREN, SCHOOLS AND FAMILIES-RR128.pdf.

Kelly, L. (1988). *Surviving Sexual Violence*. London: Blackwell Publishing/Policy Press.

Kelly, L. and Regan, L. (2000). *Rhetorics and Realities: Sexual Exploitation of Children in Europe*. London: CWASU. www.cwasu.org/filedown.asp?file=Rhetorics_Realities(1).pdf.

Kelly, L., Wingfield, R., Burton, S. and Regan, L. (1995). *Splintered lives: Sexual exploitation in the context of children's rights and child protection*. London: Barnardo's. www.barnardos.org.uk/splintered_lives_report.pdf.

Khanum, N. (2008). *Forced Marriage, Family Cohesion and Community Engagement: National Learning through a Case Study of Luton*. Luton: Equality in Diversity. www.reducingtherisk.org.uk/cms/sites/reducingtherisk/files/folders/resources/hbv_forced_marriage/FM_family_cohesion_community_engagement.pdf.

Meetoo, V. and Mirza, H. S. (2007). Lives at risk: Multiculturalism, young women and 'honour' killings. In B. Thom, R. Sales and J. Pearce (eds), *Growing Up With Risk* (pp. 149–164). Bristol: Policy Press.

Ministry of Justice (2009). *Forced Marriage (Civil Protection) Act 2007: Guidance for Local Authorities as Relevant Third Party and Information Relevant To Multiagency Partnership Working*. www.justice.gov.uk/downloads/protecting-the-vulnerable/forced-marriage/forced-marriage.pdf.

Ministry of Justice (2010). *Findings of the Forced Marriage IDVA Support Pilot*. www.forcedmarriage.net/media/images/report-on-forced-marriage-pilot-a_136.pdf.

Newiss, G. (1999). *Missing Presumed…? The Police Response to Missing Persons*. London: Police Research Series Paper 114.

NPIA (2009). *Guidance on Investigating Child Abuse and Safeguarding Children* (2nd edition). London: ACPO/CEOP. www.ceop.police.uk/Documents/ACPOGuidance2009.pdf.

NPIA (2010). *Guidance on the Management, Recording and Investigation of Missing Persons*, 2nd edition. London: National Policing Improvement Agency.

O'Brien, C. and Scott, C. (2007). The role of the family. In J. Coleman, and A. Hagell (eds), *Adolescence, Risk and Resilience: Against the Odds* (pp. 17–40). London: Wiley.

Phillips, A. (2007). *Multiculturalism Without Culture*. New Jersey, US: Princeton University Press.

Phillips, A. and Dustin, M. (2004). *UK initiatives on Forced Marriage: Regulation, Dialogue and Exit*. London: LSE Research Online. http://eprints.lse.ac.uk/546/1/Forced_marriage.pdf.

Quilgars, D. and Pleace, N. (2010). *Meeting the Needs of Households at Risk of Domestic Violence in England*. London: Communities and Local Government. www.gov.uk/government/uploads/system/uploads/attachment_data/file/6337/1778600.pdf.

Rees, G. (1993). *Hidden Truths: Young People's Experiences of Running Away*. London: The Children's Society in Social Care Online.

Rees, G. (2011). *Still Running 3: Early Findings from Our Third National Survey of Young Runaways*. London: The Children's Society. http://makerunawayssafe.org.uk/sites/default/files/Still-Running-3_Full-Report_FINAL.pdf.

Rees, G. and Lee, J. (2005). *Still Running 2: Findings from the Second National Survey of Young Runaways*. London: The Children's Society. www.childrenssociety.org.uk/sites/default/files/tcs/research_docs/Still per cent20running per cent202 per cent20- per cent20Findings per cent20from per cent20the per cent20second per cent20national per cent20survey per cent20of per cent20young per cent20runaways_0.pdf.

Richardson, D., Poudel, M. and Laurie, N. (2009). Sexual trafficking in Nepal: Constructing citizenship and livelihoods. *Gender, Place and Culture: A Journal of Feminist Geography*, 16(3): 259–278.

Safe on the Streets Research Team (1999). *Still Running: Children on the Streets in the UK*. London: The University of York, Aberlour, Extern, Children's Promise and the Children's Society. www.streetchildren.org.uk/_uploads/Publications/2.Still_Running_Children_Streets_UK.pdf.

Samad, Y. and Eade, J. (2002). Community perceptions of forced marriage. London: Foreign and Commonwealth Office. core.kmi.open.ac.uk/download/pdf/135337.pdf.

Shachar, S. (2001). *Multicultural Jurisdictions: Cultural Differences and Women's Rights*. Cambridge: Cambridge University Press.

Sharp, N. (2010). *Forced Marriage in the UK: A Scoping Study on the Experience of Women from Middle Eastern and North East African communities*. London: Refuge. http://refuge.org.uk/files/1001-Forced-Marriage-Middle-East-North-East-Africa.pdf.

Sharp, N. (2013). Missing from discourse: South Asian young women and sexual exploitation. In M. Melrose and J. Pearce (eds), *Critical Perspectives on Child Sexual Exploitation and Related Trafficking* (pp. 96–109). London: Palgrave Macmillan.

Siddiqui, X. (2005). 'There is no honour in domestic violence only shame!' Women's struggles against 'honour' crimes in the UK. In L. Welchman and S. Hossain (eds), *'Honour' Crimes, Paradigms, and Violence against Women* (pp. 263–281). London: Spinifex Press and Zed Books.

SOCA (2012). *Missing Persons: Data and Analysis 2011/12*. London: UK Missing Persons Bureau. www.issingpersons.police.uk/download/29.

Social Exclusion Unit (2002). *Young Runaways*. London: Office of the Deputy Prime Minister and University of York. www.bristol.ac.uk/poverty/downloads/keyofficialdocuments/Young per cent20Runaways.pdf.

Stein, M., Rees, G. and Frost, N. (1994). *Running the Risk: Young People on the Streets of Britain Today*. London: The Children's Society.

Tarling, R. and Burrows, J. (2003). The nature and outcome of going missing: The challenge of developing effective risk assessment procedures. *International Journal of Police Science and Management*, 6(1): 16–26.

11

Geography of Missing Adults

Penny S. Woolnough, Olivia Stevenson,
Hester Parr and Nicholas R. Fyfe

Introduction

> Every case is different […] routine kills. I demand from my people that they look at every
> case from scratch as if they know nothing and it's from looking at a case from that way
> that you will see some details. Some specific elements that make a case unique. […] Never
> exclude anything […] everything is possible.
>
> (Alain Remue, Head of the Belgium Federal Police's
> Missing Person's Unit, 17 May 2013)

Alain Remue, in a recent address to a European meeting of researchers on missing people,
reminds us of the need to regard each missing person episode as a unique single event.
Understanding the way in which people interact with the environments around them is an
integral part of comprehending the behaviour of missing people and their unique journeys, and
as such is the focus of this chapter. Whenever a person is reported missing to the police, there
is an obvious need to locate an individual in space and time. ACPO provides a definition of
'missing' equating to 'anyone whose whereabouts cannot be established', and a definition of
'absent' as 'a person not at a place where they are expected or required to be' (ACPO, 2013,
p. 5), clearly indicating that when someone is reported as missing to the police it is because their
geographical location at that moment in time is unknown or uncertain. To complicate matters,
the individual may not be static in their situation or behaviour and may move over time and
through space, navigating the environment on an evolving journey, which could also be considered uncertain in terms of its intentionality (Stevenson et al., 2013). Consequently, searching
for a missing person can be a complicated process for any agency, involving interpreting the
interplay of spatial, environmental and human elements at stake. In this chapter, we elaborate
these complexities and seek to use recent research evidence to shed new light on missing adult
geographies and journeys.

In the first section we review the research evidence that exists around where people reported
as missing travel to and discuss the associated development of quantitative spatial profiling used
in the search for them. In discussing these developments, we consider the categorical knowledge

emergent from large-scale empirical data sets of missing persons enquiries that seek to unify experience and direct search tactics, against and alongside the more 'specific' and 'particular' details of lived missing experience that qualitative data produce (Edkins, 2011; Stevenson et al., 2013). By using the latter, we seek to provide new ways of understanding missing journeys from the inside and across different adults' narrated experience. We do this specifically through the use of qualitative data generated as part of the Economic and Social Research Council-funded research project 'Geographies of Missing People: Processes, experiences, responses'.[1] This project provides insights into the social and spatial dimensions of adult missing journeys with an emphasis on decision making, planning, mobility choices, environmental resourcefulness and return. The material contributes to the evidence base around adult missing persons (a field where research is still in its infancy) and provides insights for policing education and operations (see Stevenson et al., 2013).

What Do We Know About Geographies of Missing Adults from Existing Research?

While there is a slowly increasing body of literature on missing persons only a very small amount of research to date has considered missing adults (Hirschel and Lab, 1988; Henderson and Henderson, 1998; Biehal et al., 2003; Tarling and Burrows, 2004; Stevenson et al., 2013). One of the original and largest studies which explored missing persons' experience using case records held by Missing People (then the National Missing Persons Helpline), and a survey of 114 former missing people, presented a typology of missing experience making a clear distinction between intentional and unintentional absences, understood on a continuum (Biehal et al., 2003). Importantly, this research suggested that an adult's intentions or motivations will affect how they travel, where they go and what they do. For example, a person who intentionally removes themselves from a situation (such as a woman leaving home to avoid a situation of domestic abuse) is likely to engage in a very different journey and behaviour than someone who is unintentionally missing (for example, an elderly male who becomes lost due to cognitive impairments associated with dementia).

One of the key geographical anchor points relevant to the search for any missing person is their place of residence. This usually represents the beginning of their journey and may contain crucial clues about their disappearance, such as a suicide note or the absence or presence of key objects like bank cards or a passport (ACPO, 2013). It appears, however, that people are not always reported missing from their home address. A study by Tarling and Burrows (2004), based on 1,000 cases of both adult and child missing gathered from the Metropolitan Police in London, found that just under half of the people had been reported missing from their home address, a quarter from hospitals and the remaining were split equally between being reported missing from a care environment or other location (such as work). Echoing this work, Shalev et al. (2009) also found that just under half were reported missing from home and the remaining were reported from a variety of locations including: work, institutions, public places and friends' and relatives' addresses (and see Stevenson et al., 2013). This highlights the potentially complex relationship between different geographical anchor points (such as work and home) and the missing person's intentional or unintentional journey as well as the perceptions of those left behind who report the person missing (see Parr et al., in press).

In terms of missing journeys, very little is known about where people go or stay while they are away. The only published study to touch on this reports a diversity of experiences, finding that 60 per cent stayed in one place while away and just 9 per cent moved more than once (these more often slept in temporary accommodation/shelters and moving more or less did not appear to be related to time away) (Biehal et al., 2003). Additionally, sleeping rough was engaged in by more than a quarter of the sample and over a third felt themselves to be in danger at some point while they were missing. However, this work was based on charity recorded data and included people who had lost contact with friends and family rather than exclusively those who had been reported missing to the police. So the extent to which it can be generalised to missing persons falling within new police definitions is unknown (ACPO, 2013).

In terms of return and the end points to missing episodes, some research has begun to throw light on this issue, with studies of police-recorded data suggesting that approximately 50 per cent of missing adults return to their home address of their own accord (Henderson and Henderson, 1998; Tarling and Burrows, 2004; Hirschel and Lab, 1988) and approximately 10 per cent are found in the street or an open public place (Tarling and Burrows, 2004). Furthermore, Tarling and Burrows (2004) found that over three-quarters of cases were resolved within 48 hours of persons being reported missing. Of course, where a person is found and the timescales in which they are found may be a function of the search efforts and strategies used to locate them. While these initial studies have attempted to explore some of the issues which may be relevant to an understanding of the geographies of missing persons, they only 'skim the surface', providing little in the way of in-depth understanding of this important area or direct guidance to support agency responses to missing people.

Spatial Profiling in Search and Rescue

A body of research which predates much of the research specifically on missing persons but has relevance to the geographies of missing adults relates to the behaviour of 'lost persons'. In terms of search planning, a more scientific approach to search management was initially developed in America by National Park rangers and mountain rescue personnel who were responsible for 'lost person' searches in the many large National Parks throughout the US and Canada (Syrotuck, 1975, 1976; Hill, 1991, 1999). Consequently, this work was based on those who had become disorientated and had a desire to be found, or persons who were simply overdue in their return from an outing or activity in which they were involved (such as unintentionally absent). By collating and analysing search and rescue statistics accumulated by civilian search and rescue teams they found they could separate lost persons into different behavioural categories and predict the distances these people would travel from the point they were last seen or went missing from, to where they were found (Syrotuck, 1975, 1976; Hill, 1991). Subsequent similar research has been conducted in many other countries including Australia (Twardy et al., 2006) and the UK (Perkins et al., 2011) and has incorporated wider categories of lost and missing persons such as missing dementia patients (Koester and Stooksbury, 1992; Koester, 1998). This work has illustrated the importance of spatial profiling in helping to define search areas and, as a result of this work, a number of composite guides have been published to aid search planning and management (Koester, 2008). Of course, not all missing persons are lost, and not all are in very rural environments, so while this data has proven useful in more extreme or particularly rural locations, its application to the full range of more urban or 'everyday' missing persons, particularly those encountered by the police, has limitations.

Developing Quantitative Spatial Profiling for Missing Persons Reported to the Police

Building on the theory of spatial profiling in wilderness environments, research conducted by Grampian Police presented the first attempt to provide normative spatial profiles to specifically aid police missing person investigations (ACPO, 2006; Gibb and Woolnough, 2007). Based on a UK-wide analysis of 2,198 closed police recorded missing person cases, Gibb and Woolnough (2007) used 'predictive' variables (for example, age, sex, suicide attempts, previous missing episodes and mental condition) to 'predict' outcome characteristics (such as distance travelled, where they will be located, and timescales in which they will be traced/found), presenting geographical and temporal profiles associated with these. This work is currently used by police and search and rescue agencies throughout the UK (ACPO, 2006). Like the wilderness search and rescue work (Syrotuck, 1975), this work is based on the premise that missing people behave in similar ways depending on particular elements of their specific circumstances. However, the main drawback of the research is that cases were gathered from police forces in a quasi-random manner and so the data cannot claim to be representative of all missing persons. Nevertheless, Shalev et al. (2009) also argue for the use of spatial analysis techniques to explore the behaviour of missing persons and its successful application by police suggests that such an approach can help expedite the safe, efficient and cost-effective location of missing persons.

Geographies of Missing People: Qualitative Insights

While the development of quantitative spatial profiling appears to have helped the police improve their understanding and response to missing person investigations, there is a paucity of evidence based on missing experiences as articulated by missing adults. Against this backdrop, we attempt to address the gaps by reporting empirical findings from the Geographies of Missing People research project mentioned above. Through empirical findings from in-depth interviews with adults reported as missing during 2009–2011, we fill in gaps on what is known about missing journeys from insider perspectives.

Adults reported as missing were selected based on their age (18 years and over), police force areas and time away. Working with two police force databases (Police Scotland and the Metropolitan Police Service), potential interviewees were identified and contacted through the police in line with the 1998 Data Protection Act. In addition, post-14-day cases were proactively sampled to ensure the opportunity to potentially interview longer-term missing persons. Face-to-face in-depth and semi-structured interviews took place with 45 adults in a location of their choosing. Interview data was transcribed verbatim and analysed using QSR NVivo8 software. Not all the sample self-identified with the ACPO (2013) definition (given above) of a missing person, but did recognise themselves as 'absent'. However, the study has not sought to refine these definitions of missing (ACPO, 2013; Payne, 1995) nor has it sought to sample adults reported as missing on the basis of particular 'types' of missing experience. Rather, the interviews focused on the journeys undertaken whilst being reported as missing and reflections on these (see Stevenson et al., 2013, Parr and Stevenson, 2013). The remainder of this chapter draws on this qualitative evidence to provide insights into the social and spatial dimensions of adult missing journeys and reports on decision making and choices in relation to planning and leaving, mobility, resourcing and return.

Leaving to Go Missing

Many people reported as missing are absent for relatively short periods of time (Tarling and Burrows, 2004; NPIA, 2011; Stevenson et al., 2013) and as a result journeys may appear 'meaningless' beyond the leaving and return (if this occurs). However, this research suggests that even short journeys have profound effects for adults themselves and their families and friends, and can require huge amount of police resources (see Shalev Greene and Pakes, 2012). As previous studies have shown (James et al., 2008) and the latest research evidence reflects (Stevenson et al.,

Table 11.1 Planning window before the act of leaving

Planning	% of adults (n = 58)	
	Male	Female
Days before	5%	7%
Night before	7%	16%
Moments before	29%	24%
Mention plan to others	3%	7%
Unclassified	2%	

Note: Column does not total 100% as people planned to go missing more than once

2013), the main drivers that adults report influence their decisions to go absent are: mental health crisis, drug and alcohol issues, relationship breakdowns and debt. Whilst vital to understanding the 'exceedingly complex web of behaviours and responses that surround the phenomenon of missing persons' (James et al., 2008, p. 2), it is equally important to understand what happens at the point of leaving and how people affected by the drivers for missing decide *where* to go, *when* and *if* to go, and *when* and *how* to return. Confirming findings from previous studies (Tarling and Burrows, 2004; Shalev et al., 2009; NPIA, 2011), our research shows that persons reported as missing go from a range of locations, with the most frequently reported location being the home address, followed by psychiatric wards.

In terms of planning, Table 11.1 shows how the level of consideration over whether to leave varied amongst the adult interviewees. While for the majority (53 per cent) the decision to leave was instantaneous, 23 per cent planned to leave the night before and 13 per cent made plans several days in advance. An example of advance planning is illustrated by Darren as he discusses the time leading up to his leaving:

> I didn't speak to anybody except to one of my close mates. I felt very, very guilty and it put me quite emotionally on the edge so I just blanked. I had actually packed a few days beforehand so I had made it as easy for myself as I possibly could. All the tools for my disappearance were there. The flight, the car booked in safely. All the money that I had got for spending money went on a travel card.

Darren's experience and those of other interviewees illustrate planning strategies ranging from: withdrawing money from bank accounts in small quantities to avoid detection from a spouse; changing SIM cards in mobile phones; reserving hotel rooms in advance; arranging to meet friends for companionship and/or shelter; and devising routes out of psychiatric wards, which included plans to use time out from a ward to abscond. Importantly, planning to leave days in advance was not associated with being missing for longer periods, nor was it associated with choosing exact destinations to go to. However, the findings suggest females were more likely than males to plan in advance to go absent and a minority (7 per cent) of women indicated their intentions to others before or at the point of leaving. Signs were exhibited to service providers and significant others through verbal and behavioural clues related to stress and depression. For example, in three cases interviewees had not turned up for work and did not call in sick, which was unusual for them. Three people had been to see their doctor showing signs of physical and emotional stresses before going missing and one female interviewee reported that 'one of my trigger factors is I cut all my hair off and I put bleach in it. That is one of my signs that I'm due to go'. Furthermore, for those adult interviewees who were suicidal (33 per cent), signalling intent to leave was noted especially for those in psychiatric institutions. Importantly, each person at risk of going missing may have their own personal indicative sign and, while observing trigger points and predicting missing episodes is complex, it could be helpful to families, health agencies and care services to learn to be more attentive to signs of impending 'missingness' which may offer opportunities for intervention and prevention.

Where Will I Go? Decision Making During the Missing Journey

The importance of obtaining accurate information on distance travelled by adults reported as missing is described by Shalev et al. (2009). Distance travelled is perceived as a valuable factor for building response scenarios and search planning, usually aimed at police specialist search advisors and volunteer search and rescue teams. However, placing too much emphasis on linear relationships of distance and time runs the risk of search being focused on location of departure and destination, rather than journey experience, mobility and encounters. Indeed, the empirical data below suggests a wider appreciation of missing experience relating to *all* stages of the journey is important. As Parr and Fyfe (2012) remind us, missing adults are a highly mobile and varied 'group' and the complexity of the *journey-making* experience (see Crang, 2001) is critical to better understanding.

Despite elements of planning described above, nearly all adults reported that their missing journey was not predetermined in terms of how long it would last or the exact location they would end up. Rather, the first few hours of a journey were spent focused on decisions of *where* to go and *how* to travel, suggesting a kind of 'crisis mobility' (Parr and Fyfe, 2012, p. 9).

Figure 11.1 shows that equal use was made of buses (18 per cent) and cars (18 per cent) as a mode of transport. Importantly, participants stated that using public transport meant the scheduling of journeys was largely outside their control and waiting at bus stops added to the anxiety of being caught. An awareness of the ability of CCTV or other systems, such as Automatic Number Plate Recognition or Oyster card technology, to track movements in time and space also influenced decisions around mode of travel and movement through environments, as explained by Max when he discusses why he doesn't use a car or Oyster card:

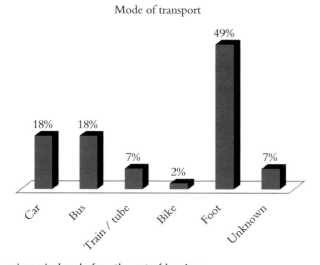

Mode of transport

Figure 11.1 Planning window before the act of leaving

I drive, but straight away it has to be registered and especially nowadays and the police know straight away through their computers. So to get a car and be anonymous is very, very hard and [to have an Oyster card], you know, I don't have anything that can be traced back to me.

The salience of Max's account in relation to the linkages between mobility choices and technological tracking partially accounts for why walking is the majority mode of mobility for the interviewees. Many recognised the advantages that walking offered as they could move with less fear of observation and choose their own routes: 'I decided to walk up the High Street and then I joined some back streets and they were quiet. I was able to walk along there for a bit and avoid the crowds' (John). As Middleton (2009) suggests, walking opens up the possibility of doing other things in a way that other forms of urban transport do not. For John, choosing back streets and less crowded routes enabled him to perceive his journey as undetected. John's narrative further reflects the points made by Solnit (2001, p. 5), who asserts, 'walking leaves us free to think without being wholly lost in our thoughts' and is 'an observer's state, cool, withdrawn, with senses sharpened, a good state for anybody who needs to reflect or create' (p. 186). Walking, then, for those reported as missing, allows more than mere transportation and avoidance of surveillance technology, and as Rhianna and Amanda describe, it is both a psychically and therapeutically important response to help deal with the thoughts and emotions experienced during these crisis mobilities (see also Parr, 1999).

[The] actual physical sensation of walking meant I felt free and I felt getting all the blood pumping back to my heart. And that type of walking, where you don't really know where you're going, it's liberating.

(Rhianna)

It was about 2 o'clock in the morning and I was just walking. I was just wandering the streets, just having this need to keep going forward, but at the same time not having any clue as to where I was going to end up.

(Amanda)

Confusion is a commonly reported state of mind on missing journeys and rather than moving from point A to point B in linear ways, journeys were often characterised by wandering in circles, loops or squares. This is not to suggest a presence of aimlessness, but rather is a reflection on deliberate decisions about where to walk and the geographies of walk taken. For 46 per cent of interviewees staying local and going to familiar or significant places was important. Many specifically steered clear of their home street and neighbouring streets in the areas they lived for fear that they would be detected. So, going to familiar places and staying local was recognised as a risky strategy as it could lead to being seen. But the risk was balanced by the recognition that: 'If I had gone somewhere I didn't know it would have been a lot harder to get through the next few days because I wouldn't know where anything was' (Mathew). Knowing streets, as Mathew's quote shows, and being able to navigate areas comfortably, allowed interviewees to blend in and not appear out of place or lost. In fact, to be lost was perceived as a significantly different experience to being missing. Choosing where to go, then, is often a conscious deliberative process, as well as an act of memory and crisis.

Environments as Resources

Johnsen et al. (2008, p. 197) found that the common everyday needs of homeless people were 'subsistence, ablutions, socialising and sustaining themselves financially', which are, they suggest, in many ways no different to those of housed people. The narratives in this research concur with such understandings as interviewees described the myriad of ways they used the built and natural environment on their missing journeys to meet these needs. In trying to do so, however, this temporarily mobile group did not readily identify with nor have knowledge of homeless service provision and support networks on the streets, and this, coupled with their need to hide throughout their journeys, made for stressful experiences. Even if adults might not be aware that they had formally been reported as missing, they were attentive to resources that could facilitate their perceived need to hide. Hiding behaviours which utilised environmental resources ranged from: taking shelter to avoid detection, changing their physical appearance, going by a false name, avoiding CCTV, changing their clothing by stealing new clothes off washing lines or from charity bins, or staying with friends who wouldn't disclose their whereabouts. In the following interview extract, Amanda reflects upon the ways she employed hiding behaviours:

> I got worried every time I heard a car because not many cars and so, I would duck into someone's garden quickly and come out again.
>
> (Amanda)

As Amanda explains, she understands the potentiality for discovery and uses tactics to lower the chances of being seen. She draws attention to how missing people are attuned to surveillance and how they use the built and natural environment as resources to avoid this. Importantly, as Table 11.2 shows, males and females used both the built and natural environment to hide with minimal differences between them.

Wooded areas, shady parks and derelict buildings were deliberately chosen and small and large parks in (semi-)residential areas featured in 46 per cent of missing journeys as popular resting places: 'There's like a park. I remember sitting on a bench for ages watching basically drunks walk past and the cops were on the go and, the trees sort of shaded and nobody noticed you' (Trish). As journeys continued in the constant cycle of motion and emotion, places to rest both momentarily and for longer periods of time increased in importance. Transport hubs, such as bus and train stations, as well as airports, offered opportunities for adults to rest, eat, wash and sleep masked by the rhythms of these spaces. This is clearly indicated by Daniel as he reflects on visiting and staying overnight at an airport, saying: 'Lot of people arrive early for flights they've

Table 11.2 Hiding behaviours

Hiding behaviours	% of adults (n = 39)	
	Males	Females
Changed physical appearance		5%
Changed clothes	5%	8%
Wore dark clothing or clothing to conceal face	8%	5%
False name	10%	3%
Hid in natural environment other places (including parks, woods)	18%	10%
Hid in built environment (including friends, sheds and derelict buildings)	13%	16%

Note: Column does not total 100% as adults may have been involved in more than one type of hiding practice or none at all.

got to catch early in the morning and they stay over at the airport so you don't really stick out'. Although such places offer access to facilities, there was recognition that transport hubs didn't provide cover indefinitely as they are heavily policed and surveyed environments. Still, many were drawn to these places, not only for restorative practices but because they acted as symbolic spaces providing a series of possibilities for travel, an associated sense of hopefulness and even feelings of happiness in some cases. This suggests that being immersed in sites for 'legitimate' mobility is helpful for some people as they go absent. On this basis, such places could be targeted sites of education and intervention around the issue of missing persons.

Return

Previous research found that the majority of missing persons incidents are resolved quickly (Tarling and Burrows, 2004; NPIA, 2011), which is broadly consistent with the findings of this latest work, where the majority (54 per cent) of adults returned or were located within 48 hours and 24 per cent were missing between 48 hours and seven days (Stevenson et al., 2013). Importantly, all the interviewees in the *geographies of missing people* study returned or were traced, and in discussing considerations for return, memories of this are of a transition filled with practical considerations and emotions of guilt, uncertainty, fear and relief amongst others. These were often caused by uncertainly in *how* to return, as two interviewees, Amanda and Max, suggest:

> I wasn't sure if I was in trouble with the police or not. I didn't know and I thought if they found me I would get arrested. You don't know what procedures are.
>
> (Amanda)

> When you get to that situation and you are about to go back, your mind is thinking about 'what am I going to go back to face'. It's just like the whole situation and you get a cramp in your stomach. It makes you feel anxious.
>
> (Max)

There are multiple drivers for return and mechanisms for being reconnected, from being located by the police, friends or family to 'running out of steam' or feeling the need to re-engage with regular routines. Uncertainty about what going missing *means* in terms of police procedure, as well as wondering what family responses would be, loom large in anxieties about return. Ninety-three per cent of interviewees reported police involvement in their journeys and showed varied experiences of return and police interaction, ranging from Wilma, commenting 'the police are the soundest. They're the ones that are least judging', to Angela revealing how police interaction was embarrassing and induced feelings of being a 'criminal'. In cases where missing adults felt like a criminal they were provided with limited opportunities to discuss the geographies of their missing journeys despite many having the personal need to do so. This also leads to lost opportunities for data capture and 'informed' policing (cf. Shalev et al., 2009; Parr and Fyfe, 2012). The research evidence suggests that what officers *say* and *explain* about being a missing person is very important in helping people cope, not just at the time of return but for years after the event. Key messages, such as 'it's our job. It's what we are here for, we're just glad that you're safe now' were critical to generating a positive police adult experience. This suggests there are further opportunities for police and partner agency policy development and training that focus on *where, when* and *how* to conduct 'return' interviews that take place after someone is located.

Conclusion

In conclusion, this chapter has reviewed the research evidence that exists around missing persons' geographies and introduced new empirical data in an attempt to expand the limited evidence base in this field. We have argued for the importance of including people's narrated experience of being missing in relation to informing future policing practice. We also assert that qualitative evidence helps to 'people' missing persons enquiries and exists as a complement to the more categorical knowledges that are produced as a result of working with large data sets related to spatial behaviour profiles. Returning to the words of Alain Remue, who reminds us that every missing person case is different and unique, we argue that it is important to be attentive to personal characteristics and specific geographical preferences, such as those discussed above, as these provide insights into the planning, mobility choices, resourcing and return that characterise missing journeys. Although most people who are reported as missing return within a relatively short space of time, this does not mean their journeys are without meaning or consequence. We are better equipped to intervene and assist people at risk of going missing if we regard them as active agents, agents who hold knowledge about the geographies of their journey, as well as relational actors, who need to make sense of their 'crisis mobility' after the event. People who are reported as missing are a rich source of information and taking time to talk and listen to them on return in an empathic manner is both beneficial for their recovery and reconnection, but may also have the potential to enrich future investigations that may lead to increased successful outcomes.

Acknowledgements

We would like to thank all the adult participants for taking part in the interviews, for their openness, generosity and willingness to talk about their experiences; without them the research would not have been possible. Special thanks to Police Scotland and the Metropolitan Police Service for their support with sampling and recruitment and in particular Detective Sergeant David Bullamore.

Funding Acknowledgement

The research on which this paper is based was funded by ESRC [RES-062-23-2492] as part of the project 'Geographies of missing people: Processes, experiences, responses'. Further research findings, reports and information are available at www.geographiesofmissingpeople. org.uk.

Note

1 ESRC RES-062-23-2492.

References

ACPO (2006). *Practice Advice on Search Management and Procedures*. Wyboston: National Centre for Policing Excellence.

ACPO (2013). *Interim Guidance on the Management, Recording and Investigation of Missing Persons*. Wyboston: College of Policing.

Biehal, N., Mitchel, F. and Wade, J. (2003). *Lost from View: A study of Missing Persons in the UK*. Bristol: Policy Press.

Crang, M. (2001). Rhythms of the city: Temporalised space and motion. In J. May and N. Thrift (eds), *Timespace: Geographies of Temporality* (pp. 187–207). London: Routledge.

Edkins, J. (2011). *Missing: Persons and Politics*. Ithaca, NY: Cornell University Press.

Gibb, G. J. and Woolnough, P. S. (2007). *Missing Persons: Understanding, Planning, Responding*. Aberdeen: Grampian Police.

Henderson, M. and Henderson P. (1998). *Missing People: Issues for the Australian Community*. Canberra, Commonwealth of Australia: Australian Institute of Criminology.

Hill, K. (1991). *Predicting the Behaviour of Lost Persons*. Paper presented to the 20th Annual Conference of the National Association for Search and Rescue, Fairfax, Virginia.

Hill, K. (1999). *Lost Person Behaviour*. Ottawa: National Search and Rescue Secretariat.

Hirschel, J. D. and Lab, S. P. (1988). Who is missing? The realities of the missing persons problem. *Journal of Criminal Justice*, 16(1): 35–45.

James M., Anderson, J. and Putt, J. (2008). *Missing Persons in Australia*. Canberra: Australian Institute of Criminology Research and Public Policy Series, No. 86.

Johnsen, S., May, J. and Cloke, P. (2008). Imag(in)ing 'homeless places': Using autophotography to (re) examine the geographies of homelessness. *Area*, 40(2): 194–207.

Koester, R. J. (1998). *The Lost Alzheimer's and Related Disorders Search Subject: New Research and Perspectives*. Response 98, NASAR Proceedings. Chantilly: Virginia, National Association for Search and Rescue.

Koester, R. (2008). *Lost Person Behavior: A Search and Rescue Guide on Where to Look for Land, Air and Water*. Charlottesville: VA: dbS Productions LLC.

Koester, R. J. and Stooksbury D. E. (1992). Lost Alzheimer's subjects, profiles and statistics. *Response: The Journal of the National Association for Search and Rescue*, 11(4): 20–26.

Middleton, J. (2009). 'Stepping in time': Walking, time, and space in the city. *Environment and Planning A*, 41: 1943–1961.

NPIA (2011). *Missing Persons: Data and Analysis 2009/10*. Bramshill: National Policing Improvement Agency.

Parr, H. (1999). 'Delusional geographies: The experiential worlds of people during madness and illness'. *Environment and Planning D: Society and Space*, 17: 673–690.

Parr, H. and Fyfe, N. (2012). 'Missing geographies'. *Progress in Human Geography*, 37(5): 615–638.

Parr, H. and Stevenson, O. (2013). *Missing People, Missing Voices: Stories of Missing Experience*. [online] www.geographiesofmissingpeople.org.uk.

Parr, H., Stevenson, O. and Woolnough, P. (in press). Searching for missing people: Families and missing experience. *Emotion, Space and Society*. doi:10.1016/j.emospa.2015.09.004.

Payne, M. (1995). Understanding 'going missing': Issues for social work and social services. *British Journal of Social Work*, 25: 333–348.

Perkins, D., Roberts, P. and Feeney, G. (2011). *Missing Person Behaviour: A UK Study*. Northumberland: Centre for Search Research.

Shalev, K., Schaefer, M. and Morgan, A. (2009). Investigating missing person cases: How can we learn where they go or how far they travel? *International Journal of Police Science and Management*, 11(2): 123–129.

Shalev Greene, K. and Pakes, F. (2012). *Establishing the Cost of Missing Person Investigations*. Portsmouth: University of Portsmouth.

Solnit, R. (2001). *Wanderlust: A history of Walking*. Verso: London.

Stevenson, O., Parr, H., Woolnough, P. and Fyfe, N. (2013). *Geographies of Missing People: Processes, Experiences, Responses*. [online] www.geographiesofmissingpeople.org.uk (accessed 19 June 2013).

Syrotuck, W. G. (1975). *An Introduction to Land Search: Probabilities and Calculations*. Mechanicsburg, PA: Barkleigh Productions, Inc.

Syrotuck, W. G. (1976). *Analysis of Lost Person Behavior: An Aid to Search Planning*. Mechanicsburg, PA: Barkleigh Productions, Inc.

Tarling, R., and Burrows J. (2004). The nature and outcome of going missing: The challenge of developing effective risk assessment procedures. *International Journal of Police Science and Management*, 6(1): 16–26.

Twardy, C. R., Koester, R. and Gatt, R. (2006). *Missing Person Behaviour: An Australian Study*. Technical report to Australian National Search and Rescue Council.

Part III
Investigation of a Missing Person Case

12

Managing a Missing Person Investigation

Charlie Hedges and Karen Shalev Greene

The initial evaluation of a report of a missing person, the assessment of risk and determination of the type of response that is required are all critical to the quality of the investigation. The challenge is recognising those cases that require immediate and urgent action out of the many that are reported to the police. Data gathered by the UK Missing Persons Bureau has shown slightly declining figures for three years' collection, slightly in excess of 300,000 reports made to the police in the UK per year (NCA, 2015). Such numbers require a sifting process, as it is not possible to conduct a full investigation into every report and a discerning approach is required.

This chapter will explain the procedures of a typical missing person investigation, drawing attention to policy considerations and good practice. It will discuss the process of initial assessment and response, investigative process and the broader subject of management of a missing person investigation. The chapter will explore how to manage expectations (for example, those of the missing person's relatives) regarding what an investigation can and should include. There will also be discussion of challenging cases and the chapter will map the operational services available to support police investigations.

Initial Assessment and Response

It has not been possible thus far to develop an accurate or clinical risk assessment model, although a 'decision-making guide' is available. It poses some relevant questions to guide the investigator towards the correct level of risk (for more details see ACPO, 2010, 2013). The initial questioning of the informant is critical to gather information to establish the circumstances of disappearance. Continued information gathering should allow for corroboration or reassessment of the circumstances.

Early information can be gathered over the telephone to assess the initial response, which will determine the investigative actions that follow. In any case where a full investigation is required, the best assessment is gained from a personal visit. Further enquiries with other family members, friends, work colleagues and associates will also give a broader picture and often information that is not known to the initial informant.

Application of the word 'investigation' to cases is significant in setting the standard that is required and moving away from the previous nomenclature of 'enquiry', as this implies something of much less importance.

Type of Investigative Response: Absent/Missing

A new approach has been adopted, which is intended to move investigations away from applying a formulaic response to each case towards something that is more considered. Failure to follow this type of response often leads to a form-filling style and ticking some boxes. Each case should be considered as an investigation, with the fact that someone has gone missing being an indicator or symptom of something that is happening to them and as a cause for them to act in that way. It is only when that cause is understood that appropriate interventions and responses can be made. An analogy would be a patient who is seeking treatment from a doctor who prescribes a painkiller for an aching arm without assessing the fact that a bone is broken.

This change has been driven by the need to reconsider all facets of how missing persons are dealt with and to determine a process that will enable the risks to be addressed in a discerning manner. The process should be adopted by all relevant agencies and involves them all in working together to solve problems and make vulnerable people safer. It is an issue that cannot be tackled by the police alone and impacts on health, social care, education, private and local authority care providers and the voluntary sector. If all agencies do everything that they should in partnership with each other, the risks can be effectively tackled.

A consideration of risk has been added to the missing person definition together with a category of absent that allows this more discerning approach to be made. These new definitions are (ACPO, 2013, p. 5):

> Missing: 'Anyone whose whereabouts cannot be established and where the circumstances are out of character or the context suggests the person may be subject of crime or at risk of harm to themselves or another.'
>
> Absent: 'A person not at a place where they are expected or required to be and there is no apparent risk.'

It is essential that those classified as absent are monitored within agreed timescales to ensure that risk is managed properly and appropriate actions are taken to recover or safeguard the missing person (ACPO, 2013).

Investigative Process

There are six key elements to any case, which are: early actions, interview, search, use of publicity, the return of the missing person and responding to the information gathered during the investigation.

Early Actions

Following from the discussion above, the effectiveness of early actions can negatively or positively influence the progress and resolution of the case. They are the building blocks upon which future actions are constructed and failure to do things properly at an early stage can mean that they have to be redone or the later stages are not properly informed.

Investigation requires an open and enquiring mind set, asking probing questions to understand what is known, what is not known and what needs to be discovered. Taking the approach that 'this is just another missing person' is not conducive to a good outcome and tends to ignore what the underlying causes of the person going missing are. One often-quoted phrase is 'if in doubt, think murder', recognising that it is easier to work back from such a scenario rather than having to play catch up with the relevant enquiries.

Interview

Speaking to the right people and asking the right questions is a basic principle of any investigation and applies in this area as much as any other. Understanding the position and perspective of the informant will indicate whether or not they are able to supply all of the information that is required and any bias that they may have. Their information may not be complete because they are not aware of everything or because they have a reason to withhold it.

Not being aware of information can result from their relationship with the missing person, especially in the case of children, who will often confide more to their friends and not wish to share information with their parents. This can be as a result of normal relations between parents and children as they grow up, or something more sinister where they are being coerced into actions through contacts on the Internet or personal contacts. Clearly it is in the best interests of those who wish to exploit young people that they create a divide between them and their parents or carers. Adults can have difficulty in expressing their true concerns, emotional issues, frustrations and so on, whether relating to themselves or another. It may take some time for trust to be built and information shared.

Interviewing starts from the first report of a missing person, which could involve a police officer or police staff, often those who work in the police contact centre or control room. Questions must be asked that will elicit information about the disappearance and lead to the person's discovery. Good interviewing skills include listening and understanding what is, and what is not being said. Just what those questions are will depend on the circumstances but should be open questions aimed at finding out as much as possible about the person, their background and the circumstances of the disappearance.

Interviewing those connected to the missing person and other witnesses will continue throughout the investigation and may involve speaking to some people on more than one occasion. Ensuring that they have an ongoing point of contact is also important to enable them to share new information that comes to light or facts that are recalled at a later stage.

The other important aspect of interviewing relates to when a person returns and this will be discussed later in this chapter.

Search

Search is a key element of finding a missing person and is inextricably linked to investigation and interview, with each part providing and feeding from information related to the others. The level of search will be determined by the circumstances and must be proportionate and justifiable, with consideration of the purpose of the search. It would not, for example, be correct to take up floorboards in a house to look for someone without appropriate justification in the circumstances.

Any search will initially consider personal effects, the place missing from and any external search areas. Personal effects may reveal information about plans or arrangements made by the missing person prior to their disappearance and personal contacts. Inference may be drawn from what is, or is not, present. For example, the presence or not of items that are considered essential, such as credit cards, keys, and money, may indicate a planned or unplanned absence. The intrusiveness of the search will depend on the circumstances and the legal powers that they may confer.

The place a person is missing from must be searched, usually with the consent of the owner or person in charge of the property. It can be difficult for a concerned relative or family member to understand why this must be done but it is an essential action and should be explained as part of gathering the best picture possible surrounding the disappearance. Using the knowledge of a person familiar with what items should or should not be in a particular place in conjunction with the observation skills and enquiring mind of a competent investigator, is a good combination to identify what is being sought. For example, a husband or wife will usually know what clothes or other possessions could be expected to be in place or notice if they are not there. This should not, however, be left for another person to carry out the search, as it will not be possible to be sure of the quality and extent of the search nor will it be possible to be clear about any ulterior motives they might have.

If searches are not conducted effectively, critical items will be missed or the missing person not found. There have been cases where a note with critical information on it has not been found, for example 'I have gone to the lake to drown myself', whilst searches have been taking place elsewhere and their body was found in the lake in a short space of time after finding the note. In other cases a person has hanged themselves in their attic or their body has been hidden there following a homicide. Children will hide behind furniture or within freezers and similar items and their presence overlooked, sometimes with tragic outcomes.

The initial search should be thorough, to ensure that all reasonable steps are taken to locate the person or clues as to their whereabouts. If more intrusive searches are considered necessary, involving the removal of floorboards, for example, the use of relevant powers and the advice of a Police Search Advisor (PolSA) should be sought. It is particularly difficult for families when this level of search is taking place and ensuring that they are informed about the progress of the investigation is of utmost importance.

Correct use of search assets is also important and these can include dogs, helicopters, search volunteers and so on. What is being sought and the area in which it is looked for will have an influence on the assets that are used. Misuse of search assets can be seen in overuse of inappropriate facilities (a helicopter may seem like an exciting asset to use, but what is its benefit in each particular case?).

The responsibility for the conduct of a search lies with the police and should not be abdicated to others when deploying assets, including volunteer search teams. They should be considered as agents acting on behalf of the police. There are occasions when nonpolice search teams are used and, at the very least, the police should set their objectives and coordinate the activities that they are conducting. None of the issues raised above precludes the police from taking advice or guidance from others who are expert in their field.

Furthermore, the adage 'clear the ground under your feet' is an important one and is a reminder not to spread the search too wide before dealing with the local area. So often doing the basics and looking close to home is overlooked, resulting in vital things being missed. It is sometimes tempting to go off and conduct extensive searches when in fact the critical location is near at hand. An example would be sending search teams off to work in the surrounding countryside when the land immediately surrounding the home or place of last sighting has not yet been searched.

Search can be a sensitive area and may need careful explanation to the family or the person reporting as this will be an uncertain time for them and they are unlikely to understand police procedures. As with many similar issues, it is important to take the time to explain why something is, or is not being done, to allay fears and uncertainty.

The need to obtain items that will provide DNA is an important but difficult issue. Not having such items can be a major hindrance later on, but it is important not to infer that taking them implies a more sinister outcome. It is simply good practice to get this early on and should be explained as such.

The Use of Publicity

Publicity can play an important part in any investigation but must be considered as part of the investigation strategy, not just as another box to be ticked on the form, and is not always given sufficient thought. It should be recognised that there are risks in using publicity, such as in the case of a missing child whose parent was a drug dealer, owing a significant amount of money to their supplier. Publicising the child as being missing was considered to increase vulnerability by advertising this to the criminal network, who may have been tempted to seek out the child as part of their retribution. Conversely, publicity can be extremely effective. It has been used in a number of cases of missing teenagers subject to sexual exploitation. In these cases, a high-profile campaign in a specific geographic area has resulted in those providing shelter withdrawing it so as to avoid the disruption to their criminal lifestyle.

Consideration of the use of publicity can also raise tensions between the police and families or carers and generally should only be done with their consent. It is justifiable to overrule this consent where the police have sufficient grounds for doing so and the safe recovery of the child would be hindered by not publicising the disappearance. Objections can be on personal or cultural grounds and these must be carefully considered against the benefits of publicity. In one case, the parent opposed publicity on the basis that it would bring shame on the family, but a publicity campaign was the only viable strategy left after nine months of investigation. The family wishes were overruled and the young person found with two weeks of doing so.

With the proliferation of information available on the Internet and social networks, an important consideration is the impact on a person's life at a later stage when they apply for a job or the information is otherwise accessed. The information is very difficult to remove from the Internet and may have a negative effect on the person's life.

Used wisely, publicity can be extremely effective in locating missing persons. It is a way of engaging the public in looking for the missing person or can alert the missing person to the fact that they are being looked for, as it is sometimes the case that people do not realise that they have been reported to the police as being missing. Also, where the person is being provided with shelter by a third party, publicity can persuade them that they should not be doing so. However, overuse of publicity can also reduce the impact on the public mind so that they become inured to the need to look out for missing persons (ACPO, 2013).

The Return

This must be considered to be part of the investigation. All too often the fact that the person has returned is seen as an end and an opportunity to take no further action. Without a satisfactory conclusion, the investigation cannot be complete. It is accepted that this is not always an easy stage to conclude but nevertheless all reasonable efforts must be made to do it properly. There is a variety of responses across the UK, with each police force and local authority delivering different ways of managing this.

There are four stages to consider when a person returns:

1   A strategy for the management of the return.
2   The safe and well check.
3   The return interview.
4   Responding to the information gathered.

A Strategy for the Management of the Return

How the return is to be managed should be thought about while the person is still missing. Families, carers and others who are reporting the person missing should be asked to consider how they will react and deal with the person when they are found, as being missing will have an impact on all concerned. There is little point in putting a lot of effort into finding the person, only for them to go missing again because the root causes have not been dealt with or consideration has not been made as to how best to respond to the person when they return.

If the person has particular vulnerabilities or is looked after within adult or childcare placements, consideration must be given to what processes should be in place when they get back. Who is the best person to speak to them? Is the existing placement still suitable? What interventions may be necessary? All of these questions and more should be considered, possibly in a multiagency meeting to determine the best course of action. It should not be forgotten that organisations such as the charity Missing People can offer support to families and work with them around the return to help them manage some of the difficult issues. They are also able to offer this support over a longer timescale as statutory agencies are forced to move on to deal with other emerging problems.

The Safe and Well Check

This is traditionally a responsibility of the police with the purpose being to ascertain whether they have suffered any harm, been involved in crime or to identify any other factors that are relevant.

Where the person goes missing from a care setting on multiple occasions, it is not unreasonable for some of the checks to be done by the carers. It is important that there is trust between professionals and it may not be the best response for the police to turn up on every occasion. It is also important to consider how this may criminalise a vulnerable person.

Giving training to care professionals to enable them to conduct safe and well checks effectively can prove effective and there are examples of this training enabling them to seize items for evidential purposes in the correct manner. It should be remembered that they may be the first person in any sort of authority to see the individual after they have been the victim of crime.

Even if the missing person is unwilling to engage in the safe and well check, noting their demeanour, clothing, physical characteristics or anything unusual may be of importance at a later stage. Observations such as these are fundamental to a professional investigation.

The Return Interview

This is separate from the safe and well check and can be conducted at an appropriate time, but there is nothing to stop a fuller interview being conducted at the same time as the safe and well check if it evolves from that encounter.

Usually there is the need to build trust and understanding, although this may naturally evolve from the provision of an effective service within a particular area. Guidance from the Department for Education states:

When a child is found, they must be offered an independent return interview. Independent return interviews provide an opportunity to uncover information that can help protect children from the risk of going missing again, from risks they may have been exposed to while missing or from risk factors in their home.

The interview should be carried out within 72 hours of the child returning to their home or care setting. This should be an in-depth interview and is normally best carried out by an independent person (someone not involved in caring for the child) who is trained to carry out these interviews and is able to follow up any actions that emerge. Children sometimes need to build up trust with a person before they will discuss in depth the reasons why they ran away (Department for Education, 2014).

The key consideration is that it must be someone that the missing person can relate to and share his or her experiences with. It is also important to consider why they have gone missing and the presence of a person related to that reason may inhibit them from giving a true account of the causes. Experience with existing schemes tells us that being honest with the interviewee and letting them know confidentiality may be breached and information shared with the police does not inhibit them in discussing issues and sharing information with the interviewer.

When they are victims of crime where the perpetrator has or is likely to threaten them or cause them actual harm, it is essential that the victim has the assurance that their interests will be protected and that effective action will be taken. For example, trafficking victims will be subject to a range of threats that are likely to significantly contribute to their fears and impact on their willingness to engage with the authorities.

Responding to the Information Gathered

The information gathered at all of the preceding stages must inform future actions. These could relate to an investigation into criminal activity, a care plan, strategies to deal with future incidents of going missing or information that indicates particular vulnerabilities in an area, to an individual or to groups of people. How this information is gathered and shared amongst agencies is important.

Intelligence and Information

It has been seen on numerous occasions that failure to share information can have a significant impact on how risky situations are not recognised or not dealt with. This information lies with a range of different agencies and it is wrong to hide behind legislation or other concerns about sharing information. Where there are child protection issues, the rule is that there must be good reasons for not sharing information.

Barriers to sharing information lie in not knowing who to give the information to; not presenting it in a usable format; and, having given information, not getting any feedback about its value, as this discourages future sharing. Most of these issues can be overcome by agencies having good relationships and engaging in joint training exercises. Examples of this include sharing information known to other statutory and voluntary agencies from which they know about vulnerable situations and events which may not be known to the police; high incidences of reporting of types of injuries or sexual health issues to the health service; and information about behaviours, truanting, unusual behaviours or unusual people seen in the vicinity of schools.

Engaging with Victims/Young People

Good investigative activity should include consideration of how best to work with victims and on terms that they can deal with. It should also include a thorough understanding of the pressures and influences that cause them to go missing. Looking behind the behaviour that they are presenting to try to identify the causes will enable a better understanding of what they are going through. Children and adults are not always in a position to give true consent to what others are expecting or coercing them to do. Grooming will distort an individual's cognitive functions causing them to act or react in a way that is different to what is considered 'normal'. Because someone, for example, appears willing to go with another person or carry out some act, they will not necessarily have done so freely.

As frustrating as it may be, it is often necessary to allow the victim to engage on their terms and when they are ready, not by those imposed by officials. It may also be beyond their capacity to immediately stop doing something that is wrong. It is important to be aware of 'survival offending' which may provide the only way that an individual can manage to eat, drink or avoid violence against them due to the situation they find themselves in. In some situations, a way of escaping or deflecting personal harm or abuse is to entice others into being victims. These are extremely complex cases to investigate and require a high level of empathy and understanding to conduct them correctly.

The investigator must remember that not everyone thinks or reacts in the same way and their upbringing and situational development may mean that they have a different set of standards, different motivations or an altered moral compass to other people, none of which may be of their making. It is not appropriate to consider persistent missing persons to be a nuisance, a waste of time or that there are other, better things to do than 'chase after' them. It is at this time that consideration should be given to which agencies are best placed to intervene to try to support the person. It is clear that the police service is not a 'one stop shop' for all of this.

Management of Missing Person Cases

A missing person investigation will always benefit from the appointment of an individual who has overall responsibility and has a clear view of progress. This may be an Investigating Officer or Senior Investigating Officer depending on the seriousness of the case and may also lead to the setting up of a major incident investigation team should suspicions raised in relation to the disappearance be sufficient for this. The decision as to whether or not this is necessary will lie with the police force that is in charge of the investigation. Due to the number of missing person reports that are made, this cannot happen in every case and many will be managed through the rotating pattern of supervision for the police area as outlined below. Another way of establishing ongoing oversight of outstanding missing persons is through the appointment of Missing Persons Coordinators, with their role being described later in this chapter.

An Investigating Officer or Senior Investigating Officer or whoever has overall responsibility should establish an investigative strategy with related actions being documented in a policy record, leading to oversight of those actions, their outcomes and how that influences future actions and enquiries. There is a risk that, if missing person investigations are not effectively managed, there will be a drift in focus with actions and enquiries being missed or duplicated. To move away from this style of ownership is difficult, bearing in mind the number of cases involved, and can be effectively managed through the duty supervisor, provided actions are managed and the investigation reviewed at each point of handover. Lax supervision and poor continuity of ownership and management can lead to failure to investigate cases properly, sometimes resulting in disciplinary action, and reflects negatively on the police service.

The National Intelligence Model (National Centre for Policing Excellence, 2005) sets out a process for reviewing and managing incidents on a police force area. Part of that process is the daily tasking management meeting that considers all significant activity and demands on a police area, determines priorities and arbitrates the use of resources. Missing persons should be considered as a part of this to ensure that cases are reviewed in light of the progress of the investigation and to place them in the correct order of priority for that day.

It is not possible for the police to manage cases without the support and assistance of other agencies and some cases will be the sole or shared responsibility of those other agencies. An effective referral process is therefore essential and will be part of standard local arrangements. This sharing of information allows a complete picture to be built up of the circumstances of disappearance and risk to the individual. The process of notification may be as an electronic notification from a missing persons management system or under standard child or adult protection processes. For example, a report by Ofsted (2013) recently cited the high quality of information sharing in Staffordshire that led to the better understanding of issues relating to sexual exploitation and an increased capability to deal with the issue.

Repeat Incidents

Recognition of patterns of behaviour, particularly in cases of repeat missing episodes, is essential to dealing effectively with the risks related to going missing. Taking a holistic view with consideration of the reasons for going missing is more likely to result in effective outcomes than simply focusing on individual cases and getting the person back on each occasion.

There are two interwoven factors that are important. First is that, unless the instance of going missing is truly an isolated occasion, risk does not cease just because the person is found and is no longer recorded as a missing person. The factor(s) driving someone to go missing are the critical issues to identify and understand, with each missing episode being a symptom of those factors. It may be, for example, that the person is being drawn into an exploitative situation or escaping from an abusive one. Going missing in these cases is the symptom and failing to recognise and deal with the cause does not remove the risk. The risk continues whether the person is missing or not. Second is the need to deal with these repeat incidents as a whole and not in isolation. Recognising this continuum of risk as a multiagency issue and response will lead to the best outcomes for the individual or individuals who are presenting with missing behaviour.

In some local policies, triggers are used to indicate when the response to incidents of going missing is escalated. An escalation would include engagement with other agencies, formal referrals and strategy meetings. These triggers usually relate to a person being reported missing on multiple occasions over a set period of time. However, flexibility is required, with recognition that the first time a person is reported missing can be the ideal opportunity to intervene, tackle the reason for them going missing and prevent or reduce further incidents. In some of the cases that arise, where the individual has been missing on scores of occasions, sometimes for long periods of time, it is extremely difficult to engage with them and commence any sort of intervention. Doing this at the outset of the pattern of behaviour is likely to be much more effective.

The Role of the Missing Person Coordinator or Missing Person Unit

One of the challenges of managing missing person investigations is achieving continuity of tasks and continual oversight of how the investigation is progressing. This is difficult in an environment where cases are managed as part of a rotating shift pattern, but this is where the majority of cases must sit. The role of the missing person coordinator or unit (ACPO, 2010, 2013) assists with such oversight, providing quality assurance and highlighting where actions are needed. While they are generally not responsible for the investigation, the role should include having an overview of cases and the capability to provide an easily accessible point of contact for other agencies and families. Coordinators have a particular role to play in the oversight of absences to identify trends and patterns, working with other agencies where appropriate to ensure that warning signs are not missed.

The other functions that should be provided by this role will include liaison with other agencies and those providing care to those who go missing; specialist knowledge of issues related to the subject area, such as local intelligence and trends; identification of individuals and cases that require additional attention; and in some areas, coordinators will build relationships with individuals or premises that are the source of high numbers of missing person reports; and ensure that return interviews are completed.

Roles of Various Agencies

The police will be the lead investigation agency in response to any missing person report but all relevant agencies need to work together in preventing and detecting issues related to those who go missing.

Care providers must monitor missing and absences and can have information vital to an investigation, some of which may be general information about persons and locations associated with individuals who go, or are at risk of going, missing.

The health sector will have information about individuals that will be pertinent to their going missing. Examples of sharing information with the health sector include highlighting high incidences of sexually transmitted diseases and in one case, a high volume of sales of pregnancy testing kits in one particular area revealed the locality and then the address where sexual exploitation of young girls was taking place.

Schools may be aware of individuals frequenting the close proximity of their premises who appear to be there for inappropriate reasons. They can also play a proactive part in monitoring absence from education and engaging with pupils to understand why they have been absent and who with.

Social services have responsibilities for those within their area who are 'looked after' and for children who go missing. Good relationships and information-sharing arrangements will identify issues that individual agencies are less likely to be aware of.

A strategy meeting is the forum where agencies relevant to a particular case come together to understand the problems relating to those who are particularly at risk of harm and going missing. They should promote actions that achieve better safeguarding for those who are the subject of the meetings. It is essential that strategy meetings have measurable outcomes that benefit the individuals that they are held for. There are reported cases of appropriate meeting structures being in place but resulting in few, if any, beneficial outcomes. In other words, they should not just be a talking shop.

Conclusion

The investigation of missing persons is a complex issue and, thankfully, the vast majority return quickly, having suffered little harm. Of those reported missing, the identification of individuals who are at risk of serious harm can be difficult. Despite the forgoing, any tendency to be complacent and lulled into thinking that the people will return anyway must be resisted and all cases treated seriously.

Further information can be found in the documents referred to, with more detailed descriptions of the recommended processes that should be employed.

References

ACPO (2010). *Guidance on the Management, Recording and Investigation of Missing Persons* (2nd edition). London: National Policing Improvement Agency.

ACPO (2013). *Guidance on the Management, Recording and Investigation of Missing Persons* (3rd edition). London: National Policing Improvement Agency.

Department for Education (2014). *Statutory Guidance on Children Who Run Away or Go Missing from Home or Care*. London: Department for Education.

National Centre for Policing Excellence (2005). *Code of Practice. National Intelligence Model*. London: National Centre for Policing Excellence.

NCA (2015). *Missing Persons Data and Analysis 2012/2013*. London: National Crime Agency.

Ofsted (2013). *Children and young People Who Go Missing and Child Sexual Exploitation. A Partnership Approach*. Staffordshire County Council. London: Ofsted.

13

Search and Rescue

Dave Perkins, Pete Roberts and Colin Hope

Introduction

In the UK, when a person is reported as 'missing' it remains the statutory responsibility of the police service to investigate what has happened. Legislation places a positive obligation on police officers 'to take all reasonable action within their powers to safeguard the rights of individuals who may be at risk' (ACPO, 2013). A failure to investigate a report effectively may leave the missing person in danger and the police service vulnerable to legal challenge and criticism. Missing person investigations represent a real risk to the life and wellbeing of the missing person. They should therefore be treated at an appropriate level of priority, with proportionate resourcing applied and using the best assets available. These assets may include those sitting both within and externally to the police service.

Whilst the majority of reports received by the police relate to those people who go missing in the urban environment such as towns and cities, a significant number of cases occur in rural locations that are potentially hostile, such as in hilly or mountainous regions. In these environments, missing person incidents are likely to require an immediate search and rescue response and one that should involve trained, experienced and well-equipped personnel. Whilst police resources will be involved in coordinating this response, the expertise of search and rescue (SAR) organisations will be called upon, due to the significant and enhanced capabilities for conducting search operations in these types of location that they can bring to bear.

Search and rescue is defined as 'the activity of locating and recovering persons either in distress, potential distress or missing and delivering them to a place of safety' (Maritime and Coastguard Agency, 2008). In the context of this chapter, search and rescue relates primarily to those incidents involving a missing or lost person that occur inland.

In the UK, the police service has the primary responsibility for coordinating the role of other agencies in search and rescue, including the specialist support provided by voluntary organisations. Deciding where to search, what parameters to set and how searchers will operate are among the challenges faced when searching for a missing or lost person. This chapter therefore aims to provide an introduction to search and rescue in the UK. An outline of the processes involved during the initiation and management of a search and rescue operation is provided and the importance of the effective use of best assets in search management is discussed. Research that has supported the development of search and rescue methodologies is identified, together with typical search planning structures often employed by personnel involved in managing a search and rescue operation.

Notification to the Police and Risk Assessment

A missing person investigation begins at the point of first notification to the police.[1] At this early stage, it is important that as much detail as possible is obtained from the person making the report. The report may be made in person or more usually by telephone, but in all cases and to ensure that all reports are accurately recorded, details will be entered onto an electronic reporting and management system. The operator taking the report will obtain and record as much detail as is available to ensure that the incident is responded to appropriately (ACPO, 2010). Supervisors will review the initial response grading to ensure that the correct level of priority is given. Reports will be prioritised applying a process based upon an assessment of the risk factors relating to the individual concerned and to the circumstances of the incident and by making reference to a graded response policy.

Risk assessment is the initial critical appraisal of the circumstances surrounding the missing incident and will dictate the level of response required. As an investigation develops, the circumstances and the risk assessment must be reviewed and updated as necessary. The risk assessment process is therefore dynamic and ongoing, with assessments being conducted as new information and evidence becomes available.

Initial Response

The duties of the first police officer attending a report of a missing person are to investigate, search and verify the level of risk. The level of risk can only be properly determined when an officer takes full report details (ACPO, 2010). Additional information will be obtained as a result of this initial response that will inform the ongoing risk assessment process. As the investigation develops, police supervision will continue to be involved, to oversee and manage the enquiry.

Dependent upon the nature of the incident, a number of additional police resources may be involved, including specialist investigators, Family Liaison Officers and specialist search assets. 'Fast-track' actions, which may include a search of the place at which the missing person was last seen, will be conducted (College of Policing, 2012). Any searches must be properly conducted and recorded in full. Searches carried out at this stage are intended to locate the missing person, to identify any information that may lead to their discovery and to establish whether a crime has been committed against the missing person. All searches must be proportionate to the circumstances of the disappearance and, particularly where premises searches are involved, will be conducted with sensitivity towards the needs of the affected families and local communities.

Police Search Assets

The UK police service has the benefit of trained search resources. Search training is delivered through the College of Policing at the Police National Search Centre.[2] The primary trained asset is the Police Search Advisor (PolSA), who will plan and manage a search using licensed search teams. The PolSA will provide advice and guidance on all aspects of search to their Chief Officers and is responsible for ensuring that licensed search officers remain competent to take part in search operations. There will be a number of PolSAs working within a police force area.

The PolSA has received training in the management of missing person searches and will have a strong awareness of the support available from search and rescue organisations, in terms of the strategic and tactical capability of each organisation and their personnel. Knowledge of the most appropriate assets to use for deployment in a specific environment (such as water, rivers, caves or mountains) is a critical feature of effective search management.

When engaged in a search operation, the PolSA will make an assessment regarding the most appropriate search assets and support to use for tasking relevant to the circumstances of the incident. This is likely to include the engagement and involvement of statutory and voluntary search and rescue organisations.

Police forces may have Service Level Agreements in place that provide a mechanism for contact with these organisations and that will facilitate the deployment of their resources. Early contact and liaison between all organisations involved in search and rescue operations is vital and effective multi-organisational command structures can be established to support the coordination of assets and expertise from all involved.

It is acknowledged that search and rescue organisations can bring a level of capability, experience, training and equipment to search operations that is complementary to that available within the police service. In addition to the police service, authorities and organisations with responsibility for, or significant involvement in, national search and rescue include the Fire and Rescue Service, the Ambulance Service, the Royal National Lifeboat Institute and voluntary inland search and rescue organisations (Maritime and Coastguard Agency, 2008).

Voluntary Inland Search and Rescue Organisations

In the UK, voluntary search and rescue organisations are represented by the following oversight bodies:

1 Mountain Rescue England and Wales (MREW).
2 Scottish Mountain Rescue (SMR).
3 Mountain Rescue Ireland.
4 British Cave Rescue Council (BCRC represented at MREW).
5 Association of Lowland Search and Rescue (ALSAR).

Specialist search dog teams also exist, which include the Search and Rescue Dog Association (SARDA) of England, SARDA Wales, SARDA South Wales, Lake District Mountain Rescue Search Dogs (MRSD) and the National Search and Rescue Dog Association (NSARDA). These are often represented by the national Mountain Rescue oversight groups.

Where support is requested from search and rescue organisations, their personnel can help in the planning of a search as well as physically going out to search for a missing person. These searches take place not only in remote mountain and moorland areas but also in non-mountainous and urban environments. Individual teams have a great deal of autonomy in deciding their approach to a search and rescue incident; local arrangements with police may vary from area to area but in reality there is very little difference in the fundamental concepts that are used under the umbrella term of search management.

Search Planning

Essentially, if someone is missing, they are not where they are supposed to be and finding them can be seen as a problem to be solved. *Where* searchers look and *how* they look are fundamental to the success of a search and rescue incident.

A number of planning methodologies can be relied upon by those charged with managing a search. For example, PolSA officers will be taught to apply the SCENARIO-based search framework. This involves the consideration and assessment of all known facts combined with the application of hypotheses regarding the nature of the missing episode that lead to search strategies being developed. The use of this process is particularly useful in the early stages of a missing person search when there is often confusion and uncertainty due to a lack of information regarding the behaviour of the missing person. Adding structure to search at the initial stages helps avoid 'speculative' searching, which can often lack focus. Using a methodology such as SCENARIO can provide a more effective, justifiable, proportionate, accountable and necessary search response (College of Policing, 2012: 11).

A similar approach is the 'Six Step Process', a planning methodology that is typically applied by SAR volunteers following a request for support from the police. This process is currently recommended and taught by the Centre for Search Research for managing the initial response to a search and rescue incident and is described in detail below.

The six steps are:

1   Size up the situation … what has happened – the facts.
2   Contingencies … what are the *maybes* and the possibilities.
3   Objectives … develop a plan of action to solve the problem.
4   Resources … who can help us deliver our plan.
5   Planning … manage and organise the incident.
6   Action … go ahead and do it.

The process is not executed to a set time and it takes as long as is needed. It may take just ten minutes to establish a plan for the 'initial response'. It is cyclical, and once search groups are out in the field then the search planners return to Step 1 to size up the current situation; any new information will feed into a new run through the six steps.

The first two steps are about the incident itself and the next four are about the response to it. The process is supported by documentation which helps deal with the developing incident and provides valuable structure for the initial call from the police for assistance.

Step 1 What are the Facts?

In Step 1 search controllers focus on all the known facts about the missing person and their circumstances. They consider what they were doing, where they were at the time they went missing, where they were last seen or known to be, any sightings and who by, whether they were prepared and equipped for the terrain they went missing in, what the weather was like, what the forecast is, and what they were wearing. This is essential planning data and also information that will be used by the teams who go out to look for the missing person. A detailed subject profile, which helps in predicting possible behaviours, is developed beyond the initial information through further investigation.

To be successful search managers must be looking in the right place with the best resources. This may sound obvious but it is a fundamental of search management – success is a function of *where* you look and *how* you look. The Six Step Process will help plan and manage the deployment of search resources.

Step 2 Consider the Possibilities

In Step 2 we consider what might have happened and likely scenarios that might account for where the missing person could be. It is important to empathise with the missing person and to put yourself in their shoes: what they might have done, how they got there, why they followed this course of action. Scenarios are the result of a careful blending of:

- incident history
- missing person behaviour statistics
- map analysis (terrain)
- subject profile
- local knowledge.

Missing Person Behaviour Statistics

Statistics are used to help create scenarios, or explanations of what might have happened, what the missing person might have done, where they might be and how far they might have travelled. Their use is a planning tool dealing with generalities and not absolutes. If 99 people in a particular category (such as walkers, children or dementia sufferers) in a similar situation behaved in a particular way, then there is a good chance that the 100th will do something similar.

Statistics are an important component of search management and are used by mountain rescue teams in helping to plan *where* to search. Information from past incidents is expressed in the form of statistics so that the search planner is able to consider the overall behaviour of missing persons of particular types rather than individual cases.

Where information regarding the missing person is limited, the search planning process can be informed by referring to statistical data based upon research conducted into missing and lost person behaviour in the UK. Information of this type includes the two data sets of Missing Person Behaviour statistics produced by the Centre for Search Research[3] that are available for use in the UK. Typically they are used at different stages of the search. The fatal/nonfatal statistics are most suitable for the start of the incident, when there may not be many specialist search resources and it is essential that a search plan is produced as quickly as possible. Statistics from the report of the Missing Person Behaviour study can be used to make a more thorough search plan for the initial response (Perkins et al., 2011).

Analysis of the data from missing person incidents has shown that there is a significant difference between the locations at which missing persons who are alive are found compared with locations at which deceased missing persons are found. These are referred to as the fatal/nonfatal statistics. Overall, in incidents in the UK almost two-thirds of missing persons who are found alive are found either in a building or on a travel aid, for example a road, path or track, whereas a roughly similar proportion of missing persons who are found dead are found in water or among trees.

This allows for a simple search strategy at the very start of a search: it is usual to assume that the missing person will be still alive, and therefore the search will focus on buildings that the missing person might be in and routes from where they were last known to be that they might have used to get to those places. After these likely locations and possible routes have been searched, then more experienced search managers and specialist resources are likely to have arrived on the scene, and the planning for the initial response can begin. The period of time just described is referred to as the immediate response, and can be organised and managed by non-specialist resources such as police officers. The immediate response will generally consist of a telephone enquiry to the likely locations combined with a tour of the area by police cars.

The initial response will make use of the complete set of statistics available in order to create scenarios. A scenario is a story that describes what might have happened after the missing person left their last known location. Search planners will typically make use of four or five different scenarios in Step 2 of the Six Step Process. These will suggest areas where searching should take place.

UK Missing Person Behaviour statistics are given for 16 different types of missing person, referred to as categories. Between them they cover the vast majority of missing person incidents, ranging from people who are missing because of some impairment (for example, dementia sufferers) to people missing while taking part in some recreational activity (for example, walkers).

As an example, suppose that an elderly male dementia sufferer living in a rural area is reported missing. The immediate response is to assume that they are still alive and to identify possible buildings that they might have headed for and routes that they might have taken. These can usually be checked by telephone calls and a police car. If that fails to find the missing person then the initial response will begin. The search planner will study the full set of Missing Person Behaviour statistics for dementia sufferers, and would note the following:

- About one-third of missing dementia sufferers are found either deceased or injured; searchers should therefore not assume that the missing person will respond to any noises (shouts or whistle blasts) that they make.
- In farmland the most frequently occurring places where missing male dementia sufferers are found are on a travel aid (road, path or track) or by a linear feature (wall, fence, hedge, stream or ditch). These are followed by buildings and open ground. Thus, a set of scenarios can be created to describe what might have happened to the missing person and from them a search plan can be produced.

The degree to which Missing Person Behaviour statistics provide useful information is largely dependent on the volume of data for each category. For example, the amount of detail given for the category 'despondents' is far greater than that given for the category 'solo walkers'. Nevertheless, the statistics for solo walkers provide unexpected and useful information, for example, female solo walkers are most frequently found on a travel aid or in a building, whereas about half of the missing male solo walkers are found in open ground, typically off their intended route or on difficult terrain. In addition, male solo walkers have a far higher fatality rate.

The category 'despondents' relates to the type of person who most frequently appears in missing person incidents. A despondent is defined as someone who is thought to have disappeared deliberately, due perhaps to depression or stress, and is often linked to threats of suicide or self-harm. These statistics show that a thorough investigation into the missing person can reveal useful information. The fatality rate is highly variable and appears to depend not only on the type of terrain in which the person is missing, but for males in particular, appears to be linked to a history of suicide attempts and depression. Furthermore, for males, the fact that the scenarios suggest that they are in or near a location of some special significance to them (such as a place they visited regularly or had particular memories associated with it) more than doubles the likelihood of a fatality.

There are many results in these statistics that are both interesting and extremely useful to the search planner. Among these are the significant differences between the locations at which fatalities are found compared with non-fatalities, the variability in the fatality rates for 'despondents' and what they would seem to be linked to, and the relevance of significant locations to fatalities of male 'despondents'. As more data is collected, then further useful insights will be gained.

Another seminal study is that conducted by Gibb and Woolnough (2007), known as the Grampian Data. This provides spatial behavioural profiles for categories of missing people. This guide has become an important planning tool that is regularly used by PolSA engaged in the search for missing people in the urban and rural environments. The data is based upon an analysis of over 3,000 missing person cases in the UK, where the behaviour of the missing person in terms of time missing, distance travelled and locations visited was examined. Published as a guide for operational police officers by Grampian Police in 2007, the guide provides predictive data relating to various categories of missing persons and includes figures relevant to the most commonly encountered forms of mental illness. The data set is currently being expanded as a result of research being conducted within the UK Missing Persons Bureau.

Building on the success of the Grampian Data, the NCA UK Missing Persons Bureau has created iFIND (to be published), an evidenced-informed search tool available to those trained in the search for missing persons. It is based upon a brand new data set of over 4,000 missing person cases drawn from a sample of 14 rural and urban forces across England and Wales. The researchers have used feedback from PolSAs and other subject matter experts to ensure it can be applied in a real-time, operational environment.

Similar to Grampian Data, iFIND provides statistics regarding distance travelled, length of time missing and likely locations found. iFIND has expanded the categories of missing persons and now includes additional ones such as autism, intellectual impairment, post-traumatic stress disorder and personality disorder, to name but a few. Other alterations include the time missing, which has now been measured from the 'time they were last seen' (rather than as 'time reported' in the Grampian data) to time located. Additional information has been provided about where and who the missing person was with whilst missing, along with accompanying percentages. For example, for autistic males, 41 per cent spent the missing episode outside on the streets; 54% per cent of autistic males were alone whilst missing. The booklet also provides further information in relation to the place located; for example, for males living with dementia, 14 per cent were located at place last seen, with further information including 'shed in the garden' and 'car in their garage'. In essence, iFIND will provide an effective and timely response in the search for missing persons.

Predicting likely behaviour demands a thorough subject profile and investigation into the missing person's state of mind, their capabilities and how they might be responding to their current situation. At this stage it is important to try 'to get inside the missing person's head' to try to predict what they might have done, where they might have gone, how they got there and where they might be now. The scenarios that will answer all of these questions will form the Incident Action Plan, which will inform where search and rescue teams go and look. If a likely scenario is that the missing person came out of their front gate and turned left and took the path to the remote country park then that is where we will look – along the path (a line) and their destination of the country park (point). Searching lines and points is fundamental to search in the initial response.

Step 3 The Incident Action Plan

Scenarios are the result of a careful *blend* of key points and they lead directly into the Incident Action Plan, as illustrated in Figure 13.1. The whole purpose of Step 3 is to produce an Incident Action Plan.

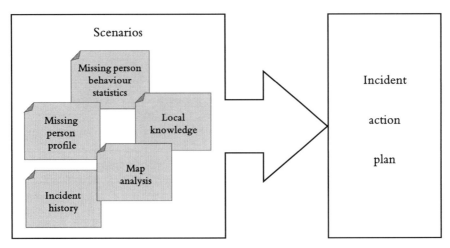

Figure 13.1 Illustration to show how scenarios are constructed

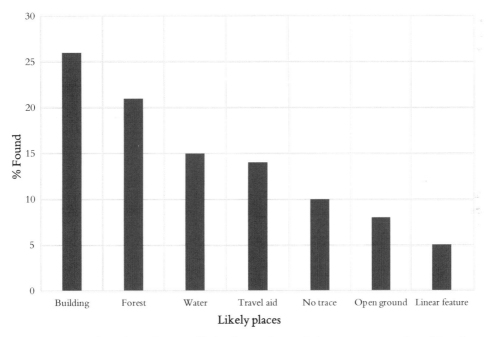

Figure 13.2 Graph to show the most likely places where missing persons were found for all categories

The example of a scenario, mentioned above, considered that when the missing person, a despond-ent male, left his house and came out of the garden gate he turned left to walk along the riverside path. This is readily turned into a search task to form part of the Incident Action Plan by identifying a *line* of travel and destination or *point*. His route and the riverside path would be important areas to search and would be identified as such in the plan. An alternative scenario might be that he turned left out of his garden gate and took the path to the nearby country park and well-known beauty spot that he frequently visited. Both scenarios, and others, can be incorporated into an Incident Action Plan. See below for a further discussion of the concept of lines and points and also Figure 13.2.

Step 4 Resources

Once there is an Incident Action Plan, resources need to be assigned to deliver the plan. The main search asset will most probably be small groups of trained mountain rescue or search and rescue personnel, which will include air-scenting search dogs. Specific search problems in the area to be searched will determine if any specialist resources are needed. For example, if there is a body of water, trained divers or coastguard may be needed to search it. Search managers should know how to access various specialist resources quickly and efficiently to help deliver their action plan.

Step 5 Control Organisation

Management of the missing person incident should be well organised and structured. Key functions should be completed by qualified personnel. A typical organisational structure is shown in Figure 13.3 and is generally self-explanatory. In the first instance this might all be done by just one or two people, but as the incident grows over time and becomes more complex each of the main functions of Controller, Planning, Operations, Investigation and Communications should have someone at the head of it. Investigation will be an adjunct to Planning and similarly Communications to Operations and each will work closely with the other. The person in charge will ensure that everyone works together and with a common purpose.

Step 6 Take Action

The final step in the Six Step Process is to go ahead and do it, for example put the action plan into operation. The search tactics advocated by the Centre for Search Research in the initial response phase of the incident are to search lines and points. Figure 13.2 shows the most likely

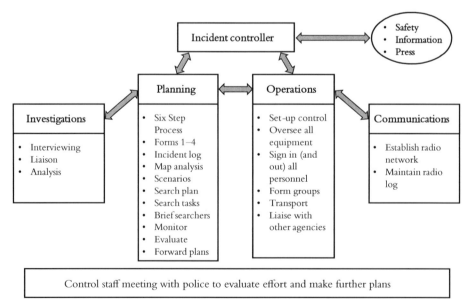

Figure 13.3 A typical control organisation structure, from 'Managing the Initial Response' training course

places where missing people are found for all categories of missing people in the most recent UK study (Perkins et al., 2011). It should be noted that the percentage figures for each likely place are different for some categories to these overall statistics. For example, for the male dementia category, travel aids and linear features are more likely than the other places compared to the overall statistics shown in Figure 13.3. Nevertheless, the guiding principle of lines and points still holds good for all categories, but some will have different more likely places than others.

Search Tactics

Trained searchers should know the basic principles of searching and the individual skills that can be applied whether searching lines and points or area searching. Searchers will have an understanding of the theory behind search and the visual process and be able to apply these in the field.

In the initial response phase small groups of two or three searchers will be deployed along lines and points identified in the Incident Action Plan. Generally these will be paths, tracks, roads, streams, edges of woods or forests and places of shelter or refuge. They should have a good 'visual image' of the person they are looking for in terms of size and colour and be able to detect them in the ambient conditions where they are searching. This will be practised in the search area by placing an item such as a rucksack to represent what they are looking for and will help in the detection process. If they move away from the rucksack they will be able to determine the maximum distance that they can see the object. This is called the *critical distance* for the object in the terrain and ambient conditions where the search is going to be completed. As searchers move along at about half walking pace they are trained to:

- stop at regular intervals to look and listen
- look all around, up, over, under and behind
- focus on the 'sphere of visibility' around them
- be visually vigilant and 'guide' their search efforts
- monitor and assess their search effort and performance.

Trained searchers should be aware of the concepts of critical separation and purposeful wandering, which are now used extensively by search teams. Essentially, critical separation tells searchers how far apart they should be when conducting an area search (often called grid searching) and is illustrated in Figure 13.4.

Critical Separation and Purposeful Wandering

When spaced at critical separation searchers will have a *corridor of responsibility* such that they can see either side only as far as the specified object is detectable, such as the critical distance. Critical separation is twice the critical distance. Each searcher will have a corridor which they will search and be responsible for and they will follow a notional central line along this. Adjacent searchers will have similar corridors to search (see Figure 13.5).

This method is fine as long as the terrain is regular and vegetation generally the same, but that is often not the case. So, within their *corridor of responsibility*, searchers wander to search any bumps or hollows or denser patches of vegetation that might conceal a missing person. Searchers move to either side of their corridor to investigate such features but then always return to the point on the notional central line to resume searching. This is known as *purposeful wandering* and this tactic enhances the chances of detection.

Critical Separation

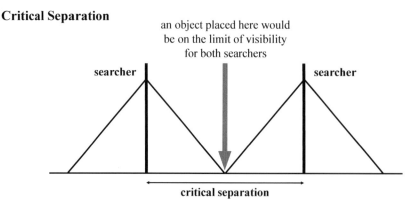

Figure 13.4 Illustration to show the concept of critical separation
Source: TCSR, 2012

Grid Searching in Open Ground

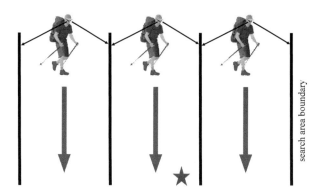

The application of critical separation in practice by line searchers showing their
corridor of responsibility – adapted from Field Search Skills Course, TCSR (2012)

Figure 13.5 The application of critical separation in practice by line searchers showing their
corridor of responsibility
Source: Adapted from Field Search Skills course, TCSR 2012

Conclusion

The initial response phase of a missing person incident is important and thus the response to it by search and rescue resources should be urgent and well organised. The incident can be seen as a problem to be solved and appropriate processes and resources should be used to solve it. Clues as to the whereabouts of the missing person have to be found through good investigation and planning. The Six Step Process provides a structure for contemporary search management concepts, such as missing person behaviour, and is fundamental to the successful outcome of a search for a missing person. It provides structure and organisation to an uncertain situation.

Acknowledgements

The authors would like to thank Naomi Eales for her contribution and assistance in explaining iFIND. All illustrations in this chapter were developed by Carl Hamilton of the Centre for Search Research, are original, and are the copyright of the Centre for Search Research (TCSR). They are taken from TCSR's course materials: *Managing the Initial Response to a SAR Incident* and *Field Skills: A Practical Teaching Course* – see www.search research.org.uk.

Notes

1 The police service coordinates land-based SAR operations including the inland aspects of those incidents that originate at sea or in the air and provides coordination of all emergency services and other authorities where appropriate. In coastal locations and a number of inland waterways, the Maritime and Coastguard Agency may be the agency receiving the first notification.
2 The Police National Search Centre sits within the UK College of Policing. It is the only service provider approved by the National Police Chiefs Council (NPCC, previously ACPO) to deliver training in search and has over 30 years of experience in developing and delivering search training to UK and other law enforcement agencies.
3 The Centre for Search Research carries out research and training in areas relating to searching for lost and missing persons: www.searchresearch.org.uk.

References

ACPO (2010). *Guidance on the Management, Recording and Investigation of Missing Persons* (2nd edition). London: NPIA.
ACPO (2013). *Interim Guidance on the Management, Recording and Investigation of Missing Persons*. London: College of Policing.
College of Policing (2012). *Police Search Management. Missing Persons*. London: College of Policing.
Gibb, G. and Woolnough, P. (2007). *Missing Persons: Understanding, Planning, Responding*. Aberdeen: Grampian Police Headquarters. www.searchresearch.org.uk.
Maritime and Coastguard Agency (2008). *Search and Rescue Framework for the United Kingdom of Great Britain and Northern Ireland*. London: Crown Printers.
Perkins, D., Roberts, P. and Feeney, G. (2011). *The UK Missing Person Behaviour Study*. August 2011. The Centre for Search Research. www.searchresearch.org.uk/www/ukmpbs/current_report.
TCSR (2012). Field search skills course. The Centre for Search Research. www.searchresearch.org.uk/www/training_courses/.

14

Risk Assessment

Naomi Eales

Various publications inform us that the term risk entered our vocabulary in the 17th century (Breakwell, 2014; Kemshall, 2003) and was associated with definitions like 'peril' and 'danger'. Kemshall (2003) goes on to explain the usage of the term risk was also associated with gambling in terms of 'taking a chance'. It is easy to see how this transformed into mathematical models of probabilities and associated statistical analysis to quantify risk and harm which became so favoured in the commercial world, particularly the insurance industry, where risk calculations were later extended to people.

From the police perspective, risk assessment of missing persons is an important topic as it provides the basis for how cases are prioritised and how resources are allocated. This chapter will examine the current process of risk assessment in missing person investigations and the challenges that police face. The chapter will also highlight areas where future research activities will assist in developing better predictors of risk and improving early classification of risk.

Risk is inherent in everything we do on a daily basis and we are largely unaware of our behaviour in minimising many of those risks in our environment. Risk is defined as 'a situation that could be dangerous or have an undesirable outcome' as well as 'a person or thing regarded as a likely source of danger or harm' (Waite, 2007). The Health and Safety Executive defines risk as:

> the likelihood that a hazard will actually cause its adverse effect, together with a measure of the effect … for example, the annual risk of a worker in Great Britain experiencing a fatal accident (effect) at work (hazard) is less than one in 100,000 (likelihood).

Although the Health and Safety Executive provides information and guidance for workplace safety in the UK, their definition provides the key elements of the risk construct, which are reiterated by Carson and Bain (2008), such as harm (effect), uncertainty (hazard) and likelihood.

Risk Assessment

Risk assessment is a method to describe the probability of a specific event occurring in a given situation as well as making a judgement regarding the severity of that event. In any decision-making situation, risk assessment will form an integral element of that process. As such, consideration needs to be given to the likelihood of harm if no action is taken as well as looking at the risks that would remain if certain actions were taken (National Research Council, 2008).

Risk assessment and management are complex processes for three main reasons (Haimes, 2005). First, there is the uncertainty of decisions being made at a time when information is often unavailable, illustrating that timeliness is one of the key issues of risk assessment. Second, the decisions will necessitate the inclusion of demands from a multidisciplinary environment. And thirdly, there will be a need to make a trade-off between competing costs and benefits without assigning undue weight to any of the risk variables.

To increase our understanding of risk, it is perhaps worthwhile making a mention of risk factors, which are frequently described in terms of being static and dynamic. As the name suggests, static factors are those which cannot be changed or are not amenable to intervention, for example age and historical events. Dynamic risk factors are those which are potentially changeable and can fluctuate over short periods of time, for example substance abuse, associates and health. Oftentimes the effects of static and dynamic risks can be mitigated by protective factors which enable a person to be more resilient at times of stress. These can come from the person themselves in terms of coping strategies and self-esteem, families by way of support and boundary setting, or community by way of safe neighbourhoods (Vanderbilt-Adriance and Shaw, 2008).

Risk Generations

In many forensic settings, there have been efforts to improve decision making and, as a result, a body of literature on risk assessment instruments has emerged. A popular view of these can be taken by looking at risk generations (Bonta, 1996).

First generation is unstructured clinical assessment where the decision maker or clinician formulates a judgement based on their knowledge and experience. This approach has been critiqued as 'informal' and 'subjective' (Grove and Meehl, 1996) and lacking interrater reliability (Singh et al., 2011). The structured professional judgement is described as a variation of this first-generation assessment method according to Andrews et al. (2006).

Second generation is actuarial risk assessment. The decision maker arrives at a judgement using an evidence-informed tool based on static factors. This numerical approach assigns values to risk variables associated with the area of interest, such as reoffending, violence and child abuse, to arrive at a probability of some outcome. This approach has been described as 'consistent' (Kemshall, 2003), 'formal' (Grove and Meehl, 1996) and 'atheoretical' (Andrews et al., 2006). Whilst this method has been considered an improvement, especially in interrater reliability, to the first-generation approaches (Grove and Meehl, 1996), the actuarial approach has also been criticised for its 'rigidity and lack of sensitivity to change' (Douglas et al., 2003).

Third-generation assessment tools aimed to 'individualise risk' (Scottish Centre for Crime and Justice Research, 2007). This type of assessment is described as being empirically based, inclusive of dynamic risk items (also referred to as criminogenic needs) and theoretically informed (Andrews et al., 2006).

Fourth-generation risk tools aim to link predicted behaviour and a wider range of dynamic factors with outcomes following treatment and is frequently referred to as the Risk Need Responsivity (RNR) model (Bonta and Andrews, 2007).

This generation approach to examining assessment methods is useful to show how risk tools have developed over recent decades. There are a wide variety of tools addressing violent behaviour, sexual violence, and sexual offending as well as tools for examining children and young offenders, to name but a few. Risk assessment tools have been evaluated on several criteria:

- Validation history, such as predictive validity or usefulness for assessment and management of risk of harm to others.
- Their foundation in evidence.
- Consistency between users (interrater reliability).
- Predictive power, or in other words how sensitive it is at predicting whether a person will reoffend or behave in a certain undesirable way.
- Their ability to identify risk factors.

This examination process is useful to consider when exploring alternatives to existing risk systems.

Risk Assessment in Relation to Missing Persons

Historically, the basis of risk assessment for missing persons was based upon their categorisation. The Council of Europe (1979) recommendation and explanatory memorandum categorised missing persons into four main groups: minors, persons disappearing under suspicious circumstances, victims of accidents, and persons unable to provide for their own needs physically, mentally or due to poverty. This classification system assisted UK police to define what it termed 'vulnerable' missing persons in 1987 and was defined as:

(a) all persons under 18 years of age.
(b) persons over 18 years of age who suffer from epilepsy, diabetes or amnesia, or who have suicidal tendencies or some other special feature which makes it desirable to have them on record without delay.
(c) persons who are 65 years of age or over.
(d) informal mental patients who are reported by next of kin, relatives or neighbours.
(e) persons whose disappearance gives reason for suspecting that some harm may befall them.

(Police Gazette, 25 November 1987)

In 1994, the first UK national unit for missing persons was established within the Metropolitan Police (Police National Missing Persons Bureau, PNMPB) and these five classifications of 'vulnerable' were continued with two further groups added: UK residents missing abroad and foreign nationals missing in the UK (Home Office, 1994).

This method of classifying missing persons was adopted by many forces, but not all, and perhaps provides an early indication of risk where cases could be prioritised into urgent and nonurgent cases thus enabling police resources to be allocated appropriately. Newiss and Webb (1999) argued that the classification of 'vulnerable' did not provide any clear indications of the particular risk facing the missing person or the justification for concern by police. Furthermore, they suggested future research should examine the risks in terms of combinations of factors such as individual characteristics as well as the circumstances under which they went missing and the person reporting them missing.

This suggestion was examined by Tarling and Burrows (2004) who researched types of missing people and their outcomes to highlight some of the challenges for any risk assessment model. They found a great deal of variety and complexity within the cases examined in terms of reasons for going missing, circumstances whilst missing, demographics and outcomes. Attempts were made to classify in terms of gender, age, marital status, employment, where they missing from as well as who had reported them missing.

None of these characteristics served as a particularly useful classification system, with often the results of 'age' (teenagers form one of the highest population groups) skewing the results of others, such as marital status where there would be a higher proportion of single people reflected. The outcomes were classified initially in four ways: 'not traced', 'deceased', 'seriously injured or in poor health' and 'found safe and well'. The majority (96 per cent) were found safe and well. The researchers also looked at the length of time missing and found that the majority (76 per cent) of missing persons were located or returned within two days and 92 per cent within one week. Once again this highlights the difficulty of identifying those cases which may be at greater risk than others.

The location of where the missing person was found did not provide any particular insight into the risk of a missing person, with almost half returning to the place they were missing from. Tarling and Burrows also looked at 132 'problem cases' in an attempt to classify missing person incidents. These were made up of missing persons who were not found (n = 10), were not safe and well when located (n = 29), who had been missing for more than a year (n = 30) and 63 incidents which were deemed 'problematic' by officers within the Metropolitan Police Service boroughs. The breakdown consisted of a mixture of lifestyle factors (involved in prostitution), outcomes (such as suicide) and circumstances (such as escaping from financial problems). The researchers concluded that the 'problem' incidents, like the nonproblem cases, reflected a wide variety of situations, circumstances and outcomes which were difficult to categorise. This study highlights the complexity of missing and illustrates the difficulties of classifying this phenomenon, especially on the basis of a single variable type.

The classification method of vulnerable and not vulnerable was followed by a more actuarial approach. A method was devised to weight each of the risk factors so that a missing person would be given a score relating to the risk variables they hit. The risk matrix was split into two parts. Part one dealt with personal circumstances and included factors related to age, for example 'ten years old or under', whether on a 'child at risk' register, their need for essential medication, their physical ability to interact with the environment, mental illness, and whether they were alcohol or drug dependent. Each of these factors was awarded a single score or weighting (such as over 65 years equals 6 points) or could be judged on a scale (for example, mental illness was scored on a scale between 10 and 15).

Part two examined the circumstances of disappearance and included factors such as 'out of character behaviour', which was awarded a weighting of 16, or 'inclement weather conditions', which had a weighting of 4. The score of the missing person would be added together and result in an indication of risk level. A score exceeding 20 would be deemed high risk and any below 12 would be classed as low risk. The score sheet provided an opportunity to add information regarding 'other factors' and this could be used to adjust the level of risk assessment as the officer felt appropriate.

The major problem with this method was that it created too many incorrectly classified cases (Hedges, 2002; Schouten and van den Eshof, 2006). Even from the examples provided above it can be seen that a person's score could quickly reach the amount required to assess the case as high risk. In addition, this method was not evidence based but rather the amalgamation of police officers' knowledge of missing persons, albeit they were experienced in missing person investigations.

This actuarial approach was followed by the current assessment method which utilises three grades of risk: 'high', 'medium' and 'low', each having a specific explanation or definition and each prompting varying operational activity as well as deployment of resources. An initial assessment takes place at the time the missing person is reported. The call handler will gather basic information about the missing person, for example name, age, description, location missing from and circumstances of going missing. In addition, a set of risk questions will be asked to determine whether the missing person is at risk to themselves or to others. The responses to these questions will ascertain whether the person is 'missing' or 'absent'.

It is prudent to make a brief mention of the 'absent' category here, although this is likely to have been mentioned elsewhere in this volume. An 'absent' person is described as 'a person not at a place where they are expected or required to be and there is no apparent risk' (ACPO/ACPOS, 2013). The inclusion of an 'absent' category came about as result of the Reducing Bureaucracy programme initiated by the Home Office and ACPO (now the National Police Chiefs' Council). The rationale for this additional category was for the police response to be proportionate to the level of perceived risk of each case rather than responding to all reports, regardless of the risk. This new categorisation was piloted in three forces (Greater Manchester, Staffordshire and the West Midlands) for a three-month period in 2011. The call handlers in the three sites were requested to monitor the newly categorised 'absent' incidents and to not deploy an immediate police response. If any information was received in relation to an 'absent' case to suggest any risk to the missing individual, then the categorisation could be altered to 'missing person' status thus enabling an appropriate response. An evaluation of the scheme was carried out by the College of Policing (2013) which found:

> promising qualitative evidence of the pilot having achieved its primary aim – to make the initial police response to missing person reports more proportionate to risk. It was thought – as a side benefit – that a more proportionate approach might also help free up police capacity. The evaluation found consistent evidence of the pilot having achieved this secondary aim.

As mentioned previously, if a person is classified as a missing person a risk grade is awarded to the incident at the point of the initial reporting. An extract taken from the Authorised Professional Practice (ACPO/NPIA, 2010) document on Missing Persons provides the definitions of risk categories and suggested police response, as shown in Table 14.1.

Once a person is classified as a missing person, a 'full' missing person report will be taken from the informant reporting someone missing. The reporting form includes a set of approximately 20 risk questions and is used to assess a person's risk of harm either to themselves or others. This may alter the risk grade taken at the point of initial contact. The risk grade is reviewed at regular intervals throughout an investigation as further intelligence is received.

Key Challenges of the Existing System

There are a number of key challenges of the current system, the first being the sheer volume of cases. The NCA UK Missing Persons Bureau reports an annual figure of 306,000 missing incidents for 2012/13, which equates to over 800 cases a day (NCA, 2014). This illustrates the considerable task police have in deciding which cases require a more focused response. As mentioned previously, the introduction of the 'absent' category is believed to relieve some of the 'workload' so attention to cases is proportionate to risk. However, a related issue may also be the extensive diversity of missing person cases in terms of reasons for going missing and outcome, which leads to considerable difficulty when attempting to categorise cases (Tarling and Burrows, 2004). In terms of risk, a missing person case will be categorised as high, medium or low.

Table 14.1 Classification of risk and response

High risk	
The risk posed is immediate and there are substantial grounds for believing that the subject is in danger through their own vulnerability; or may have been the victim of a serious crime; or the risk posed is immediate and there are substantial grounds for believing that the public is in danger.	This category requires the immediate deployment of police resources. A member of the Basic Command Unit senior management team or similar command level must be involved in the examination of initial enquiry lines and approval of appropriate staffing levels. Such cases should lead to the appointment of an Investigating Officer and possibly a Senior Investigating Officer and a Police Search Advisor (PolSA). There should be a press/media strategy and/or close contact with outside agencies. Family support should be put in place. The NCA Missing Persons Bureau should be notified of the case without undue delay. Children's Services should also be notified (only if the person is under 18).
Medium risk	
The risk posed is likely to place the subject in danger or they are a threat to themselves or others.	This category requires an active and measured response by police and other agencies in order to trace the missing person and support the person reporting.
Low risk	
There is no apparent threat of danger to either the subject or the public. Children and young people under 18 years of age should not be included in this classification.	In addition to recording the information on the police national computer, the police will advise the person reporting the disappearance that once all active enquiries have been exhausted, the case will be deferred to a regular review pending any further information coming to notice. In these cases, they may be filed on the computer system as 'inactive' provided the review process continues.

Source: ACPO, 2010, p. 21

The NCA (2014) report illustrates that 73 per cent of cases are classified as medium risk with 13 per cent of cases each being classified as high and low. Are three categories enough or too many? Considering the variety of cases, there are likely to be profound differences between the risk factors for those classified as medium, which calls into question whether this should be split into possibly 'medium high' and 'medium low'. An alternative to increasing the number of risk categories could be reducing it to two, with perhaps just 'standard' and high risk to further simplify the classification.

The Dutch police operate two classification systems (low and high) and have demonstrated that 35 per cent of cases will be graded as high risk, with approximately 90 per cent of those included to be 'actual high risk', with case outcomes demonstrating only 5 per cent were a real high risk (Schouten and van den Eshof, 2006).

In the current system, risk and operational activity are strongly linked and only certain resources are available dependent upon the classification of the incident. There are some possible dangers with this approach in terms of how they may influence each other, particularly when weighted against the volume of cases. When resources are minimised, such as annual leave, night shifts and sickness, forces are at risk of making classifications to reflect reduced capability in order to manage the workload. This can ultimately put the force at risk if someone is inappropriately assessed and comes to harm.

Alternatively, some incidents potentially could be awarded a higher level of assessment in order to make use of extra resources available to that category, for example financial checks or telecommunications. Access to these resources may enable a missing person to be located quicker than through other channels of enquiry. With competing demands on officers' time and limits to the number of enquiries that can be made there exists a further challenge from the use of the low-risk category where a reduced response is accepted. There is a danger of interpreting this as 'low risk means no risk', which once again could potentially put a police force in jeopardy if this is inappropriately used.

Consistency at a number of levels is also a challenge for risk assessment. At officer level there is potential for inconsistency between investigators in how missing persons are classified. Despite the existence of the current risk assessment system, officers involved in the process are still required to use their professional judgement (Hayden and Goodship, 2013). In the Learning the Lessons bulletins, the Independent Police Complaint Commissioner (2009) has provided instances where risk has not been properly recognised. An extract from Bulletin 7 (June 2009) illustrates this:

> All staff need to be equipped to recognise and act on risk: a man hanged himself after a 'high priority' call was downgraded without any check of the PNC or other intelligence; the lack of a single electronic record for enquiries and reasoned risk assessments can hamper decisions about risk in a missing person investigation; when an elderly man went missing from hospital, grading it on the computer as 'concern for safety' did not include a prompt to assess risk as 'missing person' would have done.

In recognition of the benefits of multiagency working there is likely to be an inconsistency of what is understood by the term 'risk' between the different parties involved. Meetings are conducted between police, local authority, voluntary organisations, and health and education professionals to discuss specific individuals who have a repeated pattern of missing. It would be beneficial to all parties for there to be mutually understood terms and definitions to ensure the best communication possible.

Recording of information can also test the current system in terms of adequacy and accuracy. For some forces a case may pass from officer to officer as shifts change therefore it is key that all information is recorded, especially for when risk reviews need to be carried out. There can be additional issues dependent upon the system/s the missing person investigation is being run on. For some this will be on a dedicated case management system and allow for the available information to be held in one place, thus making a review easier. However, there are others which may operate using both the Command and Control system as well as a dedicated missing person system thus requiring an officer to consult with both to base their review. Regardless of where the information is held, the quality of the information is key to enabling a senior officer to assess the information available and be aware of all facts to determine the correct classification for that missing person.

A further challenge to the current approach is training. There is no formal training for risk assessing missing persons. However, there is guidance (ACPO, 2013; College of Policing, 2015), and forces have a version of this adapted to their police area. In this chapter, reference has been made to risk in terms of harm which can be misunderstood, particularly by those who are inexperienced in this area. Harm can mean many things over and above the obvious, and may not always be immediately apparent. Recent news stories have highlighted the extent and prevalence of child sexual exploitation which, in the arena of missing, may only have an indicator of someone who goes missing regularly for short periods of time. The inherent 'silence' of the victim may make this type of harm difficult to identify unless an officer is very experienced. Other forms of harm may stem from human trafficking, domestic servitude and forced labour. Better understanding of the breadth that harm may manifest needs to be better understood through training.

A final challenge affecting risk assessment is the lack of evidence-informed research in the area. A current drive within academia is for a greater practical application of research and to identify 'what works'. The study of missing persons has historically received very little attention; however, this is now changing and an increasing amount of research is now being published.

One of the key areas which warrants further investigation is that of risk variables. This is an area which can impact the number and quality of risk questions asked. The national reporting form includes a list of 21 questions which have been adopted by many forces as part of their standard practice. Interestingly, the NCA UK Missing Persons Bureau recently collated all the risk factor questions asked by forces, which summed to more than 80 different questions. Naturally, some forces will have questions relating specifically to their area, for example their geography to reflect the popularity of outdoor pursuits such as hiking or skiing.

In view of the volume of cases it would be unreasonable to expect a questionnaire of this length to form the basis of a risk questionnaire for every case. Furthermore in that list of 20 questions, some could be awarded more weight than others when determining risk. There are instances where the only indicator a person is at risk is that their behaviour is 'out of character' and how this will be evident is assessed on a case-by-case basis.

A more pragmatic solution needs to be found and this needs to be based upon evidence. A study by Newiss (2011) looked at fatal disappearances and examined a number of police reported and nonpolice reported (reported to the charity Missing People) cases. A number of 'indicators of vulnerability' were examined, such as schizophrenia, dementia, vulnerable profession and divorce/family breakdown, which were then grouped into 'types' as circumstance-, lifestyle- or health-related. This enabled Newiss (2011) to examine the missing person incidents by both the number of indicators present as well as by type; for example, 11 per cent of cases had two indicators which were lifestyle-related. This approach may form a more useful basis upon which to base a risk framework.

The challenges presented above provide ideal opportunities for further enquiry. An examination of those incidents graded as medium risk to determine any perceived differences could add to discussions and possible decisions around the number of useful categories for classifying risk. The provided example of the Dutch police and its use of two categories is a useful illustration where an alternative approach appears to work. In particular, it would be useful to explore further the amalgamation of low and medium risk and whether this improves the response for low-risk cases or whether this negatively impacts those graded as medium. Examination of how other countries adopt risk classification could yield further material for the discussion.

For practitioners, it is important to identify training needs to better assist those involved at all levels. Additionally, how missing person investigations are 'staffed' can impact how well risk assessments are carried out. For some police areas there may be a dedicated team who benefit from experience and expertise to manage and assess cases; however, for others this may not be so. Therefore, it is important to ascertain how such forces can best be supported. Guidance and best practice documents are available and there may be a need to identify better ways to disseminate information to ensure that officers are as well informed as they can be.

Conclusion

This chapter provides an overview of risk and risk assessment processes within the arena of police-reported missing person cases. It highlights implications for both operational practice and research development with challenges arising from volume of cases, variety of types of incidents inherent within missing, consistency, information sharing, data quality and lack of training.

There is much to be gained and learned from multiagency working, sharing and practice to better understand the nature of missing and to better inform risk assessment processes. Academically, risk assessment can be better informed by evidence-informed research and reference to risk literature within the forensic field. In essence, risk assessment is about good decision making irrespective of outcome.

References

ACPO/NPIA. (2010). *Guidance on the Management, Recording and Investigation of Missing Persons*, 2nd edition. Bramshill: National Policing Improvement Agency.

ACPO/ACPOS (2013). *Manual of Guidance for the Management of Missing Persons*. Ryton: College of Policing.

Andrews, D. A., Bonta, J. and Wormith, J. S. (2006). The recent past and near future of risk and/or need assessment. *Crime and Delinquency*, 52(1): 7.

Bonta, J. (1996). Risk–needs assessment and treatment. In A. T. Harland (ed.), *Choosing Correctional Options that Work: Defining the Demand and Evaluating the Supply* (pp. 18–32). Thousand Oaks, CA: Sage.

Bonta, J. and Andrews, D. A. (2007). Risk need responsivity model for offender assessment and rehabilitation. *Rehabilitation*, 6: 1–22.

Breakwell, G. M. (2014). *The Psychology of Risk*. Cambridge University Press.

Carson, D. and Bain, A. (2008). *Professional Risk and Working with People: Decision Making in Health, Social Care and Criminal Justice*. London: Jessica Kingsley Publishers.

College of Policing (2013). *Risk, Bureaucracy and Missing Persons: An evaluation of a New Approach to the Initial Response* [online]. http://whatworks.college.police.uk/Research/Documents/Missing_persons_PUBLICATION_PQ.pdf#search=missing per cent20persons (accessed 25 August 2015).

College of Policing (2015). *Assessment (consultation)* [online]. www.app.college.police.uk/consultation/missing-persons-consultation/assessment-consultation/ (accessed 25 August 2015).

Council of Europe. (1979). *Search for Missing Persons*: Recommendation No. R (79) 6 and Explanatory Memorandum. Strasbourg.

Douglas, K. S., Ogloff, J. R. and Hart, S. D. (2003). Evaluation of a model of violence risk assessment among forensic psychiatric patients. *Psychiatric Services*, 54(10): 1372–1379.

Grove, W. M. and Meehl, P. E. (1996). Comparative efficiency of informal (subjective, impressionistic) and formal (mechanical, algorithmic) prediction procedures: The clinical–statistical controversy. *Psychology, Public Policy, and Law*, 2(2): 293.

Haimes, Y. Y. (2005). *Risk Modeling, Assessment, and Management* (Vol. 40). Hoboken, NJ: John Wiley and Sons.

Hayden, C. and Goodship, J. (2013). Children reported 'missing' to the police: Is it possible to 'risk assess' every incident? *British Journal of Social Work*, 43(6): 1–17.

Health and Safety Executive [online]. www.hse.gov.uk/risk/theory/alarpglance.htm (accessed 25 August 2015).

Hedges, C. (2002). *Missing You Already: A Guide to the Investigation of Missing Persons*. London: Home Office.

Home Office (1994). *Circular 12/1994*. London: HMSO.

Independent Police Complaint Commissioner (2009). *Learning the Lessons; Bulletin 7*. Sale: Independent Police Complaints Commission.

Kemshall, H. (2003). *Understanding Risk in Criminal Justice*. Maidenhead: Open University Press.

National Research Council (2008). *Science and Decisions: Advancing Risk Assessment*. Washington DC, USA: National Academies Press.

NCA (2014). *Missing Persons: Data and Analysis 2012/2013*. London: National Crime Agency.

Newiss, G. (2011). *Learning from Fatal Disappearances*. London: Missing People.

Newiss, G. and Webb, B. (1999). *Missing Presumed...?: The Police Response To Missing Persons*. Home Office, Policing and Reducing Crime Unit, Research, Development and Statistics Directorate.

Police Gazette (1987). Supplement to Police Gazette, November 25, 1987.

Schouten, S. A., and van den Eshof, P. (2006). *Police Investigations of Missing Persons*. Netherlands Police Agency/National Criminal Intelligence Department, in cooperation with the Utrecht University.

Scottish Centre for Crime and Justice Research (2007). *Research and Practice in Risk Assessment and Risk Management of Children and Young People Engaging in Offending Behaviours*. Glasgow: Risk Management Authority Research.

Singh, J. P., Grann, M. and Fazel, S. (2011). A comparative study of violence risk assessment tools: A systematic review and metaregression analysis of 68 studies involving 25,980 participants. *Clinical Psychology Review*, 31(3): 499–513.

Tarling, R. and Burrows, J. (2004). The nature and outcome of going missing: The challenge of developing effective risk assessment procedures. *International Journal of Police Science and Management*, 6(1): 16–26.

Vanderbilt-Adriance, E. and Shaw, D. S. (2008). Conceptualizing and reevaluating resilience across levels of risk, time, and domains of competence. *Clinical Child and Family Psychology Review*, 11(1–2): 30–58.

Waite, M. (ed.) (2007). *Oxford Dictionary and Thesaurus*. Oxford: Oxford University Press.

15

Cold Case Investigation

Louise Vesely-Shore and Jane Birkett

The aim of this chapter is to provide an overview of the importance of conducting cold case reviews for missing person cases. It touches on the procedures in the UK, giving an idea of some of the good practice that is in place to ensure all relevant opportunities are progressed to resolve these cases, and then identifies some of the limitations and areas where further research could aid the search.

The mystery of missing person cases and unidentified human remains sparks intrigue among both professionals and the public, with protracted cases causing frustration and often resource-intensive enquiries. Cases that seem intractable and for which future reviews are conducted are commonly known as 'cold case' investigations, or a status more locally (prereview) known as 'inactive, 'filed' or 'historic'. There is no approved definition of a 'cold case' in the UK or a set point in time when an investigation will go 'cold'. It is largely accepted that a case will become cold when all practical leads in an investigation have been exhausted and the Senior Investigating Officer considers there is nothing further that can be progressed in the investigation at that time. Missing person cases can be compared to other police investigations, such as murder and stranger rape, in that they can become dormant for many years pending additional information coming to light. This is not an unusual element of policing today in the UK; however, it can be particularly challenging in missing persons cases.

The term 'cold case' appears to have come to the UK from the US in the early 1990s[1] and has since received debate, with some arguing that the term is outdated and misleading – for example, when exactly does a case become 'cold'? Is a case that was undiscovered but clearly 'old' due to the state of the human remains already 'cold'? Is a case that is being reviewed regardless of how old the enquiries are no longer 'cold' because it has been 'warmed up'? Despite these questions being posed there currently are no more suitable or commonly known terms to use.

What Is a 'Cold' Missing Person Case?

The term 'cold' is problematic for missing person cases as the incident under scrutiny is often not complete in the same way that a crime such as murder or rape has happened and must now be detected. In a missing person investigation it may not always be obvious whether the person is alive or dead, an aspect which has obvious considerations for the investigation and what enquiries may be relevant. In Western society, it is generally accepted that if an individual is alive it will be difficult for them to remain 'under the radar' for a significant length of time. If the person left with a certain amount of money they may be able to spend days, weeks or months living off this without having to access other funds to support themselves, but will ultimately need to do so, and this will often bring them to the attention of one or more formal organisations, leading to their detection. Therefore, it can be argued that there are always some practical lines of enquiry which can be pursued. However, if an individual is suspected to be dead, whether due to misadventure, suicide or the actions of a third party, then the passage of time is unlikely to 'change' the situation and the case is more like that of a traditional cold crime investigation. Therefore the assessment undertaken by the investigating officers as to the likely reason for the disappearance is likely to influence the determination of when the case 'goes cold'.

There is also the added complication of distinguishing wanted individuals from missing individuals. Such a distinction can be important as the nature and level of enquiries for either will differ. Where an individual is sought by the police they may be actively trying to avoid coming to the attention of the authorities. Whilst a missing person is unlikely to expend significant efforts to avoid being located, a wanted person may do so, including employing an alternative identity. This would make traditional enquiries utilising the person's name unlikely to locate them, and attempts such as this are often only detected when the person is stopped in relation to another offence and their fingerprints or DNA, which cannot be changed, are taken. However the two categories are not mutually exclusive, and in some cases it is relevant to treat a wanted individual as a missing person, particularly where it is suspected some harm may have befallen them. Generally, however, unless the individual is sought for a serious offence, little resource will be expended in trying to locate a wanted person, and such wanted/missing person cases may be made 'inactive' sooner than other cases due to this ambiguity over the agency of the person involved.

Outstanding Missing Persons

In England and Wales, around 84 per cent of missing people are found within 48 hours and only 5 per cent remain missing for more than one week, which equates to approximately 10,500 reports (NCA, 2016). These are known as 'open' cases and Tarling and Burrows' (2004) research goes on to suggest that only 1 per cent of missing person cases remain open after one year (and half of these for various reasons were no longer considered actual missing persons enquiries). The UK Missing Persons Bureau, which is part of the National Crime Agency, maintains a database, Hermes, which stores missing reports that are high risk or remain outstanding for 72 hours and contains reports dating back to the mid-1900s. Although the specific number of outstanding cases will vary on a daily basis as forces report new incidents and locate people, there were approximately 5,800 outstanding cases in 2015.[2] Although this is a minute proportion of reported missing person cases, they represent a significant number of families who do not know what happened to their loved one. The term 'living in limbo' was coined by the charity Missing People (Holmes, 2008) and provides a rich account of the emotional turmoil and practical impact that ensues following the disappearance of a loved one. Without cold case reviews and ongoing investigations these families may remain forever in limbo so it is vital that cases do not remain 'cold' and everything possible is done to find their missing person.

Research suggests that adult males, with over-representation from minority ethnic backgrounds, are most likely to be outstanding for more than one year (Newiss, 2005). Equally, Tarling and Burrows (2004) found the majority of long-term missing persons to be adult females, but this can be attributed to immigration matters involving foreign nationals. For example, this frequently involves domestic maids from all over the world being reported by employers and being marked as 'immigration overstayers'. Reasons for some disappearances will often remain a mystery, however disappearances are known to be motivated by suicide, to assume new identities or as a result of crime. Characteristics of each of the different groups of the missing person population may vary considerably, allowing different profiles to be established dependent on the circumstances; however, the long-term absence of the person and reason for their being outstanding typically remain an uncertain entity. In the majority of fatal outcome missing person cases, it is probable that individuals may have committed suicide or been subject to other causes of death, including accidents and misadventure (such as drowning, a fall or dying of exposure), natural causes (such as heart attack or ill health) or the person may have been a victim of violent crime. Studies like Newiss' (1999 and 2005) offer an opportunity for police risk assessments to identify the relative likelihood of certain types of people becoming long-term missing and consequently the appropriate response to be deployed.

Unidentified Cases

Whilst only a very small proportion of missing person cases will result in a fatality (somewhere between 0.2 and 1 per cent of reports depending on the criteria used), each year a small but significant number of people and remains are found which cannot immediately be identified. Although the exact number in which the identity of the person is under question is not known (there is considered to be an underestimate, potentially as a consequence of under-reporting), the very nature of these incidents renders police forces and support agencies under pressure to resolve them.[3]

The UK, being a collection of islands with a vast shoreline, often results in bodies or body parts being found on the coast or in nearby waters. Evidence from the UK Missing Persons Bureau tells us that when people are successfully identified they are not always UK nationals but have ended up on our coastline having travelled through the water from neighbouring European countries. Likewise, the possibility of a number of UK missing persons being located on our neighbours' shores and remaining unidentified as a consequence is just as high. Efforts are made by police and support agencies to resolve such international cases. However, these are fraught with legislative and logistical problems, often resulting in lengthy delays.

In addition to recording missing person reports, the UK Missing Persons Bureau also records details of unidentified people/body cases which have not been identified after 48 hours. This allows the UK Missing Persons Bureau to manage a national and international reconciliation service between the 'lost and found', typically resulting in a rolling 50 per cent success rate. As with the missing person reports, the UK Missing Persons Bureau holds records of outstanding unidentified cases dating from the 1950s, of which approximately 850 relate to long-term unidentified remains or people found in the UK. An additional 280 relate to cases found abroad which have been notified to the UK through INTERPOL in a bid to assist with identifying them.

In November 2012, the UK Missing Persons Bureau launched its website of outstanding unidentified persons inviting the public to assist in providing information and clues as to their identities.[4] Not all unresolved cases are included on this public forum as publication relies on two conditions: one, that there is something individual about the body/body part (be it a distinguishing tattoo or birth mark or a distinctive item of clothing or jewellery) and, two, that the condition of the body/body part is such that it will not distress the public. Unless deemed appropriate, photographs of the individual/remains will not be shown on the website, and instead images such as artist impressions and photographs of replica possessions or specific features such as tattoos will be used in the hope that it will trigger someone's memory.

Cold Case Reviews

In both the UK and the US, cold case reviews have become increasingly common and generally involve undetected murders or serious sexual offences (Innes and Clarke, 2009). In the UK, these reviews have largely been energised by the advancements in forensic science, enabling the reanalysis of old evidence or identification of new evidence. It was recognised that for a relatively small investment previously undetected crimes could be solved, and this led the UK government to actively promote such work through the provision of central funding for cases meeting set criteria. The first such initiative focused only on stranger rapes (known as Operation Advance) but was later expanded to include undetected murders (Operation Stealth) and has resulted in some high-profile successes, such as the 2010 conviction of Paul Stewart Hutchinson for the 1983 murder of Collete Aram (Allsop, 2013).

Whilst similar forensic work may be a focus for cold case reviews of unidentified remains, cold case missing person investigations do not generally afford the same forensic possibilities for advancement, and as such have not to date received the same sort of national review. The aim for forensic reviews of missing person cases also differs, as in many instances the driver is to obtain a DNA profile for the missing person in order to be able to identify any bodies or remains located, rather than to identify a possible suspect. Such work is less likely to be required for recent cases due to the increasing recognition of the value in obtaining such samples during the early stages of a missing person investigation, which since 2009 has been a statutory requirement for forces. Cold case reviews of missing person investigations therefore generally require a different focus, with greater emphasis on the use of passive data sources, such as telephone or financial enquiries, or revisiting witnesses to determine more about the individual's lifestyle.

The Importance of Resolution

Given the significant number of current cases UK forces are managing, and the current limitations on police force budgets due to the economic situation, it is important to highlight the value in undertaking reviews of 'cold' cases. Whilst the justification for doing so has not been explored for missing person cases specifically, Allsop (2013) posited four reasons police cite for undertaking cold case (crime) reviews, which include:

1 For victims and families.
2 For justice.
3 For prevention of further crime.
4 Because we can.

Whilst not all missing person cases will involve a crime, and therefore do not need to be investigated in order bring someone to justice and/or to prevent further crimes, the impact of having a missing loved one should not be underestimated, and the commitment to review missing and unidentified cases in order to potentially resolve the mystery for those left behind is often the motivating factor behind such reviews. The latter motive is also becoming increasingly more influential, as the ability to access multitudes of information about individuals without leaving the office becomes ever greater and the opportunities to resolve these cases increase. There is also increasing recognition of the vulnerability of some of the individuals previously treated as low-risk missing persons (such as those with transient lifestyles) and growing concern that some of these individuals who may have 'lost contact' with family have in fact been murdered. A recent example is that of Rebecca Godden–Edwards, whose remains were only found after the murderer of another high-profile missing person (Sian O'Callaghan) led police to where she had been buried.[5]

The UK has seen a rise in police forces conducting proactive cold case reviews of both missing and unidentified cases in recent years with the advent of the UK Missing Persons Bureau's 'Operation Kharon'[6] in 2009. This initiative involved the UK Missing Persons Bureau collaborating with forces specifically in relation to historic unidentified bodies and has accomplished the resolution of 15 cases.

Although the resource implication for long-term and cold case reviews in missing person and unidentified body cases is large, the benefits can be seen too (however, there is little evidence to suggest which actually outweighs the other). Nevertheless, innovations in forensic science and technology are proving invaluable but, potentially more importantly, successes can stimulate public confidence and satisfaction in policing.

When Should a Review Take Place?

The police response must not only be open and transparent with 'good family police liaison' (Parr and Stevenson, 2013) but also be proportionate to the established risk assessment and likely outcome. This is based on background knowledge of the missing person, empirical evidence and professional expertise. Such assessments remain dynamic throughout the duration of the police investigation of the missing incident; however, there is no mandated time within which the police are required to review cases, often resulting in an inconsistent police response. National guidance for the police suggests that,

> Reviews take place every twenty eight days for the first three months, then at six monthly and twelve monthly intervals, then annually thereafter. Should any significant information come to light, this should trigger an immediate review.[7]

What this 'review' actually entails is somewhat open to interpretation and often reliant on the availability of resources.

In 1999 Newiss carried out research into the police response in the UK to missing persons. The report found that there was an inconsistent approach to case reviews across police forces and it recommended that 'each force should agree the necessary personnel, timing and terms of reference for the effective review of missing person reports. The inclusion of members of the Criminal Investigation Department is recommended.' UK policing has heeded this advice and now has more formal guidance in place to assist in the planning and execution of cold case reviews. It has a more formal and accountable recording and management process that stores decisions and policy logs that will allow a holistic and systematic review should the investigation require reopening.

With the introduction of dedicated missing person databases in many police forces, the means for managing and reviewing missing person investigations is becoming more regulated and standardised. However, not all forces have undertaken a review process to ensure all historic missing persons reported prior to the introduction of their system have been recorded, and in many cases this may only be done following a family member coming forward to ask about what has happened with the case.

Some missing person cases may become the subject of review as part of a cold unidentified case review. Operation Kharon is one such example; Operation Monton is another, where hundreds of missing women were investigated as a result of Norfolk Police undertaking a review into the unidentified remains of a young woman which were found near Swaffham in 1974.

Operation Monton

On 27 August 1974, the body of a woman believed to be in her twenties was found on farmland near Cockley Cley, Swaffham, Norfolk. Her head had been cut off, her hands were bound with string and her body was badly decomposed. In 2008, Norfolk police reopened the case and undertook the task of collating a list of all missing women last seen in the early 1970s. Over 500 names were put forward, and the investigating team undertook various checks to trace/eliminate them from the enquiry. The work completed by the team led to over 470 women being eliminated from the enquiry, nearly 60 per cent of whom were traced alive and well and a further 10 per cent were established as alive after they had been reported missing, although they had subsequently died.[8]

What Is Involved in a Review?

It is standard practice to begin the process by undertaking a comprehensive review of the entire original case file. Generally, this will aim to quality assure the actions already completed and identify any new or outstanding lines of enquiry which may be considered in order to ensure that all opportunities to resolve the case have been exploited (Vesely and Lloyd-Evans, 2012). The review may identify no further actions which can feasibly be undertaken, and may lead to the case being refiled with a new review date set in due course. Alternatively, some or all of the new lines of enquiry may be assigned to an officer or a team to complete, depending on the nature of the case and the scale of the enquiries. However, it is important to highlight that, even where a review of a case has identified additional actions, the police force involved may delay undertaking some or all of these based on an assessment of the resources required and those currently available to do the work.

Possible Lines of Enquiry in Cold Case Missing Person Reviews

As indicated above, due to the slightly unusual ongoing nature of missing person investigations, it is likely that some further actions will be identified and completed in order to ensure the person has been found unidentified or come to the attention of authorities without the police being made aware. Whilst, as with any investigation, the relevance of any enquiry will be dependent on the case circumstances, there are a number of actions which are likely to be relevant and beneficial to most missing person case reviews.

Public Databases

Particularly for very long-term cases where the amount of original documentation may be limited, researching the family tree of the missing person can be an important first step. There are a number of databases publicly available for a relatively minimal subscription, such as Ancestry, Findmypast and ScotlandsPeople, which provide access to the register of births, deaths and marriages. Searches of these databases may indicate if the individual has married/remarried, given birth or even died. It should be noted that the registers for England and Wales, Scotland and Northern Ireland are not held within one database, and therefore checks on multiple databases may be required in order to ensure nothing is missed.

Unfortunately, it is possible that an individual may die in nonsuspicious circumstances some years after last being seen and be formally registered as deceased without the police being informed. For example, in one such case, Wiltshire Police found that a 56-year-old man who had mental health issues and had been reported missing to them in 2005 had subsequently been found in another county in 2006 having died of a heart attack. His death had been recorded as natural and registered with the General Register Office, but there was no reason to investigate his death and therefore it was not realised he was recorded as missing. As a result of a review in 2014, a death certificate was found and subsequent enquiries confirmed the male was the same individual.

Other databases provide access to collections of address data such as the electoral roll and what is referred to as 'consented' data (GB's IQ database). This is personal information about an individual that they have agreed can be shared with third parties (for example, completion of a person's details as part of a consumer survey) and may contain a recent address or phone number for them. In addition to potentially providing a new address or contact number for the missing person, these databases may provide useful contact details for next of kin if the police have since lost touch with them, and can be researched to identify potential witnesses who may know more about the missing person (for example, neighbours of the person who may or may not have been spoken to at the time).

Restricted Databases

With advances in technology, the police now have access to a number of databases which can assist with determining if the person has since come to attention. This includes the Police National Database, which is a national information management system which allows the police service to share, access and search information held by forces at a local level. Although if a missing person comes to the attention of another police force they should inform the investigating force, there are reasons why this may not always occur. It is not uncommon for names to be misspelt, particularly for unusual names, which may result in the force not realising the person is reported missing. It is therefore important that any checks on these systems consider the alternative ways in which the name could be spelt. Additionally, the information may relate to a contact with police prior to the person being reported missing, and may provide further useful information which may suggest further lines of enquiry.

Other such databases which are restricted from public access include databases relating to financial transactions, health service records and benefits/pensions, some of which are directly accessible by appropriately trained members of the police, whilst others require requests for checks to be completed by the owning agency. A challenge for investigators reviewing cold case missing persons is the ambiguity surrounding the disappearance and the need to balance such intrusive investigations in order to determine if someone has come to harm with their right to a private life. Individuals have the right to go missing, and many formal institutions, such as the Department for Work and Pensions and the health service, will only share information if there are sufficient grounds to suggest the person has been the subject of crime. In many missing person investigations this is not the case, but such checks can prove crucial in resolving or progressing the investigation. Applications for such information should be made on a case-by-case basis, with due consideration to the individual's rights. Often a compelling argument can be made, especially if other checks fail to show that the person is alive and well, as this may be indicative that they have come to harm, particularly as time passes.

National Circulations

An important aspect of any review is to ensure that all relevant lines of enquiry have been pursued. For many long-term missing person cases this will involve ensuring that the details are registered in the relevant national databases, including the UK Missing Persons Bureau's database (known as Hermes). It is recommended forces contact the UK Missing Persons Bureau when undertaking a review in order for new checks of any unidentified cases to be completed. Whilst these searches are regularly completed when new unidentified cases are received, the volume of reports and varying levels of information associated with the unidentified cases (especially very decomposed remains) can make such checks challenging, and a new search may highlight matches which may previously have been overlooked or discounted (particularly if new information has been located about the missing persons). The UK Missing Persons Bureau also manages a number of subsidiary databases which aid the identification of individuals should they be found (alive or deceased), and will be able to confirm if relevant samples are held.

National Missing Persons DNA Database

The National Missing Persons DNA Database, formally established in 2010 by the UK Missing Persons Bureau, enables DNA profiles for missing people to be kept separately to those of criminals which are held on the National DNA Database (NDNAD). This ensures that for legal and ethical reasons missing individuals are not linked to any crimes as a result of going missing, and enables DNA profiles from family members to be collected and stored if a sample from the missing person is not available. Any profiles loaded to the National Missing Persons DNA Database are checked against any existing profiles held for unidentified cases, as well as any subsequent profiles submitted, as bodies may be found years after the individual went missing.

Fingerprints

The UK Missing Persons Bureau established a process for retaining fingerprints for missing individuals alongside those from unidentified people/remains for future comparison. Although fingerprints are unlikely to be available from remains that have been deceased for some time and degraded significantly, it can take some time for prints from bodies/people found abroad to be sent to the UK for comparison, and so should be considered even if the person has not been seen for some time.

Dental Records

The UK Missing Persons Bureau maintains a dental index for all missing and unidentified cases, and utilises these to assist with identifying possible matches between cases, which can then be formally reviewed by an experienced forensic odontologist to confirm or eliminate the match.

It may be beneficial to consider re-publicising the case, in an attempt to elicit new information from members of the public. Any decision to do so must consider the potential impact on the family of the missing person and should be discussed with them prior to any media release. The charity Missing People can aid forces with both local and national publicity, and consideration should also be given to circulation of the individual's details in niche publications associated with the person's interests, hobbies or lifestyle.

Outcome of Reviews

The outcome of a review, including any decisions not to pursue further actions, should be discussed with the family of the missing person. Any new information identified as a result of the review should be shared with the UK Missing Persons Bureau, and it is good practice to send a copy of any review report to the UK Missing Persons Bureau. To aid forces, the UK Missing Persons Bureau, in conjunction with South Wales Police, compiled an informative guide to long-term missing person reviews, detailing checklists for officers and investigative suggestions, and proffering advice on 'cold case' reviews of long-term missing persons and unidentified found bodies (Vesely and Lloyd–Evans, 2012).

Limitations

There are two significant limitations which hinder not only cold case reviews of missing persons but also live investigations. The first is the challenge related to balancing an individual's right to a private life with the police's duty to investigate and ensure the individual has not come to harm. Many organisations will refuse to share information which could be crucial to progressing the investigation, and can often lead to officers spending significant time and effort continuing to try to trace individuals without access to relevant information. Such refusals are predicated on the assumption that many of these individuals have chosen to go missing, as is their right. Whilst the significant majority of individuals return or are found quickly, it is not known how many of these long-term cases actually involve individuals who are being exploited/harmed or are in fact the subject of crime, such as Becky Godden-Edwards. Such cases are quite rightly the purport of police investigation, but no research has been completed which can aid investigators with distinguishing these cases from those where the individual has truly chosen to go missing and does not wish to be traced.

Linked to this is the inability for many enquiries to effectively account for individuals who may change their name/utilise a false identity in order to remain missing. Many of the lines of enquiry available to police are reliant on the name and date of birth provided by the individual, and little is known about the means and ease with which individuals may be able to obtain a new identity. In one murder enquiry, the suspect who had been investigated as missing was only traced after he came to police attention under a new identity. Enquiries established that he had turned up at a homeless shelter claiming not to remember who he was. The helpful individuals at the shelter assisted him with getting a new name and National Insurance number so that he could work, not realising they were being duped by a dangerous individual. It is unknown how many other instances of identity fraud like this are undertaken by 'missing' individuals.

Additional Considerations

The emotional impact of undertaking such reviews should not be underestimated. If the family have not been instrumental in initiating the review, careful consideration should be given to how they may react. Whilst some will welcome the review, many may find it difficult to revisit the trauma of the incident and may not be supportive of the review. Where an individual has been missing for many years, it may also be distressing for them to be contacted by police and informed they have been the subject of such an investigation. There will often be reasons why they left in the manner they did, and being contacted may remind them of experiences they had attempted to move on from. Those involved in the review will need to be prepared that some individuals will not want their whereabouts to be disclosed to the family seeking them and will have to respect this decision, which may be extremely difficult for the family to deal with. Support from the charity Missing People may be beneficial in such cases, as they can support both the family and the missing individual and may be able to assist with negotiating contact through their helplines.

Further Research

In recent years there has been greater interest in research related to missing enquiries, and this has begun to touch on the actions and experiences of those who are reported missing. However, to date, limited work has been completed in interviewing those who have returned in order to identify what enquiries by the police may have been effective in tracing them sooner. As indicated, little is known about the avenues open to individuals who wish to establish themselves under a new identity, and research would be welcomed into how people can obtain new details such as NHS numbers and NI numbers, which are needed in order to gain certain benefits. If more were known about these processes, it might be possible to plug any gaps in these systems, as well as inform the work of missing person investigation teams.

Additionally, it would be interesting to explore if there are any consistencies/patterns in the names which people adopt when they create a new identity, as these may be beneficial when undertaking 'proof of life' enquiries with formal agencies, particularly in no body murder enquiries. Whilst experience from Operation Monton showed that many of the married women had reverted to their maiden name after leaving, such observations are only anecdotal, and what proportion does this and whether men would utilise family names in a similar way is currently unknown.

For unidentified remains found, little has been done to investigate the effectiveness of facial reconstructions, and what factors may impact on the likelihood that the image will be sufficiently similar to the person in life to initiate contact from the person's family or friends. It would be interesting to explore whether similar work could be done to age 'regress' the images of unidentified individuals in a similar manner to the work done to age progress long-term missing person images, based upon what is known about the way in which we age.

Acknowledgements

The authors would like to thank the Unsolved Cases Team of Norfolk and Suffolk Major Crime Investigation Team for sharing their experiences and the lessons they learnt trying to identify the unidentified woman found at Cockley Cley, in particular Tony Deacon and Claire Rheinhold. We would also like to thank Martyn Lloyd-Evans from South Wales Police's Review Unit for sharing his insights.

Useful Websites

UK Missing Persons Bureau – for information regarding missing persons in the UK and a list of outstanding unidentified cases: http://missingpersons.police.uk.

Missing People – for details of support available, a list of those currently missing, and research into the nature and impact of going missing: www.missingpeople.org.uk.

College of Policing – for details of UK police procedures when investigating missing or unidentified cases: www.app.college.police.uk/app-cntent/major-investigation-and-public-protection/missing-persons/.

Notes

1 Source: http://criminology.research.southwales.ac.uk/features/cold-case-reviews/.
2 Source: UK Missing Persons Bureau Hermes Database, December 2014.
3 Further reading available in: Mallett, X., Blythe, T. and Berry, R. (eds) (2014). Advances in Forensic Human Identification, *Two Sides of the Same Coin – Missing and Unidentified People*. Florida: CRC Press.
4 http://missingpersons.police.uk/.
5 Further information available at: www.theguardian.com/uk/2012/oct/19/sian-ocallaghan-murder-detective.
6 Op Kharon overview.
7 Further reading available in: Vesely, L. and Lloyd-Evans, M. (2012) 'Reviews of long term missing persons and unidentified found bodies', *The Journal of Homicide and Major Incident Investigation*, 8(1).

8 Further information available at: www.norfolk.police.uk/newsandevents/unsolvedcases/homicide attemptedhomicides/cockleycley1.aspx.

References

Allsop, C. (2013). Motivations, money and modern policing: Accounting for cold case reviews in an age of austerity. *Policing and Society: An International Journal of Research and Policy*, 23(3): 362–375.

Holmes, L. (2008). Living in limbo: The experiences of, and impacts on, the families of missing people. [online] www.missingpeople.org.uk.

Innes, M. and Clarke, A. (2009). Policing the past: Cold case studies, forensic evidence and retroactive social control. *British Journal of Sociology*, 60(3): 544–563.

NCA (2016). *UK Missing Persons Bureau: Missing Persons Data Report 2014/2015*. London: NCA.

Newiss, G. (1999). *Missing Presumed …? The Police Response to Missing Persons* (Police Research Series Paper 114). London: Home Office.

Newiss, G. (2005). A study of the characteristics of outstanding missing persons: Implications for the development of police risk assessment. *Policing and Society*, 15(2): 212–225.

Parr, H. and Stevenson, O. (2013). *Families Living with Absence: Searching for Missing People*. Glasgow: University of Glasgow Press. [online] www.geographiesofmisisngpeople.org.uk.

Tarling, R. and Burrows, J. (2004). The nature and outcome of going missing: The challenge of developing effective risk assessment procedures. *International Journal of Police Science and Management*, 6(1): 16–26.

Vesely, L. and Lloyd-Evans, M. (2012). Reviews of long term missing persons and unidentified found bodies. *The Journal of Homicide and Major Incident Investigation*, 8(1).

16
Missing Abroad

Joe Apps

Introduction

With modern migration patterns, there are large numbers of people going overseas from the UK, some temporarily for study, holiday and business trips and many permanently to work and to retire abroad. A person going missing is often seen as a symptom of something that has gone wrong in someone's life. It is, therefore, inevitable that British citizens will also go missing whilst overseas. As a corollary, it is expected that a large number of foreign citizens will go missing every year whilst in the UK.

Foreign and Commonwealth Office data shows that 3,059 UK citizens went missing while in a foreign country in the five years between 2009 and 2014, an average of 600 people each year (Foreign and Commonwealth Office, 2014). People are reported as missing for a number of reasons, which include leaving home, getting lost, mental health problems or going missing due a third-party intervention, such as cases of extortion, abduction and homicide. Whilst this last category will be referenced in the chapter, it is not the intention to cover criminal enterprises here.

This chapter sets out circumstances in which people go missing, explaining the situation surrounding people who go missing abroad. The chapter describes the key agencies and bodies responsible for searching for missing people and investigating cases and the challenges and restrictions faced when conducting policing enquiries in other countries. British police procedures will also be explained. Also discussed is the support available to families, friends and found missing people from the voluntary sector both here in the UK and abroad. Meeting the expectations of families and friends is a crucial part of the investigative and supportive functions of the state and its third-sector partners and comments on this issue are weaved into the sections of the chapter. Reconstructions of cases and case studies will be used to illustrate work conducted to find and repatriate missing people.

Explaining the Situation

A person going missing can be linked to all aspects of personal, family and business life. It is not something in itself, but rather a symptom of something else affecting a person. People regularly travel abroad to find themselves, to take time for themselves, and in doing so, they may go missing intentionally to avoid some consequence. They may get lost or fall ill whilst trekking, hiking or engaged in other outdoor pursuits. Once they have not arrived at or returned to an agreed location, the person may be reported missing to local law enforcement officers, to consular officials or to a British police force. Families and friends may lose contact with a person and seek to report them as being missing. Most often, lost contact cases are not dealt with by policing agencies here in the UK and referrals to the voluntary sector for support are commonplace. Services may need to be sought from a solicitor or a tracing agency. People who have lost contact with families and friends overseas may seek the assistance of the police abroad. In most cases, it is unlikely that any assistance will be offered for reasons discussed later in this chapter.

Key Agencies and Bodies

Whatever the circumstances of a disappearance, the impact on family and friends can be a deeply traumatic one. Often the impact is exacerbated by long distances, language barriers, legal systems and bureaucracy as well as by differing cultures and policing standards. Within the UK there are many resources available to investigate a disappearance, assist and support family and friends of those missing abroad.

Her Majesty's Government has responsibility for all British citizens wherever they are in the world. On a day-to-day basis the responsibility for safeguarding British citizens abroad is exercised by the Foreign and Commonwealth Office (the Foreign Office). In cases of service personnel and their families the Ministry of Defence undertakes the role.

The Foreign Office contributes a great deal in the search for missing people, in case investigation and in coordinating repatriation of people. Through 'the UK abroad' network of embassies, high commissions and consulates, the Foreign Office is able to act as a very effective central hub to coordinate support agencies. The Foreign Office can be particularly effective on a diplomatic level when challenging relationships in other countries are making investigations and family enquiries difficult to conduct. The Foreign Office leaflet 'Missing Persons Abroad' provides further details of Foreign Office services.[1] The leaflet explains what practical help consular staff members of the Foreign Office are able to provide.

The police in the UK have a responsibility to investigate missing persons abroad.[2] Set out in College of Policing guidance, known as authorised professional practice, are guidelines for police officers investigating disappearances abroad. British policing is assisted in international enquiries by INTERPOL on a worldwide basis. INTERPOL is a contraction of 'international police'. The Schengen Information System and SIRENE network supports cooperation and coordination between law enforcement agencies in the European Union member states. Both the INTERPOL National Central Bureau and the SIRENE Bureau are hosted by the National Crime Agency as part of its International Crime Bureau.[3]

The UK Missing Persons Bureau[4] also plays an important role. It is the UK national and international point of contact for all missing persons and unidentified body cases. The UK Missing Persons Bureau is the centre for information exchange and expertise on missing persons issues. Part of the services it offers is to support police forces with investigations overseas. The UK Missing Persons Bureau has an extensive network of partners in law enforcement and the voluntary sector across Europe and the wider world and uses INTERPOL and Schengen Information System and SIRENE arrangements, as necessary, to conduct investigations with and on behalf of the police.

The UK Missing Persons Bureau operates the national database of missing and found persons or human remains (Hermes) which lists all missing British nationals as well as foreign nationals missing in the UK. The database enables the national and international reconciliation of the 'lost' and the 'found'. The UK Missing Person Bureau's website provides publicity for found persons and bodies as a way of crowdsourcing investigations to identify people and bodies, thus bringing comfort to families missing loved ones.

The UK Missing Persons Bureau also maintains the Missing Persons DNA Database as part of the National DNA Database. DNA profiles of missing persons as well as found bodies are contained on the database to assist the identification of people. Part of IDENT1, the national fingerprint register maintained by the Home Office, is set aside for missing and found persons collections, again to assist the identification of people. A dental index is kept by the UK Missing Persons Bureau for the same purposes.

A voluntary sector organisation, the Lucy Blackman Trust, is able to support missing person investigations overseas. It was designed to fill gaps in family support in missing person episodes and help families and friends understand the limits of police investigations. The Trust is able to provide publicity through social media, translation services and introductions and referrals to specialist support agencies and partners abroad. Further details about the Trust are provided in the section on support to families and friends.

Police Procedures

When a person goes missing overseas, a report will usually be made by family, friends or employer to the local police in the country where the person is missing. Sometimes this is not possible, perhaps because the missing person has been travelling or working abroad unaccompanied by family or friends and a report should be made to the police in the UK where the person is normally resident. The local policing response abroad to missing episodes varies by country and region. In some countries it is difficult to get local police to pay attention to missing adults. Adults may do as they wish. Thus, it is necessary to ensure that local police understand the risk to and vulnerabilities of the person missing.

It is the local police that will conduct any searches for the missing person and conduct an investigation into the disappearance. Local police may request the assistance of the British police but this is rarely done. The capability and capacity of local police is also highly varied across the world. Sophisticated and intensive searches and investigations may not be possible. But many countries have highly trained volunteer search and rescue groups which are used to assist the local police. Developing nations may have limited police resources and be technologically ill-equipped to conduct substantial and necessary enquiries around a missing person. In Europe, missing adult alerts on the Schengen Information System may only be raised when the case is considered high risk, with the missing adult being considered as in need of care and support. INTERPOL messaging may only be used in high-risk missing person cases.

To ensure the best possible police and agency service, it is advised that the person is also reported missing to the police in the UK. This report should be made to the police in the area where the missing person is usually resident. If the person is not a resident of the UK, the report can be made in the area where any extended family is living. The UK Missing Persons Bureau is able to offer support to families when making reports to the British police.

British police cannot travel to a foreign country to assist a local police force or conduct its own investigation into a disappearance without an invitation from the foreign government of that country. With an invitation, permission must be sought from the Home Office under mutual legal assistance arrangements; there can be no UK invasion of sovereign territory.

Families, friends and employers, through the 'UK Abroad', a British High Commission, embassy or consulate in a foreign country, can make immediate enquiries of the local police to establish progress in any investigation. British citizens reported missing to the Foreign Office will have details entered on the Foreign Office global consular system and a desk officer will be allocated to the case at the Foreign Office in London. Across Europe there is a very strong Foreign Office missing persons consular network dealing with the high numbers of missing British people each year.

Given that a missing episode is often an indicator that something has gone wrong in someone's life, any police investigation, at home or abroad, into a missing person should consider the circumstances of the disappearance, the risk to the missing person, witness testimony and, inevitably, whether there is a connection between the disappearance and a crime that has taken place. It is not the intention of this chapter to consider criminal elements to missing episodes. However, the reader will realise that being the victim of crime may lead to a person being reported as missing to the police. Without any fuller detail, crimes may include homicide, kidnap and extortion, abduction, parental child abduction or forced marriage, amongst others. Police investigations will follow all these types of crime allegations. Missing and crime investigations follow the same sort of path, pursue the same sorts of lines of enquiry and are supported in the same way by the Foreign Office and the voluntary sector when they occur abroad.

Case Study: Rebecca Coriam

The Rebecca Coriam case provides an example of a 'missing abroad' investigation. Rebecca, a British national and a crew member of the cruise ship *Disney Wonder*, disappeared in March 2011 when the ship was off the Pacific coast of Mexico. She could not be found on board the cruise ship and despite sea searches by coastguard and navy vessels, Rebecca was still not found. As the *Disney Wonder* is registered in the Bahamas, it fell to the Royal Bahamas Police Force to conduct an investigation. Cheshire Police, the home police service of Rebecca's parents in the UK, was also involved in reviewing the investigation. It is reported that the Disney company forwarded on-board video (CCTV) to the Federal Bureau of Investigation in the US, although the law enforcement body has no jurisdiction on the ship. The Federal Bureau does have authority and competence under American federal law to investigate the disappearance or death of American citizens from vessels anywhere in the world. After Rebecca's disappearance, the British government announced that the Marine Accident Investigation Branch would investigate similar cases, mirroring the American provision, and that international cooperation on investigations would be increased through the International Maritime Organisation. Rebecca's case remains unresolved.

Resolution of Cases

Unresolved cases will always lead to difficulties, but especially so when a person is missing overseas. British police services are frequently asked to intervene with reviews of investigations or asked to conduct investigations with or on behalf of a foreign law enforcement body. As an example, the Madeleine McCann case has been investigated by the Metropolitan Police Service in conjunction with the judicial police of Portugal. Families are likely to face 'ambiguous loss' (Boss, 1999) and may be described as 'living in limbo' (Holmes, 2013).

There will be occasions when a missing person is found dead. Obtaining the necessary papers to repatriate the body is likely to be a distressing issue at a time when families are going through the first stages of bereavement. Assistance with repatriation can be provided by the Foreign Office consular representatives as well as by the Lucy Blackman Trust. Specialist funeral director services are available to conduct repatriations.

As a result of a Court of Appeal ruling in 1982, a duty was imposed upon coroners of England and Wales to inquire into any deaths abroad which were violent or unnatural and where the body was repatriated. This followed the case of a British nurse, Helen Smith, who fell from a hotel balcony in Saudi Arabia in 1979 (Pavia, 2009). Now a coroner, for the area to which the body is taken, will hold an inquest, investigating the cause and circumstances of the death.

Support from the Voluntary Sector

In the UK, the primary charities supporting missing people and their families are the Lucy Blackman Trust[5] and Missing People. Formerly known as Missing Abroad, the Lucy Blackman Trust is also able to assist with publicity across social media, with poster campaigns and web banners. The charity can provide assistance coordinating international searches through local networks and contacts. The Trust is able to facilitate travel and searching in foreign countries, discussing the benefits and risks involved for family and friends. Discounted flights, car hire and accommodation for a family is a possibility through the Trust, enabling a family to travel and stay abroad to understand the police response, volunteer and charity support and, of course, to conduct their own enquiries and searches.

Missing People[6] is the only charity in the UK which specialises in, and is dedicated to, bringing missing children and adults back together with their families. For families missing a loved one, life without them can be a desperate and unbearable struggle (Holmes, 2013). Missing People offers services for families as well as people who are missing, such as setting up three-way telephone calls, helping send a message home and returning home or reconnecting with family and friends, as well as creating publicity appeals for missing persons.

Across Europe, a special number, 116 000, has been established as the missing children 'hotline'. Calling or texting this number enables to caller to report a missing child (and sometimes a missing adult) as well as enabling a missing child (and sometimes an adult) to reach out for help. 116 000 is one of the harmonised numbers of social value available in most member states. Operated by NGOs in European member states, 116 000 is quickly becoming the number to call for missing people (Missing Children Europe, 2014).

In the wider world, charities provide services to complement law enforcement agencies in the search and investigation of missing persons. The largest network is that provided by the International Centre for Missing and Exploited Children.[7] Based in Washington, DC, the International Centre operates the Global Missing Children Network, which is a group of 30 countries represented by a leading charity for missing children and associated law enforcement body. Part of the services of the International Centre is to manage the Network's website, www.missingkids.com, which provides publicity appeals for missing children across the world as well as displaying the Network's online content of guidance and support materials.

Meeting Expectations

Adults have the right to travel as they please under the constraints of law, local customs and cultural practice. Across Europe, Article 8 of the European Convention on Human Rights applies to all member states. In short, this is the right to a private life. A right to respect for one's 'private and family life, his home [sic] and his correspondence' subject to certain restrictions that are 'in accordance with law' and 'necessary in a democratic society'. In missing person investigations there is always a balance between the search for a person and the person's right to remain unfound. In circumstances where a missing person is found but wishes to remain 'forgotten', police will seek permission to let the person's family know that they are, hopefully, safe and well. Some charities offer a 'reconnection' service enabling three-way conversations to be mediated. On occasions, the found missing person will not wish to have any information passed back to family or friends, not even 'I'm alive'. The lack of information can be very difficult for a family to come to terms with and the emotional support provided by the Lucy Blackman Trust or Missing People can be crucial for a family. Often a negotiation between the found missing person and a support worker from one of the charities will result in the charity being able to pass on 'good news' information to a family.

For the police, it is essential that the course of investigations overseas is explained carefully and in detail to the relatives of the missing person. In some cases, police Family Liaison Officers are used to relay news of investigations to families. In other cases, a family may have to rely on support from either Missing People or the Trust.

Meeting the expectations of family and friends missing a loved one can be difficult to achieve for the police, despite much hard work and good will on both sides. Research is starting to indicate (for example, Stevenson et al., 2013; Parr and Stevenson, 2014; Wayland, 2015) that having the police listen completely to the family narrative will help a family come to terms with the 'missing' event. Even when a missing person is not found, a family may be satisfied and have their expectation met because of the trust and care built up between the police investigative team and the family.

Conclusions

Examples of missing British persons are in media stories daily but it is essential that the best service to support families through charities is available alongside thorough and effective police investigations coordinated, as far as is possible, by police in the UK. Understanding how to prevent people from going missing is key, but producing the most effective ways to contribute to a person's safe recovery through international multi-agency partnerships is essential in conjunction with practical and emotional support for families through the trauma of a missing person episode.

Acknowledgement

The author would like to thank Neville Blackwood for his assistance.

Notes

1 Missing Persons Abroad: www.gov.uk/government/publications/missing-persons.
2 Authorised professional practice (forthcoming at www.app.college.police.uk).
3 Regarding services provided by both INTERPOL and SIRENE, see www.interpol.int; www.app. college.police.uk/app-content/investigations/european–investigations/Schengen-information-system; www.nationalcrimeagency.gov.uk/about-us/working-in-partnership/international-cooperation.
4 The UK Missing Persons Bureau: http://missingpersons.police.uk.
5 The Lucy Blackman Trust: www.lbtrust.org.
6 Missing People: www.missingpeople.org.uk.
7 International Centre for Missing and Exploited Children: www.icmec.org.

References

Boss, P. (1999). *Ambiguous Loss: Learning to Live with Unresolved Grief.* Cambridge, MA: Harvard University Press.
European Convention on Human Rights. www.echr.coe.int; also see Human Rights Act, 1998 at: www.legislation.gov.uk/ukpga/1998/42/schedule/1.
Foreign and Commonwealth Office (2014). *Freedom of Information Request Answer Number: 0136-14.*

Holmes, L. (2013). *Living in Limbo*. London: Missing People. www.missingpeople.org.uk.

Missing Children Europe (2014). *Annual Report*. Brussels: Missing Children Europe. http://missingchildren europe.eu.

Parr, H. and Stevenson, O. (2014). 'No news today': Talk of witnessing with families of missing people. *Cultural Geographies*, 22(2): 297–315.

Pavia, W. (2009). Funeral to be held for nurse who died in Saudi Arabia 30 years ago. *The Times*, 28 October. http://thetimes.co.uk/tto/news/uk/article1945672.ece (accessed 10 May, 2016).

Stevenson, O., Parr, H., Woolnough, P. and Fyfe, N. (2013). *Geographies of Missing People: Processes, Experiences, Responses*. http://geographiesofmissingpeople.org.uk.

Wayland, S. (2015). *'I Still Hope, But What I Hope for Now Has Changed': A Narrative Inquiry Study of Hope and Ambiguous Loss When Someone Is Missing*. Unpublished PhD thesis, University of New England, Australia.

17

Forensic Identification

Sue Black and Jan Bikker

Introduction

The police receive many calls relating to missing persons who have disappeared without explanation, are very vulnerable or dangerous or are not at a place where they are expected or required to be (also referred to as an 'absent person' rather than a missing person; see ACPO, 2013). Each missing person report is categorised based on an assessment of risk factors such as vulnerability, suicide risk or circumstances of disappearance, and actions appropriate for each category initiated. For the highest risk categories, samples for identification purposes will be collated in the early stages of the investigation to avoid degradation and loss of evidence. While the majority of persons reported missing return soon after their disappearance, in a small number of cases the requirement of forensic identification of unidentified remains may be necessary to reunite a missing person with their families. It is in those cases that the importance of identification evidence becomes apparent.

The forensic specialities required to identify an unidentified body may depend on the physical state and completeness of the remains. Certainly, the identification process may be further complicated if no leads are available that point to the identity of the deceased such as identification documents. The Senior Identification Manager (SIM), in consultation with the pathologist, may consult forensic experts such as a forensic anthropologist when the remains are badly decomposed or skeletonised to obtain a biological profile to narrow down the list of possible missing persons. It is pivotal that the authority leading the investigation has an understanding of not only the available identification methods they can utilise, but also the limitations of the techniques employed to aid in the identification of unidentified remains. Indeed, every identification method has a potential for inherent errors and those limitations have to be weighed on a case-by-case basis by the authority leading the identification process. This chapter describes the identification process and discusses the potential and limitations of the most commonly deployed identification methods. A case study to illustrate the process of forensic identification using a multifactorial approach is provided at the end of this chapter.

Identification

The word 'identification' originates from the Latin 'idem' meaning 'the same' or 'identical'. Therefore, to confirm that an 'identification' has been achieved, regardless of whether the individual is alive or dead, requires that two sets of directly comparable data be brought together to provide an identical match. On one hand this will be data relating to the reported missing person collected by trained police investigators from direct family members, referred to as antemortem information, and those data collected from an unidentified body, referred to as postmortem information. The comparison of those data sets in itself may be a complicated and time-consuming exercise and an exact match can rarely be achieved as all means of assessing indicators or markers of identity carry inherent practical error and most biometrics (physiological markers) change with time (Ratha et al., 2003; Jain et al., 2004). Those complicating factors may include postmortem changes of the body, time between disappearance and reporting of the missing person and loss of identification evidence over time (due to degradation of potential samples or memory loss of direct family members). Thus the investigator must balance and consider all the available identification information and assess any discrepancies between the antemortem and postmortem data before reaching a conclusion that sufficient evidence is available to confirm a positive identification. Further, it is generally acknowledged that an identification must be scientifically rigorous and this imposes a minimum level of concordance between the two data sets to satisfy the judicial authority, the HM Coroner or the Procurator Fiscal, who investigates or confirms the identity of an unknown person who has been found dead within their jurisdiction, that a match has been achieved (Robertson and Vignaux, 1995; Dessimoz and Champod, 2008; Bouchrika et al., 2011; Ferguson and Raitt, 2013). Therefore, confirmation of forensic identification is predicated on the strength of a match between two comparable but not necessarily identical sets of data, to a standard that is deemed acceptable to a judicial authority.

It is extremely important for all concerned to understand that there is unavoidable inherent error associated with forensic identification and that it is important to establish how much error can be tolerated to ensure that the correct identity has been attributed to the right individual (Lucy, 2005; AFSP, 2009; Aitken et al., 2010). For this reason, confirmation of identity is rarely a rapid process as it requires that all avenues be explored and every inconsistency scrutinised to ensure that the degree of certainty in a match is maximised and to determine whether the associated error can be tolerated (Black et al., 2010). This can be extremely difficult for families and friends to understand when what they want more than anything is a swift answer and the remains of their loved ones returned to them expeditiously (Jensen, 2000; PAHO, 2006). But misidentification is to be avoided at all costs because it is not a single event: if one person is assigned to the wrong identity then it has also been denied to the correct person who should own it and so in a misidentification there are at least two mistakes made (Mundorff et al., 2008).

The similarity between the processes of identification regardless of whether the individual is alive or dead, is evident in the recording mechanisms operated by INTERPOL (Black et al., 2010, INTERPOL, n.d.). INTERPOL is the world's largest international police organisation, with 192 member countries and aims to facilitate international police cooperation in criminal matters. When a person is notified as missing, INTERPOL's General Secretariat, at the request of a National Central Bureau (NCB) in one of its 192 member countries, will distribute what is known as a 'yellow notice' and this same form is completed whether the individual is thought to be alive or dead. When an unidentified dead body is found, a 'black notice' is distributed, with the anticipation that a yellow notice may be found that will be sufficiently close in content to facilitate further investigation with regards to a possible match. In disaster victim identification (see Chapter 18 in this volume) antemortem information is collected on the yellow recording form (comparable to the missing persons form) and postmortem information is recorded on pink forms (comparable to those generated from a black notice). Antemortem information is any identification data related to the reported missing person obtained from relatives, friends, neighbours or others who knew the victim. Therefore, there is an inherent understanding that identity is not something that is lost with death and that the means by which scientists are able to establish a close link between indicators of identity are robust regardless of whether the missing person is alive or deceased (PAHO, 2006).

Primary Methods of Identification

INTERPOL ranks its identifiers as being either primary or secondary in nature (INTERPOL, 2009). Primary identifiers are those which may be accepted in isolation as reliable indicators of identity with a high probability of securing a match. Secondary identifiers carry more likelihood of error and, to reach an accepted level of agreement that identification has most likely been achieved, may require that several of these identifiers are utilised. In this chapter we will concentrate on the primary identifiers and will mention only briefly some of the secondary identifiers that may be of greatest value. We will then conclude this chapter with a case study that remains unidentified at the time of publication to illustrate the utilisation of primary and secondary identifiers.

INTERPOL recognises three primary indicators of identity – DNA, fingerprints and dental information (INTERPOL, 2009). Although it is unquestionably true that confirmation of identity is more secure the greater the number of indicators that are in agreement, any one of these three may be utilised in the absence of any other indicator, but obviously it cannot be contrary to other accepted indicators. It is the duty of the legal authority such as HM Coroner to ensure that the probability of a correct identification is as high as it is possible to achieve. Only by ensuring the highest scientific standards used in the identification process will there be sufficient confidence in the decision making required to permit legal notification and subsequent release of the body to the person's family and friends. Lacking standards may result in doubts from relatives about the identity of the deceased, not only resulting in delays in releasing the body but also undermining confidence in the coronial system.

DNA, the molecular barcode of life, is present in virtually every cell in the body in one of two forms – either as nuclear DNA or as mitochondrial DNA. Nuclear DNA is a product of half the genetic component from the person's father and half from their mother whereas mitochondrial DNA is only passed down from the maternal source, although recent clinical observations have challenged this bold statement (Schwartz and Vissing, 2002). It is generally accepted that mitochondrial DNA possesses a preferential survival rate compared to nuclear DNA and this is important when identification is being attempted from remains which are badly decomposed, burned or fragmented (Foran, 2006). All individuals in the maternal line will have the same mitochondrial DNA profile (or mitotype), apart for possible mutations. Therefore it is easier to obtain sample mitochondrial DNA from several possible generations for a match. However, identification will not be statistically as positive because nuclear DNA families may share the same maternal ancestors, and this is especially so in population groups where mating of closely related individuals is common.

Furthermore, an individual's mitochondrial DNA contains no information about the individual's father. It is well known that DNA can now be extracted from extremely small samples but it is important to know which site will give the optimal chance of good recovery and equally how and where to collect antemortem or familial DNA for the purposes of comparison. It is equally important to ensure that the quality of the antemortem DNA is secured as there is no value in concentrating on quality or quantity on only one side of the identification equation. DNA that can be sourced directly from the missing person is preferred, such as direct profile matching. This may necessitate sampling from sources including toothbrushes, razors, brushes, combs, hats, underwear and dental appliances where it is known that the missing person's DNA is most likely to be located (Montelius and Lindblom, 2012). The Family Liaison Officer assigned to the relatives of the reported missing person will ensure that the appropriate items are collected for DNA testing. Depending on the missing person risk assessment, the collection of samples is normally carried out within 24 hours in high-risk cases and within seven days in medium-risk cases (ACPO, 2009). To avoid erroneous DNA mixtures, the expert has to ensure that the items can only have been used by the missing person and cross-checking between these different sources will ensure that a robust profile is secured. In the absence of such information, perhaps because of the passage of time in securing confirmed sources of the victim's DNA, for example when the person is homeless or has no known fixed abode, then familial DNA can be substituted but this will not confirm the identity of the deceased with the same degree of reliability as direct match profiling will (Ge et al., 2011). Familial DNA will confirm only the familial relationship of the individual to the DNA donors. The closer the relationship to the missing person, then the more confident will be the potential match. In line with common practice, parents, siblings and offspring are the primary target sources, with more distant relations being of lesser confirmatory value. Unfortunately, complete parentage trios are not always available.

Antemortem DNA will be collected by a trained forensic practitioner, commonly the Police Family Liaison Officer, and stored so that it can be compared with the postmortem samples. The source of the DNA recovered from the mortuary will be dependent on the state of preservation of the remains. Often samples of muscle tissue are sufficient if the body is relatively recent but if decomposition is advanced then it may be necessary to take samples of bone or tooth (Collins et al., 2002). The rate of decomposition is variable and dependent on the interaction of many variables, including temperature, humidity, season of death, indoor or outdoor location of the body, cause of death, trauma, presence of scavengers and other biotic and abiotic factors. DNA too may prove to be of limited or less value if the body is perhaps cremated or fragmented and environmental factors such as heat, humidity or a salt water environment are detrimental to the survival of DNA. The more fragmented and denatured the DNA samples then the greater the difficulty in obtaining a full profile and consequently there is a reduction in the strength of match for identification. This may be further compounded if only familial DNA is available for comparison.

Confirmation of identification through DNA analysis is generally the preferred route and the one that carries the greatest degree of assurance. The UK Missing Persons Bureau maintains a DNA database which is solely used for the identification of missing persons or unidentified remains. The database is a collection of DNA profiles from reported missing persons, their close relatives, unidentified people or human remains.

Fragmented or denatured DNA from the deceased, no match to a DNA database and no match to a known missing person, means that this route may not provide the desired outcome of being able to ascribe a name to the deceased. Once a missing person has been located or an unidentified person or human remains are identified, the DNA profiles are deleted from the database. If the body is incomplete, for example as may occur following a death at sea or as a result of animal scavenging, the DNA profile will be retained on the database until all the remaining body parts have been found.

Fingerprints are the next most favoured approach to determining identity but this biometric faces the same issues as DNA in terms of likelihood of a successful outcome (Maltoni et al., 2005). Although fingerprints are generally identified as the preferred latent print, other prints may also be considered, including palm prints, foot prints, toe prints and, less commonly used, ear prints and lip prints (Champod et al., 2004). Although until relatively recently fingerprints were placed within the same category of strength of evidence as DNA, this has changed with the outcome of the Shirley McKie investigation[1] (McKie and Wallace, 2007; Cole, 2008). Antemortem fingerprints may be difficult to find if the person is not already on a database and so successful location and retrieval will again require the involvement of a trained forensic fingerprint expert. Prints may be lifted for example from windows, computer screens, books, electronic readers, mobile phones, door handles, drinking glasses, photographs in frames and so on. The ingenuity and experience of the police's scene of crime officer is invaluable in this regard as, unlike DNA analysis, there is no familial substitute that can assist.

As with DNA, the ability to recover fingerprints in the mortuary will also be dependent on the condition of the body and the degree of advanced decomposition. Skin slippage can occur relatively soon after death and if the sloughed epidermal glove is retained then a print can be retrieved (Robb, 1999). However, if it is lost then a dermal print obtained from the layer of skin underneath the (epidermal) top layer may be used but this will not match perfectly to an epidermal print, which will be the basis for the antemortem comparison (Champod et al., 2004). Following the Asian tsunami of 2004, fingerprints proved to be of greater assistance for countries who issued biometric identification cards to their citizens, which meant that they had a centralised fingerprint database.

Teeth survive decomposition well and are frequently preserved even after long-term exposure to soil conditions and immersion. Resistance of the dentition against excessive heat and fragmentation is due to the high inorganic content of teeth and the relative protection afforded by the soft tissues of the mouth. The human dentition has been regarded as highly individualistic, especially when there has been odontological intervention. It has been said that over 2.5 billion different possibilities exist for charting the human dentition, based on the combinations of missing teeth, filling materials, lesions and prostheses involving the total number of 160 dental surfaces (Frearnead, 1961; Heras et al., 2005). Any restorative work or dental intervention undertaken can result in an antemortem record that is invaluable for comparison purposes with the deceased. Under these circumstances it is vital for there to be a known missing person to match with the deceased as there are no general dental records kept as a searchable database in most countries. In the UK, dental records for a reported missing person (if they are registered with a dentist) will be added to the National Missing Persons Dental Record Collection, held at the UK National Missing Persons Bureau for comparison with dental information retrieved from unidentified bodies. In the Asian tsunami of 2004 dental identification proved to be the most reliable means of confirming identity for Western citizens as decomposition severely impacted on the ability to extract viable fingerprints or DNA profiles (Petju et al., 2007; Schuller-Gotzburg and Suchanek, 2007).

Secondary Methods of Identification

When a deceased person or remains are found and none of the three primary identifiers described prove to be of assistance, then forensic investigators must rely on what are called secondary source identifiers. Those may include personal effects (for example, jewellery, clothing, documents), medical matters (such as scars, diseases, trauma), body modifications (tattoos, piercings and so on), photographs and descriptive appearances of the individual (Black et al., 2010). Family Liaison Officers will try to collect as much of this personal information as possible during antemortem interviews. Depending on the condition of remains found, it may be impossible to tell which postmortem information can be collected and it is therefore important to collect as much information as possible, not only to ultimately identify the remains but also to establish other intelligence, such as sightings. Where possible, photos showing specific pieces of jewellery, personal effects and body modifications will be collected from relatives for later comparison to items and adornments found on recovered remains. Social media such as Facebook often may provide valuable photos. It must be noted however that these indicators of identity do not carry sufficient individualisation power to be utilised in isolation, but when considered in combination they may pass a threshold whereby identification may be confirmed. A case study is included at the end of this chapter which, at the time of publication, has not resulted in confirmation of an identity but illustrates how primary sources did not assist and how secondary sources have been utilised.

Secondary identifiers are features which are unlikely to be unique to the individual but which still have some discriminatory capacity. For example, body modifications are increasingly popular as a form of self-adornment and most commonly represented by tattoos and piercings (Black and Thompson, 2007). INTERPOL forms permit recording of these alterations to the body and whilst family and friends may be able to recall those which are visible, for example a tattoo on a forearm or pierced ear lobes, more intimate partners may be able to provide information on modifications that are not visible such as nipple piercings and tattoos in more private regions. In terms of tattoos, some are particularly individuating as they may include a specific date or name but the majority are freely reproduced and rarely unique. However, the location of the tattoo, its size and colour as well as its pattern are all selected by the individual and so therefore there is a strong element of individuation, especially if there is a multiplicity of modifications. Piercings tend to be less identifiable as there are limited suitable places on the body for mainstream piercings and so unless the jewellery used is unique or the location is unusual, this modification can be of restricted value for identification.

Modifications that are not mainstream, but are considered to be extreme, have a greater value for discrimination simply because they are less common (Benecke, 1999). Often those who go to extremes of body alteration are more extrovert and photographs may be available that would allow comparison of the location, number and type of modification. These may include elective amputation, tongue splitting, penile beading, corsetry, rib removal and many other alterations that are limited only by imagination. There is little or no regulation in the tattooing, piercing and implanting industry and so no recourse to a database to aid comparison. Therefore, if this is to be a successful means of identification it requires careful and accurate data collection both from the antemortem and the postmortem sources.

Personal effects may be of value but, as a transferrable commodity and frequently not being unique, they can never be considered to be more than of assistance in identification (Puxley and Thompson, 2007). Clothing, jewellery, electronic devices, luggage, documents, and so on, may give the necessary clues to permit identification teams to track down a missing person, which will permit further investigation through primary sources of identification; therefore they have a strong role to play in intelligence gathering more than in the process of identification per se.

A 'unique medical condition' refers to situations in which foreign devices, perhaps bearing a serial identification number, are implanted within the human body. These may be, for example, breast implants, a pacemaker or a hip prosthesis. Providing that they carry a unique reference number (URN) they may be matched to known medical records associated with the individual (Clarkson and Schaefer, 2007). Unfortunately, not all surgical facilities will record the serial number of the implant and without prior intelligence on the possible identity of the deceased this feature will likely prove to be of limited value as no central records or databases are commonly kept that would support random searching.

Finally, when all else has been addressed, the value of the face may be considered (Wilkinson and Rynn, 2012). It has been shown in previous mass fatality events that facial identification is inherently flawed as a process of matching antemortem and postmortem information, with the circumstances of the death often rendering environmental insults too detrimental to support an objective analysis. Ten per cent of victims of the Asian tsunami and 50 per cent of victims of the Bali bombing of 12 October 2002 were wrongly identified by facial recognition (Lain et al., 2003). The family member who is asked to look at the faces of the deceased to find their loved one is not a reliable source of identification; they have not seen their family member in such circumstances before, they will be severely distressed, they may be desperate for closure and, despite best intentions, past experience has taught that mistakes will be made (PAHO, 2006). Therefore, INTERPOL does not advocate that facial identification be utilised as a primary means of identification, only as a supporting indicator of possible identity. However, when all other avenues have been explored and if the body is badly decomposed or skeletonised then the reconstruction of a face may provide the intelligence required for a cold case to direct towards potential primary sources of identification. Facial reconstruction (also referred to as facial approximation) is the process used to reproduce the facial appearance of an individual by relating the skeletal structure to the overlying soft tissue using a combination of scientific, artistic and anatomical skills; essentially a facial reconstruction *estimates* the facial appearance of the individual in life. This may jog the memory of members of the public who may recognise the victim. A facial reconstruction can be created from a skull after consultation with an experienced facial anthropologist and is normally attempted after other lines of enquiries into an unidentified body have failed to produce any leads. This is the situation illustrated in the case study below.

There is also a third category: tertiary methods of identification. These include physical characteristics such as eye and hair colour, body shape, hairstyle and other visual identifiers. Visual identification has proved unreliable in a number of cases and as such is not recommended.

Case Study

A case study will be presented here to illustrate how a re-examination of a long-term unidentified body can provide additional intelligence for further police investigations using advances in forensic anthropology and forensic sciences. This is by no means a common occurrence and many unidentified remains are still being stored in mortuaries around the UK. Indeed, not all missing persons are reported missing and remains found may therefore remain unidentified for a considerable time. It is therefore important to collect as many clues as possible which may ultimately lead to the identification of this person. Thanks to the support of the investigative authorities it was possible to review the case presented below.

On 16 October 2011 badly decomposed remains were found by a member of the public in woodlands in East Dunbartonshire in Scotland.[2] The Procurator Fiscal[3] was content that the circumstances surrounding the death were not suspicious and a one-doctor postmortem examination was performed. Tissue samples were taken for DNA analysis but despite an extensive missing person's check including DNA profiling and examination of the personal effects associated with the remains, no identification was forthcoming. After completion of all possible avenues of investigation the Procurator Fiscal gave permission for burial as an 'unknown' but the investigative authorities requested that a full forensic anthropological assessment be undertaken to see if there was any information that had not been uncovered in the initial examination that might subsequently assist with securing an identification.

This case was used as an opportunity for the forensic anthropology team at the University of Dundee to obtain collective team training in forensic casework and a second postmortem examination was performed at the Southern General Hospital on 30 January 2013 in the presence of the Serious Organised Crime Agency (NCA) and Strathclyde Police. At the time of publication, this individual remains unidentified.

The first step in the process was to identify the biological profile of the deceased. Sex was determined as being male, evidenced primarily from the morphology of the skull and the pelvis but this also fitted with the

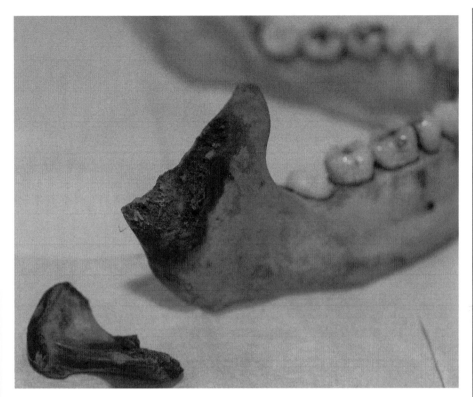

Figure 17.1   Unhealed fracture to the right mandibular ramus
Source: Centre for Anatomy and Human Identification

clothing recovered. Age was determined to be adult and most likely in the region of 25–35 years of age. This was determined through assessment of various areas of the skeleton that display age-related characteristics, for example the pubic symphysis, the sacrum, the sternum and the clavicles. Ancestry was determined from his facial morphology and was considered to be consistent with Caucasian. The stature of the individual was calculated from the long bones of the upper and lower limbs and calculated to be between 174.5–185.4cm (5'8'–6'1').

He had a fracture to his left nasal bone which had fully healed, suggesting it had occurred some considerable time before his death. He had also sustained a blow to the right side of his jaw. This fractured the bone across the ramus and because he did not seek medical attention for this the bone did not heal (Figure 17.1). There was evidence of new bone that had attempted to repair the fracture but in reality it should have been plated by a surgeon. He also sustained a fracture to his right lateral pterygoid plate of the sphenoid bone, which is situated at the base of the skull in front of the temporals and basilar part of the occipital, but this was healed. Indeed, all three fractures could have occurred in the same violent incident. With an unhealed fracture in his mandible, eating solid food would have proved difficult and painful and this situation most likely persisted for quite some time.

His dental hygiene was poor, with alveolar resorption (wasting of the bony socket surrounding the teeth), gum disease, abscess cavities and several unfilled decay cavities. At some earlier point in his life he had had quite extensive dental intervention (consistent in style with UK NHS procedures) which consisted of fillings and root canal work. In addition, he had a longitudinal fracture to his left upper central incisor with a small chip taken out of the bite surface, which could have been linked to the rest of the fracture trauma seen in the skull but may have occurred prior to this.

Figure 17.2   Clothing similar to that worn by the deceased
Source: Centre for Anatomy and Human Identification

His upper body showed an asymmetry. His right and left clavicles were of a different size as were his right and left scapulae, which showed a marked narrowing in width. This could not be explained and may have no bearing on his identification but may represent some, as yet unknown, clinical condition or syndrome. The hyoid bone was fractured which was consistent with his suspected cause of death, suicide by hanging.

Stable isotope analysis can provide further intelligence for police investigations. Human tissues may yield valuable information about a person's life history and geographic origin. Hair, nail and bone samples were taken for stable isotope analysis, but at the time of writing, these results had not been disclosed.

His clothing consisted of a woollen cardigan, polo shirt, boxer briefs, jeans, ankle socks and trainers (Figures 17.2–17.3). The cardigan was long-sleeved and dark blue with a front zip. The brand was MAX, which is not common in the UK and is traded in the Middle East. This size was small. The light blue/green polo shirt was from Top Man and was size small with a distinctive white print covering most of the front. The boxer briefs were not a brand that was readily identifiable. The jeans are exclusively sold at Officers Club and Petroleum Stores and were a size 30L which was consistent with his anticipated stature and suggests that he was of slim build, which would fit with the small size of his polo shirt and cardigan. The hem of the right leg showed greater wear than the hem of the left leg. The ankle socks were unremarkable. The trainers were black with grey and red markings. They carried the label SHOCK X, which is a low-cost brand sold in Lidl stores in the UK. His shoe size was UK 11 (EU 45). There was greater wear on the heel of the right than the left shoe and this may be of relevance given the extra wear seen on the right hem of the jeans.

His face was anatomically reconstructed in 3D software using the biological profile determined by the forensic anthropologists, incorporated a hairstyle that was consistent with the short fair hair identified at the postmortem and reflected his slim build as identified from his clothing. Also incorporated into the reconstruction was his deviated nose as a result of the nasal fracture (Figure 17.3).

Despite so much information being available about an individual, including features that are primary identifiers, this case illustrates that, if the individual is not listed as missing, then reuniting antemortem and postmortem information to achieve a positive identification can be extremely challenging. It is therefore extremely important to collect as much information as possible since it cannot be predicted which fact may ultimately aid in the identification of an individual or provide further intelligence that can be followed up by the investigating officer(s).

Figure 17.3   Facial reconstruction of the deceased
Source: Centre for Anatomy and Human Identification

Acknowledgements

We wish to acknowledge the following, who were involved in the work undertaken for the case study listed above:

University of Dundee, Forensic Anthropology: Dr Craig Cunningham, Dr Lucina Hackman, Ms Catriona Davies, Ms Eilidh Ferguson and Ms Seaneen Tennant. Facial reconstruction: Dr Chris Rynn, Mr Tobias Houlton and Prof Caroline Wilkinson.

Dental advice: Dr Phil Marsden.

SOCA: DS Kerr Duncan, NFSA Kirsty Potter.

Police Service of Scotland: A.DI Graeme Lannigan and PC Iain Gibb.

Notes

1 In this particular case, a fingerprint found at a murder scene was wrongly attributed by Scottish Criminal Record Office (SCRO) examiners to Shirley McKie, a former Scottish police detective who denied ever having been in this house. The SCRO's fingerprint evidence was later rejected and McKie was unanimously found not guilty of perjury. An inquiry later recommended that fingerprint evidence should be treated as opinion-based rather than fact in Scottish courts.

2 For more details about this case, see http://stv.tv/news/west-central/244831-balmore-body-find-facial-construction-of-torrance-dead-man-released/.

3 The Procurator Fiscal investigates all sudden and suspicious deaths in Scotland. In England and Wales, this role is performed by a HM Coroner of the jurisdiction in which the death has occurred.

References

ACPO (2009). *Collection of Missing Person Data: Code of Practice for the Police Service on Collecting and Sharing Data on Missing Persons with Public Authorities* [online]. www.acpo.police.uk/documents/crime/2009/200907CRIMPD01.pdf (accessed 30 August 2013).

ACPO (2013). *Interim Guidance on the Management, Recording and Investigation of Missing Persons* [online]. http://library.college.police.uk/docs/college-of-policing/Interim-Missing-Persons-Guidance-2013.pdf.

Aitken, C.G.G., Roberts, P. and Jackson, G. (2010). *Fundamentals of Probability and Statistical Evidence in Criminal Proceedings*. London: Royal Statistical Society.

Association of Forensic Science Providers (AFSP) (2009). Standards for the formulation of evaluative forensic science expert opinion. *Science and Justice,* 49: 161–164.

Benecke, M. (1999). First report of nonpsychotic self-cannibalism (autophagy), tongue splitting, and scar patterns (scarification) as an extreme form of cultural body modification in a western civilization. *Forensic, Medicine and Pathology*, 20(3): 281–285.

Black, S. and Thompson, T. (2007). Body modification. In T. Thompson and S. Black (eds), *Forensic Human Identification: An Introduction* (pp. 379–400). Florida: CRC Press.

Black, S., Walker, G., Hackman, L. and Brooks, C. (2010). *Disaster Victim Identification: The Practitioner's Guide*. Dundee: Dundee University Press.

Bouchrika, I., Goffredo, M., Carter, J. and Nixon, M. (2011). On using gait in forensic biometrics. *Journal of Forensic Sciences*, 56(4): 882–889.

Champod, C., Lennard, C. J., Margot, P. and Stoilovic, M. (2004). *Fingerprints and Other Ridge Skin Impressions*. Florida: CRC Press.

Clarkson, J. and Schaefer, M. (2007). Surgical intervention. In T. Thompson and S. Black (eds), *Forensic Human Identification: An Introduction* (pp. 127–146). Florida: CRC Press.

Cole, S. A. (2008). The 'opinionization' of fingerprint evidence. *Biosocieties*, 3(1): 105–113.

Collins, M. J., Nielsen-Marsh, C. M., Hiller, J., Smith, C. I., Roberts, J. P., Prigodich, R. V., Wess, T. J., Csapo, J., Millard, A. R. and Turner-Walker, G. (2002). The survival of organic matter in bone: A review. *Archaeometry*, 44(3): 383–394.

Dessimoz, D. and Champod, C. (2008). Linkages between biometrics and forensic science. In A. K. Jain, P. Flynn and A. A. Ross (eds), *Handbook of Biometrics* (pp. 425–459). Berlin: Springer.

Ferguson, P. R. and Raitt, F. E. (2013). If a picture paints a thousand words … the development of human identification techniques in forensic anthropology and their implications for human rights in the criminal process. *The International Journal of Evidence and Proof*, 17(2): 127–156.

Foran, D. R. (2006). Relative degradation of nuclear and mitochondrial DNA: An experimental approach. *Journal of Forensic Sciences*, 51(4): 766–770.

Frearnead, R. W. (1961). Facilities for forensic odontology. *Medicine, Science and the Law*, 1: 273.

Ge, J., Chakraborty, R., Eisenberg, A. and Budowle, B. (2011). Comparisons of familial DNA database searching strategies. *Journal of Forensic Sciences*, 56(6): 1448–1456.

Heras, S. M., Valenzuela, A., Ogayar, C., Valverda, A. J. and Torras, J. C. (2005). Computer based production of comparison overlays from 3D-scanned dental casts for bite mark analysis. *Journal of Forensic Sciences*, 50(1): 1–7.

INTERPOL (2009). Disaster victim identification guide [online]. www.interpol.int/content/download/9158/68001/version/5/file/Guide.pdf (accessed 30 June 2013).

INTERPOL (n.d.). Notices [online]. www.interpol.int/interpol-expertise/Notices (accessed 30 June 2013).

Jain, A. K., Prabhakar, S., Hong, L., Ross, A. and Wayman, J. L. (2004). Biometrics: A grand challenge. *Pattern Recognition*, 2: 935–942.

Jensen, R. A. (2000). *Mass Fatality and Casualty Incidents: A Field Guide*. Florida: CRC Press.

Lain, R., Griffiths, C. and Hilton, J. M. N. (2003). Forensic dental and medical response to the Bali bombing – a personal perspective. *Medical Journal of Australia*, 179: 362–365.

Lucy, D. (2005). *Introduction to Statistics for Forensic Scientists*. Chichester, UK: John Wiley and Sons Ltd.

McKie, I. and Wallace, M. (2007). *Shirley McKie: The Price of Innocence*. London: Berlinn Ltd.

Maltoni, D., Maio, D., Jain, A. K. and Prabhakar, S. (2005). *Handbook of Fingerprint Recognition*. New York: Springer.

Montelius, K. and Lindblom, B. (2012). DNA analysis in disaster victim identification. *Forensic Science, Medicine and Pathology*, 8: 140–147.

Mundorff, A. Z., Shaler, R., Bieschke, E. and Mar-Cash, E. (2008). Marrying anthropology and DNA: Essential for solving complex commingling problems in cases of extreme fragmentation. In B. Adams and J. Byrd (eds), *Recovery, Analysis and Identification of Commingled Human Remains* (pp. 285–299). New Jersey: Humana Press.

PAHO (2006). *Management of Dead Bodies after Disasters: A Field Manual for First Responders* [online] www.ifrc.org/docs/idrl/I967EN.pdf (accessed 30 June 2013).

Petju, M., Suteerayongprasert, A., Thongpud, R. and Hassin, K. (2007). Importance of dental records for victim identification following the Indian Ocean tsunami disaster in Thailand. *Public Health*, 121(4): 251–257.

Puxley, A. and Thompson, T. (2007). Personal effects. In T. Thompson and S. Black (eds), *Forensic Human Identification: An Introduction* (pp. 365–378). Florida: CRC Press.

Ratha, N. K., Connell, J. H. and Bolle, R. M. (2003). Biometrics break ins and band aids. *Pattern Recognition Letters*, 24(13): 2105–2113.

Robb, N. (1999). 229 people, 15,000 body parts: Pathologists help solve Swissair 111's grisly puzzles. *Canadian Medical Association Journal*, 160(2): 241–243.

Robertson, B. and Vignaux, G. A. (1995). *Interpreting Evidence*. Chichester, UK: John Wiley and Sons.

Schuller-Gotzburg, P. and Suchanek, J. (2007). Forensic odontologists successfully identify tsunami victims in Phuket, Thailand. *Forensic Science International*, 171(2–3): 204–207.

Schwartz, M. and Vissing, J. (2002). Paternal inheritance of mitochondrial DNA. *New England Journal of Medicine*, 347: 576–580.

Wilkinson, C. and Rynn, C. (2012). *Craniofacial Identification*. Cambridge: Cambridge University Press.

18

Disaster Victim Identification

Jan Bikker

Introduction

Disaster Victim Identification is the internationally accepted term to describe the processes and procedures for recovering and identifying the deceased in a disaster. A (major) disaster has been commonly defined as 'an episode in which the number of fatalities is in excess of that which can be dealt with using the normal mortuary facilities' (Busuttil et al., 2000) and as such is dependent on the local infrastructure and mass fatality protocols in place. Other authors have based the operational definition of a disaster on a subjective number of fatalities ranging from 12 or more (Knight, 1991) to 50 (Gilliland et al., 1986) in a single event. Indeed, the latter definitions ignore the impact of the event on the (local) community and relatives of the victims involved. The use of a subjective number is often justified by policy makers as the minimum number of fatalities after which a mass fatality response protocol must be activated.

A disaster, irrespective of whether it is a man–made or natural event, creates many challenges in terms of the number of individuals killed and the humanitarian response to identify the deceased. It has been estimated that more than 150,000 people go missing after a disaster each year (ICMP, 2012). The identification of unidentified remains and missing persons in disasters is a fundamental requirement for any Disaster Victim Identification deployment and can be 'a highly complex and sensitive procedure' (London Assembly, 2006, p. 1). Recovery, identification and proper burial are basic humanitarian rights which must be respected and enacted not only to address the social and emotional needs of the relatives but also for legal considerations such as inheritance, compensation and remarriage. The Disaster Victim Identification process and the procedures are subject to international agreement through INTERPOL, although they may be modified to accommodate national legislation and locally accepted practices.

Following the 1989 *Marchioness* disaster,[1] Lord Justice Clarke (2001) in his report of Public Inquiry into the Identification of Victims following Major Transport Accidents made 36 recommendations that have been instrumental in laying out the current best practice guidelines for dealing with multiple fatality incidents. In his report, Lord Justice Clarke stressed the importance of respecting the dead and their relatives and of working with sensitivity throughout; of ensuring that full, honest and accurate information is given to the relatives at every stage; and of respecting the request of a relative to view the body. These fundamental practices are now integrated widely in Disaster Victim Identification procedures.

National Disaster Response

In the event of a mass casualty incident in the UK the Metropolitan Police Service is responsible for informing the Foreign and Commonwealth Office if any of their nationals are known to have been affected. The Foreign and Commonwealth Office is the government department responsible for UK foreign policy and protecting the UK's interests abroad. The Foreign and Commonwealth Office plays an important role in a mass fatality incident that occurs in the UK that involves citizens of another country and when a mass fatality incident occurs abroad that may involve British citizens. In 2006, a UK Disaster Victim Identification Team was established consisting of police officers and police staff, together with nonpolice forensic experts including pathologists, mortuary technicians, radiographers and anthropologists. Members of UK Disaster Victim Identification are trained and equipped for deployment nationally and internationally. UK Disaster Victim Identification international response will be provided where British nationals are involved, at the request of the Foreign and Commonwealth Office or when the support of the UK has been requested by the country in which the incident has occurred. The Foreign and Commonwealth Office will lead on the UK's international relations. In a disaster involving foreign nationals in the UK, Disaster Victim Identification personnel from other countries may be invited to attend and they can provide invaluable assistance in the identification process.

Following a disaster, a number of operational activities will be conducted: search and recovery, identification of the victims and repatriation of those identified. The response is often directed by the characteristics of a disaster. A disaster may be characterised as open or closed. In an open disaster, it is uncertain who and how many may be missing, for example the 2004 South East Asia tsunami. An aircraft accident may be considered a closed disaster as a passenger manifest with the names of those involved is available. It must be noted however that passenger lists may not always be correct. A combination of a closed and open disaster may also be seen, for example an aircraft accident in a residential area. In the UK, natural disasters are scarce and the majority of incidents with multiple fatalities are often technological or structural in nature requiring a criminal investigation, for insurance and liability purposes or judicial procedures. A rigorous (scientific) approach to the identification of those involved and the collection of potential evidence to determine the cause(s) of the incident is therefore of vital importance for it to stand up in potential court proceedings.

This chapter will focus on general procedures in Disaster Victim Identification. The same principles of identification in the context of identifying missing persons and unidentified bodies apply in disasters, and the applications and limitations of those methods have already been discussed in Chapter 17 on forensic identification in this volume. They will therefore not be discussed here in more detail, but the remainder of the chapter will rather focus on the organisational and procedural aspects of identifying a multitude of fatalities in a single event according to UK practices.

Search and Recovery

Depending on the characteristics of a disaster, the boundaries of the site may be confined to a limited area or stretch across a wide area or multiple independent sites. A high-impact aviation accident of an intact plane may be limited to a confined area (such as Flight 93 in Somerset, Pennsylvania) while a mid-air break-up may spread plane parts, personal effects and human remains over a large area, for example as witnessed in the 1988 Lockerbie disaster which covered a search area of approximately 845 square miles (Galloway and Mallett, 2011, p. 99). A scene parameter, site security and access routes should be established as soon as possible. Emergency services have first priority to treat the wounded while search and rescue teams are mobilised to trace survivors trapped in the wreckage or building structure. After the rescue mission is called off and/or no survivors are likely to be found, the body recovery process can commence. A Disaster Victim Identification team or pathologist may be on the scene to assist with the recovery of remains. Both visual and written documentation of the location of personal effects and remains are essential for the purposes of reassociation and evidential reasons. In civilian settings, nonhuman tissue (for example, domestic pets) may be co-mingled with the remains of the victims and forensic anthropologists may be called in at this stage to separate those tissues. The remains and personal effects are bagged and transported to the mortuary facility for further examination and documentation. Many agencies and parties may be present on the scene including emergency responders, forensic experts, accident investigators, press and families of the deceased and missing wishing to visit the scene. A coordinated effort is therefore essential.

Survivor Reception Centre and Casualty Bureau

One of the initial responses is to record all information relating to individuals involved in the disaster. A Survivor Reception Centre will normally be established within a couple of hours following a disaster. This centre is located close to the scene, within the inner cordon, and provides humanitarian assistance to the survivors. It furthermore acts as a central location to document the details of casualties and survivors which will feed directly into the missing person list maintained by the Casualty Bureau (also referred to as a Casualty Call Centre). In the UK, a Casualty Bureau will be activated that acts as 'a single point of contact to receive and access information relating to persons who have, or are believed to have, been involved in an incident' (ACPO/ACPOS, 2008). Its primary aims are to provide information for the investigation process relating to an incident, trace and identify people involved in an incident, reconcile missing person records with casualty, survivor and evacuee records and collate this information accurately for relevant parties. A media strategy will be decided and an information website for the general public is often launched as soon as possible, accompanied with an announcement of a Casualty Bureau phone number to report missing persons. It is the responsibility of the Casualty Bureau to assess the degree of likely involvement for each reported missing person by applying 'grading' parameters. This is achieved by asking predetermined questions which are specified beforehand: was the missing person travelling on this particular train (to go to work)? Was he/she working in the affected building at the time of the disaster? Have you tried to contact him (by phone)? This strategy ensures that all the calls to the Casualty Bureau are filtered and the available call capacity is not overwhelmed with requests for general information.

As seen in previous disasters, the number of reported missing persons may exceed the actual number of missing persons by a ratio of 10:1 or more (INTERPOL, 2009). Following the 7 July bombings in 2005, a total of 7,823 people were reported missing (Home Office, 2006). As a result, it may take considerable time to establish the final victim list, which in some cases may even take up to three years, such as seen in the World Trade Centre terrorist attacks (Brondolo, 2004). Continuous comparison with the lists kept by search and rescue teams (list of injured and uninjured survivors), hospitals and located survivors can result in a systematic reduction of the presumed number of victims. A mechanism must be in place to be check the casualty list for misspellings, incorrect statuses and duplicate records, for example when the same missing person is reported multiple times by different family members or when aliases are being used. By using aforementioned quality control procedures an actual missing person list can be established that will form the blueprint for activation of Family Liaison Officers (FLOs) to relatives of those highly likely to be involved. Challenges may arise when foreign nationals are involved, for example the Morecambe Bay cockling disaster in 2004, which claimed the lives of 23 Chinese immigrants. In this particular disaster, the illegal immigrants were unknown to the authorities and many of the surviving witnesses did not speak English and fled to different parts of the UK in the days after the incident for fear of deportation and retaliation of gang leaders behind the human trafficking scheme (The Investigator, 2010).

Methods of Identification

Identification relies on the comparison of identifying features of the missing person (antemortem data) and those present on human remains (postmortem data). Positive identification is achieved when the antemortem and postmortem data match in sufficient detail to establish that they are from the same individual and no irreconcilable discrepancies are found (Higgins and James, 2006). The primary and scientific means of identification are fingerprint analysis, odontology and DNA. Secondary means of identification include personal description and unique medical findings as well as evidence and clothing found on the body. The latter serves to support primary identifiers and are ordinarily not sufficient to positively identify a victim on its own. Particularly in overseas disasters requiring an international response of Disaster Victim Identification teams from multiple countries, it is important to define a uniform scientifically rigorous identification strategy as soon as possible as the culturally accepted methods of identification may differ from accepted standards elsewhere in the world. For example, in many countries and jurisdictions, visual identification is still legally accepted as proof of identification (Ruwanpura, 2012) even though cases of misidentification have been reported, most notably the 2002 Bali bombings in which one-third of the victims were incorrectly identified by visual means (Lain et al., 2003). The use of inappropriate identification protocols has led to misidentifications and subsequent mass grave exhumations and re-examination of foreign nationals' bodies in previous disasters, as seen recently in the 2010 Polish Air Force Tu 154 plane crash in Smolensk. In one rare case of a 2003 YAK 42 aircraft crash near the town of Macka (Turkey) involving peacekeeping forces, the use of inappropriate identification protocols resulting in 30 misidentified victims has led to charges of negligence (BBC, 2009). In Europe, the Parliamentary Assembly of the Council of Europe in the Memorandum of Recommendation R(99)3 on the harmonisation of medico-legal autopsy rules recommends the use of the internationally recognised INTERPOL Disaster Victim Identification forms to record any identifying information, particularly when foreign nationals are involved, to facilitate international data exchange.

The identification process can be divided into three phases: antemortem data collection, postmortem data collection, and reconciliation. It is important to explain the complexities of the process to family members of the missing and provide them with a realistic timeframe.

Antemortem Data Collection

Antemortem information is any identifying data obtained from families of the missing person or records which may be directly or indirectly comparable to the missing person. Families in this context include partners, parents, siblings, children, guardians and others who have had a direct and close relationship with the victim. Antemortem information can be obtained via a number of ways: from an interview with family members; through medical, dental or fingerprint records held; by third parties or directly obtained from personal belongings of the missing persons; or by gathering DNA reference samples. Antemortem records are pivotal to corroborate a positive identification (Blau et al., 2006; Rai and Anand, 2007) and the availability and accuracy of these records determine the success of the identification process (Avon, 2004; Leclair et al., 2004; Calacal et al., 2005; González-Andrade and Sánchez, 2005; Petju et al., 2007). This may be further complicated in scenarios where entire families have perished (De Valck, 2006).

Family Liaison Officers have a crucial role to play in the response to a mass fatality incident and the identification of the dead. INTERPOL recommends that a Family Liaison Strategy is immediately implemented following a mass fatality incident, which will include the deployment of a trained police investigator to every family believed to have lost a relative in the incident (INTERPOL, 2009). Family Liaison Officers will undertake the day-to-day interaction with the family of the deceased. They will complete the yellow INTERPOL Disaster Victim Identification antemortem forms and undertake the collection of antemortem evidence on behalf of the Senior Identification Manager (SIM). Interviews to collect this information can take place at a relative's home or in a designated Family and Friends Reception Centre located away from the scene, where relatives of those people directly involved in the disaster can provide the relevant documentation, and information regarding the disaster can be disseminated (ACPO, 2009).

A disaster may involve victims and family members from different social, religious and cultural backgrounds. This requires appropriate, tactful and sensitive consideration by the Family Liaison Officers. A personal approach is desirable; it is important to ask questions in the present time and to address the missing person by name rather than as 'the missing person'. Realistic, factual and honest information regarding the identification process should always be given to family members if requested. Communication and provision of accurate information is a vital coping mechanism for the relatives of those people directly involved. Family Liaison Officers are also key in managing potential family tensions, for example, where the deceased may have been estranged from the whole or part of their family prior to their death, or may have a forbidden relationship with someone unknown to other members of the family due to religious circumstances.

Postmortem Data Collection

Postmortem information is technically similar to that collected following the discovery of unidentified remains in missing persons investigations. Simultaneous processing of multiple fatalities requires, however, different logistical, scientific and operational approaches and necessitates close coordination between agencies and parties involved in the disaster response.

Regional mass fatality plans have normally identified the local capacity of bodies that can be dealt with or, if this number is exceeded, other temporary locations where the identification process can be facilitated. This can be an existing mortuary facility in a hospital for example; however, the available capacity should take into account the normal day-to-day working operations. If no building is available, a temporary mortuary facility[2] can be set up at a designated location. Several considerations will be made when setting up a temporary mortuary in a structure not designed for this type of work. This will include security and temporary flooring. Refrigeration trucks to temporarily hold the bodies have to be arranged.

The bodies typically arrive at the reception area of the facility. Prior to examination, the body bag with the remains may be radiographed and screened for potential evidence such as shrapnel, to corroborate or support medical findings, to assess the extent of commingling or presence of nonhuman remains, or as a safety precaution to detect unexploded ordnances.

Particularly in burned remains, the radiography may reveal otherwise hidden personal effects such as piercings and rings (Shkrum and Ramsay, 2007, p. 189). Radiography is considered a viable alternative in chemical, biological, radiological and nuclear (CBRN) incidents in which handling of human remains is potentially hazardous but is also increasingly utilised in other types of disasters (for example see O'Donnell et al., 2011; Rutty et al., 2007) or as an alternative to an invasive autopsy in cases where religious or cultural objections may be present (Rutty 2012). Depending on the state of the body or degree of fragmentation, examinations will normally be carried out in a number of consecutive stations or simultaneously by a number of experts.

Disaster Victim Identification teams are frequently composed of a pathologist, odontologist, exhibits officer, scribe, photographer, fingerprint officer and other experts including forensic anthropologists. A multidisciplinary approach is essential to the success of these operations (Byard and Winskog, 2010) as well a structured process of collecting identification information. Clothing items, personal effects and body modifications such as tattoos and piercings found on the deceased will be photographed and accurately recorded on the pink (postmortem) INTERPOL Disaster Victim Identification forms. Those photographs may become important for comparison to antemortem photographs of personal items or as a means to show to relatives to assist with the identification process. Personal effects, no matter how insignificant they may seem, are of emotional importance to relatives and should therefore be treated with respect as they may signify the last tangible objects the deceased was wearing at the time of his or her death. Medical findings which may aid identification such as surgical interventions, healed fractures, disease processes and evidence of the cause of death will be recorded by a pathologist. Fingerprints will be taken where possible. Forensic odontologists (dentists) document visually and radiographically any dental findings including restorations, crowns, implants, tooth extractions and other features that may aid identification. The Family Liaison Officers will aim to collect the most recent dental records from dentists, as well as medical information and fingerprints for comparison. In cases of fragmentation of bodies, such as often experienced in aircraft accidents or explosions, additional complexities arise due to a potentially large number of body parts and/or unrecognisable tissues. Correct identification of the anatomical location of a body part is essential to establish the number of individuals involved and the reassociation of the remains (Budimlija et al., 2003). This may be a time-consuming and lengthy process but one that is necessary to ascertain that all missing persons are accounted for. DNA identification is increasingly used for the reunification of body parts to a body. Associated body parts show identical DNA profiles and can hence aid in the reunification process (Leclair et al., 2004; Piccinini et al., 2004). More complex matching problems are likely to occur where the remains are extensively fragmented, commingled and exposed to conditions promoting DNA degradation (Brenner and Weir, 2003; Budimlija et al., 2003) and this may confound the identification or regrouping of remains. Once all the postmortem information has been collected and quality checks have been completed to assure all the information is correctly entered onto the forms, the data will be entered into a software system to allow for automated comparisons and searches to be performed.

It is important that those working at the scene or mortuary are experienced in dealing with a large number of deceased. Professional social work intervention and support can assist disaster response workers and volunteers assigned to the morgue to cope with the unique stresses associated with recovering and handling dead bodies (Newhill and Sites, 2000) and to reduce the risk of post-traumatic stress disorders (Brondolo et al., 2008). Not only is the wellbeing of the relatives of those involved important, but also that of the responders and forensic experts working in such challenging environments.

Reconciliation

Reconciliation is the final phase in the identification process and aims to match the collected postmortem data with the antemortem data in order to establish the identity of the victim 'on the balance of probabilities' or 'beyond reasonable doubt'. As Keiser-Nielsen (1969) pointed out, antemortem and postmortem data is initially collected blindly, without prior knowledge as to which particular identification feature will be reported in the other set. In disasters and missing person investigations it is therefore pivotal that both the antemortem and postmortem data collected is as comprehensive, detailed and accurate as feasibly possible. It is not uncommon that discrepancies are found between antemortem and postmortem data. Relatives may have forgotten certain physical features or personal effects the missing person was wearing, particularly so in a state of emotional distress in the immediate aftermath of a disaster or when the missing person had not been seen for a considerable time. Dental inconsistencies may also be present, particularly when no up-to-date dental records are available or if the missing person had switched dentists regularly. It is the responsibility of the reconciliation team, in collaboration with scientific experts, to provide plausible explanations to resolve those discrepancies. If a potential identification is made, the antemortem and postmortem files of the reported missing person and deceased, respectively, are presented to the Identification Commission for final verification. The Identification Commission is chaired by the HM Coroner of the jurisdiction in which the disaster occurred and may further consist of relevant identification experts including forensic pathologists, odontologists, DNA scientists, fingerprint examiners, reconciliation manager, exhibit officers and other experts deemed relevant. For each putative identification, the experts provide their opinion on the strength of the antemortem and postmortem evidence presented to them. If in agreement, the identification is confirmed and necessary repatriation and funeral arrangements may be made. Under certain circumstances the Identification Commission may decide to postpone releasing the remains until all the bodies or body parts have been identified, frequently in disasters involving fragmentation. Although this delay may cause frustration to relatives (Edkins, 2007), an accurate process must be followed to ensure that all the remains are correctly identified prior to release and no unanswered questions relating to the identity of the victims remain, which may cause additional distress to descendants of disaster victims. Indeed, it should be kept in mind that if one person is misidentified another family will also have been presented with a wrong body.

The management of the dead may raise many ethical questions which are unique to every disaster. Those questions may include what resources should be allocated to the identification process, should all fragmentary remains be tested or only a select sample, how will unidentifiable tissues be disposed of and how long should the process continue if not all remains can be identified due to limitations in technological advances. The answers to those questions depend on the expectations of relatives and family groups, cultural and societal beliefs, the comparability of antemortem data, forensic technology and resources available, and the characteristics of the disaster itself. Following the World Trade Centre 9/11 terrorist attacks, it was decided to take DNA samples from every bone fragment, no matter how small, in light of the degree of fragmentation, sample disintegration and the unknown number of victims (Budimlija et al., 2003). Pressure of the relatives of those missing further reinforced this decision as many would not want their loved ones' remains to be reinterred with those of the hijackers (Conant, 2009). This also meant that relatives were given a choice to bury the remains of their loved ones once the identification process was completed or to be notified every time a fragment was identified; in the latter the relatives have to relive the loss over and over again. Following the 7 July terrorist bombings in London, however, although an open incident, size and relative identifiability were considered when deciding which remains to sample for DNA (Mundorff, 2008). In large-scale destructive disasters, it is not uncommon that bodies may never be found because they have been washed away or buried in the immediate, chaotic aftermath of a disaster. This 'ambiguous loss' may have a profound effect on the relatives as there is no closure, verification of death or certainty that the person will return (Boss, 2002).

The Role of Families of Disaster Victims

Many of the manuals and guidelines for Disaster Victim Identification have been developed from the perspective of responders' operational needs in terms of plans, procedures and protocols rather than the needs and interests of the bereaved (Eyre, 2002). Furthermore, while detailed mass fatality plans are in operation in the UK, which include activation of Casualty Bureau, and coordination between hospitals, search and rescue teams and other agencies in the response unit, this is by no means fully implemented and operational in other countries. Relatives may travel to the country itself, enquiring at hospitals or searching through galleries of missing person information or photos of deceased posted online in a bid to establish the fate of their loved one. The right of families to conduct religious and cultural funeral rites should be respected (Pan American Health Organization, 2004) as well as allowing family members to visit the scene of the disaster. The right to view the body should be granted if relatives wish to do so, even though the remains may be disfigured by trauma or decomposition (Chapple and Ziebland, 2010). Websites have been created to facilitate the search for missing persons in overseas disasters such as Google PersonFinder[3] and the American Red Cross' Safe and Well list.[4] Social media, most notably Facebook, are playing an increasingly important role not only for locating missing persons but also as a means to stay updated on the search and rescue efforts, sharing of identification information or as a means of public grieving and memorialisation. Several instances of abuse of these media have been reported, including fake death notifications and 'trolling' following a disaster, and no framework is currently in place to deal with those excesses. Moderation of online memorials is often ungoverned and the creation unsanctioned by close relatives of those deceased (Moncur and Waller, 2010). In the UK, members of DisasterAction,[5] all of whom are survivors and bereaved people from disasters, have written and published documents with guidance for families, Police Family Liaison Officers and Coroner's Officers.

International Coordination and the Identification of British Nationals Abroad

Operating in an external jurisdiction following a disaster abroad may create complex legal and cultural issues (Byard and Winskog, 2010). INTERPOL Resolution AGN/65/RES/13, adopted by the ICPO-INTERPOL General Assembly at its 65th session in Antalya, recommends that member countries seek the assistance, as participants or observers, of Disaster Victim Identification Liaison Officers and/or teams from countries whose citizens are victims of the disaster to assist with the identification process and enhance cooperation, liaison and information exchange. Jurisdiction to deal with a disaster lies with the host country in which the incident occurs and all processes are governed by the laws, legislation and conventions of the affected country. If the crisis overseas involves mass fatalities with the possibility of British nationals being involved, the Foreign and Commonwealth Office may request UK Disaster Victim Identification Team resources.

INTERPOL's Disaster Victim Identification unit, part of the Operational Police Support Directorate, is supported by a Steering Group and a Standing Committee on Disaster Victim Identification. The Steering Group formulates INTERPOL Disaster Victim Identification policy and strategic planning while the Standing Committee meets regularly to discuss improvements to procedures and standards in Disaster Victim Identification matters. Cross-border coordination between agencies and organisations can be facilitated by INTERPOL in case of an international disaster. An INTERPOL Incident Response Team (IRT) may be deployed at the request of a member country during a crisis situation to coordinate the Disaster Victim Identification response through a wide network of international experts and laboratories. This support network ensures compliance with international standards and forensic quality assurance controls, information sharing and exchange between member countries via national NCBs and operational assistance to countries which lack Disaster Victim Identification capacity. The INTERPOL Disaster Victim Identification guide states that,

> the specific religious and cultural needs and national idiosyncrasies or laws and directives of the Member States must be taken into consideration during an operation, but will not be discussed any further in the explanations of the Guide. It is also not possible to deal with all conceivable operational scenarios.
>
> (INTERPOL, 2009)

As stated in the INTERPOL guidance, national laws and directives need to be followed, although the guidance acknowledges that application of international standards should apply in multinational Disaster Victim Identification operations. However, management of Disaster Victim Identification operations cannot rely solely on standardised protocols alone and should also consider lessons learned from previous disasters (Perrier et al., 2006).

While INTERPOL promotes the highest international identification standards, it should be recognised that the host country has the jurisdiction of the disaster and different standards may be accepted. Foreign Disaster Victim Identification teams may want to implement identification criteria so that, as far as foreign victims are concerned, the identification is also recognised in their countries of origin. On the other hand, however, forensic experts from the host country may wish to conduct the identification process based on locally accepted standards, which may be further reinforced by pressure from families, religious organisations and political influences.

A uniform approach is of vital importance to the identification process and a coordinated effort can significantly speed up the victim recovery and identification process, enabling victims' families to begin the healing process and communities to rebuild (INTERPOL, 2009). The organisation of the identification process differs from country to country, and within the countries, depending on the historical and political structures and on the kind of disaster (Lessig and Rothschild, 2012). Indeed, an uncoordinated approach may lead to errors in comparability, exchange and translation of identification data (Keiser-Nielsen, 1969) and may significantly delay the process. Important lessons have been learned from previous disasters. In the immediate aftermath of the 2004 tsunami, for example, different identification protocols were followed resulting in misidentification, exhumation and re-examination of the deceased (Morgan et al., 2006). Particular problems may occur when the disaster occurs in weakened, failed or collapsed states with limited infrastructure, forensic capability or authoritative control. Geographic isolation and destruction of infrastructure and resources are other factors that have to be considered. It is imperative that foreign Disaster Victim Identification teams assisting with the identification process are briefed on local traditions, religious and cultural attitudes and sensitivities, or find assistance from a local interpreter or professional with a thorough understanding of the language and cultural customs (Berketa et al., 2012). During the 2011 east Japan earthquake and tsunami, language issues caused problems between Disaster Victim Identification and search and rescue teams (Kubo, 2012). Following (natural) disasters and resultant loss of income and livelihood, stories of theft of bodies from local hospitals for ransom, looting and grave robbing by locals have been reported. Reports of stolen jewellery, money and other personal items have emerged in a number of disasters such as the 2004 tsunami (Teh, 2008; Rohan et al., 2009). Cadavers may be recovered and buried by family members, neighbours, the local community or even the state before proper identification procedures can be established (Gupta and Sadiq, 2010). It is therefore vital that an appropriate disaster response mechanism is in place to avoid any additional distress for the relatives of those missing.

Conclusion

Disasters, whether relatively small or large in terms of fatalities, are challenging and complex. Preparedness is the key to success in Disaster Victim Identification (Pretty et al., 2001). Any preplanning must include adequate provisions for the collection, accommodation, examination, identification and disposal of large numbers of dead victims (Hussain et al., 2006). Many factors play a role in a successful Disaster Victim Identification operation, including the quality and quantity of antemortem information, characteristics of the disaster, communication and cooperation between agencies and facilities available. It is therefore important that uniform standards are adopted and promoted, not only in relation to the identification process but that also take into account the (humanitarian) needs of the relatives of those directly involved, disaster responders and forensic experts. For any Disaster Victim Identification deployment, transfer of knowledge by experienced practitioners and succession planning must be encouraged (Winskog et al., 2012).

Notes

1 The *Marchioness* disaster was a fatal collision between the *Marchioness* passenger boat and the aggregate dredger *Bowbelle* on the River Thames on 20 August 1989 resulting in the sinking of the *Marchioness* and the loss of 51 lives. A nonstatutory inquiry into the identification of victims following major transport accidents began on 30 November 2000. The report by Lord Justice Clarke made 36 main recommendations, the most important of which was that a detailed review should be undertaken as to the role of the coroner with a code introduced laying out his powers, duties and responsibilities and listed the general principles which should be kept in mind throughout the identification process after a major disaster.
2 In the UK those arrangements are commonly referred to as a National Emergency Mortuary Arrangements (NEMA) facility.
3 http://google.org/personfinder/global/home.html.
4 https://safeandwell.communityos.org/zf/safe/add.
5 www.disasteraction.org.

References

ACPO/ACPOS (2008). *Guidance on Casualty Bureau Standard Administrative Procedures (CBSAP)* [online]. www.acpo.police.uk/documents/uniformed/2008/200803UNCBS01.pdf (accessed 1 July 2013).

ACPO (2009). *Guidance on Emergency Procedures* [online]. www.acpo.police.uk/documents/uniformed/2009/200904UNGEP01.pdf (accessed 3 July 2013).

Avon, S. L. (2004). Forensic odontology: The roles and responsibilities of the dentist. *Journal of the Canadian Dental Association*, 70(7): 453–458.

BBC (2009). Spanish general jailed over crash [online]. http://news.bbc.co.uk/1/hi/8057983.stm. (accessed 16 June 2013).

Berketa, J. W., James, H. and Lake, A. W. (2012). Forensic odontology involvement in disaster victim identification. *Forensic Science Medicine and Pathology*, 8(2): 148–156.

Blau, S., Hill, A., and Briggs, C. A. (2006). Missing persons–missing data: The need to collect antemortem dental records of missing persons. *Journal of Forensic Sciences*, 51(2): 386–389.

Boss, P. (2002). Ambiguous loss in families of the missing. *The Lancet*, 360: s39–s40.

Brenner, C. H. and Weir, B. S. (2003). Issues and strategies in the DNA identification of World Trade Center victims. *Theoretical Population Biolology*, 63(3): 173–178.

Brondolo, E., Wellington, R., Brady, N., Libby, D. and Brondolo, T. J. (2008). Mechanism and strategies for preventing post-traumatic stress disorder in forensic workers responding to mass fatality incidents. *Journal of Forensic and Legal Medicine*, 15(2): 78–88.

Brondolo, T. J. (2004). Resource requirements for medical examiner response to mass fatality incidents. *MedicoLegal Journal of Ireland*, 10(2): 91–102.

Budimlija, Z. M., Prinz, M. K., Zelson-Mundorff, A., Wiersema, J., Bartelink, E., MacKinnon, G., Nazzaruolo, B. L., Estacio, S. M., Hennessey, M. J. and Shaler, R. C. (2003). World Trade Center human identification project: Experiences with individual body identification cases. *Croatian Medical Journal*, 44(3): 259–263.

Busuttil, A., Green, M. and Jones, J.S.P. (2000). *Deaths in Major Disasters — The Pathologist's Role*. London: Royal College of Pathologists.

Byard, R. W. and Winskog, C. (2010). Potential problems arising during international disaster victim identification exercises. *Forensic Science, Medicine, and Pathology*, 6(1): 1–2.

Calacal, G. C., Delfin, F. C., Tan, M. M., Roewer, L., Magtanong, D. L., Lara, M. C., Fortun, R. and De Ungria, M. C. (2005). Identification of exhumed remains of fire tragedy victims using conventional methods and autosomal/Y-chromosomal short tandem repeat DNA profiling. *American Journal of Forensic Medicine and Patholology*, 26(3): 285–291.

Chapple, A. and Ziebland S. (2010). Viewing the body after bereavement due to a traumatic death: Qualitative study in the UK. *British Medical Journal*, 340: c2032.

Clarke, Lord Justice (2001). *Public Inquiry into the Identification of Victims Following Major Transport Accidents*. Norwich: HMSO.

Conant, E. (2009). Nineteen hijackers died on 9/11. What should be done with what's left of them? [online]. The DailyBeast. www.thedailybeast.com/newsweek/2009/01/02/remains-of-the-day.html (accessed 19 June 2013).

De Valck, E. (2006). Major incident response: Collecting antemortem data. *Forensic Science International*, 159: S15–19.

Edkins, J. (2007). *Missing Persons London*, July 2005 [online]. www.st-andrews.ac.uk/intrel/media/Edkins_missing_persons.pdf (accessed 17 June 2013).

Eyre, A. (2002). Improving procedures and minimising distress: Issues in the identification of victims following disasters. *Australian Journal of Emergency Management*, 17(1): 9–14.

Galloway, G. and Mallett, X. (2011). The Lockerbie bombing, December 21, 1988. In S. Black, G. Sunderland, L. Hackman, and X. Mallett (eds), *The Disaster Victim Identification Casebook: Experience and Practice* (pp. 89–107). Boca Raton: CRC Press.

Gilliland, M. G., McDonough, E. T., Fossum, R. M., Dowling, G. P., Besant-Matthews, P. E. and Petty, C. S. (1986). Disaster planning for air crashes. A retrospective analysis of Delta Airlines flight 191. *American Journal of Forensic Medicine and Pathology*, 7(4): 308–316.

González-Andrade, F. and Sánchez, D. (2005). DNA typing from skeletal remains following an explosion in a military fort first experience in Ecuador (South America). *Legal Medicine (Tokyo)*, 7(5): 314–318.

Gupta, K. and Sadiq, A. (2010). Responses to mass fatalities in the aftermath of 2010 Haiti earthquake [online]. www.colorado.edu/hazards/research/qr/submitted/gupta_2010.pdf (accessed 17 June 2013).

Higgins, D. and James, H. (2006). Classifications used by Australian forensic odontologists in identification reports. *The Journal of Forensic Odonto-Stomatology*, 24: 32–35.

Home Office (2006). The emergency response to the London bombings – lessons learned [online]. www.scribd.com/doc/34643696/Addressing-Lessons-From-the-Emergency-Response-to-the-7-July-2005-London-Bombings-What-we-learned-and-what-we-are-doing-about-it-22-September-2006 (accessed 14 June 2013).

Hussain, S., Hafeez, N., Munawar, A. Z. and Khalil, I. R. (2006). Disaster victim identification – are we prepared? [online] *Pakistan Armed Forces Medical Journal*, 4. www.pafmj.org/showdetails.php?id=18andt=r (accessed 2 July 2013).

ICMP (2012). U.S. Helsinki commission hearing: 'Healing the wounds of conflict and disaster: Clarifying the fate of missing persons in the Osce area'. Intervention by Her Majesty Queen Noor. ICMP Commissioner, 28 February 2012 [online]. www.ic-mp.org/wp-content/uploads/2012/02/icmp-dg-415-4-doc.pdf (accessed 11 June 2013).

INTERPOL (2009). *Disaster Victim Identification Guide* [online]. www.interpol.int/interpol-expertise/Forensics/DVI (accessed 4 December 2015).

Keiser-Nielsen, S. (1969). Forensic odontology. *University of Toledo Law Review*, 1: 633–639.

Knight, B. (1991). *Forensic Pathology* (1st edition). London: Arnold.

Kubo, S. I. (2012). Great East Japan earthquake: Postmortem examinations and personal identifications of victims. *Rechtsmedizin*, 22: 12–16.

Lain, R., Griffiths, C. and Hilton, M. (2003). Forensic dental and medical response to the Bali bombing. *Medical Journal of Australia*, 179: 362–365.

Leclair, B., Frégeau, C. J., Bowen, K. L. and Fourney, R. M. (2004). Enhanced kinship analysis and STR-based DNA typing for human identification in mass fatality incidents: The Swissair flight 111 disaster. *Journal of Forensic Sciences*, 49(5): 939–953.

Lessig, R. and Rothschild, M. (2012). International standards in cases of mass disaster victim identification. *Forensic Science, Medicine and Pathology*, 8: 197–199.

London Assembly (2006). *Report of the 7 July Review Committee* [online]. www.london.gov.uk/sites/default/files/archives/assembly-reports-7july-report.pdf (accessed 1 July 2013).

Moncur, W. and Waller A. (2010). *Digital Inheritance* [online]. www.computing.dundee.ac.uk/staff/wmoncur/publications/2010-rcuk-digitalFutures.pdf (accessed 15 June 2013).

Morgan, O. W., Sribanditmongkol, P., Perera, C., Sulasmi, Y., Van Alphen, D. and Sondorp, E. (2006). Mass fatality management following the South Asian tsunami disaster: Case studies in Thailand, Indonesia, and Sri Lanka. *PLoS Med*, 3(6): e195.

Mundorff, A. Z. (2008). Anthropologist-directed triage: Three distinct mass fatality events involving fragmentation of human remains. In B. Adams and J. Byrd (eds), *Recovery, Analysis, and identification of Commingled Human Remains* (pp. 123–144). Totowa: Humana Press.

Newhill, C. E. and Sites, E. W. (2000). Identifying human remains following an air disaster: The role of social work. *Social Work in Health Care*, 31(4): 85–105.

O'Donnell, C., Iino, M., Mansharan, K., Leditscke, J. and Woodford, N. (2011). Contribution of post-mortem multidetector CT scanning to identification of the deceased in a mass disaster: Experience gained from the 2009 Victorian bushfires. *Forensic Science International*, 205(1–3): 15–28.

Pan American Health Organization (2004). *Management of Dead Bodies in Disaster Situations*. Washington, DC: Pan American Health Organization.

Perrier, M., Bollmann, M., Girod, A. and Mangin, P. (2006). Swiss disaster victim identification at the tsunami disaster: Expect the unexpected. *Forensic Science International*, 159 (Suppl.): S30–S32.

Petju, M., Suteerayongprasert, A., Thongpud, R. and Hassiri, K. (2007). Importance of dental records for victim identification following the Indian Ocean tsunami disaster in Thailand. *Public Health*, 121(4): 251–257.

Piccinini, A., Betti, F., Capra, M. and Cattaneo, C. (2004). The identification of the victims of the Linate air crash by DNA analysis. *International Congress Series*, 1261: 39–41.

Pretty, I. A., Webb, D. A. and Sweet, D. (2001). The design and assessment of mock mass disasters for dental personnel. *Journal of Forensic Sciences*, 46: 74–79.

Rai, B. and Anand, S. C. (2007). Role of forensic odontology in tsunami disasters. *Internet Journal of Forensic Science*, 2: 1540–2622.

Rohan, R. P., Hettiarachchi, M., Vidanapathirana, M. and Perera, S. (2009). Management of dead and missing: Aftermath tsunami in Galle. *Legal Medicine*, 11: S86–S88.

Rutty, G. (2012). *Can Cross Sectional Imaging as an Adjunct and/or Alternative to the Invasive Autopsy Be Implemented Within the NHS?* NHS Implementation Subgroup of the Department of Health Post Mortem, Forensic and Disaster Imaging Group (PMFDI).

Rutty, G. N., Robinson, C. E., BouHaidar, R., Jeffery, A. J. and Morgan, B. (2007). The role of mobile computed tomography in mass fatality incidents. *Journal of Forensic Sciences*, 52(6): 1343–1349.

Ruwanpura, R. (2012). Medicolegal practice and its interaction with multitude of socioreligious rites in Sri Lanka. *Sri Lanka Journal of Forensic Medicine, Science and Law*, 2(2): 4–6.

Shkrum, M. J. and Ramsey, D. A. (2007). Thermal injury. In M. J. Shkrum and D. A. Ramsey (eds), *Forensic Pathology of Trauma: Common Problems for the Pathologist* (pp. 181–242). Totowa, NJ: Humana Press.

Teh, Y. K. (2008). The abuses and offences committed during the tsunami crisis. *Asian Criminology*, 3: 201–211.

The Investigator (2010). Operation Lune: The Morecambe Bay cockling disaster [online]. www.the-investigator.co.uk/files/The_Investigator_Aug-Sept_2010.pdf. (accessed 1 July 2013).

Winskog, C., Tonkin, A. and Byard, R.W. (2012). The educational value of Disaster Victim Identification (Disaster Victim Identification) missions transfer of knowledge. *Forensic Science, Medicine and Pathology*, 8(2): 84–87.

Part IV
Families of Missing Persons

The Emotional Impact on Families When a Loved One Goes Missing

Jo Youle and Helen Alves

For someone you love to go missing, and then not to find them for days, weeks, months or years is an unimaginable experience for many. The emotional impact is significant. It is not the same as bereavement, although there is grieving. To miss someone and not know if they are alive or dead means for many an inability to move on and generates emotions that are nearly impossible to cope with. This chapter explores the key themes in research about the emotional impact on families when someone goes, and stays, missing. Furthermore, this chapter will introduce new testimony collected from 12 families of missing people, some of whom were interviewed in spring 2013. The family members involved wished their names to be used, reflecting a desire to openly share their personal story.

Much is known about the impacts on the families of long-term missing people, and this chapter is primarily focused on people missing through accident, crime or individual choice. There are other sources that focus on what it is like to live with having somebody missing as a result of political unrest, war and mass migration. Examples include Edkins, 2011; Finucane, 2010; Luster et al., 2009; and Cassia, 2006.

When a loved one is missing, the experience of loss can be described as ambiguous. Pauline Boss (1999, 2002, 2006; Boss et al., 2003) used the phrase 'ambiguous loss' to describe what families face when a loved person is missing. The phrase is also used in a wider context whereby the object of loss is not wholly absent or wholly present. It describes the loss experienced by families of people living with dementia and the loss faced by people who have lost touch with family members following natural disaster, mass migration or other large-scale events, and people who have themselves migrated and have 'lost' the place and life they left behind (Vargas, 2008).

Boss (1999, 2002, 2006; Boss et al., 2003) talks of the experience of missing: the unresolved grief and the fluctuations between hope and hopelessness. She details how 'ambiguous loss is inherently traumatic because the inability to resolve the situation causes pain, confusion, shock, distress and often immobilisation. Without closure, the trauma of this unique kind of loss becomes "chronic"' (Boss, 2006, p. 4). The UK charity Missing People supports families, sometimes over many years, for as long as is needed. Descriptions of this support can be found in Steyne et al. (2013). Some people experience the intensity of emotions as painfully in the later years as in the first months. Valerie Nettles, whose son Damien has been missing since November 1996, describes her sorrow as 'the beast within'.

Ambiguous loss differs from other types of loss, despite ostensible similarities. The experience of someone close being missing is unique. De Young and Buzzi (2003) found marked differences in the experiences and coping strategies of parents of murdered children compared to parents of abducted, long-term missing children, identifying that,

> both groups suffered comparable bereavement manifestations and utilized similar coping strategies during times of ambiguous loss. The two groups mirrored each other emotionally until the time that parents of murdered children attained the first stage of resolution: clarification of the ambiguous loss through outcome determination. At this point, parents of murdered children were then able to embark on the different emotional and physiological tracks toward the identifiable stages of resolution, which is grieving the loss of their child.
>
> (De Young and Buzzi, 2003, p. 343)

Pauline Green, whose son Matt went missing in April 2010, talks about how people do not understand unless they are going through it themselves: 'They say, well, it is like a death, and I say, well no, because if it is a bereavement or a death, you've got an end, and you can focus forward, but with this we've got no end and it's just day in and day out.' Maureen Trask, whose son Daniel went missing in November 2011, says: 'How do you grieve when someone is missing … if you don't know whether they are alive or dead?' She continues, 'Having a son go missing is so very different from a death. It's a never ending uncertainty.'

The emotional impact on a family may be affected by their understanding or perception of why their loved one went missing. For example, it might feel different to be the partner of someone who has gone missing after a night out, compared to being the parent of a child where there is simply no explanation of why they went missing, leading to endless speculation.

Missing People supports those who are missing and their families across the whole continuum. We recognise the importance of perceived 'intent' to leave. Even though this intent is generally assumed rather than known by a family, it has a huge effect on their feelings and their ability to cope. Holmes explains in more detail how families may feel, based on their understanding of why someone is missing. Figure 6.2 in Chapter 6 of this volume further illustrates the potential range of emotions based on a sense of why someone is missing and the likelihood that they will be found safe.

Sarah Wayland refers to the sense of trauma experienced by family members responding to an unanticipated event of a loved one going missing whereby 'families respond in similar ways to those exposed to a sudden trauma: shock, distress, confusion, ambivalence and a considerable sense of being overwhelmed' (Wayland, 2007, p. 11). Valerie Nettles wrote of the sense of 'incredulity that this was actually happening and I was actually unable to find my son and nobody knew where he was'. She went on to describe the terror that her child was 'out there somewhere'. Elizabeth Templeton, mother of Alan, who was missing from November 2006 until his body was found in March 2012, put into words that the early days when she realised her son was missing were like 'stepping on a step that wasn't there' and described a feeling that 'this can't be happening'.

In the early days of his son Andrew going missing in September 2007, Kevin Gosden describes sleeping on the floor waiting for news by the phone 'so if he rang any time'. Nicki Durbin remembers when Luke her son first went missing in May 2006, 'the amount of times I would buy all the stuff he liked, put it in the fridge, just in case he came home, and you know it'd just be thrown away'. Valerie Nettles said, 'initially family and friends flocked to my house, the kettle was always on and there was someone to hold my hand or just sit quietly and keep me company. Eventually and inevitably people drifted back to their own lives as it became apparent there wasn't going to be a quick solution.'

Denise Allan, mother of Charles who went missing in May 1989, describes herself in the early days as 'demented', with days of uncontrollable sobbing. She describes a day when she thought Charles had come back home: 'Somebody rang the doorbell at the house, and I turned round to look out the window to see the porch, and … Charles is home, and I ran like a lunatic to the front door, and opened the door, and it wasn't him. I was hysterical … cracking up.' Trish Cooper describes 'four days with no sleep' when her brother Steven first went missing in January 2008. She explains how in the early days they would drive 'all through the night, miles and miles and miles … all the places we thought he would be, with the weather as bad as it was … and you're looking on moors where Myra Hindley and that guy buried bodies'.

The family members' testimonies suggest that families go through different stages as they live without knowing where their loved one is and without resolution. Pauline Green says that 'the hardest bit was like the first six months; maybe the first year was difficult for the pair of us … because we've never been in this situation before'. Some families describe the difficulty of being encouraged to move on. Elizabeth Templeton, whose son was sadly found dead after being missing for six years, described how it had felt 'awful' when a police officer said, 'I advise you to get on with the rest of your lives.'

Sandra Flintoft, mother of Craig who went missing in February 2003, said,

> When Craig first went missing I was so worried and sad. Where had I gone so wrong, what had I done to let him down so much … what more could or should I have done to help him sort himself out … after the first year my feelings changed. I felt sorry for myself … I was distraught with worry … I was angry with him. I wondered why he did not care that I was so unhappy.

The next stage followed: 'I felt guilty that life continued for me and my family.' Glenys Gosden, mum of Andrew, says, 'I had to be back at work, for psychologically, work was a sort of haven, something that was a constant and normality that I was in control of.' Glenys went on to say, 'I almost have to stop expecting that I'll see him [Andrew] … 'cos I don't think I will.' Kate McCann, mother of Madeleine McCann who went missing in May 2007, said,

> Everyone reaches phases at different times, and you know … me and Gerry, we're good example of that … he got to each stage … much quicker than I did … it doesn't mean he didn't have days when he totally lost it … and I was actually the stronger one.

The strength and range of emotions felt by families when a loved one is missing are considerable. Families and loved ones can go through stages of guilt, regret and also of intense anger – one participant in Living in Limbo said: 'I was furious I just wanted to bloody kill him you know for putting us through this' (Holmes, 2008, p. 20). Several families imagined how they would respond if their missing person turned up. Sandra Flintoft said,

> if he came home … hug him first, kick him next and then never let him out of my sight again … I forget that my boy will be 33 years old now. How sad that I have missed so much time.

Monique Leslie, whose sister Jacqueline was missing from October 2007 until her body was found in August 2015, had pored over her sister's diary, piecing together information and snippets that might help find her. 'I think what struck me, is how alone she was' and that 'it hurt me … for some reason I felt I should have been there … in some way'. She says, 'sometimes people are crying out and … you're not really listening … I just wish I'd put myself out more for her.' Trish Cooper describes how she has 'beaten herself up' over her brother's party she was supposed to go to and did not, asking the question, 'was it 'cos he thought we didn't care?' One mother describes the strong feelings – deep unhappiness, overwhelming anxiety, anguish, distress and despair: 'I had never in my life and still haven't experienced such excruciating pain' (Holmes, 2008, p. 19), and Kate McCann says, 'It's that feeling of uncertainly … lack of knowledge … helplessness … which is a killer.'

Family members can struggle with conflicting ideas about what has happened to their missing person within themselves. Valerie Nettles said, 'It began to be, in my head possible that he was dead; though I found it odd that a mother wouldn't know by instinct if her son was dead.' She continues,

> I tried to be calm and philosophical and tell myself this is just a mistake … this is not ha pening and stop panicking, there is a logical explanation and he will come waltzing through the door. But all the time deep down I knew, something was terribly wrong and it was terrifying.

Pauline Boss explains: 'persons who tolerate best this kind of loss … are able to hold two opposing ideas in their mind at the same time: "My son is gone, but he is also still here and always will be in some ways"' (Boss, 2002, p. 17). Trish Cooper highlights the contradictory hopes of a family in this position: 'You don't want him to be dead – 'cos you want him to be found alive somewhere … but you want … an end to the suffering.'

There may be differing views or thinking within a family about the missing person. Alan Pike from the Centre for Crisis Psychology, which specialises in support for people experiencing trauma, notes that different views within a family can also be an additional cause of distress and conflict and put immense pressure on a relationship, particularly if it is perceived that a family member could have 'contributed to' someone going missing. Mendenhall and Berge note that 'individual members of the same family frequently espouse different viewpoints regarding the missing person's status as a person who is alive or a person who is dead' (Mendenhall and Berge, 2010, p. 48). Glenys Gosden, whose son Andrew is missing, said,

> I was clutching at something so small, a tiny bit of hope and, you know, I still had to rationalise it, probably at lot earlier than you (referring to her husband Kevin), I would say my best conclusion is that he's not there and he's taken his own life.

She says it was unbearable to cope with disappointment upon disappointment after potential sightings came to nothing. She also says, 'I almost have to stop expecting that I'll see him again. 'Cos I don't think I will; at least not this side of heaven.' Kevin, her husband, says, '*still* in the back of your mind there's that little nagging thing that maybe this time, that article or whatever will find somebody who knows something about what happened to Andrew'.

Kate McCann describes herself as a 'glass is half empty person' and is thankful that her husband Gerry is 'the opposite'. She uses the example of people who refer to statistics that 'there is more likelihood that your child will be dead than alive', noting that Gerry will say: 'It doesn't matter what the statistics show – if you're in that small group – then the statistics mean nothing!' Pauline Green says,

> It was pushing us apart … you could feel it … because I was in my world and I think Jim [her husband] was in his world, he couldn't give me any answers and I obviously couldn't give him the answers.

Clark et al. note the 'pervasive, constant, protracted and debilitating' process of speculation (Clark et al., 2009, p. 273). Alan Pike notes that 'people who experience the trauma of missing will sometimes "catastrophise", imagining worse outcomes than that which has happened or may happen'. This is conversely tinged with hope that an unidentified body might be their relative; at least that would be an answer; at least they could get their special person back. Trish Cooper said, 'Like everyone else that has someone missing long term, they've got loads of questions that they're not going to get answered … because people can't answer them.' Kevin Gosden says, 'To this day we have no idea why Andrew disappeared as he did.' He continues: 'Nobody was aware that he was unhappy or anything … right up to the evening before he vanished he was a perfectly normal Andrew, and maybe that compounds it for us.' He says: 'That's the ongoing torture isn't it, you just end up thinking of every possibility that might fit in, but you can never reach any conclusion.' Waring's (2001) paper, 'It's the hope that hurts', refers to the 'untold number of other unanswerable questions' (Waring, 2001, p. 18).

Sandra Flintoft fears that her son could 'be laid dead and no one knows he is there, rotting, only bones left'. The New South Wales Department of Justice and Attorney General, in 2010, explain how 'family members may experience constant thoughts about the missing person, imagining terrible fates and pervading feelings of doom' (Missing People, 2012a, p. 10). At Missing People, research found that in cases of missing people around 1 in 10 of the missing people searched for are found dead (Newiss, 2011, p. 9), and so families also live with fears which may become reality. In Waring's paper, parents who have a child missing are described as being 'consumed with fear' (Waring, 2001, p. 10). Families tell support workers at Missing People how terrified and anxious they feel whenever there are news reports on the TV about a body being found. Trish Cooper says, 'the worst thing is when you hear … an unidentified body has been found and … you instantly think Christ, is that him?' Kate McCann talks about being haunted by a crippling fear: 'I kept thinking she'll open her eyes and she's going to be terrified and she'll want mummy and daddy and we're not there.' She talks about the early days when you 'can't stop speculating and you do go to the darkest places'. She says that more recently 'I can block things out' and that 'it comes with the knowledge that speculation does not help'.

The effect of the passage of time may not reduce the emotional pain, and presents other challenges. Hogben characterises this as a disruption to a family's 'private calendar', which causes confusion and distress. As an example, Hogben discusses the difficulties surrounding a missing person's birthday. It is not usual to send a birthday card to a dead person, yet not sending a card to a missing person 'would indicate the erasure [of that person's birthday from the family's] private calendar and, thus, the tacit acceptance of a permanent end to that suspended relationship' (Hogben, 2006, p. 331). Trish Cooper is resolved that 'something's happened [to Steve] and we don't know … I don't think we'll ever know.' She says, 'I feel calmer … because there isn't anything else we can do.' Monique Leslie's quest to find her sister Jacqueline had become a life's mission, as it is with other families, saying, 'she's missing, there's work to be done … maybe it's part of me proving to her that she is loved and we have not given up hope in finding her.' Nicki Durbin, mother of Luke, is thinking about moving from their family home, explaining she's seven years on and 'it just doesn't stop … living in the same house', she says, 'there's something I find really difficult about being in this house. It's like another season and Luke's not here.' Kevin Gosden says,

> In some senses the feelings that I have now five years on, are incredibly similar to some of the feelings that I had five years ago, you know you just walk around sometimes with this sort of tight feeling in your chest and your guts just thinking you know, I just want to give him a hug and make sure he's OK.

Denise Allan often thinks of her own mortality, explaining,

> It's gets harder because you know time's running out. I'm 64 this year … I won't live for-
> ever … my mother's already died, his Godfather's died, his father's died … there's nobody
> left … as long as I can stand, walk, talk, I'll search for my child until the day I die.

Pauline Green says,

> We had to sell his car … it was just sitting up there and it was rotting, and it was such a
> shame. His room, other than the fact that we've decorated it … everything in his wardrobe
> is as he left it … everything in his room is as he left it.

She says, 'If we had a closure, then obviously … we could grieve … but at the moment it's just
open … and it's continuous.' They won't move house, and until 'someone tells me and shows
me, 100 per cent differently he will always be alive.' Valerie Nettles concludes, 'I have learned
to live a "normal life" one foot firmly in the present and the other even more firmly in the past.'

Living in Limbo (2008) highlights physical issues such as sleep disruption, high blood pressure
and worsening ill health, especially amongst those already vulnerable to this. Waring's paper
(2001) talks of the interference with daily routines: 'irregular meals, late nights, disturbed sleep'
(Hunter Institute of Mental Health, 2001, p. 9). Stephanie Hynard, whose husband Brian went
missing in March 2011 and was found dead in May 2013, said, 'Even on antidepressants, there is
a sense that my feelings are just under control.' She goes on, 'Waking with heart beating, sudden
panic when things go wrong, a sadness when in stressful places.' Nicki Durbin noted, 'It's not
about what you're going to do for the day, it's like, how am I even going to get through the
day, it's so bleak.' Denise Allan says, 'It's only since the 21st anniversary that I've gone really
downhill with depression.'

The charity Missing People conducts annual surveys with people who use their services, in
order to understand more about their experiences. Over the last three years 462 family members were asked whether they had experienced any mental health problems as a result of their
relative being missing; 222 (48 per cent of them) said that they had (Missing People, 2011,
2012b, 2013).

Clark et al. (2009) focus on the lesser considered impact when a brother or sister goes missing
and describe sibling relationship as often the 'enduring family relationship', the lifelong friend
and confidante who is lost (Clark et al., 2009, pp. 268–269). Coping with the same emotions as
parents they often have the added worry of parental grief which is 'disconcerting' for children
(Clark et al., 2009, p. 273). Furthermore, she notes that siblings often felt that their grief was
'secondary' to parental grief or even unrecognised; a 'disenfranchised grief' (Clark et al., 2009,
p. 274). Trish Cooper said, 'I don't know how my mother does it, 'cos … it's her son – I don't
have that bond, 'cos I don't have kids, I can't imagine.'

> The loss of a sibling during early developmental stages is one of the most unique and
> intense losses one can sustain (Robinson and Mahon, 1997; Schwab, 1997). Research
> shows that the impact often continues into adulthood (Horsley and Patterson, 2006;
> Rosen, 1984–1985; Stahlman, 1996).
>
> (Greif and Bowers, 2007, p. 203)

Many families remain ever hopeful for news of their loved one: hope of seeing them again, hope
of finding an answer, even if it is the worst news. 'Worry and hope both reveal the future to be

uncertain and both tend, though in contrasting modes, to work towards an outcome that can reduce the uncertainty on which each is premised and thrives' (Bradac, 2001). Worry, while implying a future, is also stasis inducing because, as Phillips (1993, p. 41) also argues, it also 'fixes the worrier in the present' (Hogben, 2006, p. 333).

Kevin Gosden said, 'I've kicked myself because I find it so difficult to let go of that one little last bit of hope', and Denise Allen said, 'Your brain tries to accept, and you know in your heart that he's gone … but, there's always hope … maybe, what if, maybe you know that call, one day.' Alan Pike notes that it could be an 'irresistible and sometimes unsaid thought that to find a missing person's body would be preferred to living the rest of one's life never "knowing".'

Other chapters in this book focus on a family's interactions with different agencies when a loved one is missing. The nature of interactions can affect how families cope with their experience. Greif and Bowers note,

> All concerned parties become focused on 'the search' at the same time that police and media become involved. Their involvement can have a significant impact on family functioning by the way they interview family members, respond to their concerns, and report the news.
>
> (Greif and Bowers, 2007, p. 204)

Valerie Nettles describes how she 'felt foolish turning up at the police station and telling them my son was missing'. She goes on, 'I was confused by the reaction of the police who seemed unconcerned when this was my child, my son.' Elizabeth Templeton said, 'We were, I recognise retrospectively, extremely lucky with the officer who … couldn't have been more diligent and communicative' and goes on to describe that the level of (police) activity helped them to feel that 'something was happening'.

Missing People Family Support Manager Helen Alves (formerly Morrell) notes,

> The family's acceptance of the police's response to scale down an investigation is dependent upon their belief in sufficient effort and the thoroughness of the investigation … As the ultimate goal of finding the missing person has not been achieved, many families do not feel that enough has been done, or they have not updated enough in the steps that have been taken. Relationships with police may become fractured as trust becomes challenged.
>
> (Morrell, 2011, p. 25)

Even when the official search activity is scaled down, 'the internal search and the individual's ongoing need to search, remember and to hope can increase or at least remain as profound' (Steyne et al., 2013, p. 10).

Nicki Durbin talks about trying to get hold of an officer 'he didn't … wouldn't respond to my email … it took him ten days' (and he still didn't respond personally) and she describes how she was 'just so worn down' and describes one occasion where she remembers thinking, 'I can't do this anymore', and considered hurling herself through a plate glass window. She talks about the 'absolute desperation that no one … not one of those police would really listen … and I knew my son, but they were telling me how my son was.' Nicki explains the stress of fighting: 'Everyone who stands in your way to try and find your child.' She notes in recent years 'they've [the police] been brilliant'.

Kate McCann talks about how some comments have not helped over time.

Someone saying in the early days, 'you'll get through this, you'll get stronger' didn't necessarily help, 'cos I didn't want it, I just wanted to have Madeleine back, so the thought of getting strong and Madeleine still not being here grated.

Kate also refers to some friends who 'don't know how to react and it's almost like they try and block it out themselves because it's so painful … part of it is they don't know how to reach out to you and the other part is they are trying to protect themselves … that's human nature.'

Denise Allen said there's exasperation at the question asked by people: '"Why do [you] keep looking?" – and I say, well, I only had one child … you know … I couldn't get another one, I didn't lose my car; I lost my only child.' Monique Leslie recognises 'well-meaning' comments from people, but struggles with comments such as 'let it go … move on'. She thinks 'there's no going, where's it gonna go?' Monique also refers to her interaction with the media: 'I had to learn … because they put things in the newspaper that I didn't quite say … I thought OK I need to be a little bit guarded here.'

Other people may also speculate about the missing person. Pauline Green says some people think that her son must be selfish to be missing and she may say, or think: 'You don't know the reasons around this … even I don't know … so I can't see where selfishness comes into it…'

Waring's paper (2001) notes that families of missing people are somewhat comforted and consoled by basic human contact and the opportunity to share their experience. The charity Missing People's annual surveys with people who use their services note the importance of empathy: 'You showed so much empathy. You offered more than I thought you could offer. You took a lot of the pressure off me.' Another family said, 'We were in such a state. It was a godsend that the charity made contact with us to help' (Missing People, 2013). In the *Promoting Connectedness* guidelines (NSW Department of Attorney General and Justice, 2010) families identify the following as useful, in summary: the chance to talk and acknowledge the loss of the missing loved one; recognition of their need to talk about the impact of having someone missing, both emotionally and physically; receiving emotional support quickly to reduce feelings of isolation and despair; understanding that ambiguous loss is very hard to endure and live with. They recommend staying away from words like 'acceptance', 'closure' or 'resolution' or from focusing on the unknown outcome or fate of the missing person. As noted by families, emotions change over time, and from day to day, but the intensity of the emotion is often not far from the surface.

Pauline Boss talks about the importance of accepting the ambiguity when a loved one is missing:

> One's need for mastery must give way to more acceptance if there is to be resilience. Specifically, this translates into being able to tolerate ambiguity or lack of closure. Keeping loved ones present in one's mind, without preoccupation, is a way to live with the ambiguity and lack of closure.
>
> (Boss, 2006, p. 29)

One way that people cope, particularly with a missing incident that they categorise as intentional, is by,

> exploiting a range of time referents to account for the missing person's lack of communication. The emergent formula, glossed here as, the longer you leave it the harder it is, identifies the duration of the absence, rather than the missing person's potentially wilful withdrawal, as the obstacle to renewing contact.
>
> (Hogben, 2006, p. 338)

Families of missing people face unimaginable and intensely painful emotions. There does not seem to be any words to describe this loss, this ambiguous loss, unending not knowing, living in limbo. Families are not able to move on in the way that might be expected when someone dies. Whilst someone remains missing there is always hope of seeing them again one day or finding answers. Hope can be a vital way of survival and is enduring through the years. Families are often driven by searching, sometimes feeling embattled on top of it all, feeling that not everything is being done to find their special person.

Thank you to the families who contributed and who kindly shared their experiences for the purpose of this chapter. Reading their personal accounts, feeling the empty spaces, contemplating the unanswered questions and the endlessness of it all, helps us to empathise, helps us to not forget. To get in touch even when there is nothing to say. To sit alongside someone when there are no words. To ensure that everything that can be done, is being done. It is a vast world out there and not knowing where someone is, not being able to place them anywhere, not to know if they are living, breathing, fighting or dead is unbearable and yet must be borne. Families yearn to see their loved one again. Families yearn to find them. Families yearn to at least to find an answer. Sometimes families die without ever knowing.

Postscript

Matthew Green has been found alive in Europe, and Pauline and Jim Green are hoping to see him soon. May 2016.

References

Boss, P. (1999). *Ambiguous Loss: Learning to Live with Unresolved Grief*. Cambridge, MA: Harvard University Press.

Boss, P. G. (2002). Ambiguous loss: Working with families of the missing. *Family Process*, 41: 14–17.

Boss, P. (2006). *Loss, Trauma and Resilience: Therapeutic Work with Ambiguous Loss*. New York: W.W. Norton and Co.

Boss, P., Beaulieu, L., Weiling, E., Turner, W. and Lacruz, S. (2003). Healing loss, ambiguity and trauma. A community based intervention with families of union workers missing after 9/11 attack in New York City. *Journal of Marital and Family Therapy*, 29(4): 455–467.

Cassia, P. S. (2006). Guarding each other's dead, mourning one's own: The problem of missing persons and missing pasts in Cyprus. *South European Society and Politics*, 11(1): 111–128.

Clark, J., Warburton, J. and Tilse, C. (2009). Missing siblings: Seeking more adequate social responses. *Child and Family Social Work*, 14: 267–277.

De Young, R. and Buzzi, B. (2003). Ultimate coping strategies: The differences among parents of murdered or abducted, long term missing children. *OMEGA Journal of Death and Dying*, 47(4): 343–360.

Edkins, J. (2011). *Missing: Persons and Politics*. Ithaca and London: Cornell University Press.

Finucane, B. (2010). Enforced disappearance as a crime under international law: A neglected origin in the laws of war. *The Yale Journal of International Law*, 35: 171–197.

Greif, G. L. and Bowers, D. T. (2007). Unresolved loss: Issues in working with adults whose siblings were kidnapped years ago. *The American Journal of Family Therapy*, 35(3): 203–219.

Hogben, S. (2006). Life's on hold: Missing people, private calendars and waiting. *Time and Society*, 15(2–3): 327–342.

Holmes, L. (2008). *Living in Limbo: The Experiences of, and Impacts on, the Families of Missing People*. London: Missing People.

Hunter Institute of Mental Health (2001). *It's the Hope That Hurts: Best Practice in Counselling Models Relevant to Families and Friends of Missing Persons*. Sydney: Families and Friends of Missing Persons Unit, Attorney General's Department of New South Wales.

Luster, T., Qin, D., Bates, L., Johnson, D. and Rana, M. (2009). The Lost Boys of Sudan: Coping with ambiguous loss and separation from parents. *American Journal of Orthopsychiatry*, 79(2): 203.

Mendenhall, T. J. and Berge, J. M. (2010). Family therapists in trauma-response teams: Bringing systems thinking into interdisciplinary fieldwork. *Journal of Family Therapy*, 32(1): 43–57.

Missing People (2011). *Family Feedback Survey*. www.missingpeople.org.uk.

Missing People (2012a). *An Uncertain Hope: Missing People's Overview of the Theory, Research and Learning About How It Feels for Families When a Loved One Goes Missing*. www.missingpeople.org.uk/missing-people/professionals.

Missing People (2012b). *Family Feedback Survey*. www.missingpeople.org.uk.

Missing People (2013). *Family Feedback Survey*. www.missingpeople.org.uk.

Morrell, H. (2011). *Lessons from Australia: Churchill Report*. www.wcmt.org.uk/reports/976_1.pdf.

Newiss, G. (2011). *Learning from Fatal Disappearances*. London: Missing People. www.missingpeople.org.uk/about-us/about-the-issue/research/12-missing-people-research.html.

NSW Department of Attorney General and Justice (2010). *Promoting Connectedness: Guidelines for Working with Families of Missing People*. www.missingpersons.justice.nsw.gov.au/Documents/fmp32_promote-connect.pdf.

Steyne, R., Alves, H., Robinson, K., Towell, H. and Holmes, L. (2013). *Living in Limbo Five Years On: A Summary of Work to Improve the Support Available to Families of Missing People*. London: Missing People.

Vargas, L. (2008). Ambiguous loss and the media practices of transnational Latina teens: A qualitative study. *Popular Communication*, 6(1): 37–52.

Waring, T. (2001). *'It's the Hope that Hurts': Best Practice in Counselling Models Relevant to Families and Friends of Missing Persons*. www.missingpersons.justice.nsw.gov.au/Documents/fmp08_hope-that-hurts.pdf.

Wayland, S. (2007). *Supporting Those Who Are Left Behind: A Counselling Framework to Support Families of Missing Persons*. National Missing Persons Coordination Centre, Australian Federal Police, Commonwealth of Australia, ACT.

20

Presumption of Death and Guardianship

Holly Towell

The loss of one's partner is one of the worst things in life; to lose your partner without knowing for sure what happened to them, not to have their body, not to be able to organise a funeral, is unbearable. There is no sense of closure … At this time I have no idea when my partner's estate will be settled. I wish to see things resolved primarily for my partner's sake, but also to allow me to at least attempt to get on with my life without this constant worry about his affairs.

(Partner of a missing man; Justice Select Committee, 2012, Ev25)

Introduction

Each year approximately 250,000 people are reported missing to the police and other agencies in the United Kingdom (Home Office, 2010, p. 5). Whilst the majority of these adults and children are found or return within days of a disappearance (NCA, 2014, p. 21), some remain missing for weeks, months, or even years, creating a legacy of unresolved disappearances.

Whilst there is a clear need to establish the whereabouts and safety of these longer-term missing people, it is important to additionally consider the wellbeing of the family[1] that they leave behind. Awaiting news of their loved one, relatives often experience emotional trauma as a result of a disappearance and are left in a limbo state (Holmes, 2008), unable to move on without answers as to what has become of their loved one and, for those who believe the missing person has died, the rituals that accompany death.

Yet, further to these emotional repercussions, families of missing people can also encounter complex issues if there are not appropriate provisions in place to enable them to either manage or protect the missing person's affairs whilst they are away, or to administer them if it is believed they have died. This can cause significant additional stress to families, and may be particularly pressing for those whose financial security is linked to the missing person, including dependents and those who share joint assets with them, such as a home or business.

If families are unable to intervene in their missing loved one's legal and financial affairs, a myriad of assets and liabilities can be left unmanaged. From banking, benefits and insurance policies to pensions, subscriptions, and rent and mortgage payments, the missing person's affairs may waste in their absence. The longer a person remains missing, the more devastating this lack of oversight can be on their financial and practical wellbeing, and in the worst cases, bank accounts drain, contracts lapse and homes can be lost.

This can be hugely distressing for families, as many feel duty bound to protect the life they hope their missing loved one will return to. Maintaining their relative's affairs can feel of utmost importance to families and, for those contemplating the possible death of their loved one, they may additionally be keen to maintain these so that they can be administered in accordance with their relative's wishes if this is the case or presumed in law to be so.

In addition to families, any absence of provisions to manage or resolve a missing person's affairs can also be problematic for institutions holding a missing person's assets or liabilities (APPG, 2011, p. 14). This can include banks, insurers, creditors, utility companies and public sector bodies, such as local authorities, which have contracted directly with the missing person, and are therefore generally unable to take instruction from anyone other than the account holder to either terminate or vary the terms of the contract. When the only person able to do so is missing, the family left behind, as well as the institutions, can be left in a stalemate situation.

Families facing legal and financial issues following a disappearance generally look to under-take one of two courses of action: to manage and maintain their missing loved one's affairs so that their relative will have them in order to return to, or to resolve and conclude them on the basis that it is believed they have died. These two approaches tend to be referred to, respectively, as guardianship and presumption of death.

This chapter explores these two areas in detail, including the issues families can encounter when attempting to manage or resolve a missing loved one's affairs (or their own if these are shared with the missing person), when families tend to explore their legal options and what provisions they can access. While it may appear counterintuitive, the first area explored is pre-sumption of death as there is now much greater legal clarity as regards the steps families can take when a person is presumed to be dead than in the situation where a person is simply missing and the aim is to manage the person's affairs until they return.[2]

UK Charity Missing People

Whilst presumption of death is a well-known concept across many countries, the practical and legal impact experienced by families of missing people following a disappearance has not been explored a great deal in research literature. As the specialist needs of this group have become better understood however, interest has grown in exploring how they can be better provided for in policy and law.

The needs of this group have been explored, notably, by various agencies in Australia, and the UK charity Missing People, which provides services to families of missing people; these include a helpline, practical and legal guidance sheets and a bespoke counselling service. As the author spent more than five years at Missing People working on the practical and legal issues following a disappearance, much of this article has been informed by her experiences there.

Resolving a Missing Person's Affairs: Presumption of Death

> I feel very strongly that it would be a disservice to my partner if there were never any resolution of his affairs and his estate was not settled as he instructed in his will.
>
> (Partner of a missing man; Justice Select Committee, 2012, Ev25)

Whilst the majority of missing person reports are resolved relatively quickly, approximately 1 per cent of disappearances reported annually remain open for a year or more, and some for much longer (Tarling and Burrows, 2004, p. 20). As time passes, some families of long-term missing people come to the conclusion that their relative is likely to have died. Others, however, may conclude this much sooner as a result of the circumstances of the disappearance; for example, if a suicide note had been left, if it is known that the missing person faced immediate peril at the time they went missing, or if the disappearance was starkly out of character:

> The one thing that he did love was his kids and to not see them for ten years, I can't believe that. The sad thing is that you know he has missed a lifetime of them. I believe he has died somewhere and they just haven't found his body yet.
>
> (Former wife of a missing man, as told to Missing People)

In both instances, families may seek to administer their relative's affairs on the basis that they are no longer alive, accessing provisions commonly referred to as 'presumption of death'. This is a process through which, in the absence of a body, a person can be legally declared as presumed dead and, following this, their estate can be administered as if they were dead.

Families Seek Presumption of Death for a Missing Relative

Families of missing people tend to pursue presumption of death for their relative for one of two reasons, or a combination of both. First, families may use it to help with emotional closure, and so may look to use this legal procedure to confirm the likely death of their relative in the absence of the rituals of a regular death. Second, they may use it to administer the missing person's financial and legal affairs, which, if left unattended, may be falling into disarray in their absence:

> I have got to wait until seven years … then he would be pronounced dead and only then would the mortgage be sorted out and shares and things sorted out.
>
> (Wife of a missing man, as told to Missing People)

Those seeking presumption of death to resolve their loved one's affairs may be driven to do so out of want or need, with a thin line standing between these in some instances. For example, some may want to deal with their loved one's estate so that it may be administered and distributed in line with their will, if one had been left, or what they believe were their relative's wishes. Some report the importance of undertaking this, explaining that they want to honour their loved one: 'My partner deserves to have his estate settled as he wished' (partner of a missing man, Justice Select Committee, 2012, Ev24).

Part of this process may be additionally driven by members of the family wanting to ensure that the missing person's inheritors, such as their partner or children, receive what they are due. This may become particularly pressing in longer-term disappearances, when older family members might feel duty bound to resolve the estate so that the younger generations (who may not be as knowledgeable of the circumstances of the disappearance and subsequent search) are not left to do this. For example, the daughter of a missing man may look to resolve her father's estate so that her children will not have to undertake this in her absence.

Other families may be compelled to resolve their relative's affairs as a result of need, which may be driven by a range of factors. For example, the family might be aware that their relative's estate has fallen into disarray and as such may look to administer it. Dependents of the missing person may alternatively look to sort out their relative's estate by way of being able to better provide for the family's new circumstances, such as selling a property in order to downsize and save on mortgage payments. Others who share assets or liabilities with the missing person may look to sort out their relative's estate so that they are able to resolve issues that have complicated their own affairs whilst their loved one has been missing (for example, those with joint property may have to pay the full balance on their own, and be unable to sell it without the missing person's signature):

> There is absolutely nothing I can do with my mortgage. My husband's name is on that mortgage, and he is not around to sign it over to myself.
>
> (Wife of a missing man; Justice Select Committee, 2012, p. 9)

Exploring a Presumption of Death Declaration

The time at which families look into presumption of death varies widely. Those who are certain that their missing loved one has died, perhaps due to the circumstances of the disappearance (for example if there was a suicide note, if they went missing at sea or following a natural disaster), may look into seeking a declaration in the weeks following the disappearance. For others, however, some years might pass before they consider making an application. There may even be an assumption that the family cannot apply for a declaration until seven years has elapsed since the disappearance of the missing person (this is addressed further in the next section).

Whilst a family might explore presumption of death at any given time following a disappearance, whether they are able to successfully pursue a legal declaration at that moment is likely to depend on the circumstances of the disappearance and the provisions of the applicable law. Not all countries, and not all states within countries, have specific presumption of death processes in place. Those with developed forms of presumption of death law include: Scotland (the Presumption of Death (Scotland) Act 1977), Northern Ireland (the Presumption of Death Act (Northern Ireland) 2009), England and Wales (the Presumption of Death Act 2013), and several states within both Australia (including Victoria (the Administration and Probate Act 1958 (Vic)) and Canada.

Legal Processes Families Are Able to Access

While the legal concept of presumption of death is well established in a number of countries, the model or quality of provisions in place can differ. There may be a process set out in legislation which enables families or other interested parties to apply for a certificate of presumed death. This is likely to provide the clearest and easiest to follow route. In countries where there is no such legislative provision there may be ad hoc provisions that have grown up to deal with situations on a case-by-case basis, possibly similar to the position in England and Wales before the Presumption of Death Act 2013 came into effect.

One element common to many processes is a requirement that a prescribed period of time (frequently seven years) must have elapsed in cases where death is not certain before a declaration of presumed death can be made. For example, the English common-law 'seven-year rule' holds that, where there is no evidence to suggest that the missing person has died, the missing person is presumed to be alive for a period of seven years. If, after seven years, there has been no evidence of life (for example, those who would be likely to have heard from the individual have not and attempts to find them have been unsuccessful), a declaration may be granted. In contrast, where there is evidence to suggest that the missing person has died, perhaps from the circumstances in which they vanished, a declaration can be sought and may be granted almost immediately. In either case, applicants will need to provide evidence to demonstrate that either there is no proof of life with respect to the missing person or that there is evidence of their likely death. This will be assessed by the relevant court and a judgment made based on it.

Some debate has taken place over whether the seven-year rule remains relevant given the advances in technology in recent decades and people's so-called digital footprint, and whether this timeframe is now too lengthy. Nevertheless, as it stands, this remains in place for many systems, including newer ones. The Presumption of Death Act 2013, introduced for England and Wales, for example, included the seven-year period in its text, though it is perhaps noteworthy that the Act also contains provision for this period to be reviewed and altered as deemed appropriate. Families do not have to wait for seven years before applying under the Presumption of Death Act 2013, but the Act provides that the court must make a declaration of presumed death if satisfied that the missing person has not been known to be alive for at least seven years.

The seven-year period is also to be found in a 2009 Council of Europe Recommendation (Principles concerning missing persons and the presumption of death, Recommendation CM/Rec (2009)12 and explanatory memorandum). This recommends that, where the death of the missing person can be taken as certain, there should be no required waiting period. Where it is reasonable to conclude that death is likely, there should be one year at the most from the disappearance (or the last news that the person was alive) before being able to request a declaration of presumed death. Finally, where the death of the missing person is uncertain, the maximum waiting period proposed by the Recommendation is seven years.

Families in countries without presumption of death provisions may well face difficulties in, for example, obtaining probate, since, typically, probate is granted following proof of death, most commonly a medical certificate following examination of a body. Although in England and Wales there was a process prior to the 2013 Act that families could follow to obtain probate in the absence of a death certificate (Rule 53, NonContentious Probate Rules 1987 (SI 1987/2024)), the process was little used and not well known, resulting in delays and issues for families trying to use the process. Additionally, professionals unfamiliar with such processes may be hesitant to take action where they are unsure whether there are appropriate safeguards to protect them if they make an error:

> The Probate system [is] just not set up to deal with such cases … the case being passed from person to person, the excuse being that it was an unusual case which had no death certificate.
>
> (Brother of a missing man; Justice Select Committee, 2012, Ev18)

Managing and Protecting a Missing Person's Affairs (Guardianship)

> [My daughter] has her own house, almost inevitably with a mortgage, house insurance, car insurance, bank accounts and investments. It was literally a very few weeks before I realised the difficulty in trying to deal with these matters when she is missing.
>
> (Father of a missing woman, APPG, 2011, p. 12)

The presumption of death process helps those seeking to wind up a missing loved one's affairs where the missing person is likely to be dead; however, a number of families will instead want to manage and maintain the missing person's affairs in the hope of their return. Such families may look to ensure that the missing person's finances (including banking, insurance policies, mortgage or rent payments, benefits and other outgoings and incomings), property and legal affairs are looked after and do not fall into disarray, and that any dependents are cared for, in their absence. If family members share assets or liabilities with the missing person, this may be particularly pressing:

> When my husband first went missing there was the huge impact of suddenly going from being a couple and having two wages to suddenly overnight becoming a single mum who could only work part time, with a mortgage and bills to pay. There was this traumatic thing going on that my husband was missing, and that in itself was traumatic enough, but there was still the everyday living to do as well.
>
> (Wife of missing man, as told to Missing People)

While there are now some established processes as regards presumption of death, the maintenance of a missing person's estate in their absence is a less mature area of policy and practice. This is reflected in the lack of uniformity used by countries to describe it. For example, in the US, some states (including Delaware, Ohio and California) refer to it as conservatorship, whereas others, including some Australian states, and the UK Ministry of Justice in a 2014 consultation paper (Ministry of Justice, 2014), use the term guardianship. For the purposes of this chapter, the latter term will be used.

Managing or Maintaining a Relative's Affairs

Families may look at whether they can be granted guardianship over their missing relative's affairs for emotional or financial reasons, or a combination of both. Emotionally, taking active steps to protect a relative's affairs can help allay the feelings of helplessness families of missing persons can feel, and such steps can assume enormous importance for the family left behind. Families tend to be concerned with ensuring that, should the missing person return, they will be able to easily assimilate back into their previous life without having practical issues to contend with. Some can feel duty bound to try to achieve this for their loved one, out of a sense of honour:

> His bank was going overdrawn, and I know it sounds so petty in the great scheme of what's happened, but I didn't want my son's account to go overdrawn. It mattered so much to me.
>
> (Mother of a missing man; Holmes, 2008, p. 32)

Others may worry about the impact on their missing relative if they return to find their affairs in disarray. As such, families may seek to monitor their relative's affairs or make alterations to arrangements (for example, cancelling unnecessary contracts which are draining a bank account, such as newspaper or magazine subscriptions or gym or club memberships) by way of protecting them. For others, there may be a financial need to seek guardianship if they share assets or liabilities with the missing person, such as a mortgage or a joint business, or if they are dependent on them as a breadwinner.

Whether the drivers are emotional or financial, families are likely to face difficulties in taking steps to protect or alter the missing person's affairs if they do not have a legal mandate. As outlined at the start of this chapter, families may be unable to alter contracts without the missing person's signature, or may not be able to access information or money without the permission or intervention of the missing person. If the missing person was in receipt of benefits, and is not present to sign for these, this may disrupt the family's finances and can lead to real hardship.

In addition, however, it is also important to recognise that a further pocket of families seek to pursue guardianship because they are not yet able, or do not want, to obtain a presumption of death declaration for their missing relative. Families that are seeking to rely on the so-called seven-year rule and who are waiting for seven years to pass before seeking a declaration of presumed death, will tend to want to try to manage their relative's affairs until this point so that they are maintained and can be administered in line with their loved one's wishes.

Others, even if they believe it is likely that their missing relative has died, may not want to pursue a presumption of death declaration because they find the thought of this and the perceived finality of it too emotionally difficult. They may feel it is 'giving up' on their loved one, and may have questions as to whether it will have a negative effect on the search for their relative who, for all intents and purposes, will still remain missing regardless of a declaration. Others may find the process of applying for a presumption of death declaration daunting and be dissuaded from pursuing one for practical reasons. In both instances, however, it is likely that a number of these families will seek guardianship to preserve their missing relative's affairs.

Families Explore Guardianship

Families may look into issues relating to guardianship very soon after their relative's disappearance. Initially, they may try to deal with individual issues as they present themselves. For example, within the first week or two they may look at whether they are able to draw a benefit payment which their relative is responsible for collecting. After a few weeks, they may seek to cancel or freeze direct debits or standing orders from their missing relative's account that are not deemed to be strictly necessary and which could be diverting resources from other payments seen as vital. After a few months, a family might consider altering mortgage payments, and after a year or more, they may look at whether they can sell a shared property.

Some families tend to assume that there will be a legal system, perhaps like Power of Attorney, that will enable them to cope with the missing person's affairs, or that they will be able to access bespoke policies or provisions used within institutions such as banks and insurance companies, and may try to explore this with legal advisors or directly with the institutions themselves.

Available Legal Solutions

While legal provisions on presumption of death are by no means universal, guardianship provisions are to be found even less frequently. As such, the provisions in place for those left behind to manage or resolve a missing person's affairs vary.

Guardianship, in some form, exists in several countries, with Canada, Australia and the US each containing states that have relevant provisions. In 2015, the United Kingdom government signalled its intention to introduce a system of guardianship for England and Wales (it does not have the jurisdiction to make such legislation for Scotland and Northern Ireland as a result of devolved powers) following a public consultation (Ministry of Justice, 2015, p. 3).

In the US, 'conservatorship' law exists in varying forms across states, providing a legal mechanism through which matters connected to a person's affairs can be determined by another person or body. Some states, such as Florida, provide for scenarios in which conservatorship can be granted in missing person cases (therein termed 'absentees'), such as if an individual has gone missing as a result of a mental health issue or amnesia (Florida Statute Title XLIII, Domestic Relations Ch. 747). States in Canada and Australia (for example, Victoria, through the Guardianship and Administration Act 1986) have similar systems whereby an application can be made to a relevant court to manage a missing person's estate once a person has been absent for 90 days and attempts to find them have been unsuccessful.

For those in countries without guardianship provisions, families of missing people are left to attempt to negotiate with individuals and institutions on a case-by-case basis. Laws prohibiting third parties from interfering with contracts, and laws on data protection, mean that many struggle to achieve what they set out to do and may be left feeling helpless and unsupported. These families may have to stand by and watch as their missing loved one's estate disintegrates, and perhaps their own finances too if they hold liabilities or assets with the person: 'My mortgage is in mine and my husband's name … My mortgage rate has gone up – the bank won't have anything to do with it – I am potentially going to lose my home' (Wife of a missing man; APPG, 2011, p. 10).

In conclusion, families may explore presumption of death or guardianship for a number of reasons relating to emotional or financial issues, and for many the drive will be to preserve a loved one's estate in case of a return, or to administer it in line with their will or known wishes.

While presumption of death systems exist in a number of countries or states in the West, there are still those where legislation is either not in place or does not meet the needs of families; for example, the debate as to whether the seven-year period often referred to in decision making is too long in the modern era continues. Guardianship remains an area of new and emerging law which, whilst slowly gaining traction, is not progressing at a speed which is quick enough to meet the needs of families of missing people.

Overall, it is clear that families of missing people (and indeed missing people themselves if they are found or return) need adequate legislation in place to enable them to protect and manage their relative's affairs, and their own if they have joint assets or liabilities. Without this, both parties can suffer damage to their estates, possibly beyond repair. It is important that governments consider providing for this group so that they do not suffer as a result of the law of unintended consequences from provisions intended to protect individuals, such as contract law.

For more information on the issues contained in this chapter, the following may be of interest:

Further Information

United Kingdom
Missing People: The charity Missing People provides a range of support for families of missing people, as well as missing people themselves, and undertakes policy, research and campaigning on connected issues. For information, visit www.missingpeople.org.uk.

UK Missing Persons Bureau: Part of the National Crime Agency, the Bureau has a variety of information on missing persons, including factsheets and how to make a report to the police. It also has a directory of unidentified cases. See www.missingpersons.police.uk.

Australia
The National Missing Persons Coordination Centre: This Centre has information on missing persons in Australia, and resources for those impacted by a disappearance. Visit www.missingpersons. gov.au for more information.

Missing Persons Advocacy Network: This organisation looks to provide practical support to those with a missing loved one. See www.mpan.com.au.

Notes

1 The term 'family' here is used in the broadest sense to take in all of those close to the missing person, such as immediate family and partners.
2 This chapter contains parliamentary information licensed under the Open Parliament Licence v3.0. For information on this, see www.parliament.uk/site-information/copyright/open-parliament-licence/.

References

APPG for Runaway and Missing Children and Adults (2011). *Inquiry into Support for Families of Missing People*. London: Missing People.

Holmes, L. (2008). *Living in Limbo: The Experiences of, And Impacts on, Families of Missing People*. London: Missing People.

Home Office (2010). *The Missing Persons Task Force: A Report with Recommendations for Improving the Multiagency Response to Missing Incidents*. London: Home Office.

Justice Select Committee (2012). *Presumption of Death, Twelfth Report of Session 2010–12*. London: The Stationery Office Limited.

Ministry of Justice (2014). *Guardianship of the Property and Affairs of Missing Persons: A Consultation*. London: Ministry of Justice.

Ministry of Justice (2015). *Guardianship of the Property and Affairs of Missing Persons: A Response to Consultation*. London: Ministry of Justice.

NCA (2014). *Missing Persons: Data and Analysis 2012/2013*. London: National Crime Agency.

Tarling, R. and Burrows, J. (2004). The nature and outcome of going missing: The challenge of developing effective risk assessment procedures. *International Journal of Police Science and Management*, 6(1): 16–26.

21

Resolution of Missing Incidents

Lucy Holmes

By far the majority of missing person incidents are resolved in some way. Research studies around the world have shown that in the United Kingdom, the United States of America, Australia and New Zealand, location rates are well over 90 per cent of police missing person cases and in many areas more than 99 per cent of cases were resolved within a year (Henderson and Henderson, 1998; Newiss, 1999; Biehal, Mitchell and Wade, 2003; Tarling and Burrows, 2004; James, Anderson and Putt, 2008; National Crime Information Center, 2011; New Zealand Police, 2013).

Case resolution can take many forms, depending on the circumstances of the missing incident, the choices made by the missing person and the response of the people searching for them or the people to whom the missing individual reaches out. If a missing person considers that they have left their normal life (even if they have not been reported missing) the missing incident might be considered resolved when they reach out to a person or place of safety for help or support. If, however, a person has been reported missing to an agency such as the police or a search agency, case resolution may take many forms including the possibilities of the person being found alive and the person's body being located. This chapter will explore the range of ways in which missing incidents can be resolved, with the understanding that resolution means that at least one person or organisation that is searching has had contact with the missing person, or that an unreported missing person has made contact with family, carers or a support agency.

It is important to recognise that a missing incident may appear resolved to just some of the people searching for a missing person. For example, if a missing adult is found by the police but chooses to remain out of contact with their family, the incident will be considered resolved by the police and search agencies, but the family might feel that the incident remains unresolved and the individual is still missing. This highlights that there may be a difference between the resolution of an investigation and emotional resolution for the people searching.

Figure 21.1 shows the phases of a missing incident. It represents a single incident, but also acknowledges that an individual who has been missing can loop back to the beginning and go missing again. A great deal of attention on missing persons has focused on what is labelled here as the primary phase – the investigation, family support and services for missing people. Some work has been done to identify causal factors and to consider preventative measures, for

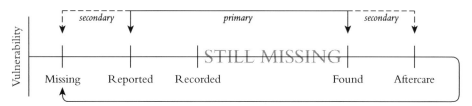

Figure 21.1 The cycle of missing
Source: Developed by Newiss in 2009; Holmes, 2013

example efforts made on mental health hospital wards to reduce the likelihood of patients leaving the ward (Bartholomew et al., 2009), or the resources available for children to dissuade them from running away in response to problems. For example, the national charity The Children's Society (2013) provides a free lesson plan for teachers, aimed at Key Stage 2 children, which includes lessons about running away. There has also been some effort made to consider how best to respond when incidents are resolved, although there is still a way to go in this respect.

It is vital that more work is done to understand the issues surrounding the resolution of missing incidents. What happens after a missing incident will potentially have an impact on the missing person's wellbeing and that of the others in their lives. It is also important to recognise that the period following a missing incident presents opportunities to: 1) reduce the likelihood of that person going missing again; 2) reduce the risks they face should they go missing again; 3) change the pattern of their future missing incidents (for example, duration and distance); and 4) inform future investigations (through intelligence gathering).

How Incidents are Resolved

Missing people may be found or traced in many different ways. They may be traced by individuals or organisations using social networks, public databases or through contact brokered by a third party using a private database. In some instances, the missing person may not have known they were considered missing, or that anyone was searching for them, until they received that contact. Some missing people do not choose to end the missing incident but are, instead, located by someone who is aware that they are missing. This may be a result of intelligence (such as a reported sighting), physical searching or a range of other methods.

Research using data from the Metropolitan Police Service in 1999 found that, of more than 32,000 incidents, 37 per cent had been resolved when the missing person returned of their own accord, 17 per cent when the person was located or returned by police, and 1.5 per cent when the person was arrested. The remainder of the incidents were unsolved, ended in fatality, ended for other reasons, or there was no reason for cancellation recorded (Newiss, 1999, p. 4).

Holmes (2014) explored incidents of people who had been reported missing to the police. Of a sample of 471 people who were found alive, in most cases (240, 51 per cent) the charity was not informed of how the person was found, but in the remaining 231 cases, 117 people returned of their own accord. This represents around half of the cases where the details of the resolution were known. A further 76 people were found by the police and 15 by their families (Holmes, 2014).

When missing people decide to return of their own volition this may be prompted by a number of things, such as becoming aware of an ongoing search. In other incidents, the missing person may not have been reported missing, or been actively searched for, but they may have made a decision to sever contact and later decided to make contact with family, friends, carers or support organisations such as the police, social care services or charities. The Geographies of Missing People research team interviewed a large number of formerly missing adults and found that 'decisions over if, when and how to reconnect were prompted by an aspiration to end the constant motion/emotion of the journey' (Stevenson et al., 2013, p. 81).

The Geographies of Missing People project found that, of 65 respondents, the most common prompt to return was the desire to return or reconnect (23 per cent of men and 18 per cent of women), followed by the pull of relationships with friends or family (18 per cent of men and 11 per cent of women), awareness of being looked for, safety or security, and concern about pets (Stevenson et al., 2013, p. 78).

One way in which people are able to make contact is via a third party, such as a charity helpline. Between July 2010 and June 2011 Missing People logged 1,139 dialogue calls to its helpline from children and adults away from home. Of these, 362 people chose to connect either to their family or carers, or to a professional agency that could provide ongoing support. Of the people who chose to connect, either by passing a message, by being connected on a three-way call, or by being directly referred into a service, more than half were connected to police or social care services. Three per cent were connected to a care home or foster carer and 17 per cent to a family member (Holmes, 2014).

Outcomes of Missing Incidents

Research has shown that most missing person cases are resolved quickly. Tarling and Burrows examined a sample of cases from London's Metropolitan Police Service and found that 59 per cent of missing people were found within two days of last being seen, and 76 per cent were closed within two days of the case being opened (Tarling and Burrows, 2004). More recent analysis of police reports has found that around 90 per cent of police reports are resolved within two days (UK Missing Persons Bureau, 2013, p. 26). There is some variation between groups of missing people. For example, there is a reasonably significant correlation between being female and being found within two days. Similarly, children are significantly more likely to be found within two days than adults (Holmes et al., 2013).

Holmes (2014) further explored the outcomes of missing incidents that have been resolved. In a recent 12-month period the charity supported police investigations for 557 missing people. Of these, 72 (12.9 per cent) were found deceased, 14 (2.5 per cent) remained missing for more than one year, and the remaining 471 (84.6 per cent) were found alive. The charity works on more than the national proportion of fatal missing person incidents because of the nature of the cases referred to the charity. The cases the charity works on tend to be longer-term, higher-risk cases, because lower-risk or shorter-term cases do not require publicity or emotional support for families (for more detail see Newiss, 2011). During the same period, Missing People opened 193 new family tracing cases, in order to trace adults who had lost contact with family members. Of these: 5 (2 per cent) were found to have died; 107 (55 per cent) remained missing after a year; and 81 cases (42 per cent) were closed when the person was found alive within a year (Holmes, 2014).

Missing People Found Deceased

Sadly, not all missing person incidents are resolved by the person being found alive. UK research has shown that a very small minority of missing person cases are resolved when the missing person's body is located or identified. While estimates vary, UK research suggests that less than 1 per cent of police reported missing person incidents end in fatality (Newiss, 1999; Tarling and Burrows, 2004; Newiss, 2006). This tallies with overseas estimates: Hirschel and Lab (1988) found that 0.3 per cent of found missing persons in a large American city were located dead (Henderson and Henderson, 1998, p. 15).

Newiss (2011) examined missing person cases reported to the charity Missing People over a two-year period which ended in fatality. The study found that, while in 42 per cent of these cases the cause of death was unexplained, in one-fifth the cause of death was recorded as suicide, one-fifth was attributed to natural causes, 9 per cent to accident and 6 per cent to homicide (Newiss, 2011, p. 16).

In the UK the Missing Persons Bureau hosts a website containing details of unidentified bodies and remains, which may be found at www.missingpersons.police.uk. The site, created in 2012, allows members of the public, including the families of missing people, to view photographs of unidentified people and remains and to contact the Bureau if they can help with identification. The site has received around 10,000 views per month and has, at the time of writing, confirmed one match already (The Investigator, 2013, pp. 12–15). This site has the potential to resolve some of the UK's most intractable missing person cases, by creating a joined-up and publically searchable repository for unidentified people's details.

Missing People Found Alive

In the majority of incidences where the missing person is found alive, there are a number of potential outcomes. Once found or located, missing people are able to make certain choices. The scope of these choices will be limited by their legal status; children, for example, are not permitted to live independently, and an individual who is subject to an arrest warrant will be arrested if found. However, support organisations, including the police, will seek to respect the person's wishes where possible and to ensure that any risk factors or vulnerabilities are taken into account. Adults who have been missing, whether reported to the police or another organisation or not reported at all, have three main options available to them: to be fully reunited with the people searching for them; to be partially reconnected to the people searching or others; or to choose to remain out of contact completely.

Biehal et al. (2003) explored the outcomes of a sample of cases held by the charity Missing People. This sample included people who were not subject to police investigation, but had lost contact and whose family were attempting to trace them. They found that, of a sample of 1,148 missing people (of all ages) who were found alive, 470 (39 per cent) renewed contact, 228 (20 per cent) returned home and 450 (41 per cent) refused contact (Biehal et al., 2003, p. 39).

The UK charity Missing People supports families who have a missing family member and conducts an annual survey with these families to gather information and feedback, the findings of which are available to download from the charity's website. Over three years of this survey, nearly 300 family members whose search had ended were surveyed. Of the missing children and adults who had been found alive: 26 per cent had returned home to live with family; 33 per cent had resumed face-to-face contact; 25 per cent had established contact via phone, email or letter; and 17 per cent of the formerly missing people had decided not to resume contact with family members. There was a slight variation between cases of vulnerable missing people whose disappearance had been investigated by the police and people who had lost contact with their families and were subsequently traced by Missing People. Nearly a quarter of people who had lost contact and were then traced by the charity decided to have no further contact, compared with just 14 per cent of people reported missing to the police.

Similarly, around a third of people reported missing to police returned to live with the person who reported them missing while none of those traced did. Finally, more than half of people traced subsequently resumed letter, phone or email contact, compared to just under a fifth of people reported missing to police. From many years of experience supporting missing children and adults via helpline services, UK charity Missing People is aware that making contact can be extremely daunting for missing people. Individuals' decisions about what to do when found, or when choosing to reach out for support, may be informed by many factors including how and when they are located by search agencies. No research has been done, to date, exploring whether and how the way in which a missing person is found affects their decisions about whether and how to reconnect with the people searching for them.

The situation is different for children aged 15 or under than for adults, as children of this age are not permitted to live independently. If it is not suitable for them to return home, a child must be looked after by their local authority or another responsible adult (such as another family member) until they can return home or reach an age when they can live independently. In the long term, this might mean the child becoming Looked After and living in foster care or a children's home. In the short term, a shortage of emergency accommodation means that young people may be encouraged to stay with family members, or even accommodated in a police cell overnight (Rees et al., 2009; Evans et al., 2007).

For Looked After children who run away from care placements, they are likely to be returned to that placement unless or until another suitable placement is found for them. The UK charity the NSPCC (2012) explored the experiences of children returning to care placements after being missing. A key finding of the study was that young people reported a lack of support on return, as well as a lack of boundaries and consequences for running away. In particular, the young people who took part in the research emphasised the need for 'firm boundaries, reinforced not with actions of power, but rather, empathy, understanding, support, respect and a listening ear' (NSPCC, 2012, p. 15)

Responding to Return

The need to manage missing people's return is recognised in police guidance and best practice across organisations. Key to managing the return is the need to debrief each missing person using a police 'Safe and Well' check and, where possible, a return interview. ACPO guidance for police devotes several pages to managing a missing person's return. It emphasises the need to make sure that any place of return is safe and that missing adults are allowed to make choices about what information is revealed to the person who made the missing report. It emphasises that Safe and Well checks must be conducted as soon as possible post return (section 4.12.1) and that return interviews 'are relevant to all missing persons' (section 4.12.2) and should, ideally, be conducted within 72 hours (NPIA, 2010, p. 55).

Return interviews are recognised to be particularly important for young people who go missing and may have faced significant risks to their welfare. The 2010 *Missing Children and Adults: A Cross-government Strategy* largely addresses incident resolution in terms of reducing repeat episodes. The strategy emphasises that early intervention is appropriate when children, young people or adults start going missing, in order to prevent future episodes, and that agencies should work in partnership to intervene effectively (Home Office, 2010, p. 13). The 2014 statutory guidance on children who run away and go missing from home or care also contains the instruction that, 'When a child is found, they must be offered an independent return interview' (Department for Education, 2014, p. 14). These interviews provide the opportunity to identify and understand the reasons for running away, any harm the child has experienced, and to provide help and support, including signposting and advice (Department for Education, 2014).

The use of return interviews will continue to be relevant as many police forces roll out a new approach to responding to missing person reports, using a new tiered response to missing incidents and cases where the person is simply absent. This new approach means forces conduct risk assessment at an earlier stage and then respond differently to people who are 'missing' compared to people who are 'absent'. In cases where a person is absent, the police maintain a watching brief, whilst supporting the person making the report to conduct their own enquiries. Cases can move between a missing response and an absent report, according to regular reassessments of risk. Currently, return interviews are not provided to all missing children and adults in all areas, and it remains to be seen whether they will be provided to people who have received the new absent response (College of Policing, 2013a, 2013b).

The Impact of Return

How families are affected by their missing relative's body being found may be somewhat related to the nature of the missing incident (such as circumstances and duration). Families with a long-term missing relative may yearn for resolution, even if that means a body being found and identified. In some instances families already have a strong belief that the person has died, and may even have pursued legal procedures to have this recognised (Holmes, 2008, pp. 23–26). More needs to be understood about the nature of bereavement following a missing incident and the ways in which this loss may differ from other types of bereavement.

Once a missing person has been found alive, families may experience a range of emotions. As well as relief that the person has been found, some families experience frustration with questions not being answered, fear that the person will disappear again, ongoing concern for the person's wellbeing, and the physical, emotional and practical effects of the missing incident. Some families, when the missing person has chosen not to resume contact, may experience acute rejection, worry and frustration at the investigation or search being concluded (Holmes, 2014).

Currently, there is relatively little support for families and missing people post-resolution. The charity Missing People is currently developing a pilot programme of support services for missing people and their families post-resolution, in a confined geographical area of the UK. Aside from this, services for missing people after they reconnect is largely focused on services for young people. Although some tailored runaways services provide family support, such as SAFE@LAST in South Yorkshire, UK, this is not consistently available nationally and is not usually available to missing adults and their families. Young missing people may also receive a referral to local social services for assessment, which may result in ongoing support for them and their family.

When missing adults return, there is no guarantee of any support being provided, once the police have conducted a Safe and Well check. In difficult circumstances, such as when the missing adult has experienced serious mental illness, their return may be the beginning of the family's efforts to help them engage, or re-engage, with support services. In other situations, such as an adult with dementia who has been missing, it might be possible for carers to access mainstream services. Given the high proportion of missing people who have experienced mental ill health (estimates range as high as 80 per cent) (see Chapter 7 in this volume), the likelihood of returning missing adults requiring further support would seem high.

Adults who have been missing are not, however, automatically referred into any service (statutory or otherwise) for assessment of their support needs. This is an issue that would bear further investigation, with the aim of exploring how future incidents might be reduced through improved response to incidents of adults going missing. Evidence of need for improved support may be found in the Geographies of Missing People project findings, which recommend that 'for adults that are repeatedly missing, a service intervention enabling prevention or swift return needs to be established' (Stevenson et al., 2013, p. 81).

Conclusion

A number of themes emerge from the literature and analysis described in this chapter which, in turn, suggest a number of areas for future research and policy and practice development. First, resolution of missing incidents can be prompted by a number of factors. These prompts may be internal to the missing person, such as cold, hunger, emotional ties or the discovery that people are searching for them. Alternatively, external factors may play a part: the police or the person's own friends or family may physically locate or identify them. Better understanding of these processes would enable search agencies to reach out to missing people in the most appropriate ways, or to provide services that most effectively encourage and support the decision to make contact.

Once a person has been found, any subsequent reconnection can take place in a number of ways. It is important that a variety of options are available, in order to provide choice to missing people. For example, if a missing person is nervous about contacting the police, alternatives such as charity helplines can provide an invaluable service. Reconnection following resolution of a missing person incident may not be immediate, and it is important that people searching for someone are made aware of this. Where the missing person is permitted to decide their own fate, they may take some time to make the decision to reconnect. If they decide to reconnect via a third party, there may be a period during which messages are passed back and forth before independent contact is resumed.

Reconnection, where it does occur, should be understood as a dynamic process, rather than an instant occurrence. A formerly missing person may be reconnected temporarily, before disconnecting again, and reconnection can also be terminated by the missing person's family, if they reject attempts to reconnect. Further to this, missing people may choose to reconnect with some but not all family members, resulting in a partial reconnection. Service providers should be aware that the way in which a case is resolved may have a significant impact on any subsequent reconnection.

At the end of a missing incident, formerly missing and absent individuals should have access to appropriate support and advice, both to assist the reconnection process and to take steps to prevent future missing episodes. This might include a return interview, adequate signposting to relevant services, and advice about how to manage future episodes (such as using Missing People's Message Home service to broker contact. Message Home is a service provided by the charity Missing People. A missing person may pass a message to a family or member via the charity and the charity can pass back a return message).

Even successful reconnection may present significant challenges to the people who have been affected in three main ways: the reasons behind the disappearance may still be unresolved; dealing with the effects of the disappearance on those left behind may be troublesome; and addressing the missing person's experiences whilst away may be challenging. Support services could be provided for families following a disappearance to support those affected to come to terms with what has happened, and why, and to find ways to resolve outstanding issues.

When a missing person is found alive, in some circumstances they may choose not to reconnect to family or support agencies. Further research could shed more light on how missing people approach this decision. Improved understanding of this decision making could inform support services for people who are missing, as well as helping to prepare families for the range of potential outcomes. All agencies working with missing people and their families should be aware of the different options available to support and mediate reconnection, such as Missing People's Message Home service, and should manage the expectations of missing people and those searching to emphasise that simply resuming contact may not be an easy process.

In cases where the missing person is found to have died, much work may be done to understand the way in which the person died, when they died, how they were found and identified, and what lessons may be learned to inform the search for missing people in future. The experience of the families of deceased missing people may also be distinct from other types of bereavement, which will affect their requirements for support; further exploration of these families' support needs is required.

To date, very little research has explored the experiences of missing people as they reconnect to family, carers or support services. This chapter has demonstrated that incidents are resolved in a wide variety of ways, and that missing people reconnect to different degrees and over different periods of time. Whilst, understandably, great efforts have been focused on understanding how, why and where people go missing, it is important that the topic of incident resolution is given due consideration. If incident resolution is successful, this may have a strong influence on the likelihood of the missing person disappearing again, and on the long-term wellbeing of everyone affected. Further research would provide vital evidence to support the development of more sophisticated services to support formerly missing children and adults, and their families, after a missing incident.

References

Bartholomew, D., Duffy, D. and Figgins, N. (2009). *Strategies to Reduce Missing Patients: A Practical Workbook*. London: National Mental Health Development Unit.

Biehal, N., Mitchell, F. and Wade, J. (2003). *Lost from View: A Study of Missing People in the United Kingdom*. Bristol: Policy Press.

Children's Society (2013). *My Life, Unit 8: Young Runaways. Teachers' Notes*. www.mylife4schools.org.uk/teachers/runaways (accessed 30 October 2013).

College of Policing (2013a). *Interim Guidance on the Management, Recording and Investigation of Missing Persons*. London: College of Policing.

College of Policing (2013b). *Risk, Bureaucracy and Missing Persons: An Evaluation of a New Approach to the Initial Police Response*. London: College of Policing.

Department for Education (2014). *Statutory Guidance on Children Who Run Away or Go Missing from Home or Care*. London: Department for Education.

Evans K., Houghton-Brown M. and Rees G. (2007). *Stepping Up: The Future of Runaways Services*. London: The Children's Society.

Henderson, M. and Henderson, P. (1998). *Missing People: Issues for the Australian Community*. Canberra: Commonwealth of Australia.

Holmes, L. (2008). *Living in Limbo: The Experiences of, and Impacts on, the Families of Missing People*. London: Missing People.

Holmes, L. (2013). *Reconnecting Missing Adults and Children*. Presentation to the First International Conference on Missing Children and Adults, University of Portsmouth, 17–19 June 2013. www.port.ac.uk/departments/academic/icjs/csmp/conference/ (accessed 30 October 2013).

Holmes, L. (2014). *When the Search is Over: Reconnecting Missing Children and Adults*. London: Missing People.

Holmes, L., Woolnough, P., Gibb, G., Lee, R. J. and Crawford, M. (2013). *Missing Persons and Mental Health*. Presentation to the First International Conference on Missing Children and Adults, University of Portsmouth, 17–19 June 2013. www.port.ac.uk/departments/academic/icjs/csmp/conference/ (accessed 30 October 2013).

Home Office (2010). *Missing Children and Adults: A Cross-government Strategy*. London: Home Office.

James, M., Anderson, J. and Putt, J. (2008). *Missing Persons in Australia*. Research and public policy series no. 86. Canberra: Australian Institute of Criminology.

National Crime Information Center (2011). *Missing Person and Unidentified Person Statistics for 2011.* www.fbi.gov/about-us/cjis/ncic/ncic-missing-person-and-unidentified-person-statistics-for-2011 (accessed 30 October 2013).

NPIA (2010). *Guidance on the Management, Recording and Investigation of Missing Persons* (2nd edition). London: NPIA.

New Zealand Police (2013). *Missing Persons: An Introduction.* www.police.govt.nz/missing-persons/advice-and-support/introduction (accessed 30 October 2013).

Newiss G (1999). *Missing Presumed … ? The Police Response to Missing Persons.* London: Police Research Series.

Newiss, G. (2006). Understanding the risk of going missing: Estimating the risk of fatal outcomes in cancelled cases. *Policing: An International Journal of Police Strategies and Management,* 29(2): 246–260.

Newiss, G. (2011). *Learning from Fatal Disappearances.* London: Missing People.

NSPCC (2012). *Children Who Go Missing from Care: A Participatory Project with Young Peer Interviewers.* London: NSPCC. www.nspcc.org.uk/Inform/resourcesforprofessionals/lookedafterchildren/missing-from-care-report_wdf93502.pdf (accessed 30 October 2013).

Rees, G., Franks, M., Medforth, R. and Wade, J. (2009). *Commissioning, Delivery and Perceptions of Emergency Accommodation for Young Runaways.* London: Department for Children, Schools and Families.

Stevenson, O., Parr, H., Woolnough, P. and Fyfe, N. (2013). *Geographies of Missing People: Processes, Experiences, Responses.* Glasgow: University of Glasgow.

Tarling, R. and Burrows, J. (2004). The nature and outcome of going missing: The challenge of developing effective risk assessment procedures. *International Journal of Police Science and Management,* 6: 16–26.

The Investigator (2013). 'Missing Facts' in *The Investigator* online magazine, 2: 12–13, 2013. www.the-investigator.co.uk/files/The_Investigator_-_Issue_2_2013.pdf (accessed 10 May 2016).

UK Missing Persons Bureau (2013). *Missing Persons: Data and Analysis 2011–2012.* London: Serious and Organised Crime Agency.

Index

Locators in *italic* refer to figures/diagrams